2005

Gender Differences in Mathematics

Females consistently score lower than males on standardized tests of mathematics, yet no such differences exist in the classroom. These differences are not trivial, nor are they insignificant. Test scores help determine entrance to college and graduate school and, therefore, by extension, a person's job and future success. If females receive lower test scores, then they also receive fewer opportunities.

Why does this discrepancy exist? This book presents a series of chapters that address these issues by integrating the latest research findings and theories. Authors such as Diane Halpern, Jacquelynne Eccles, Beth Casey, Ronald Nuttal, James Byrnes, and Frank Pajares tackle these questions from a variety of perspectives. Many different branches of psychology are represented, including cognitive, social, personality/self-oriented, and psychobiological. The editors then present an integrative chapter that discusses the ideas presented and other areas that the field should explore.

Ann M. Gallagher is Research Scientist at the Law School Admission Council. Her main research interest is sources of group differences in test performance and problem solving. She has published in the *Journal of Educational Psychology*, *Journal of Educational Measurement*, *Journal of Experimental Child Psychology*, *Merrill Palmer Quarterly*, and *Teacher's College Record*.

James C. Kaufman is Assistant Professor of Psychology at the California State University at San Bernardino, where he is also Director of the Learning Research Institute. He is coauthor of *The Creativity Conundrum* (with Jean Pretz and Robert Sternberg, 2002) and was coeditor of *The Evolution of Intelligence* (with Robert Sternberg, 2002).

Gender Differences in Mathematics

An Integrative Psychological Approach

Edited by

ANN M. GALLAGHER
Law School Admission Council

JAMES C. KAUFMAN
California State University, San Bernadino

PUBLISHED BY THE PRESS SYNDICATE OF THE UNIVERSITY OF CAMBRIDGE
The Pitt Building, Trumpington Street, Cambridge, United Kingdom

CAMBRIDGE UNIVERSITY PRESS
The Edinburgh Building, Cambridge CB2 2RU, UK
40 West 20th Street, New York, NY 10011-4211, USA
477 Williamstown Road, Port Melbourne, VIC 3207, Australia
Ruiz de Alarcón 13, 28014 Madrid, Spain
Dock House, The Waterfront, Cape Town 8001, South Africa

http://www.cambridge.org

First published 2005

Printed in the United States of America

Typeface Palatino 10/12 pt.   *System* LaTeX 2_ε [TB]

A catalog record for this book is available from the British Library.

Library of Congress Cataloging in Publication Data
Gender differences in mathematics / edited by Ann Gallagher, James Kaufman.
    p.   cm.
  Includes bibliographical references and index.
  ISBN 0-521-82605-5 – ISBN 0-521-53344-9 (pbk.)
    1. Mathematical ability – Sex differences.   2. Mathematics – Study and
teaching – Psychological aspects.   3. Sex differences in education.
I. Gallagher, Ann M.   II. Kaufman, James C.

QA27.5.G47   2004
510'.8 – dc22   2003069686

ISBN 0 521 82605 5 hardback
ISBN 0 521 53344 9 paperback

*To my sons, Patrick and Andrew, who amaze me daily and who have
changed the way I see the world.
With all my love . . .*
– AMG

*To Dr. Jennie Lynn Kaufman Singer, my sister and wonderful friend,
With pride, friendship, admiration, and love*
– JCK

Contents

Preface

Think of the stereotype of the female mathematician as the homely spinster, or the female high school student who opts out of math courses as early as possible, or the Barbie doll that says, "Math is hard!" The gender gap that exists in the field of mathematics has permeated our society and become entrenched in our culture. Unlike many such popularizations of psychological research, gender differences in the field of mathematics are persistent and tangible.

From Maccoby and Jacklin's (1974) work on the psychology of sex differences to Halpern's (2000) in-depth analyses of gender and cognition, the one consistent finding has been the performance gap in standardized tests of mathematics favoring males. Differences on mathematics tests are generally found to be one-third of a standard deviation or greater. For example, Willingham and Cole (1997) report the following standard deviation units for several tests of mathematics: 0.36 for the SAT – Mathematics, 0.25 for the ACT – Mathematics test, and 0.63 for the GRE – Quantitative. Differences in the same direction are found even when comparing scores for students in mathematical fields or for students who have taken the same math courses. The GRE – Mathematics subject test, for example, shows a male advantage close to one standard deviation (0.87) and Advanced Placement and achievement test scores show a similar, though smaller, gap (0.17 for Calculus AB, 0.20 for Calculus BC, 0.38 for Math 1 Achievement test, and 0.42 for Math 2 Achievement test). Research examining gender differences in classroom grades, however, has generally reported no differences, or differences favoring females, even in high-level mathematics courses (Bridgeman & Wendler, 1991; Kessel & Linn, 1996).

Why this discrepancy? If we just look at test performance, then we might conclude that women have less mathematical ability than men, but test performance does not tell the whole story. For example, Kessel and Linn (1996) suggest that there are two views of what constitutes mathematical ability. One view is that the kind of unfamiliar task found on some standardized tests of quantitative material is a crucial element in any assessment of quantitative reasoning ability. This line of reasoning posits that those who can apply knowledge in an unfamiliar circumstance and solve test questions quickly are more able reasoners than those who cannot. However, according to Kessel and Linn, professional mathematicians value the solution of difficult problems that require extended thought over a period of hours or days. They suggest that the former view of quantitative reasoning ability, which they call "clever and speedy," is likely to disadvantage more reflective students whose study habits and problem-solving approach may actually be more reflective of the reasoning valued by professional mathematicians. Research by Gallagher and DeLisi (1994) suggests that females as a group are less likely than males to fall into the "clever and speedy" category in solving difficult mathematical reasoning problems.

If males and females are viewed as coming to math from two distinct "cultures," then standardized test differences can be seen in a different light. Specifically, the fields of cognitive psychology, educational psychology, and social psychology provide clues to the sources of the differences and ways to measure these abilities in a more equitable fashion. Our hope is that this book will eventually lead to an expanded view of talent assessment in mathematics.

This book, *Gender Differences in Mathematics*, tries to explore these issues from a variety of viewpoints. The first section presents some more general thoughts and research. We start with an introduction to the field by a long-time researcher in the area, Susan Chipman. Next, Paula and Jeremy Caplan present their critical examination of the issue of the researcher's perspective in designing and executing studies of gender differences in mathematics. Diane Halpern, Jonathan Wai, and Amanda Saw discuss a psychobiosocial approach that integrates work from several different fields into a model for examining gender differences.

The next section offers a cognitive psychology perspective on gender differences in mathematics. James Byrnes analyzes gender differences from the perspective of his cognitive processing model. James Royer and Laura Garofoli focus on math fact retrieval as one source of gender differences in SAT mathematics performance. The late Ronald Nuttal, M. Beth Casey, and Elizabeth Pezaris look at spatial ability as a mediator of mathematical test performance. Allan Cohen and Robert Ibarra use differential item functioning analysis to understand why differences occur. They interpret these differences through Hall's multicontext theory.

The next group of chapters take their cue from social psychology and environment-based research. Paul Davies and Steve Spencer offer a review of what we know so far about stereotype threat, a relatively new and exciting area of research. Talia Ben-Zeev and her colleagues present further research on stereotype threat and suggest that specific physiological responses may warrant more investigation. Next, Alyssa Walters and Lisa

Brown examine gender differences in mathematics by ethnicity and culture. Sofia Catsambis takes a more sociological perspective, studying family, school, and community influences.

The final group of chapters look at the self (i.e., self-efficacy, self-concept, self-regulation, and socialization) and the role it plays in mathematics performance. Janis Jacobs, Pamela Davis-Kean, Martha Bleeker, Jacquelynne Eccles, and Oksana Malanchuk use the parental socialization model to write about the relationship between interests, values, and mathematical activity. Eunsook Hong, Harold O'Neil, and David Feldon analyze the role of self-regulation and its relationship to gender and mathematics performance. Finally, Frank Pajares explores gender differences in mathematics self-efficacy.

In our final chapter, we try to integrate these theories, ideas, and findings and to highlight both our own work and recent work by others that we find promising and exciting. We hope that *Gender Differences in Mathematics* will spur more research on this important topic, leading to a better understanding of the sources of gender differences in mathematics performance.

References

Bridgeman, B., & Wendler, C. (1991). Gender differences in predictors of college mathematics performance and in college mathematics course grades. *Journal of Educational Psychology, 83*, 275–284.

Gallagher, A. M., & DeLisi, R. (1994). Gender difference in Scholastic Aptitude Test: Mathematics problem solving among high-ability students. *Journal of Educational Psychology, 86*, 204–211.

Halpern, D. F. (2000). *Sex differences in cognitive abilities* (3rd ed.). Hillsdale, NJ: Erlbaum.

Kessel, C., & Linn, M. C. (1996). Grades of scores: Predicting future college mathematics performance. *Educational Measurement: Issues and Practice, 15*(4), 10–14.

Maccoby, E. E., & Jacklin, C. N. (1974). *The psychology of sex difference.* Stanford, CA: Stanford University Press.

Willingham, W. W., & Cole, N. S. (1997). *Gender and fair assessment.* Mahwah, NJ: Erlbaum.

Acknowledgments

We want to acknowledge the Law School Admission Council and California State University at San Bernardino for their support of this project. It is impossible to produce work of any substance without a wonderful and nurturing environment, and we are lucky to have found such welcoming institutions.

We also want to thank our colleagues who have provided invaluable assistance in reviewing manuscripts and making suggestions: Talia Ben-Zeev, Roja Dilmore-Rios, Jennifer Duffy, Carol Dwyer, Diane Halpern, Allison B. Kaufman, Lynda Reese, Alex Weissman, and Gita Wilder; to Phil Laughlin at Cambridge University Press, we extend special thanks for his encouragement, support, and guidance.

For individual moral support, Ann would like to thank her family for their encouragement and her husband, Horacio Furlong, for his patience in stressful times. James wants to thank his wife, Allison Kaufman; his parents, Alan and Nadeen Kaufman; and his friend, David Hecht, for putting up with him as he was working on this project.

Sadly, we have lost two valued colleagues since we began work on this project. James B. Grossman was a clinical psychologist who studied child development and autism. He passed away in June 2002, at the age of 31. His humor, brilliance, and compassion are sorely missed. Ronald L. Nuttall, senior author of one of our chapters, died suddenly, soon after completing work on this book. We join his family, friends, and colleagues in mourning the loss of such a gifted researcher.

Contributors

Talia Ben-Zeev
San Francisco State University

Martha Bleeker
Pennsylvania State University

Lisa M. Brown
University of Florida

James P. Byrnes
University of Maryland

Jeremy B. Caplan
The Rotman Research Institute,
   Baycrest Centre for
   Geriatric Care

Paula J. Caplan
Brown University

Cristina M. Carrasquillo
San Francisco State University

M. Beth Casey
Boston College

Sophia Catsambis
City University of New York and
   U.S. Department of Education

Alison M. L. Ching
San Francisco State University

Susan F. Chipman
U.S. Office of Naval Research

Allan S. Cohen
The University of Georgia

Paul G. Davies
University of California,
   Los Angeles

Pamela Davis-Kean
University of Michigan

Jacquelynne S. Eccles
University of Michigan

Steven Fein
Williams College

David Feldon
University of Southern
   California

Ann M. Gallagher
Law School Admission Council

Laura M. Garofoli
Dr. Franklin Perkins School

Diane F. Halpern
Claremont McKenna College

Eunsook Hong
University of Nevada, Las Vegas

Robert A. Ibarra
The University of New Mexico

Michael Inzlicht
New York University

Janis E. Jacobs
Pennsylvania State University

James C. Kaufman
California State University,
   San Bernardino

Tattiya J. Kliengklom
San Francisco State University

Oksana Malanchuk
University of Michigan

Kristen L. McDonald
San Francisco State University

Daniel C. Newhall
San Francisco State
   University

Ronald L. Nuttal
Boston College

Harold F. O'Neil
University of Southern
   California

Frank Pajares
Emory University

Gillian E. Patton
San Francisco State University

Elizabeth Pezaris
Northeastern University

James M. Royer
University of Massachusetts,
   Amherst

Amanda Saw
Claremont Graduate University

Steven J. Spencer
University of Waterloo

Tiffany D. Stewart
San Francisco State University

Tonya Stoddard
San Francisco State University

Jonathan Wai
Claremont McKenna College

Alyssa M. Walters
Educational Testing Service

Research on the Women and Mathematics Issue

A Personal Case History

Susan F. Chipman

The history of research on the issue of women's participation in mathematics provides an interesting case study of the psychology and sociology of research in the social sciences. Although there had been prior research on the topic, two key works of the early and mid-1970s sparked a major burst of interest. They were Lucy Sell's unpublished study of women at the University of California at Berkeley (Sells, 1973), "High school mathematics as the critical factor in the job market," and Sheila Tobias's publications on math anxiety (Tobias, 1976, 1978), the first of them an article in *MS* magazine in 1976. The study of mathematics, or the failure to study mathematics, came to be seen as a critical barrier to women's participation in a wide range of high-status and remunerative occupations during those surging years of the women's movement. Based on a random sample of freshmen entering Berkeley in 1972, Sells (1973) reported that only 8% of the females had taken four years of high school mathematics, whereas 57% of the men had. This report received a lot of attention.

The U.S. National Institute of Education (NIE) responded with plans for a special grants competition addressing this perceived problem. Background preparations for this competition were exceptionally thorough. Three review papers were commissioned to examine existing research results and opinions concerning major classes of possible influences on women's choices to study mathematics or to select occupations requiring mathematical competence: Fennema (1977) reviewed cognitive, affective, and educational influences; Fox (1977) reviewed social influences; and Sherman (1977) reviewed possible biological explanations. These papers were presented at a large, 2-day-long working conference in Washington, DC, that brought together many people concerned with the mathematics education of women, in February 1977. A grants announcement was issued (NIE, 1977). The research grants were intended to provide "a better knowledge base for designing effective educational programs to encourage women to enroll in mathematics beyond the minimal school requirements." An important underlying assumption was expressed in the opening statement describing the research requested by the announcement, "Women's lower enrollment in the study of advanced mathematics precludes them from entering a variety of occupations requiring mathematical competence."

The grants competition was sponsored by an organizational unit called the Career Awareness Division of the Education and Work Group of the NIE. By the time the research projects were completed, there had been a major reorganization of the NIE. I found myself responsible for this research program, and for a planned publication to pull the research results together, because they had been grouped with all other research on mathematics learning, in a division on Learning and Development that I was chosen to direct. The planned summary publication for the research program was to include chapters by each supported researcher as well as a research synthesis. Although my earlier involvement in the grants competition had been somewhat peripheral – I had attended the working conference and had served as a reviewer of grant proposals – I chose to take on the job of synthesizing the research myself, rather than contracting it out, as originally planned (Chipman, Brush, & Wilson, 1985; Chipman & Thomas, 1985; Chipman & Wilson, 1985). At the NIE, we were continuing to receive more grants proposals on the topic of women (or girls) and mathematics than on all other topics in mathematics education combined. This seemed disproportionate. Mathematics education was not, and still is not, a well-researched area. Many problems concerning more effective ways to teach mathematics had not been addressed. It was part of my job responsibility to define and set research priorities.

In this chapter, I discuss how I have come to understand the women and mathematics issue since the late 1970s, in all its many dimensions. I have revisited the issue many times (Chipman, 1994; Chipman, 1996a, 1996b), sometimes also considering related issues such as participation in fields of science and technology and the participation of minorities, with separate consideration of minority women (Chipman & Thomas, 1987). In addition to these review efforts, I have pursued some research into specific aspects of the issue: possible test bias (Chipman, 1988b; Chipman, Marshall, & Scott, 1991) and the impact of mathematics anxiety on choice of major field and career (Chipman, Krantz, & Silver, 1992, 1995).

As I began the task of synthesizing the set of research grants on women and mathematics, it seemed logical to first define the problem. It was then that I noticed a significant omission in the preparation for the grants competition – there had been no commissioned paper on the demographic facts of the problem. As the language of the grants announcement made clear, everyone involved was thoroughly convinced that the problem existed and that it was serious.

Very quickly, my planned research synthesis chapter turned into two chapters, a first chapter that outlined the demographic facts of the problem

(Chipman & Thomas, 1985) and a chapter attempting to synthesize the findings of the research grants (Chipman & Wilson, 1985). I soon uncovered a major surprise: mathematics has been the least sex-typed of college majors! By that, I mean that the representation of women among math majors has been as close to their representation among all recipients of Bachelor of Arts (BA) degrees as one can find for any field of study. This fact immediately casts doubt on the idea that mathematics is a particularly problematic field for women. It was revealed by a readily available and complete data set, the statistics on earned degrees conferred in the United States that have been maintained by the National Center for Education Statistics (NCES) since at least the 1949–1950 academic year. In that academic year, 24% of all BA degrees went to women and nearly 23% of BA degrees in mathematics went to women. In the 1976–1977 academic year, the last year for which statistics were available when I did these analyses, 46% of BA degrees were awarded to women and 42% of the BA degrees in mathematics. In publications over the years, I have periodically updated these figures. My latest update appears in Table 1.1. Note that women's share of the degrees awarded remains high at the BA level (although lagging their recent majority status among BA recipients) and has continued to climb at the level of graduate degrees. In the early 1980s, I concluded that if there was any problem concerning women's participation in the study of mathematics, it seemed to be at the level of continuation to the doctoral degree and that some self-examination of university math departments might be warranted. Despite some improvement, this conclusion still seems valid. Women's level of participation in the study of mathematics itself has been much higher than their level of participation in other fields that are seen as math-related, requiring mathematical competence, such as engineering, computer science, and physics. Thus, it hardly seems plausible that

TABLE 1.1. *Percent of Degrees Awarded to Women*

	BA – All	Math BA	MA – All	Math MA	PhD – All	Math PhD
1950	24	23				
1960	35	27				
1970	43	37				
1975	45	42	45	33	22	10
1980	49	42	49	36	30	13
1985	51	46	50	35	34	15
1990	53	46	53	40	36	18
2000	57	47	58	45	44	25

Source: The primary source of these data is the Series of Earned Degrees Conferred, National Center for Education Statistics. Data 1950–1970, as cited in Chipman & Thomas (1985). Data 1975–1990, as cited in National Science Board, *Science and Engineering Indicators – 1993*, Appendix Tables 2-19, 2-25, and 2-27, pp. 272–285. Data for 2000 from *Digest of Education Statistics* (2001), http://nces.ed.gov/pubs2002/digest2001/tables/.

aversion to mathematics is or was functioning as an important barrier to women's participation in those fields. Perhaps the explanation should be sought elsewhere.

No such complete data were maintained concerning the study of mathematics at the high school level. However, at the time of my synthesis effort, I was able to find a number of large representative data sets. One of the grants had been to Armstrong (1985) for a National Assessment of Educational Progress (NAEP) survey of women and mathematics that was conducted in 1978, taking a nationally representative sample of 1,700 twelfth-grade students. Thirty-one percent of the males and 27% of the females had taken some variant of the usual 4-year high school mathematics sequence. Similarly, the 1979 report of the College Entrance Examination Board (CEEB; Educational Testing Service [ETS], 1979) stated that 64% of males and 45% of females expected to have completed four years or more of high school mathematics. Of course, individuals taking the SAT are not a random sample of all students, but they constitute a large fraction of students going on to college. More than 900,000 individuals were covered by that 1979 report.

These data did indicate a sex difference in the study of high school mathematics, especially in the study of advanced courses such as calculus or optional courses beyond the standard college preparatory track: those courses tended to be about 60% male in participation. However, these differences were not nearly so extreme as most people believed or as Sells (1973) had reported. About 40% of those who were approaching college with 4 years of mathematics preparation were women and about 40% of women were entering college well prepared in mathematics, having taken the standard 4 years of high school mathematics. (For more details, see Chipman & Thomas, 1985.)

There were also older data sets that could have better informed the research planning. The National Longitudinal Sample of persons who were twelfth graders in 1972 showed that about 39% of the males and 22% of the females had taken 4 years of high school mathematics. Farther back, the 1960 Project TALENT sample showed that 33% of the boys and only 9% of the girls were taking four years of mathematics. Even so, it would have been difficult to argue that mathematics was functioning as a barrier to entry into math-related careers because only 3% of the girls were planning to go into math-related careers. Clearly, too, a significant change had occurred between 1960 and 1972: the percentage of girls studying 4 years of high school mathematics had more than doubled. The successive CEEB reports from 1973 to 1979 also showed a slow increase in female participation in the study of advanced high school mathematics. It seems that a process of change was well underway by the time the grants competition was initiated. One wonders how the research would have been different if these facts had been recognized at the time. Why weren't these facts recognized? Why weren't such analyses done in preparation for the grants competition?

Perhaps it was that the decision-makers and the lobbyists for the research harkened back to their own school experience in the 1960s, 1950s, and before and remembered that few girls had been studying advanced mathematics in those days or perhaps remembered that they themselves had not chosen to study mathematics. Although an analysis of the dimensions of the "problem" seemed like a mundane, standard thing to do when starting the research synthesis effort, perhaps I asked the question because I myself had majored in mathematics in college and had attended a high school in suburban Chicago where many girls had studied advanced mathematics in the early 1960s. A large social change in expectations for women's lives occurred during those years; undoubtedly some women found themselves hampered by the educational choices they had made when expecting to lead very different lives. Analyses of the Project TALENT data (Wise, 1985) showed that the choice to study advanced mathematics in high school in 1960 was predicted by a girl's expectation of going on to college and pursuing a career of some sort. In later years, many more girls would have such expectations. Correspondingly, it seems that by the time the 1998 High School Transcript Study was done, sex differences in high school math course participation had disappeared, or even shifted to favor females. Even calculus was shown as being taken by 11.2% of males and 10.6% of females; Advanced Placement (AP) calculus by 7.3% of males and 6.4% of females (NCES, 2001).

In summary, by the time the brouhaha concerning the mathematics preparation of young women was raised, the "problem" had already diminished significantly, and that trend has continued until the present time. Sells's highly publicized and influential data were unrepresentative of the national situation at the time; perhaps her sample size was too small or perhaps the University of California was atypical. Furthermore, the bare facts, as well as some of the analyses done in the studies that provided the facts, cast doubt on the assumptions that were held about the causal relations between the study of high school mathematics and entry into fields seen as "math-related." It might be that the intention to go into a math-related field, or even the mere intention to attend college, "causes" the study of advanced high school mathematics, rather than vice versa.

Despite what these facts show, it is obvious that the belief that there is a large "women and mathematics problem" persists today. One constantly reads of efforts to "solve" it by offering single-sex math classes and the like.

INVESTIGATING THE DETERMINANTS OF MATH COURSE ENROLLMENT AND ACHIEVEMENT

The primary focus of the research grants that NIE awarded was on understanding the factors determining enrollments and achievement in advanced high school mathematics. Beyond that, the emphasis was on examining

variables that might plausibly explain sex differences in math course enrollments. A consequence of that concern was a relative neglect of cognitive
variables in the research that was done. Despite the widespread belief that
there are sex differences in some inherent ability to learn and do mathematics, a topic to be discussed later in this section, it was already known in
1977 that sex differences in mathematical ability and/or achievement at the
beginning of high school were negligible and, therefore, had little promise
of explaining the differences in enrollment or choice of occupational field.
Measures of spatial ability were well represented in the research, but measures of general intellectual ability, or prior mathematics ability and/or
achievement, were not. Affective measures of attitudes related to mathematics, mathematics study, mathematics teachers, and so on, were well represented. As with demographic facts, the effort to synthesize the results of
the research studies brought out shortcomings in the way the research studies had been designed to address the question of determinants of course
enrollment. The grant to analyze previously collected, nationally representative Project TALENT data (Wise, 1985) revealed that the strongest
correlates or predictors of individual differences in advanced mathematics
course enrollment were measures of cognitive ability, mathematics ability,
or even verbal ability at the beginning of high school, although these measures did not serve to explain the sex differences in enrollment that were
still large at that time. The sex differences in enrollment then present did,
however, tend to account for the sex differences in mathematics achievement that were measured at the end of high school. This agreed with Fennema's (1974) earlier report that sex differences in math course-taking had
an important role in explaining what had tended to be interpreted as sex
differences in inherent mathematical ability. Project TALENT was not designed to examine decisions to enroll in advanced mathematics and science
or the sex differences in those decisions. Consequently, it did not include
measures of attitudes toward mathematics, and did not provide an opportunity to assess the relative explanatory contributions of cognitive and
affective variables. This proved to be a problem for the research program
as a whole.

The nature of this problem was evident even within the cognitive realm.
As mentioned above, the best-represented cognitive variables in this research were various measures of spatial ability. It was believed that there
were sex differences in spatial ability and that spatial ability was important to mathematics. Intuitively, the capacity to mentally rotate, translate,
and transform objects appears to be important in mathematical thinking,
at least in geometry. Fennema (1977) reported on opinions from the mathematical community that support this point of view.

There is a tendency to think that measures of ability have a stronger
theoretical, scientific basis than they actually do. Ability testing and the
definition of abilities has been a pragmatic and empirical technology.

Performance is sampled within a domain of tasks or situations, in a way limited by the practical constraints on testing. Statistical techniques, usually factor analysis, are used to identify tasks that "go together," have something in common, and those that seem to be independent of each other. The hypothetical "something" in common is called a factor, and may sometimes be labeled an ability, although the technical psychometric use of the term *ability* does not always carry with it all the implications of the popular meaning of *ability*. For instance, a psychometric *ability* sometimes consists entirely of learned knowledge. In the history of cognitive testing, it has been found that all intellectual performances have something in common: that is, persons who do well or poorly on one intellectual task also tend to do well or poorly on other, quite different intellectual tasks. This common factor has been called general intelligence or "g." Some relatively recent research is beginning to show the way to a deeper theory about the nature of general ability. For example, Carpenter, Just, and Shell (1990) showed, by constructing computational models of cognitive processes in solving Raven Progressive Matrices items, and by converging evidence from another task, that individual differences in performance on this well-accepted measure of general intelligence are largely accounted for by individual differences in the number of problem-solving goals that can be managed in working memory. Intuitively, this characterization of general intelligence also sounds much like the essence of mathematical ability, as distinct from learned mathematical knowledge.

Many different tasks, which can be performed with diverse mental strategies, have been called tests of spatial abilities. Various tests of so-called spatial abilities do not necessarily have high correlations with each other, as contrasted with their correlations with other kinds of tasks (Lohman, 1979; McGee, 1979). There is no single, unitary spatial ability that these tests are measuring. Lohman (1979, 1988, 1996) concluded that a considerable proportion of performance on spatial tests, especially complex spatial tests, is explained by variation in measures of general intelligence, what all tests of intellectual performance have in common. One of the surprises of the effort to synthesize the results of the NIE grants (Chipman & Wilson, 1985) was that the studies including measures of spatial ability did not provide any strong evidence for sex differences in spatial abilities, despite a previous review concluding that this was a reliable cognitive sex difference (Maccoby & Jacklin, 1974). The nationally representative and relatively large Armstrong (1979) study even reported a statistically significant advantage for 13-year-old females on 15 items taken from the Paper Form Board test. These unexpected results might be due to the tests used (most often the DAT Spatial Relations test, which requires the examinee to select the three-dimensional (3-D) shape that will be formed by folding a two-dimensional (2-D) shape along indicated fold lines), or due to changes over time affecting the experiential influence on "ability" measures, or due to relatively small sample sizes in many of the studies. Psychometric studies have often had huge sample sizes that make almost any observed difference statistically significant, even though it may be too small to be considered practically significant. At the time, the research studies that had shown substantial sex differences in a spatial ability (Sanders, Soares, & D'Aquila, 1982; Vandenberg & Kuse, 1979) used a test involving the rotation of objects in three-dimensional space. Indeed, a formal and thorough meta-analysis of the research on sex differences in spatial abilities done independently at about the same time (Linn & Petersen, 1985) concluded that sex differences are found primarily on that type of measure and not on the other types of measures of spatial ability. Although that review has been cited more than 400 times in the intervening years, none of the citing articles is a later review or meta-analysis that would change this picture.

Despite these results undermining the notion that putative sex differences in spatial ability might explain putative sex differences in math enrollments or achievement, it is probably worth mentioning that the evidence for a specific contribution of spatial ability to mathematics performance, distinct from the contribution of general intelligence, is surprisingly weak. Smith (1964) and Werdelin (1961) are two of the most frequently cited references on this point, but neither of them actually provides strong evidence for a relationship between spatial ability and mathematics performance. Several reviewers of the literature have concluded that no such relationship has been shown (Fruchter, 1954; Very, 1967; even for geometry: Werdelin, 1961; Lim, 1963). Fennema & Sherman (1977, 1978) and Sherman (1980) did report that the DAT Spatial Relations test shows a correlation of about 0.50 between the DAT score and general tests of mathematical achievement in a high school population enrolled in college preparatory mathematics courses. However, the DAT is the type of spatial ability test that Lohman (1979) characterized as being similar to measures of general intelligence, and Fennema and Sherman do not provide any evidence for a specific unique contribution of spatial ability either. In the larger and more broadly representative Project TALENT sample, there were two measures of spatial ability, Visualization in 2-D and Visualization in 3-D, but they were not among the variables having a correlation of 0.20 or higher with mathematics achievement (Wise, Steel, & MacDonald, 1979). One of the NIE studies that emphasized spatial ability provided an intriguing pattern of results. Stallings (1985) used the DAT and course-specific tests of mathematics. The pattern of correlations she found for the different types of mathematics is quite consistent with what one might expect: algebra I (0.49), geometry (0.53), algebra II (0.15), trigonometry (0.38), analytic geometry (0.68), and calculus (0.20). Unfortunately, the design of her study did not include a measure of general intelligence or even one of verbal ability, so it, too, cannot provide evidence of a unique contribution of spatial ability to performance in any of these mathematical fields, despite a suggestion of some promise for analytic geometry and geometry. This seems to have been an opportunity missed because of the intense focus on possible explanations for sex differences. In contrast to the general lack of evidence of a contribution of specifically spatial abilities to mathematics performance, there is such evidence for predictions of success in courses such as mechanical drawing and shop (McGee, 1979).

Within the mathematical community, there is a long-standing distinction between algebraists and geometers. Perhaps this is grounded in a difference in their reliance on spatial thinking, but both types are counted as mathematicians. There is more than one way to do mathematics. The need to do mental rotation in depth (apparently the primary locus of sex differences in spatial ability) probably does not arise all that often. Furthermore, very advanced mathematics often deals with N dimensions, not just 3. Heavy reliance on spatial thinking can prove a barrier in moving on to N dimensions.

AFFECTIVE VARIABLES

In addition to spatial ability, the NIE studies emphasized the possible role of affective variables in determining course enrollments and mathematics achievement. Fennema and Sherman (1976) developed a thorough and extensive set of attitude scales, but two variables have received the most extensive exploration: liking for mathematics and mathematics anxiety/confidence. Although these variables seem closely related conceptually and have a strong correlation with each other (0.60–0.65), they behave rather differently with respect to sex differences (Chipman & Wilson, 1985). Consistently, there is no sex difference in liking for mathematics. Thus, it may not be surprising, after all, that women have been so well represented among math majors. In contrast, there is an equally consistent sex difference in mathematics anxiety/confidence (Hyde, Fennema, Ryan, Frost, & Hopp, 1990). Although Fennema and Sherman (1977) attempted to construct separate scales for anxiety and for confidence, the two scales were found to have a correlation of −0.89 with each other, so they can be considered to have been measuring the same thing. It is not entirely clear what to make of the small mean sex differences that are observed. Because no one seems to have published the full *distributions* of male and female scores, it is not clear, for example, whether serious mathematics anxiety is more common among females than among males. It might be that, for social reasons, females are less willing to express high confidence in themselves as learners of mathematics, even if they in fact have such high confidence. The interpretation of these attitudinal variables is not entirely straightforward. The questionnaires that measure these variables are fallible yardsticks. Some people will use extreme values on the scales; others will not. The expression of true opinions may be tempered by the person's impression of what is a socially acceptable answer. Expressions of very high confidence in mathematical ability may be more socially acceptable in males than in females. Admissions of weakness, anxiety, or distress may be less socially acceptable for males. We can never be certain that the apparent sex differences in these subjective variables reflect genuine differences in the characteristic the scale purports to measure. Nevertheless, sex differences in mathematics anxiety/confidence showed some potential to explain sex differences in enrollment.

Another important affective variable is the perceived utility of mathematics study and of the resulting mathematical knowledge. Looking over the historical changes in girls' and women's study of high school mathematics, participation in higher education, and participation in the workforce over the past 50 years, it seems likely that the primary driver of change lay in this area. Among the NIE grant studies (see Chipman & Wilson, 1985, for details), the general perceived usefulness of mathematics was moderately related to enrollments, while more specific perceptions of mathematical requirements for a planned job or career or aspirations for higher education had a somewhat stronger relationship to enrollments or enrollment intentions. Wise (1985) reported that sex differences in career interests in the Project TALENT sample from the early 1960s predicted math course enrollments, preceded differences in achievement, and probably could explain the sex differences in enrollment and achievement that then prevailed. As discussed earlier, by 1998–2000, sex differences in high school mathematics enrollment had virtually disappeared and women had become the majority among BA recipients. Yet, sex differences in participation in the so-called math-related fields, engineering (23% female in 2000), physics (22% female in 2000), and computer science (28% female in 2000) remain substantial (NCES, 2001). Other sciences such as biology (58% female in 2000) and chemistry (46% female in 2000) now have an excellent representation of women. The once male-dominated fields of medicine (6% female in 1960; 43% in 2000) and law (2.5% female in 1960; 46% in 2000) changed radically between 1960, the year that Project TALENT began, and 2000. For many women, the primary utility of math study in high school may be in meeting the requirements for admission to the college of their choice rather than the inherent requirements of their occupational choice.

Thus, the historical evidence strongly suggests that the utility of mathematics study for girls and women was an important factor in changing rates of participation in advanced high school mathematics courses. However, one of the frustrations in summing up the results of the NIE math grants and similar research done at that time was the difficulty in performing analyses that would shed light on the relative importance of various cognitive, affective, and other variables in predicting mathematics enrollments, intentions to enroll, and mathematics achievement. Not surprisingly, earlier mathematics achievement, confidence in oneself as a learner of mathematics, and liking for mathematics – among other variables studied – are all related to each other. Therefore, it is difficult to say which of these variables should be regarded as more basic or "causal," to which should be attributed the effects of what these variables have in common. These data resisted efforts to define approximately independent but still meaningful variables that would make the results of regression analyses reliable and meaningful. Overall, the results suggested that general cognitive ability was the most important variable predicting individual differences in mathematics enrollments, and that mathematics confidence/anxiety probably made some independent contribution. The evidence for the independent contribution of perceived utility of mathematics was even weaker, largely because so few studies included a good representation of both cognitive and affective variables. Also, a number of studies had data only about reported intentions to enroll in advanced math courses, not about actual enrollments. The latter was a harder, more predictable variable. The NIE studies also included many efforts to measure social influences on student enrollment and achievement, including the behavior, attitudes, or perceived attitudes of parents, teachers, and peers. However, none of these variables emerged as important, and sex differences were not usually found. Disappointingly few strong conclusions could be drawn from the research because the strong focus on sex differences resulted in a poor representation of cognitive variables. Ignoring the variables with the strongest relations to the predicted variables made it difficult to gauge accurately the size of the influence of the affective variables, given the strong intercorrelations.

BARRIERS TO WOMEN'S PARTICIPATION IN MATH-RELATED CAREERS – THE BIG PICTURE

Having raised the opposite causal possibility that career expectations may influence math course participation, let us turn to consider the notion that adequacy of mathematics participation is or was functioning as a barrier to women's entry into mathematics-related careers. Dunteman, Wisenbaker, and Taylor (1979) performed analyses of the National Longitudinal Survey (circa 1972) data that attempted to understand sex and race differences in the selection of engineering and science majors. Their model for predicting the selection of a science major had four variables on which females obtained lower scores: orientation toward things (2/3 standard deviation [SD] lower) vs. orientation toward people, reported mother's educational aspirations for the child (3/10 SD lower), mathematics score (1/4 SD lower), and number of science courses taken (considerably lower). Even after these variables having a negative effect for females were taken into account, an unexplained direct negative effect of being female upon selection of college science remained, and it was about twice as important as the math score. Additional variables considered to be related to women's roles or values also failed to explain that difference. It would be interesting to know if this unexplained barrier to women's entry into those fields still exists. If so, that should probably be regarded as a social problem needing to be addressed. The large sex differences in vocational interest patterns, such as the crude dimension of interest in things vs. interest in people that Dunteman et al. (1979) constructed are probably the most important single factor in explaining the low representation of women in what have been thought of as math-related careers. It is surprising that so little research attention has been given to this explanation for sex differences in career participation. More recent research indicates that these sex differences in vocational interest patterns continue to exist (Hansen, 1988; Lippa, 1998). Unfortunately, little is known about how such vocational interests develop, except that they seem to develop rather early in life (Tyler, 1964). A citation search on Tyler's article did not reveal recent developmental research of this kind. It is not obvious to me, however, that sex differences in the area of interests, or the resulting differences in occupational choices, should be regarded as a problem.

MATHEMATICS ANXIETY AS A BARRIER

An opportunity for me to pursue the open question about the possible influence of mathematics anxiety/confidence on the selection of a field of study, separate and distinct from the influence of mathematics ability/ achievement, arose in a study of three successive classes at Barnard College (a women's college associated with Columbia, then and now a coeducational college but once a men's college), totaling about 1,360 women initially and 1,074 for whom complete data through college completion were available (Chipman, Krantz, & Silver, 1992, 1995). This study was able to demonstrate a strong influence of mathematics anxiety/confidence, independent of the effects of quantitative SAT scores. In this select population (mean QSAT about 600), QSAT had no effect on expressed interest in a scientific career at the time of college entrance, whereas mathematics anxiety/ confidence did have a significant effect. For actual biological science majors, the same picture held true at the end of college: no effect of QSAT, significant effect of mathematics anxiety/confidence. For actual physical science majors at the end of college, both QSAT and mathematics anxiety/ confidence showed significant effects on the likelihood of a major. In this population, there were some individuals with very high QSAT scores and low mathematics confidence. The results of this study indicate that the sex difference in mathematics confidence may be partially responsible for some of the underrepresentation of women in science and engineering fields, but the sex difference in math confidence seems to be quite small among able college students (Hyde et al., 1990). In the Barnard study, the full impact of that effect was expressed *prior to* college entrance, but it was substantial: the odds of becoming a science major were 5 times as great for the math confident as for the math anxious. The effect of QSAT on actual completion of a physical science major was even more substantial – the odds of being a physical science major were 16 times as great for the group with the highest QSAT (scores over 650) as for the lowest group. There are several possible interpretations of this QSAT result. It may reflect a reality that mathematical competence is important in the pursuit of a physical science field. Alternatively, it may reflect a strong belief in the college-level community – both faculty and students – that mathematical competence really matters. Students with less than the highest QSAT scores may be counseled out of physical science fields or may counsel themselves out of those fields. When interpreting these results, however, it is important to remember that the Barnard College population was an intellectually select population. According to National Science Foundation (NSF) data, the mean QSAT of the Barnard population was as high or higher than the mean QSAT of all U.S. males receiving BA degrees in physical sciences, engineering, or even mathematics at that time (NSF, 1986). The majority of those Barnard students, therefore, were probably capable of completing a physical science major. However, interest in a science career was rare at Barnard College – there were 45 physical science majors, 69 biological science majors, 572 social science majors, 357 humanities majors, 31 in creative writing or similar fields, and no mathematics majors at all. Although interest in a science major at the beginning of college was strongly predictive of an actual major, such interest was so rare in this population that there were actually more physical science majors coming from the group classified as not open to consideration of engineering or science careers at the time of college entrance than from those with high initial interest. Contrary to popular belief and some prior research results, it seems that experiences during college can result in a science major. The people vs. things dimension of vocational interests was also investigated in the Barnard study; its influence on occupational interests and major selections was substantial and had had its effect prior to college entrance.

MATHEMATICS ABILITY AND ACHIEVEMENT AS A POSSIBLE BARRIER

Finally, let us turn to the subject of possible sex differences in mathematical ability and/or achievement. As was pointed out earlier for the case of spatial abilities, there is no deep theory about the fundamental nature of mathematical ability. It has proved difficult to define mathematical ability factors that are any more predictive of success in mathematics than measures of general intelligence (Aiken, 1973). As noted above, Carpenter, Just, & Shell's (1990) characterization of the fundamental basis of general intelligence is also very plausible as a characterization of the essence of mathematical ability. Beyond general intellectual ability, the cognitive variable that predicts future mathematics performance is past mathematics achievement. Previous grades in mathematics appear to be the best available predictor of success in college mathematics (Wick, 1975).

In the United States and elsewhere, there is widespread belief that males outperform females in mathematics. However, the data for the United States do not necessarily support this belief (Chipman & Thomas, 1985; Hyde, Fennema, & Lamon, 1990). Large, representative studies of U.S. student populations have tended to find little or no sex difference in overall mathematics performance prior to the secondary school years, when the study of mathematics often becomes optional in the United States. Despite occasional reports that boys or girls in elementary school perform better on one or another type of math test item, a meta-analysis concluded that no such differences are evident prior to secondary school (Hyde et al., 1990). An exception to the general picture of equality is that searches for mathematically talented youths have generated reports that extremely high levels of mathematical performance on the SAT at a young age (about 7th or 8th grade) are much more frequently found in males (Benbow & Stanley, 1980, 1983). These reports have received much publicity and have had a substantial effect on public beliefs about male and female performance in mathematics (Eccles & Jacobs, 1986). Because of the way in which these searches are conducted, methods that do not ensure representative sampling, it is difficult to know what one should conclude about the actual incidence of high levels of mathematics performance among young male and female students in the United States. The U.S. National Assessment of Educational Progress (NAEP) (National Science Board, 1993), which does aim at achieving a nationally representative sample, reported that 0.2% of females at age 13 and 0.5% of males at age 13 attained the highest category of mathematical proficiency (p. 232) – characterized as involving multistep problem-solving and algebra, as well as various other mathematical content usually taught during high school. However, it is clear that the generalization from these reports to beliefs about the performance of more typical male and female students is not justified. In the general population, sex differences in mathematics performance prior to secondary school are negligible.

By the end of secondary school, however, sex differences in mathematics test performance that favor males have usually been reported in the United States, and the performance differences seem to arise from problem-solving tests or items (Hyde et al., 1990). For many years, the possibility that differences in course taking might account for these differences in mathematics test performance seems to have been ignored. Fennema (1974) pointed this out. Obvious as that hypothesis might seem, many seem to have concluded that such test results implied lesser mathematical ability among female students. Analysis of data from the representative survey sample of U.S. students that was collected in the early 1960s – when there were substantial sex differences in secondary school mathematics course enrollments – showed that course enrollments statistically accounted for nearly all the sex difference in mathematics performance at the end of secondary school (Wise, 1985). However, as noted above, sex differences in course enrollments diminished greatly over time. Nevertheless, a performance difference on the SAT remained circa 1993. It still remains today. The CEEB (2000) report on college bound seniors, 2000, reported no difference between males and females in number of math courses taken (3.8) but a mean difference of 35 points on the SAT math test, favoring males. Similarly the NAEP (National Science Board, 1993) results showed that 5.6% of 17-year-old females but 8.8% of 17-year-old males were attaining the highest category of proficiency in 1990 (p. 233). On the other hand, the mean results for 17-year-old males and females in 1990 showed no difference (p. 7 & 231), the culmination of a gap-closing trend.

The picture is further complicated by the fact that different measures of mathematical performance yield different messages about sex differences. In an important review paper, Kimball (1989) showed that course performance measures consistently favor females. Similarly, the results of some studies tend to indicate that examinations that are closely tied to the instructed curriculum, like the New York State Regents Exam (Felson & Trudeau, 1991) or IEA Math content, which is well represented in the "implemented curriculum" (Hanna, 1989), are more likely to favor females. This side of the story is further reinforced by another large-scale study drawing from a huge sample of students gathered to investigate the validity of the SAT exam. When males and females were matched by university math course taken (in the same institution) and by performance grade received in the course, it was found that the females had received scores nearly 50 points lower on the SAT exam (Wainer & Steinberg, 1992). In other words, the SAT underpredicted the performance of females relative to males in these mathematics courses, advanced as well as introductory. Reportedly, an earlier internal study at the Massachusetts Institute of Technology (MIT) had similar results showing that the SAT underpredicted course performance at MIT, but I was never able to obtain a report of that study. Such results suggest that the observed sex differences in performance on tests like the SAT may reflect differences in responding to the testing situation itself (Becker, 1990), or that they may arise from extracurricular differences in experience that are related to the content of some such tests.

POSSIBLE SOURCES OF SEX DIFFERENCES IN TEST PERFORMANCE

There are a variety of factors that might contribute to persisting sex differences in math test performance. Significant sex differences remained circa 1990 for course enrollments in "extra" mathematics courses like statistics and probability that are not part of the standard college preparatory curriculum. Large sex differences existed in enrollments in courses like high school physics that may provide considerable practice in solving mathematics problems. If the majority of secondary school females are taking high school mathematics simply to fulfill college or university entrance requirements rather than to prepare for further study and careers that intrinsically require mathematical competence, their degree of involvement with the subject matter may be less than is common for males taking the same courses.

Studies that have attempted to analyze sex differences in performance on the SAT or similar tests have not yielded any great insight (Chipman, 1988b). Individual test items can be found that show very large sex differences, but the reasons for those differences are not obvious. There has been little or no consistency in the apparent nature of such items from one study to the next. Occasionally, these analyses have appeared to confirm hypotheses that sex differences might be concentrated in items with geometric or spatial content, but this has not proved consistently true. (Furthermore, as discussed above, the belief in sex differences in spatial ability is also rather weakly supported by the actual evidence.) Many have hypothesized that the stereotypically masculine content of mathematics word problems might account for some of the sex differences in performance on such items. Subjective examination of items that do and do not show large sex differences does not provide obvious support for that view. Furthermore, an experimental study of this question that had high statistical power (Chipman, Marshall, & Scott, 1991) did *not* confirm the popular hypothesis that sex-stereotyped content of math word problems would affect performance. A more recent study confirmed this negative finding (Walsh, Hickey, & Duffy, 1999). In several studies of the SAT, it was found that a class of items ("data sufficiency items") that ask whether sufficient data are available to answer the question did consistently favor females (Donlon, 1973; Strassberg-Rosenberg & Donlon, 1975). It is rather hard to say why such items should have favored females: one can speculate that perhaps females tended to actually attempt problem solutions, thereby improving their ability to answer these items correctly while consuming extra time that may have hindered their performance on the rest of the examination. In any case, the historical fact that the Educational Testing Service chose to drop a class of items that consistently favored females from a test that consistently favors males should cast doubt on the tendency to treat the SAT as if it were some gold standard of mathematical ability. (Ostensibly, these items were removed for being too susceptible to coaching.) The SAT is a speeded multiple-choice test that rewards test-taking strategies such as guessing based on partial information. The characteristics that produce good performance on the SAT are undoubtedly somewhat different than the characteristics that result in good performance in mathematics courses or in mathematical work itself. Does the SAT deserve more weight than the grading judgments of college mathematics professors? Probably not. Unfortunately, the sex difference in math SAT scores does disadvantage women in the college admissions process, in the award of scholarships, and perhaps in faculty attitudes and advice about course selection. It contributes substantially to the public belief in sex differences in mathematical ability. The evidence to the contrary that is cited here has tended, in contrast, to be ignored.

MOTIVATIONAL FACTORS

External encouragement, internal confidence, and the expectation of eventual rewards in employment are among the many motivational factors that may influence persistence in the advanced study of mathematics. Competing interests and demands on the individual may be another. Although the study participants have now lived out their lives and many social changes have occurred, the Terman study of gifted children (Terman, 1954; Terman & Oden, 1959) may suggest some other factors. For men in the Terman study, the *breadth* of interests was a negative predictor of career success, and women in the Terman study differed from men both in the direction of their vocational interests and in having broader interests. The culture of the United States places a high value on being a well-rounded individual, and this continues to be even more true for women than for men. One study of attrition among female mathematics majors and female graduate students in mathematics (Maines, 1980; Maines, Sugrue, & Hardesty, 1981) at two U.S. institutions found that female students of mathematics spent much less time on mathematics than did male students of mathematics. One would expect this to result in less accomplishment. It seems that female students are less likely to develop the intense, almost obsessive involvement with mathematics that may well be critical to truly outstanding achievement. Perhaps they are less involved because the community of mathematicians does less to recruit and involve them. Regardless, it is well to remember that putative sex differences in underlying mathematical abilities are not the only possible explanation for sex differences in the extremes of mathematical accomplishment – whether it be emergence in one of Julian Stanley's talent searches, exceptional achievement in the NAEP exams, or attainment of the doctoral degree. Effort, involvement, engagement, and mentoring come into play.

The likely causal structure of phenomena such as the participation of women and minorities in mathematical, scientific, and technical careers is extremely complex. In my opinion, it can be very helpful to map out that hypothetical structure, as I attempted to do in Chipman & Thomas (1987), modeled on earlier work by Eccles, Adler, Futterman, Goff, Kaczala, Meece, & Midgley (1985). Even though the full analysis and testing of such a structure undoubtedly exceeds our methodological capabilities, it provides a sense of perspective regarding the possible importance of many variables that have figured strongly in verbal discussions of the issues.

"MATH IS POWER": CONCLUDING REMARKS

The words "Math is Power" were the sole content of the ads in a recent campaign run by the National Action Council for Minorities in Engineering. There is a mystique about mathematics, going beyond the practical utility of mathematical competence. The last 30 or so years of research on the women and mathematics question make it clear that the stereotypic views on this subject are extremely resistant to change. The actual facts seem to have little impact on those stereotypes. It seems to have made little difference when Fennema pointed out that the amount of math study could probably explain what were thought of as sex differences in mathematical ability. It seems to have made little difference when Kimball pointed out that many measures of mathematical achievement actually favor females. It seems to have made little difference when I pointed out that mathematics was the least sex-typed of college majors.

It is clear that many people *do not want to believe* that girls and women can be good at mathematics. Back in 1974, Fennema observed that researchers tended to distort their own results in the direction of their stereotyped expectations. When observed, small mean differences get mentally transformed into dichotomized stereotypes, as if every male were more or less whatever than every female. (Ironically, that phenomenon is probably due, in part, to the limitations of language and the inability of many people to think about notions such as overlapping distributions.) Whenever a statistically significant difference is found in the way males and females tend to do mathematics is observed, the male way of doing things (faster retrieval of math facts) tends to be stated in a more positive way than the supposedly female way of doing things (reliance on rote learning). Putative sex differences in cognitive abilities continue to be advanced as the preferred explanation for sex differences in career participation, even though large sex differences in other variables would seem to be more plausible. The topic of sex differences remains far too sexy a topic (Chipman, 1988a). No one is disinterested.

There are some real and unfortunate consequences of these stereotypes. If a local school system has few girls studying advanced mathematics, the situation will be regarded as normal and not the sign of a local problem, even though it is not normal. In my view, it is a problem if false beliefs lead to separate – inherently unequal, in the words of *Brown v. the Board of Education* – educational opportunities. It is a problem if possibly biased tests are seen as simple reflections of the truth. Apparently, ETS believed it was acceptable to drop a class of items that consistently favored females from a test that as a whole favored males. No doubt they believed that was the way things were supposed to be, even though at about the same time they changed the specifications for reading comprehension items because the verbal SAT somewhat favored females, a situation that apparently was not considered acceptable (Dwyer, 1979). Because the SAT is used to determine so many scholarship awards, this situation has real, negative consequences for many women college students (Rosser, 1987).

A case can be made that the primary women and mathematics problem in the U.S. today is that people keep talking about the women and mathematics problem. Sex differences in confidence in oneself as a learner of mathematics probably continue to exist, and the degree of confidence may impact individual decisions to continue in the study of mathematics or to pursue career directions perceived to require mathematical competence. There is a pervasive social stereotype that females are less capable in mathematics, achieve poorly in mathematics, and need special help in mathematics. Despite their dubious validity – as outlined above – statements making these assumptions appear regularly in the U.S. media. Ironically, many of these statements accompany stories about well-meaning efforts to assist female students, such as provision of special single-sex mathematics classes. Because of a study that they had ongoing at the time, Eccles & Jacobs (1986) were able to document that the original Benbow and Stanley (1980) report and accompanying barrage of somewhat distorted publicity had a negative impact on the expectations that both girls and their parents had for their achievement in mathematics. (Headlines at the time read: "Do males have a math gene?" [*Newsweek*], "A new study says males may be naturally abler than females" [*TIME*], and "Are girls born with less ability?" [*Science*].)

Recent experimental studies by social psychologists have shown that the invocation of such stereotypes might explain the continuing sex differences on the SAT Math (Spencer, Steele, & Quinn, 1999; Walsh, Hickey, & Duffy, 1999; Quinn & Spencer, 2001). Because the existence of sex differences on the math SAT and similar ETS tests is so well known, female examinees are always in the condition of "stereotype threat" when taking these tests. Feeling threatened can also change the selection of strategies and cognitive processes used in approaching problems. Highly practiced or *automated* skills are the ones that resist disruption by stressful circumstances (Schneider, 1999), consistent with the gender differences in processing reported by Gallagher & DeLisi (1994). So, perhaps we should stop talking about the women and mathematics problem, and then it will vanish entirely. Should that happen, many people may be upset. The report that women are now receiving a significant majority of BA degrees (see Table 1.1) provoked an almost hysterical article on the front page of the June 25, 2002 *Washington Post* (Fletcher, 2002). It was suggested that the greater participation of women in higher education would lead to serious social problems, including difficulties in filling top corporate jobs and difficulty for women in finding husbands. Education is power. Math is power. And, it seems, power positions are still not seen by many as appropriate for women.

References

Aiken, L. (1973). Ability and creativity in math. *Review of Educational Research, 43,* 405–432.

Armstrong, J. M. (1979). *A national assessment of participation and achievement of women in mathematics.* Denver: Education Commission of the States. (ERIC Document Reproduction Service No. ED 187562).

Armstrong, J. M. (1985). A national assessment of participation and achievement of women in mathematics. In S. F. Chipman, L. R. Brush, & D. M. Wilson (Eds.), *Women and mathematics: Balancing the equation* (pp. 59–94). Hillsdale, NJ: Erlbaum.

Becker, B. J. (1990). Item characteristics and gender differences on the SAT-M for mathematically able youths. *American Educational Research Journal, 27,* 65–88.

Benbow, C. P., & Stanley, J. C. (1980). Sex differences in mathematical ability: Fact or artifact? *Science, 210,* 1262–1264.

Benbow, C. P., & Stanley, J. C. (1983). Sex differences in mathematical reasoning ability: More facts. *Science, 222,* 1029–1031.

Carpenter, P. A., Just, M. A., & Shell, P. (1990). What one intelligence test measures: A theoretical account of the processing in the Raven Progressive Matrices Test. *Psychological Review, 97,* 404–431.

Chipman, S. F. (1988a). Far too sexy a topic. *Educational Researcher, 17,* 46–49. Review of J. S. Hyde & M. C. Linn (Eds.), *The Psychology of Gender: Advances Through Meta-analysis.*

Chipman, S. F. (1988b). *Word problems: Where test bias creeps in.* Paper presented at the annual meeting of the American Educational Research Association, New Orleans, April 1988. (Listed in program as: Cognitive Issues in Math Test Bias) (ERIC Document Reproduction Service No. TM 012 411).

Chipman, S. F. (1994). Gender and school learning: Mathematics. In T. Husen & T. H. Postlethwaite (Eds.), *International Encyclopedia of Education.* Pergamon Press.

Chipman, S. F. (1996a). Female participation in the study of mathematics: The U.S. situation. In G. Hanna (Ed.), *Towards Gender Equity in Mathematics Education* (pp. 285–296). Boston: Kluwer Academic.

Chipman, S. F. (1996b). Gender and school learning: Mathematics. In E. De Corte & F. E. Weinert (Eds.), *International Encyclopedia of Developmental and Instructional Psychology.* Amsterdam: Pergamon.

Chipman, S. F., Brush, L., & Wilson, D. (Eds.). (1985). *Women and mathematics: Balancing the equation.* Hillsdale, NJ: Lawrence Erlbaum Associates.

Chipman, S. F., Krantz, D. H., & Silver, R. (1992). Mathematics anxiety and science careers among able college women. *Psychological Science, 3,* 292–295.

Chipman, S. F., Krantz, D. H., & Silver, R. (1995). Mathematics anxiety/confidence and other determinants of college major selection. In B. Grevholm & G. Hanna (Eds.), *Gender and Mathematics Education: An ICMI Study* (pp. 113–120). Lund: Lund University Press.

Chipman, S. F., Marshall, S. P., & Scott, P. A. (1991). Content effects on word problem performance: A possible source of test bias? *American Educational Research Journal*, *28*, 897–915.

Chipman, S. F., & Thomas, V. G. (1985). Outlining the problem. In S. F. Chipman, L. Brush, & D. Wilson (Eds.), *Women and mathematics: Balancing the equation* (pp. 1–24). Hillsdale, NJ: Lawrence Erlbaum Associates.

Chipman, S. F., & Thomas, V. G. (1987). The participation of women and minorities in mathematics, sciences, and technology. *Review of Research in Education, XIV*, 387–430.

Chipman, S. F., & Wilson, D. (1985). Understanding mathematics course enrollment and mathematics achievement: A synthesis of the research. In S. F. Chipman, L. Brush, & D. Wilson (Eds.), *Women and mathematics: Balancing the equation* (pp. 275–328). Hillsdale, NJ: Lawrence Erlbaum Associates.

College Entrance Examination Board (CEEB). (2000). *2000 Profile of College-Bound Seniors, National Report*. http://www.collegeboard.com/sat/cbsenior/yr2000/nat/.

Donlon, T. F. (1973). *Content factors in sex differences on test questions*. (ETS RM-73-28). Princeton, NJ: Educational Testing Service.

Dunteman, G. H., Wisenbaker, J., & Taylor, M. E. (1979). *Race and sex differences in college science program participation*. Research Triangle Institute: Report submitted to the National Science Foundation under Contract No. SED77-18728. (ERIC Document Reproduction Service No. ED 199034).

Dwyer, C. A. (1979). The role of tests and their construction in producing apparent sex-related differences. In M. A. Wittig & A. C. Petersen (Eds.), *Sex-related differences in cognitive functioning: Developmental issues* (pp. 335–353). New York: Academic Press.

Eccles, J. S., & Jacobs, J. E. (1986). Social forces shape math attitudes and performance. *Signs: Journal of Women in Culture and Society, 11*, 367–380.

Eccles-Parsons, J., Adler, T. F., Futterman, R., Goff, S., Kaczala, C., Meece, J. L., & Midgely, C. (1983). Expectancies, values, and academic choice. In J. Spence (Ed.), *Achievement and academic motivation* (pp. 75–146). San Francisco: W. H. Freeman.

Educational Testing Service (ETS). (1979). *National college bound seniors, 1979*. Princeton, NJ: College Entrance Examination Board.

Felson, R. B., & Trudeau, L. (1991). Gender differences in mathematics performance. *Social Psychology Quarterly, 54*, 113–126.

Fennema, E. (1974). Mathematics learning and the sexes: A review. *Journal for Research in Mathematics Education, 5*, 126–139.

Fennema, E. (1977). Influences of selected cognitive, affective and educational variables on sex-related differences in mathematics learning and studying. In *Women and Mathematics: Research perspectives for change*. Washington, DC: The National Institute of Education.

Fennema, E., & Sherman, J. (1976). Fennema-Sherman mathematics attitudes scales. *JSAS Catalog of Selected Documents in Psychology*, 631.

Fennema, E., & Sherman, J. (1977). Sex-related differences in mathematics achievement, spatial visualization and affective factors. *American Educational Research Journal, 14*, 51–71.

Fennema, E., & Sherman, J. (1978). Sex-related differences in mathematics achievement and related factors: A further study. *Journal for Research in Mathematical Education, 9*, 189–203.

Fletcher, M. A. (2002). Degrees of separation. *Washington Post*, June 25, 2002, p. 1, A10.

Fox, L. H. (1977). The effects of sex-role socialization on mathematics participation and achievement. In *Women and Mathematics: Research perspectives for change*. Washington, DC: The National Institute of Education.

Fruchter, B. (1954). Measurement of spatial abilities: History and background. *Educational and Psychological Measurement, 14*, 387–395.

Gallagher, A. M., & DeLisi, R. (1994). Gender differences in Scholastic Aptitude Test mathematics problem solving among high ability students. *Journal of Educational Psychology, 86*, 204–211.

Hanna, G. (1989). Mathematics achievement of girls and boys in grade eight: Results from twenty countries. *Educational Studies in Mathematics, 20*, 225–232.

Hansen, J. C. (1988). Changing interests of women: Myth or reality. *Applied Psychology: An International Review, 37*, 133–150.

Hyde, J. S., Fennema, E., & Lamon, S. J. (1990). Gender differences in mathematics performance: A meta-analysis. *Psychological Bulletin, 107*, 139–155.

Hyde, J. S., Fennema, E., Ryan, M., Frost, L. A., & Hopp, C. (1990). Gender difference in mathematics attitudes and affect: A meta-analysis. *Psychology of Women Quarterly, 14*, 299–324.

Kimball, M. M. (1989). A new perspective on women's math achievement. *Psychological Bulletin, 105*, 198–214.

Lim, H. (1963). *Geometry and the space factors*. Unpublished paper for the School Mathematics Study Group.

Linn, M. C., & Petersen, A. C. (1985). Emergence and characterization of sex differences in spatial ability. *Child Development, 56*, 1479–1498.

Lippa, R. (1998). Gender-related individual differences and the structure of vocational interests: The importance of the people-things dimension. *Journal of Personality and Social Psychology, 74*, 996–1009.

Lohman, D. F. (1979). *Spatial ability: A review and reanalysis of the correlational literature*. (Technical Report No. 8). Palo Alto, CA: Aptitude Research Project, School of Education, Stanford University.

Lohman, D. F. (1988). Spatial abilities as traits, processes, and knowledge. In R. J. Sternberg (Ed.), *Advances in the psychology of human intelligence* (pp. 181–248). Hillsdale, NJ: Erlbaum.

Lohman, D. F. (1996). Spatial ability and g. In I. Dennis & P. Tapsfield (Eds.), *Human abilities: Their nature and measurement* (pp. 97–116).

Maccoby, E., & Jacklin, C. (1974). *The Psychology of Sex Differences*. Palo Alto, CA: Stanford University Press.

Maines, D. R. (1980). *Role modeling processes and educational inequity for graduate and undergraduate students in mathematics*. Unpublished manuscript, Northwestern University, 1980.

Maines, D. R., Sugrue, N. M., & Hardesty, M. J. (1981). *Social processes of sex differentiation in mathematics*. Unpublished manuscript, Northwestern University, report on NIE-G-79-0114.

McGee, M. G. (1979). Human spatial abilities: Psychometric studies and environmental, genetic, hormonal and neurological influences. *Psychological Bulletin, 86*, 889–918.

National Center for Education Statistics (NCES). (2001). *Digest of Education Statistics, 2001*. http://nces.ed.gov/pubs2002/digest2001/tables/.

National Institute of Education (NIE). (1977). *Grants for research on education and work*. Washington, DC: National Institute of Education.

National Science Board. (1993). *Science and Engineering Indicators – 1993* (NSB 93-1). Washington, DC: U.S. Government Printing Office.

National Science Foundation (NSF). (1986). *Women and minorities in science and engineering* (Report No. NSF 86-301). Washington, DC: National Science Foundation.

Quinn, D. M., & Spencer, S. J. (2001). The interference of stereotype threat with women's generation of mathematical problem-solving strategies. *Journal of Social Issues, 57*, 55–71.

Rosser, P. (1987). *Sex bias in college admissions tests: Why women lose out*. Cambridge, MA: Fair Test National Center for Fair & Open Testing. (ERIC Document Reproduction Service No. ED 285904.)

Sanders, B., Soares, M. P., & D'Aquila, J. M. (1982). The sex difference on one test of spatial visualization: A non-trivial difference. *Child Development, 53*, 1106–1110.

Schneider, W. (1999). Automaticity. *The MIT Encyclopedia of the Cognitive Sciences* (pp. 63–64). Cambridge, MA: The MIT Press.

Sells, L. (1973). High school mathematics as the critical filter in the job market. *Developing Opportunities for Minorities in Graduate Education: Proceedings of the Conference on Minority Graduate Education at the University of California, Berkeley, May, 1973*, pp. 39–47.

Sherman, J. (1977). Effects of biological factors on sex-related differences in mathematics achievement. In *Women and Mathematics: Research perspectives for change*. Washington, DC: The National Institute of Education.

Sherman, J. (1980). *Women and mathematics: Prediction and change of behavior*. Madison, WI: Women's Research Institute of Wisconsin, Inc. (ERIC Document Reproduction Service No. 182162).

Smith, I. (1964). *Spatial ability: Its educational and social significance*. San Diego: Robert Knapp.

Spencer, S. J., Steele, C. M., & Quinn, D. M. (1999). Stereotype threat and women's math performance. *Journal of Experimental Social Psychology, 35*, 4–28.

Stallings, J. (1985). School, classroom, and home influences on women's decisions to enroll in advanced mathematics courses. In S. F. Chipman, L. R. Brush, & D. M. Wilson (Eds.), *Women and mathematics: Balancing the equation* (pp. 199–223). Hillsdale, NJ: Erlbaum.

Strassberg-Rosenberg, B., & Donlon, T. P. (1975). *Content influences on sex differences in performance on aptitude tests*. Paper presented at the annual meeting of the National Council on Measurement in Education. (ED 1110 493; TM 004 766).

Terman, L. M. (1954). Scientists and non-scientists in a group of 800 gifted men. *Psychological Monographs, 68*(7), 1–44.

Terman, L. M., & Oden, M. H. (1959). *Genetic Studies of Genius. The gifted group at mid-life* (Vol. 5). Stanford, CA: Stanford University Press.

Tobias, S. (1976). Math anxiety. *MS*, September 1976, pp. 56–59, 80.

Tobias, S. (1978). *Overcoming math anxiety*. New York: Norton.

Tyler, L. E. (1964). The antecedents of two varieties of vocational interests. *Genetic Psychology Monographs, 70*(2), 177–227.

Vandenberg, S. G., & Kuse, A. R. (1979). Spatial ability: A critical review of the sex-linked major gene hypothesis. In M. Wittig & A. Petersen (Eds.), *Sex related differences in cognitive functioning: Developmental issues*. New York: Academic Press.

Very, P. S. (1967). Differential factor structures in mathematical ability. *Genetic Psychology Monographs, 75,* 169–207.

Wainer, H., & Steinberg, L. S. (1992). Sex differences in performance on the mathematics section of the Scholastic Aptitude Test: A bidirectional validity study. *Harvard Educational Review, 62,* 323–336.

Walsh, M., Hickey, C., & Duffy, J. (1999). Influence of item content and stereotype situation on gender differences in mathematical problem solving. *Sex Roles, 41,* 219–240.

Werdelin, I. (1961). *The geometrical ability and space factor analysis in boys and girls.* Lund, Sweden: University of Lund.

Wick, M. E. (1975). Study of the factors associated with success in first year college mathematics. *Mathematics Teacher, 58,* 642–648.

Wise, L. L. (1985). Project TALENT: Mathematics course participation in the 1960's and its career consequences. In S. F. Chipman, L. R. Brush, & D. M. Wilson (Eds.), *Women and mathematics: Balancing the equation* (pp. 25–58). Hillsdale, NJ: Erlbaum.

Wise, L. L., Steel, L., & MacDonald, C. (1979). *Origins and career consequences of sex differences in high school mathematics achievement.* Palo Alto, CA: American Institutes for Research. (ERIC Document Reproduction Service No. ED 180846.)

2

The Perseverative Search for Sex Differences in Mathematics Ability

Jeremy B. Caplan and Paula J. Caplan

Studying "sex differences" in cognition is not a neutral activity, any more than studying "racial differences" in cognition (Caplan & Caplan 1997, 1999). As long as our society is sexist, racist, or biased in any other way, any claim to find group differences is likely, sooner or later, to be held up as proof of the more powerful group's superiority (Eccles & Jacobs, 1986; Wine, Moses, & Smye, 1980; Wine, Smye, & Moses, 1980). One illustration of the lack of neutrality of the study of sex differences is the title of this book, which suggests that its contents will be about the nature and extent of sex differences in mathematics. Indeed, several researchers have suggested that the very presence and the volume of studies of sex differences give the impression that differences have been found (this debate is reviewed by Favreau, 1997). Notice that in the wording of the title, *Gender Differences in Mathematics*, there is no implication that there is any question about whether there are such differences. However, the field has usually been referred to as "sex differences" rather than "gender differences" research, but in contrast, the use of "gender" in the title of this book serves the important function of suggesting the possibility that, whenever sex differences are found, they may be due to socialization factors rather than to the "biological" ones usually taken to be implied by the term "sex differences."

The sheer volume of material published by researchers engaged in the persistent search for sex differences in mathematics abilities is staggering. Should we regard this research with any more seriousness or respect than we would accord the intense search for racial differences in cognition? Is it so different from the unrelenting attempts of 19th-century researchers to find some basis in the brain for what was assumed to be the innate intellectual inferiority of women and racialized people (Caplan & Caplan, 1999)? The amount of time, energy, and money that are poured into the search for sex differences in math are disproportionately large, given how difficult it is to find these differences. Even researchers who assert, when they do find sex differences, that those differences are biologically based, have rarely, if ever, designed any element of their experiments to test for either such a basis in general or a specific type of biological basis. However, this has not stopped biological determinists from claiming to know that a particular biological mechanism is the cause of these differences (e.g., Benbow & Benbow, 1987; Benbow & Stanley, 1980, 1983; Royer, Tronsky, Chan, Jackson, & Marchant, 1999).

One would urge the biological determinists to take notice of data from other cultures showing no sex difference in math. For instance, in South Africa, there was no sex difference in university math majors' mean achievement in math courses, and in fact there was some indication that women's achievement was higher than the men's (Cherian & Siweya, 1996). Research by Taal (1994) on Dutch secondary school students ages 13–16 years showed no gender differences in achievement for math or in attitudes toward math. It might be significant that in Holland, where the lack of a difference in attitudes suggests that there may be less gender discrimination in regard to math, what distinguished students who did from students who did not select math for their final examination curriculum were intellectual capacities, achievements, and feelings of adequacy in math; previous involvement in math-related activities did not play a role. It seems that, in the absence of socialization differences, both females and males were able to make choices related to math based on their actual abilities and achievement rather than on socially produced, sex-differential expectations.

Researchers have motivations. Their motivations impel them toward some research questions rather than others. Of course, factors other than personal motives, such as availability of laboratory space, funding, ease of doing research, and interest of one's colleagues and supervisors, can play roles in determining one's areas of study. However, nothing eliminates bias. Bias can lead to problems in the design as well as in the interpretation of research. When it comes to research on sex differences in mathematics abilities, researchers' bias is a huge problem with enormous consequences. An example of this is the disproportionate amount of major media coverage given to a single pair of studies, based on an atypical population and using a single test (Benbow & Benbow, 1987; Benbow & Stanley, 1980, 1983), whose authors put forward the allegation that males' abilities are superior to those of females and that this is due to hormonal differences. That allegation rapidly became accepted as true by many teachers, parents, and students themselves, and Eccles and Jacobs (1986) found that because of this news coverage, parents' ratings of the mathematical potential of their daughters was reduced. This field of research should not be discussed in the absence of explicit consideration of the researchers' motivations. Because no one is ever bias free, it is crucial to make the motivations of sex-differences researchers both transparent and central to any discussion of their work, whether the discussion is about basic questions of cognition or about how to implement social change (Gelsthorpe, 1990; Hunt, 1992). Indeed, this bias has led to a powerful belief that pervades our society (often presented as true at cocktail parties), to the effect that girls cannot do math.

WHY DO PEOPLE STUDY SEX DIFFERENCES IN COGNITION?

Table 2.1 provides a sampling of kinds of motives, ranging from those relevant to basic research to those relevant to applied research. We separate examples of motivations, which are especially likely to lead researchers to produce flawed designs and inappropriate interpretations (righthand column), from those less likely to lead to researchers' biasing of design and interpretation (lefthand column). Most bias-prone motives involve

TABLE 2.1. *Sample of Possible Motives for Doing Sex Difference Research*

Low Bias	High Bias
To understand relationships between biology and behavior	To prove that behavior is determined by biological factors
To test whether social factors cause sex differences	To prove that behavior is determined by social factors
To test "common-knowledge" notions of sex differences in cognition	To confirm/dispel influential "common knowledge" about sex differences in cognitive abilities
To understand why certain people are alienated from or drawn to specific fields of work	To justify differences in hiring practices
To test a theory of cognition that bears on sex differences	To find sex differences in order to get results published[a]
To identify and reduce or eradicate unnecessary difficulties in people's lives[b]	To develop interventions to overcome imbalances, regardless of their cause(s)[b]

[a] Editors of "scholarly" journals are vastly more likely to publish studies in which significant group differences are found than in which no group differences are found (the "file drawer" problem; Rosenthal, 1979).

[b] If one's primary aim is to improve people's quality of life, then a detected sex difference could be regarded as a sign that there is some systematic problem that should be corrected, such as in educational or social practices. Alternatively, one's primary aim might be simply to eradicate a sex difference. This is dangerous because there are many ways to eradicate a sex difference, some with socially beneficial consequences (e.g., tailoring education to individuals' needs) and some harmful (e.g., choosing different strategies for teaching math based on the students' sex rather than on their abilities and needs).

Note: Many of these are similar to motivations that were self-reported in a questionnaire study of social psychologists who had published in social psychology journals (Rotton, Foos, Van Meek, & Levitt, 1995).

advancing a preexisting personal and/or political agenda. Having a personal and/or political agenda does not *inevitably* lead to problematic designs and interpretations, but it does create a greater need for researchers to be aware of and to disclose their own motivations and biases.

Because the various motives listed in Table 2.1 may be at play, data from and claims about studies of sex differences in mathematics abilities must be received with caution, both on their own and as bases for construction of theories. Although a researcher from any viewpoint, whether it be biological determinism or socialization theory or something else, could have any of the biased aims, evidence of biological bases tends to be linked with the notion that it is futile to try to overcome "natural" forces.

OUR OWN BIAS IN REVIEWING THE RESEARCH ON SEX DIFFERENCES IN MATHEMATICS

In light of the backflips in experimental design and interpretation of data that we have seen researchers execute in order to produce sex differences in math performance, as well as of the harm caused to girls and women who believe they are inferior and also to boys and men who fail to live up to the stereotype of superiority, our own motivation has landed on the socialization theory end of the scale. More specifically, the onus is on researchers to establish a substantial and reliable (replicable) sex-difference result and to rule out major classes of systematic socialization factors before claims that there is a clear, reliable sex difference that is grounded in biology should be incorporated into theories of cognition.

WHAT BIOLOGICAL DETERMINISTS HAVE TO IGNORE

The two most common patterns of research results that appear in the literature are:

1. There is a male superiority.
2. There is no sex difference in math.

The only way to estimate ability is to examine samples of performance, but performance is often treated as though it perfectly reflected or corresponded with ability. It is crucial to keep in mind the distinction between abilities and performance in considering the following list of ways one can explain pattern 1 and pattern 2, per above. There are various possible explanations for each pattern.

If males get higher scores than females on a mathematics test, then (1) there is a biological basis for males' superior abilities, and no socialization differences change this and thus affect performance; or (2) there is a (slight or substantial) biological basis for males' superior abilities, and one or more socialization factors enhances males' performance or reduces females' performance or both; or (3) there are no biologically based sex differences in mathematics abilities, but sex-differential socialization enhances males' performance or reduces females' performance or both; or (4) there is a biologically based female superiority in abilities, but sex differences in socialization enhances males' performance or reduces females' performance or both.

If there is no sex difference in performance on mathematics tests, then (5) there is a biologically based male superiority in abilities, but sex differences in socialization enhance females' performance or reduce males' performance or both; or (6) there is a biologically based female superiority in abilities, but sex differences in socialization enhance males' performance or reduce females' performance or both; or (7) there is no biologically based sex difference in abilities, and either there are no relevant sex differences in socialization or there are two or more such differences that cancel each other out.

Most of the published research about sex differences in math is implicitly or explicitly based on explanations 1, 2, 5, or 7. Rarely have 3, 4, and 6 been considered.

Because various kinds of motivation might be at play, and because various underlying factors can lead to similar patterns of results, studies of sex differences in math abilities must be interpreted with caution, especially when they are used as bases for constructing theories about cognition. Before one begins to develop a theory of biological determinants of cognitive sex differences, one should be sure that the research yields substantial and reliable findings that warrant developing such a theory (Block, 1976). However, the literature on sex differences in mathematics abilities does not yield consistent results. Furthermore, when differences are found, they tend not to arise until around puberty and to be small and to depend on the choice of measures, other aspects of experimental design, and the particular experimental situation. Typically, they come from studies of high-achieving or gifted populations (Fan, Chen, & Matsumoto, 1997) and account for only a tiny proportion of the variance. Furthermore, as Favreau (1997) emphasizes, small but significant differences can easily (and often, in sex-difference research) arise from systematic effects in a small proportion of participants, while the majority of participants show no difference. She notes that this has profoundly different implications than a systematic difference found across the entire populations of participants; however, researchers usually refer to findings of small but significant difference as signalling a general effect of sex.

The practice of focusing one's research on a population segment (preselected by ability, age, or both) and/or a test that is the most likely to produce a significant sex difference is reminiscent of the practice followed by the 19th-century researchers who sought desperately to find a basis in the brain for what they assumed to be men's superior intelligence (see Caplan & Caplan, 1999). When their early idea that men's brains were probably bigger than women's failed to pan out (proportional to overall body size, women actually had the larger brains), they ran hither and thither throughout the brain, trying to find some bit on which they could pin men's greater intelligence. Even that tradition continues today, using more recently developed methods of investigation that therefore confer upon the research an aura of greater sophistication, among researchers who seek obsessively for sex differences in the corpus callosum, numbers of neurons in particular lobes or parts of lobes, and glucose metabolism or brain activity in various bits of the brain. The irony is that both many 19th-century researchers and many present-day researchers are jumping the gun; they are trying to explain a difference that has not been solidly shown through behavioral measures to exist. Today, the search for sex differences in neuronal activity or glucose metabolism in particular brain areas may sound highly scientific and rigorous, as, no doubt, did the 19th-century search for sex differences in brain size. However, none of these approaches make sense because they represent a search for anatomical or physiological correlates of a behavioral effect that has not been reliably demonstrated to exist, certainly not so reliably and immutably that it makes sense to posit physiological correlates.

In the realm of sex differences in mathematics abilities, the researchers who are the most famous and whose work is most widely considered to be true tend to be those who claim that their research proves that there is a male superiority. These same researchers rarely classify as a problem what they present as females' inferiority, and they do not tend to make thoughtful recommendations to help females with math, provide them with more support while they are studying math or trying to decide whether to pursue careers with heavy demands in mathematics subjects, or design studies aimed to find out what it would take to improve females' performance. Nor, for the most part, do these researchers take care to point out in their writing and media interviews that, even in the small number of studies that yield a male superiority, that superiority is only part of the picture, and that the rest of the picture includes a huge overlap between the scores of females and those of males on *all* math tests (cf. Favreau, 1997).

One glaring, and perhaps the least-discussed, omission from the vast majority of research on "sex differences" in behavior is the fact that there are more than two biological sexes, as most eloquently discussed by biologist Anne Fausto-Sterling (2000) in her book *Sexing the Body*. Fausto-Sterling points out that a decision was made in Western culture to divide humans into two categories of sex and to assign every individual to one of those two, even though there is an underlying continuum of hormonal variability and manifestations, as well as multiple sex-chromosomal combinations.

In cognitive sex-difference studies, researchers nearly always talk in terms of two sexes (the socially assigned ones) rather than using an accurate, biologically based definition of numerous sexes. It is particularly curious that researchers who seek to test biological theories of cognitive sex differences (whether or not differences exist) usually fail to investigate the hormonal and chromosomal composition of the people they study. Because roughly 1.7 births per 100 fall into 10 classes of nondimorphic sexual development, researchers will be likely to have one or more participants who do not fit the traditional Western standards for the chromosomal and hormonal "female" or "male" (Fausto-Sterling, 2000). Recognition of this fundamental and well documented fact would do nothing less than revolutionize the entire field of inquiry because the vast majority of it is based on an utterly false dichotomy. We hope the reader will keep this significant problem in mind while reading all "sex differences" research, including the rest of this chapter; we realize that may be difficult due to the fact that in most of our chapter we write in terms of two sexes because that is how the literature we address is presented, and thus we have no way of knowing how many sexes might have been represented in any study in which all participants were labeled either female or male.

Researchers and theorists bent on persuading people that males have superior math abilities and that this superiority is biologically determined have tended to ignore a great deal of the existing research. This myopia is disturbing for many reasons, not the least of which is that, when teaching children their very first lessons about science, responsible people make sure to explain to them the fundamental importance of taking into account all the available data relevant to whatever they are trying to understand. Because these determinists have received the vast majority of the attention from academics and educators alike, we focus on the published work of which they appear to take little or no note as they pursue their campaign to convince us of the accuracy of their claims. As we do this, it will also be clear how atypical are those studies they cite to support their claims.

Studies with enormous samples that were not preselected for ability show either no significant sex differences, as for the roughly 24,500 students from the National Education Longitudinal Study (Fan et al., 1997; Mau & Lynn, 2000), or small effect sizes (28,240 high school students; Osborne, 2001). In the Hyde, Fennema, and Lamon (1990) meta-analysis of 100 studies including more than 3 million participants, differences between females and males on math tests were small ($d = 0.15$). In that same meta-analysis, Hyde et al. found that girls tended to score higher than boys in elementary and middle school, and boys performed better than girls in high school. Other studies with smaller samples that have yielded no sex differences include one by Bradley and Wygant (1998), in which there was no sex difference in performance in an introductory statistics course, even though the women had indicated having greater anxiety than the men about taking the course.

Even among populations selected for their high achievement or ability – a major source of research populations for the biological determinists – males do not always perform better than females; for instance, in a study by Pajares (1996), gifted girls actually surpassed gifted boys in mathematical problem solving. Insofar as ability contributes to choice of academic courses and careers, it is noteworthy that in a recent study of 2,900 high school students (Jensen, 1998), whereas males showed more positive attitudes toward math, females in equal numbers to males chose to take higher math and aspired to math-intensive careers.

In a study of 47,000 people who completed first-year college math courses, with women and men matched for type of math course taken and grade received, women scored 21 to 55 points lower than men on the SAT-M (Wainer & Steinberg, 1992). It is extremely important to note that part of the design of the study was the matching of women and men for grades in math courses. In view of that, it is important to consider that the difference in scores may be either because (1) women who take college math are overachieving relative to men, and/or (2) men are underachieving relative to women, and/or (3) of the SAT-M and the college math course grades, one is a less adequate reflection of math ability than the other.

Spencer, Steele, and Quinn (1999) acknowledged that they had to go to great lengths to produce a large sex difference in performance by using an especially difficult test. Then, having produced this sex difference, they found it was eradicated simply by telling participants that, in the past, the test had produced no sex differences. This is a further example of the exceedingly special arrangements one has to make to produce even a reliable and sizable sex difference.

Similarly, using large, national data sets, Leahey and Guo (2001) charted gender differences in mathematical trajectories from elementary school through high school and found only slight differences in rate of acceleration in math performance. Differences only emerged late in high school and were exaggerated for higher-performing students. In addition, the small differences, when found, tended to show males performing better on multiple-choice questions and females performing better on questions on which they had to identify the appropriate method first and then perform the computation. It is not clear that one class of problems is more "mathematical" than the other. The authors note that this "slight and delayed emergence of gender differences" calls into question the strong conclusions of earlier researchers to the effect that large gender differences emerge by high school. It also further illustrates how specific the conditions need to be to produce sex differences.

Despite the vast amount of research yielding no sex differences, many researchers nonetheless persist in designing studies that are clearly based on the assumption that there are sex differences. This is curious because *when one considers the huge differences in the ways children are still socialized in North America, depending on whether they are labeled "male" or "female," it is remarkable that so many studies yield no sex difference at all and that those sex differences in performance on math tests that ever do appear are as small as they are. That is a compelling reason to keep researchers' motivations in mind.*

It is a fundamental tenet of research methodology that one must regard no-difference findings with caution. A lack of a difference (failure to reject the null hypothesis) could result from using too small a sample. The large-sample studies mentioned here overcome this problem somewhat. The persistence of null results and small effect sizes could either result from there being no underlying difference or from the use of a measure (e.g., SAT-M) that is insufficiently sensitive to an underlying difference. This highlights the fact that, although there still *could* be an underlying sex difference in some mathematical ability, we still have little idea what that ability is; for example, Gallagher and DeLisi (1994) reported differences in choice of strategy, arguing that these differences could trade off to result in small overall accuracy differences. Further, small effect sizes from very large samples could result from very specific, subtle effects confined to a small proportion of the tested population that should be interpreted quite differently than a large effect size in a more moderate sample (Cohen, 1990; Favreau, 1997).

To illustrate in some detail the many problems in methodology and interpretation that plague the researchers who persistently seek findings of sex differences (who tend to be, but are not always, biological determinists), we now describe a number of worrying aspects of two typical studies whose measures were very different from each other.

In a lengthy article in which they report no fewer than nine studies, Royer et al. (1999) introduce their paper with the statement, "Males from select populations receive better scores on standardized math achievement tests than females" (p. 181). Like most researchers who base their work on the assumption of a male superiority, they provide little or no truly critical analysis of the existing literature. Like most researchers who begin by assuming that there is a male superiority, they provide little or no critical analysis of the existing literature, for the most part critiquing studies that appear consistent with their initial assumption. Within their literature review, their choice of words is also telling. For instance, reporting that in one study of national samples using thirteen tests, they say that females had a slight advantage over males on math computation "*but* males had a somewhat larger advantage on tests measuring math concepts" (p. 181; our emphasis). Although we do not want to put too fine a point on it, their use of the word "but" in that sentence rather than "and" is only one example of their apparent focus on the superiority of males.

The stated purpose of the nine studies by Royer et al. (1999) was to explore whether "math-fact retrieval," which they define as "the ability to rapidly and automatically retrieve correct answers to addition, subtraction, and multiplication problems" (p. 196), predicts performance on math achievement tests and whether there is a sex difference in the ability to retrieve math facts. The focus of their article is on their conclusion that math fact retrieval "explains the origins of gender differences in math" (p. 181). What is far less emphasized is their finding that "speed of retrieval improves with practice" (p. 181), an important pattern in view of the greater encouragement males receive to think of good performance in math as consistent with their sex role. Furthermore, as one reads their lengthy paper with its focus on explaining a male superiority, it is easy to forget that even they mention that reviewers of research have tended to find that sex differences in math appear only sporadically before junior high school and those that do appear show a female superiority (Kimball, 1989; Willingham & Cole, 1997), as well as that females' grades in specific courses and in math overall are better than those of males through junior high and high school, and that in university, either no difference or a female superiority in math grades is usually found (Royer et al., 1999).

So at most, Royer et al. (1999) took the trouble to conduct nine studies in order to try to explain why in one very limited arena, that of the highest-scoring students on standardized math tests, mostly the SAT-M, there appears to be a male superiority. However, what is also surprising and disturbing is that, as Wigfield and Byrnes (1999) point out, it is clear from the numbers in the article by Royer et al. that the latency for math fact retrieval actually favors females. Wigfield and Byrnes also note that it is difficult to know how to interpret the various findings of Royer et al. because they do not report significance tests. One would think that this is surprising in a so-called "scholarly" journal, but this kind of glossing over of unwanted findings all too often goes past journal reviewers and editors without a ripple. In reviewing the article by Royer et al. one has to wonder whether the absence of significance tests might have anything to do with the fact that their numbers show a dramatic advantage for females in accuracy of answers and a less dramatic pattern of either a female superiority or a no-difference finding. It would have been nice to have reports of statistical analyses, particularly because the vast majority of the article is based on an alleged male superiority in math.

A somewhat different example of the kinds of distortions that appear in the literature is seen in the article by Gallagher and DeLisi (1994), titled "Gender differences in Scholastic Aptitude Test: Mathematics problem solving among high-ability students." The authors' abstract echoes their choice of title in its focus on sex differences, for the abstract's content is primarily about the report that females were more likely than males to use

TABLE 2.2. *Correct Answers (Corrected Means) by Problem Type*

	Conventional (%)	Unconventional (%)
Women	79	72
Men	66	76

Source: From the Gallagher and DeLisi (1994) study.

conventional strategies in solving the problems. What they neither mention in the abstract nor indicate in the title is the following finding from that same study: there were no sex differences in overall performance. In our culture, where it is generally assumed that there is a male superiority in math, it would have cast their findings in a very different light had they explained that there was a great deal of overlap, that nevertheless a significant sex difference emerged in the kinds of strategies used, but that these differences *did not lead to sex-differential scores on the SAT-M*. In the Gallagher and DeLisi (1994) study, of the 18 math problems included in the analyses, 9 were considered conventional, having clearly defined methods for solution, and 9 were considered unconventional, either requiring an atypical strategy for solution or "solved more quickly using some type of estimation or insight" (p. 206).

Thus, before the students were given the problems, one-half were classified as conventional and one-half as unconventional, and then the strategies they used in arriving at their answers were classified as conventional or unconventional. It is worth looking at their data in detail (see Tables 2.2 and 2.3).

Note that, although men were more likely than women to use unconventional strategies, members of both sexes were more likely to use conventional than unconventional strategies. Gallagher and DeLisi uncritically present possible accounts of their findings, relying on both social and biological factors. For example, ". . . because of both physiological differences in male and female brains and differences in socialization of male and female students, female students are generally better at tasks that require the rapid retrieval of information from memory, whereas male students are

TABLE 2.3. *Problem-Solving Strategy Used*

	Conventional (%)	Unconventional (%)
Women	70	26
Men	57	37

Source: From the Gallagher and DeLisi (1994) study.

usually better at tasks that require the manipulation of information that is already represented in memory" (p. 210).

This assertion gives the undoubtedly unintended impression of damning women with faint praise and indicates the kind of critical consideration of various factors that is important in this field. What is interesting is that, because in Western culture it is widely assumed that less intelligence is required for simply retrieving stored information than for choosing ways of manipulating stored information, the intentions of Gallagher and DeLisi to urge readers to think about various possibilities may give rise, in this culture, to the impression that males do better on higher-level cognitive tasks than do females, whereas females do better on the lower-level ones.

At their extremes, the debate between biological determinists and proponents of socialization explanations can be expressed this way: the former assume that differences in ability *necessarily* arising from biological sex lead to performance differences, whereas the latter assume that socialization differences *unnecessarily* based on biological sex lead to any performance differences that may appear.

In summary, then, the performance differences appear rarely and inconsistently. When present, they are small, and one needs to use highly selected populations and unusual measures to produce any differences. In contrast, a great number of social/motivational factors have been shown to reduce females' performance on math tests, and we address these next.

In reviewing the research about social/motivational factors, because there are so many that affect math performance and because they have been demonstrated in repeated studies, what we are about to present is a picture of just a few of the large number of hurdles that girls and women have to leap in the math arena. It is crucial to keep in mind that, even with all those hurdles to leap, girls' and women's math performance is rarely lower than that of males. It would not be out of line to wonder, then, in order to ensure that all possible kinds of theories will have been proposed, whether females' math abilities are actually superior to those of males and whether it takes a lot of hurdles to slow them down. For example, Pajares (1996) found that gifted girls who had somehow managed to leap the hurdle of the stereotype insofar as they did not differ from boys in self-efficacy in math actually surpassed gifted boys in performance on mathematical problem solving. Although all fields of research have their flaws and biases, the matter of sex differences in math requires particularly urgent attention and critique, given that so much harm has been done by claims of males' superiority. Therefore, we are not claiming that females are in fact superior in this realm. We are simply illustrating that the long-standing practice has been to focus on either a male superiority approach or a no-difference one, so the various possibilities have not had equal journal space, grant money, or air time.

Variables That Mediate Sex Differences

Some of the recent research on sex differences in math ability is motivated by the question of whether sex differences can be explained by nonbiological variables. In this kind of research, when sex differences are found, they are regarded as the canary in the mine. When miners ventured deep into the earth, they knew when the canary died that they had reached the point where the air was dangerous. A finding of sex differences can be a sign that people are treated differently, depending on their sex. If females and males are differently socialized, as in many ways they still are, then a finding of a sex difference in task performance could be a direct result of some aspect of that socialization. Variables we consider include stereotype threat, locus of control, anxiety, parents' and teachers' influences, and math-related experience.

The studies we cover in this section reveal some explanations for sex differences in performance when they occur. Equally important, and too rarely considered, is that these same variables are also covariates of *individual differences* in performance. For applied researchers, who aim to help people to improve their math test scores and/or to feel more comfortable in a math-oriented environment, understanding individual differences is far more helpful than focusing on group differences, especially because there is so much overlap in score distributions for the sexes. If a substantial sex difference is found, this means there is a correlation between sex and performance. However, correlation doesn't tell you about the causal relations between sex and performance. It is likely that a third mediating variable (e.g., self-confidence, prior experience with mathematics) influences performance and happens to be correlated (perhaps for reasons of socialization) with sex. In such cases, one can see the sex difference as the canary. If the mediating variable can explain all the variance accounted for by sex, then applications may be more effective if they are focused directly on that mediating variable, for instance, improving *all* students' self-confidence or exposing students to more mathematics in everyday life. Further, potentially, males as well as females could benefit from these proactive measures. Using an individual-differences approach, one would be likely to find that at least some of the steps that help girls who are having trouble in math would also help boys who are having trouble, rather than operating as though all boys were superior and need no help or attention, and as though all girls were inferior and need of help.

STEREOTYPE THREAT

A major factor in reducing females' math performance appears to be "stereotype threat," which Steele (1992) initially introduced in relation to race. He described stereotype threat as the worry about being judged in comparison to a negative stereotype, such as that racialized people are less intelligent than "white" people. Another such stereotype is that women have weaker math abilities than men. Spencer et al. (1999) wrote that stereotype threat ". . . can be thought of as a disruptive reaction to an imagined audience set to view one stereotypically" (p. 14). Aronson, Lustina, Good, and Keough (1999) found that even white, male undergraduates, when placed in a stereotype threat situation in which white males were compared with a group stereotyped as excelling at math (Asians), performed worse on a difficult math test than did a nonstereotype threat control group.

In two studies, Spencer et al. (1999) found that women underperformed on difficult math tests but not on easy ones. This pattern held for a highly selected sample of female and male undergraduates. It also held for a more typical population – undergraduates who had scored between 400 and 650 on the SAT-M. In a third study, Spencer et al. (1999) found that the sex difference in math performance they revealed in the first two studies could be eliminated when they lowered stereotype threat by telling the participants that that test had not in the past produced gender differences. This is similar to Tobin's (1982) finding that, when she administered a spatial ability task to female and male participants and found a male superiority in performance, then immediately afterward had them repeat the task, she eradicated the sex difference. Her finding is especially important because the task she chose had usually been said to yield a male superiority.

Inzlicht and Ben-Zeev (2000) found that, when participants completed a difficult math test in the presence of two other people, women who took the test with two men obtained lower scores than women who took the test with one or two other women. In fact, the women's deficits in performance increased as the number of males in the group increased. This supports the notion that, when sex differences emerge, they do so within the context of a rich social structure rife with stereotypes. Expectations of success or failure, based on stereotype threat, may in turn influence men and women differently. Brown and Josephs (1999) found that women who believed that a math test would indicate whether they were especially weak in math performed worse on standardized math tests than did women who believed it would test whether they were exceptionally strong. In contrast, men performed worse when told that the test would indicate whether they were exceptionally strong.

Quinn and Spencer (2001) further investigated the effect of stereotype threat on math performance. When stereotype threat was high, women performed more poorly than men on word problems in math but not on equivalent numerical problems. This suggests that stereotype threat interferes not with performance on computations *per se*, but rather with selection of appropriate mathematical operations for a given problem. In an important sense, the discovery that reducing stereotype threat, by the speaking of a *single sentence* about the lack of sex differences on a test, can immediately eliminate group differences renders uninteresting and irrelevant the massive literature of research and theory about the causes of the alleged male superiority. However, one could see how characterizing the effects of stereotype might be informative in developing interventions to remove the systematic effects of stereotype, regardless of whether they influence measurable performance on tests of mathematics ability.

OSTRACISM AND GENDER IDENTIFICATION

An important social factor is the fear of ostracism of girls who perform well in mathematics because, at least in the United States and some other countries, "femininity" is described as inconsistent with math ability. In work by Schmader (2002), when women's gender identity was linked to their performance on a math test, women with higher levels of gender identification performed worse than men, but women with lower levels of gender identification performed comparably to men. When gender identity was not linked to test performance, women performed comparably to men, regardless of the importance they placed on gender identity. Case (1984) found that, around puberty, those girls who became underachievers differed from those whose school achievement remained good in that the former had "narrower" ideas about the definition and boundaries of femaleness than did girls who continued to achieve at their previous level.

SELF-EFFICACY: BELIEF IN ONE'S OWN ABILITIES

It is not surprising that, in light of sex-role stereotypes, males tend to have a more positive assessment of their own math abilities than do females. This assessment is sometimes referred to as "self-efficacy." Brown and Josephs (1999) found that women who believed that a math test would reveal weakness in math scored lower on math tests than did women who believed it would reveal whether they were exceptionally good at math. Men showed the reverse pattern. In a study by Pajares and Miller (1994), males scored higher and had greater self-efficacy, a better self-concept, and lower anxiety than women in regard to mathematical problem solving. However, these differences were due largely to the influence of self-efficacy because gender had a direct effect only on self-efficacy and a measure of prior experience. In a comparison of gifted with average fifth-grade students, regardless of ability level, males had more self-efficacy in regard to math than did their female counterparts (Ewers & Wood, 1993). Males tended to overestimate their performance more than did females (see also Pajares & Miller, 1994).

Among eighth-grade students, males with high math achievement had both higher self-concept and higher standardized test scores than did females with high math achievement (Reis & Park, 2001). Does this suggest that standardized test scores are poor reflections of math achievement or that school achievement is? Are we overestimating boys' math ability or underestimating girls'? These questions are currently unanswered.

It is rare to find no sex difference in self-efficacy in regard to math; however, among gifted girls and boys, Pajares (1996) found no sex difference. Notably, when they controlled for self-efficacy, the girls surpassed the boys in mathematical problem solving. One interpretation of this is that girls have more social pressures with regard to math to overcome. Therefore, a given level of self-efficacy may benefit a girl more than it would benefit a boy.

In the study by Gallagher and DeLisi (1994), their highest SAT-M scorers were those who, according to self-reports, had confidence in their math abilities and were persistent when unable to solve math problems immediately. This highlights the relevance of self-efficacy as a variable mediating sex differences in math test performance.

TEACHER AND PARENT FACTORS

Sex-differential expectations and treatment contribute to sex differences in performance. Teachers provide different experiences for girls than for boys with respect to math in the classroom. Whereas teachers and counselors can be unhelpful or discouraging, female peers can be particularly important for support (Casserly, 1980). There are many subtle manifestations of sexism in the classroom that can influence girls' interest and performance in math classes (Wigfield & Byrnes, 1999). Girls and boys have been shown to have equivalent expectations about math performance when their teachers praise them equally (Parsons, Kaczala, & Meece, 1982). Math and physics, however, tend to be taught in less girl-friendly ways, a particularly troubling pattern given that girls' attitudes and performance can be improved by girl-friendly approaches (Eccles, 1994). Parents provide different experiences for girls than for boys with respect to experiences with math in the home (Beal, 1994; Ruble & Martin, 1998), and children's attitudes toward math are more influenced by their parents' attitudes about their abilities than by their own past performances (Parsons, Meece, Adler, & Kaezala, 1982). In the United States and Thailand, parents' support has been shown to be a significant predictor of 13-year-olds' attitudes toward math (Tocci & Engelhard, 1991). Given that beliefs can influence performance (Brown & Josephs, 1999), it is plausible that these attitudinal factors are relevant to performance.

MATH-RELATED EXPERIENCE

As males' and females' experiences begin to diverge, this could influence other variables, such as attitudes, effort, and interest, which could in turn feed back and influence subsequent quantity and quality of experience.

Byrnes and Takahira (1993) explained sex differences in performance on the SAT-M as a result of prior knowledge and strategies, and Pajares and Miller (1994) found that people had different prior experiences with math problem solving, depending on their gender. One important implication of experience as an important predictor of performance is that experience compounds over a lifetime.

MATH TEST ANXIETY

Girls are more likely than boys to have math test anxiety and, as Spencer et al. (1999) report, considerable evidence has shown that "test anxiety," sometimes considered dispositional but sometimes considered "a disruptive reaction to an evaluative test-taking context" (p. 14), can interfere with test performance (e.g., Sarason, 1972; Wigfield & Eccles, 1989; Wigfield & Meece, 1988; Wine, 1971). They suggest that this constitutes further support for the principle that self-evaluative stereotype threat can interfere with test performance.

Pajares and Kranzler (1995) found that even though, in their study, girls did not differ from boys in their having a sense of self-efficacy about math, girls reported feeling more math anxiety. Hunsley and Flessati (1988) showed that past experiences with math are related to the level of math anxiety, identifying a possible systematic social origin of sex differences in math anxiety. Because they measured anxiety after the math test was given, this study does not help us answer whether anxiety influenced performance or vice versa. Osborne (2001) found that anxiety only made a small contribution to females' inferior math achievement, but the small effect size appears to have been partly because the sex differences in math achievement were so small.

CHOICE OF RESEARCH QUESTION AND THE "FILE-DRAWER" PROBLEM

Up to this point in the chapter, we have discussed how motivations and bias can influence the quality of research that people do, as well as the distortions they are likely to make in interpreting their findings. As we have mentioned, different motivations can lead researchers to ask different questions. One might consider that knowledge is knowledge, and missing knowledge can be simply treated as missing and kept in mind accordingly. We argue, as others have (see Favreau, 1997, for a review), that the choice of which research to do has a powerful impact on the student who is trying to make sense of the literature and trying to draw conclusions from it. Indeed, we would venture that reading a scientific paper tells one as much about the motivations, interests, values, and biases of the researcher as it does about the nature of the world. Given how difficult it is to synthesize findings, with all their caveats and differences in design details, from many journal articles, the impression one ends up with may be dominated by "prevailing wisdom" rather than by justifiable conclusions one may draw from the published evidence.

Given this state of affairs, it is as crucial to attempt to understand what studies sex-difference researchers *don't* do as it is to master the published literature. For example, the fact that contemporary researchers are far more likely to investigate cognitive differences by sex than by race or sexual orientation or eye color doesn't so much tell us that there are differences by sex and not by race or sexual orientation or eye color. Rather, it tells us that researchers may believe this to be the case. Alternatively, they may feel social pressure from colleagues, journal editors, or the media to avoid asking politically risky questions.

In a revealing investigation of these types of effects, Rotton et al. (1995) surveyed authors who had recently had articles published in a set of social psychology journals. They identified a number of reasons that their responders stated for not publishing their data. The most frequent of these was that they had "nonsignificant results." Some of these failures to reach statistical significance may have been due to a lack of statistical power because of small sample sizes, but some may have had plenty of statistical power, with large enough sample sizes, but simply failed to reject a null hypothesis (the "file-drawer" problem), a distinction that can be tested through power analysis (Cohen, 1990). Because null results are less likely to be published than findings of significant differences, scholars conducting any meta-analysis or literature survey will tend to find inflated estimates of differences. Favreau (1997) goes further, discussing the myriad ways in which null hypothesis testing has been used to distort and misrepresent sex-difference research.

Rotton et al.'s respondents also reported that they avoided submitting data to journals if the results seemed inexplicable or if they received unfavorable reviews. Although this behavior is understandable, one can easily see how it could seriously bias the published, refereed literature toward the *status quo* view of sex differences in mathematics abilities, as well as resulting in bias against forming new views and theories of the possible existence and nature of such differences.

DISCUSSION

It has simply never been established that there is any meaningful and substantial sex difference in mathematics ability that is not massively confounded with factors related to individual experience. Therefore, researchers whose goals are to understand the biological basis of behavior still need even to produce data that suggest that there is any sex difference that can be even partly explained by biological factors. As we mentioned earlier in the chapter, (1) in cultures that are less concerned with portraying females as having inferior math abilities, there is no evidence for sex differences in performance; and (2) there are not just two biological sexes, and it is not clear how one should usefully classify biological sex in the context of a given cognitive research question. In an important sense, these two points show that the whole enterprise of research on sex differences in math is based on an utterly false dichotomy. It is interesting to examine how dichotomies of sex have been constructed within a specific social setting. However, to *begin* by assuming that scores on a cognitive measure will differ according to a socially constructed variable is simply unwarranted, especially considering the ambiguity of biological sex and the high variability found in cross-cultural data.

Researchers who assume that there is a male superiority in math ability, whatever the cause, and who aim to improve people's "quality of life" would do well to be clear about what they mean by "quality of life." Much of the applied research in this field is based on unexamined biases. Some people want to get females to perform like males, an aim that, if not carefully examined, can result from two biased assumptions: (1) that higher scores, *per se*, are worthy goals; and (2) that what males do should be the standard. Historically, the people who have, or would have, gotten the best grades in math courses or on tests have by no means always been the people who made the most significant breakthroughs in math and math-related fields. Furthermore, high-achieving males might be achieving well at little cost or at great cost, by compromising their quality of life (e.g., social life) or reducing the time and energy they invest in other areas (e.g., ability to think creatively outside the context of a test).

Some who want to recruit more people of all kinds into professions that involve a great deal of work with quantitative data may be biased about the relative social values of different kinds of work. Some people might consider these professions to be particularly worthwhile and important, whereas others may place more value on other kinds of work, like human services and the arts. Favreau (1997) makes the point that, although Garai and Scheinfeld (1968) interpreted better manual dexterity in women as a qualification for typing, it could alternatively be taken as an excellent qualification for neurosurgery. We would extend this logic and argue that typing may well be a more valuable skill than neurosurgery; this depends on what one considers socially respected. Although it might be productive to do research with a specific, biased, applied goal in mind, the bias needs to be made clear. Researchers who earnestly aim to improve students' self-confidence or open up their possible career paths need to study more directly the factors that influence self-confidence and streaming into career paths. We unequivocally feel that leveling the playing field in all arenas is a worthy goal. However, simply leveling the playing field is perhaps the very least one could do to overcome the social limitations imposed by classifying people, assuming that such classifications are correlated with types and levels of abilities, and assuming that ability in an arena should be used to limit access to people's life pursuits. Obtaining a level playing field is better thought of as the very first step on the way to ensuring that all people have diverse opportunities for self-expression and for exploration of broad ranges of creative as well as traditional activities, independent of any kind of social judgment.

Two common fallacies come into play when people consider the research on sex differences in math; both influence public opinion and the design of future research. The first fallacy is that sex differences in math are substantial and reliable. These differences are in fact elusive. The second is that, when one finds a sex difference, its social implications are clear and inevitable. The choice of social change strategies have often depended more on the social engineer's own values than on findings of sex differences. However, the effects of personal values and motivations have even greater impact when, as in the field of sex differences in math, the experimental findings are noisy and difficult to interpret and have been misinterpreted or misunderstood.

In light of all we have considered, it is clear that the best thing that researchers could do to pave the way for an open, useful look at the kinds of social changes that are needed would be to teach the public that it is simplistic and largely inaccurate to claim that researchers have found a male superiority in math and that that superiority is biologically based.

References

Aronson, J., Lustina, M. J., Good, C., & Keough, K. (1999). When white men can't do math: Necessary and sufficient factors in stereotype threat. *Journal of Experimental Social Psychology, 35*, 29–46.

Beal, C. (1994). Boys and girls: The development of gender roles. New York: McGraw-Hill.

Benbow, C. P., & Benbow, R. M. (1987). Extreme mathematical talent: A hormonally induced ability? In D. Ottoson (Ed.), *Duality and unity of the brain* (pp. 147–157). London: Macmillan.

Benbow, C. P., & Stanley, J. (1980). Sex differences in mathematical ability: Fact or artifact? *Science, 210*, 1262–1264.

Benbow, C. P., & Stanley, J. (1983). Sex differences in mathematical reasoning: More facts. *Science, 222*, 1029–1031.

Block, J. H. (1976). Issues, problems, and pitfalls in assessing sex differences: A critical review of the psychology of sex differences. *Merril-Palmer Quarterly Review, 22*, 283–308.

Bradley, D. R., & Wygant, C. R. (1998). Male and female differences in anxiety about statistics are not reflected in performance. *Psychological Reports, 82*(1), 245–246.

Brown, R. P., & Josephs, R. A. (1999). A burden of proof: Stereotype relevance and gender differences in math performance. *Journal of Personality & Social Psychology, 76*(2), 246–257.

Byrnes, J. P., & Takahira, S. (1993). Explaining gender differences on SAT-math items. *Developmental Psychology, 29*(5), 805–810.

Caplan, P. J., & Caplan, J. B. (1997). Do sex-related cognitive differences exist, and why do people seek them out? In P. J. Caplan, M. Crawford, J. S. Hyde, & J. T. E. R. Richardson (Eds.), *Gender differences in human cognition* (pp. 52–80). New York: Oxford University Press.

Caplan, P. J., & Caplan, J. B. (1999). *Thinking critically about research on sex and gender* (2nd ed.). New York: Addison-Wesley Longman Inc.

Case, L. (1984). *Female adolescents and underachievement.* Unpublished master's thesis, Ontario Institute for Studies in Education, Toronto.

Casserly, P. L. (1980). Factors affecting female participation in advanced placement programs in mathematics, chemistry, and physics. In L. H. Fox, L. Brody, & D. Tobin (Eds.), *Women and the mathematical mystique* (pp. 138–163). Baltimore: Johns Hopkins University Press.

Cherian, V. I., & Siweya, J. (1996). Gender and achievement in mathematics by indigenous African students majoring in mathematics. *Psychological Reports, 78*(1), 27–34.

Cohen, J. (1990). Things I have learned (so far). *American Psychologist, 45*(12), 1304–1312.

Eccles, J. S. (1994). Understanding women's educational and occupational choices: Applying the Eccles et al. model of achievement-related choices. *Psychology of Women Quarterly, 18*(4), 585–609.

Eccles, J. S., & Jacobs, J. E. (1986). Social forces shape math attitudes and performance. *Signs, 11*(2), 367–380.

Ewers, C. A., & Wood, N. L. (1993). Sex and ability differences in children's math self-efficacy and prediction accuracy. *Learning and Individual Differences, 5*(3), 259–267.

Fan, X., Chen, M., & Matsumoto, A. R. (1997). Gender differences in mathematics achievement: Findings from the National Education Longitudinal Study of 1988. *Journal of Experimental Education, 65*(3), 229–242.

Fausto-Sterling, A. (2000). *Sexing the body.* New York: Basic Books.

Favreau, O. E. (1997). Sex and gender comparisons: Does null hypothesis testing create a false dichotomy? *Feminism & Psychology, 7*(1), 63–81.

Gallagher, A. M., & DeLisi, R. (1994). Gender differences in Scholastic Aptitude Test: Mathematics problem solving among high-ability students. *Journal of Educational Psychology, 86*(2), 204–211.

Garai, J. E., & Scheinfeld, A. (1968). Sex differences in mental and behavioral traits. *Genetic Psychology Monographs, 77*, 169–299.

Gelsthorpe, L. (1990). Feminist methodologies in criminology: A new approach or old wine in new bottles? In L. Gelsthorpe & A. Morris (Eds.), *Feminist perspectives in criminology*. Philadelphia: Open University.

Hunsley, J., & Flessati, S. L. (1988). Gender and mathematics anxiety: The role of math-related experiences and opinions. *Anxiety Research, 1*(3), 215–224.

Hunt, D. E. (1992). *The renewal of personal energy.* Toronto: OISE Press.

Hyde, J., Fennema, E., & Lamon, S. (1990). Gender differences in mathematics performance: A meta-analysis. *Psychological Bulletin, 107*, 139–155.

Inzlicht, M., & Ben-Zeev, T. (2000). A threatening intellectual environment: Why females are susceptible to experiencing problem-solving deficits in the presence of males. *Psychological Science, 11*(5), 365–371.

Jensen, J. A. (1998). Gender differences in the relationship of attitudinal and background factors to high school students' choice of math-intensive curriculum and careers. *Dissertation Abstracts International Section A. Humanities & Social Sciences, 58*(8-A).

Kimball, M. M. (1989). A new perspective on women's math achievement. *Psychological Bulletin, 105*, 198–214.

Leahey, E., & Guo, G. (2001). Gender differences in mathematical trajectories. *Social Forces, 80*(2), 713–732.

Mau, W.-C., & Lynn, R. (2000). Gender differences in homework and test scores in mathematics, reading and science at tenth and twelfth grade. *Psychology, Evolution & Gender, 2*(2), 119–125.

Osborne, J. W. (2001). Testing stereotype threat: Does anxiety explain race and sex differences in achievement? *Contemporary Educational Psychology, 26*, 291–310.

Pajares, F. (1996). Self-efficacy beliefs and mathematical problem-solving of gifted students. *Contemporary Educational Psychology, 21*(4), 325–344.

Pajares, F., & Kranzler, J. (1995). Self-efficacy beliefs and general mental ability in mathematical problem solving. *Contemporary Educational Psychology, 20*(4), 426–443.

Pajares, F., & Miller, M. D. (1994). Role of self-efficacy and self-concept beliefs in mathematical problem solving: A path analysis. *Journal of Educational Psychology, 86*(2), 193–203.

Parsons, J. E., Kaczala, C. M., & Meece, J. L. (1982). Socialization of achievement attitudes and beliefs: Classroom influences. *Child Development, 53*(2), 322–339.

Parsons, J. E., Meece, J. L., Adler, T. F., & Kaczala, C. M. (1982). Sex differences in attributions and learned helplessness. *Sex Roles, 8*(4), 421–432.

Quinn, D. M., & Spencer, S. J. (2001). The interference of stereotype threat with women's generation of mathematical problem-solving strategies. *Journal of Social Issues, 57*(1), 55–71.

Reis, S. M., & Park, S. (2001). Gender differences in high-achieving students in math and science. *Journal for the Education of the Gifted, 25*(1), 52–73.

Rosenthal, R. (1979). The file drawer problem and tolerance for null results. *Psychological Bulletin, 86*(3), 638–641.

Rotton, J., Foos, P. W., Van Meek, L., & Levitt, M. (1995). Publication practices and the file drawer problem: A survey of published authors. *Journal of Social Behavior and Personality, 10*(1), 1–13.

Royer, J. M., Tronsky, L. N., Chan, Y., Jackson, S. J., & Marchant, H. I. (1999). Math-fact retrieval as the cognitive mechanism underlying gender differences in math performance. *Contemporary Educational Psychology, 24*, 181–266.

Ruble, D., & Martin, C. (1998). Gender development. In N. Eisenberg (Ed.), *Handbook of child psychology* (Vol. 111, 5th ed., pp. 933–1016). New York: Wiley.

Sarason, I. G. (1972). Experimental approaches to test anxiety: Attention and the uses of information. In C. Spielberger (Ed.), *Anxiety: Current trends in theory and research* (Vol. 2). New York: Academic Press.

Schmader, T. (2002). Gender identification moderates stereotype threat effects on women's math performance. *Journal of Experimental Social Psychology, 38*(2), 194–201.

Spencer, S. J., Steele, C. M., & Quinn, D. M. (1999). Stereotype threat and women's math performance. *Journal of Experimental Social Psychology, 35*, 4–28.

Steele, C. M. (1992). Race and the schooling of black Americans. *The Atlantic Monthly, 69*(4), 68–78.

Taal, M. (1994). How do mathematical experiences contribute to the choice of mathematics. *Sex Roles, 31*(11–12), 752–769.

Tobin, P. (1982). *The effects of practice and training on sex difference in performance on a spatial task.* Unpublished master's thesis, Ontario Institute for Studies in Education, University of Toronto, Toronto.

Tocci, C. M., & Engelhard, G. (1991). Achievement, parental support, and gender differences in attitudes toward mathematics. *Journal of Educational Research, 84*(5), 280–286.

Wainer, H., & Steinberg, L. S. (1992). Sex differences on the mathematics section of the scholastic aptitude test: A bidirectional validity study. *Harvard Educational Review, 62*(3), 323–336.

Wigfield, A., & Byrnes, J. P. (1999). Does math-fact retrieval explain sex differences in mathematical test performance? A commentary. *Contemporary Educational Psychology, 24,* 275–285.

Wigfield, A., & Eccles, J. (1989). Test anxiety in elementary and secondary school students. *Educational Psychologist, 24,* 159–183.

Wigfield, A., & Meece, J. (1988). Math anxiety in elementary and secondary school students. *Journal of Educational Psychology, 80,* 210–216.

Willingham, W. W., & Cole, N. S. (1997). *Gender and fair assessment.* Mahwah, NJ: Erlbaum.

Wine, J. (1971). Test anxiety and direction of attention. *Psychological Bulletin, 76,* 92–104.

Wine, J. D., Moses, B., & Smye, M. D. (1980). Female superiority in sex-difference competence comparisons: A review of the literature. In C. Stark-(Adamec) (Ed.), *Sex roles: Origins, influences, and implications for women.* Montreal: Eden Press Women's Publications.

Wine, J. D., Smye, M. D., & Moses, B. (1980). Assertiveness: Sex differences in relationships between self-report and behavioral measures. In C. Stark-(Adamec) (Ed.), *Sex roles: Origins, influences, and implications for women.* Montreal: Eden Press Women's Publications.

3

A Psychobiosocial Model

Why Females Are Sometimes Greater Than and Sometimes Less Than Males in Math Achievement

Diane F. Halpern, Jonathan Wai, and Amanda Saw

We have some numbers that may surprise you, but first you need to supply some of your own. Make your best estimate in answering the following questions: What percentage of all accountants and auditors in the United States in 1983 were female? Now answer the same question for the year 2000. What about other math-intensive professions, say economists? What percentage of economists in the United States in 1983 and in 2000 were female? What about the percentage of all engineers who were female in 1983 and in 2000? Finally, is the difference in achievement scores between girls and boys much larger on tests of reading literacy or tests of mathematical literacy?

Are you fairly confident about your answers? Give yourself a "point" for each answer you supplied that is within five percentage points of the correct answer. According to the U.S. Bureau of the Census (2001), the majority of accountants and auditors in 2000 were female (56.7%), up considerably from 1983 when females made up slightly more than one-third of this profession (36.7%). The comparable values for economists in 1983 and 2000 were 37.9% and 53.3%. Surprised that these values are so high? Most people are. What about engineers? Females were 5.9% of all engineers in 1983 and still only 9.9% in 2000 – values that are probably closer to what most people estimated for all these math-intensive professions. The final question – both U.S. and international studies show that females are substantially outscoring males in measures of reading literacy, with significant differences in every one of the thirty-one countries where the Program for International Student Assessment (PISA) was administered to fifteen-year olds in 2000 (National Center for Education Statistics [NCES], 2002). PISA showed that although there was an average advantage in mathematical literacy favoring boys in twenty-eight of the same thirty-one countries, the male advantage in mathematical literacy was much smaller than the female advantage in reading literacy, with many of the differences in mathematics failing to achieve statistical significance. The PISA data are not unusual.

48

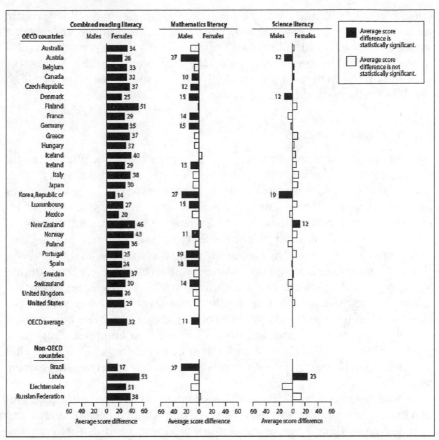

FIGURE 3.1. Comparative data from Program for International Student Assessment (2000). (From National Center for Education Statistics (2002), http://nces.ed.gov/quicktables accessed July 5, 2002.)

Numerous other national and international studies show similar patterns of results (e.g., Third International Mathematics and Science Study [NCES, 1997, 1998, 2000], National Assessment of Educational Progress [1999], and others reviewed in Halpern [2000] and Willingham & Cole [1997]). The PISA data are graphically depicted in Fig. 3.1 along with comparable data on science literacy, which shows that, overall, fifteen-year-old girls and boys around the world (at least in these thirty-one countries) were approximately equal in science literacy in 2000.

Taken together, the occupational data from three different math-intensive fields and international assessments show two parts of the complex equation that describes male and female achievement in mathematics. There is cross-national constancy in that males (at midadolescence) are outperforming females in virtually every country with (presumably) equal access to education, but the advantage to females in reading is much, much larger than the advantage to males in math, and females are entering many, but not all, occupations that require a high degree of mathematical knowledge at a higher rate than males. How can we make sense from these data and use them in ways that can help females and males achieve at high levels of mathematical literacy?

POLITICAL MINEFIELDS

Almost every poll of the American public shows that education is among the top concerns, even after the tragic events of September 11, 2001 (Jacobson, 2002), so it is not surprising that news about large differences in the academic achievement of males and females has sparked considerable and often acrimonious debate. Here is a sample of recent newspaper headlines: "Community Colleges Start to Ask, Where Are the Men? 151 women receive associate degrees for every 100 men who do" (Evelyn, 2002); "Gender Gap Dogs Nation's Vet Schools: Nearly 75% of Students are Women . . . " (MacGillis, 2001); and "Girls Not Wired for Science, Author Claims" (Swainson, 2002). The "battle of the sexes," a hackneyed phrase that has been used as the punch line for numerous jokes, has now moved into the classroom, as popular writers advance different social agendas by declaring that there is a "War Against Boys" (Sommers, 2000) or that "schools shortchange girls" (American Association of University Women, 1992).

It is little wonder that many serious scientists have opted out of the controversies surrounding the relative academic achievement of males and females, and others have urged a moratorium on studies that compare female and male academic achievement. A primary concern among psychologists who object to the study of male and female differences in academic abilities/achievement is that the findings will be used to promote discrimination and sexism (e.g., Baumeister, 1988). This is a legitimate concern given that there are many examples where data have been misused in exactly this way. The newspaper headline proclaiming that the brains of girls are not "wired for science" shows the futility of trying to prevent the misuse of scientific findings. Even though recent international studies show no difference in science literacy for girls and boys, and women are entering many science professions in numbers that equal or exceed that of men, there are still authors proclaiming that girls' brains are not compatible with science learning. This is an important point because it shows that stereotypes and prejudice exist in the absence of data and even when they are contrary to data. Stereotypes and prejudice will not be eradicated if we refuse to examine data.

Amid the cacophony of opinions on the question of comparing the academic achievement or ability of females and males, there are many psychologists who have been strong advocates of comparative studies (Eagly, 1990, 1994). A primary reason in support of scientific comparisons is that research is the only way to determine whether common beliefs about the abilities of males and females are supported by facts. Not surprisingly given the nature of this book, we believe that there is much to be gained from studies of individual differences in how and how well people learn math. Information gained from these studies can be used as a tool for understanding learning and cognitive processes in general, as well as for providing insights into better ways to teach and learn in mathematics and other disciplines.

An oft-repeated maxim (that has been attributed to many different authors) is that "there is nothing as useful as a good theory." A good theory can serve as an organizational framework that brings clarity to a diverse body of data, it can provide directions for future research, and it can move researchers away from the mental set of older assumptions that may have blinded them to alternative types of explanations. Thus, we begin with an explanatory model that strives to achieve some of these desirable outcomes.

THE PSYCHOBIOSOCIAL MODEL

It is common to think about any differences between females and males (except those directly related to reproduction) in the framework of dichotomies and ask if they are due to factors inherent in the biology of maleness or femaleness or due to differential sex-related experiences and expectations. The questions being posed here are familiar to most psychologists and educators – they are variations on the age-old question of nature and nurture.

Explanations can usually be identified as falling somewhere along a continuum anchored at one end by "nature" (or biologically oriented causes) and at the other end "nurture" (or environmentally oriented causes), with few contemporary psychologists or educators expecting that any complex human behavior would be entirely explainable by either nature or nurture. Like other scientists, psychologists tend to think about the variables they study in terms of the data analytic techniques that are used to interpret them. With the general linear model at the heart of most contemporary statistical procedures, it is common to ask about the proportion of the variance in our data that can be accounted for by biological and environmental/social variables and their interaction. An assumption inherent in a general linear model approach to the comparison of females and males is the idea that biology and environment/social variables can be separated into "independent variables," and their interaction can be separated from the main effects. Any answer to the question of "the percentage of explained variance" reifies the idea that there is a number attributable to each

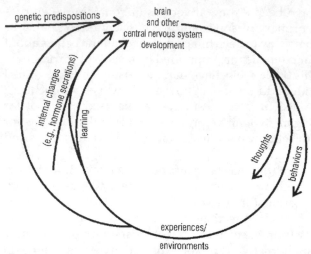

FIGURE 3.2. A psychobiosocial model as a framework for understanding cognitive sex differences. It replaces the older idea of nature vs. nurture with a circle that shows the way biological and psychosocial variables exert mutual influences on each other. (Reprinted with permission from Halpern, D. F. (2000). *Sex differences in cognitive abilities* (3ʳᵈ) ed. Mahwah, NJ: Erlbaum.)

of these sources of variance that exists in the population, and if researchers are clever in their experimental designs and analyses, they can discover the "true" population parameters. Questions about the proportion of variance explained by environmental and biological variables and their interaction are based on faulty premises about the separability of biological and environmental/social variables. The psychobiosocial model offers a better alternative to the nature–nurture dichotomy or nature–nurture continuum.

Instead of thinking about nature and nurture as making separate (i.e., independent) contributions to the development of human abilities, it is more productive to think about these influences as an interdependent relationship in which nature and nurture need each other. It is a holistic model that accounts for dynamic and reciprocal influences. A schematic diagram of the psychobiosocial model is depicted in Fig.3.2.

A psychobiosocial model is much like a puzzle with pieces that are not autonomous segments that fit into corresponding grooves, but rather, are dynamic pieces that overlap and change the shape of connecting pieces so they can continue to fit together as they undergo change. Each piece is essential to understanding the larger picture, that is, to understanding how all the elements work together to influence each individual's cognitive abilities. Researchers can and do examine separate puzzle pieces to compare female and male cognition and academic achievement, but the goal is to put the pieces together to "see" the whole picture. To take the analogy further, we can envision each piece as a piece that momentarily holds a static image of a portion of the puzzle, almost like a snapshot taken during a continuous flow of movement. Only when each piece is put together to form the whole picture and the animation is included can the picture become a vibrant and dynamic scene.

Biological Contributions to the Psychobiosocial Model

Although we are advocating an integrated approach to understanding the way biological and psychosocial variables create female and male differences in math achievement, the language we use to discuss the process is necessarily linear, which means we need to consider each type of influence separately. It should be no surprise that some scientists have looked to uncover a biological basis that can lead to a better understanding of differences in mathematical literacy. Opponents of the idea that biology has contributed even a small part to male and female differences in mathematics have labeled these types of explanations as "sexist." Despite the name-calling and labeling that is rampant in this area of study, we urge all readers to keep an open, albeit skeptical mind, as various hypotheses are considered. Biological hypotheses are not necessarily sexist. There does not have to be a "smarter" sex with a "better biology" to conclude that there are biological origins to any cognitive ability. The data (summarized below) provide strong evidence of some systematic differences in math and other cognitive areas between males and females, but sometimes the differences favor females and other times they favor males. There is no evidence of a smarter sex. Differences, even ones that may have a biologically based origin, do not imply deficiencies. If the skills and abilities that are associated with one sex are routinely valued more highly than those that are associated with the other sex, the problem lies in the social system that determines what is valued and not in the data or theory that describes the differences. Humans are biological and social organisms. Biology "works" within a context, therefore even if findings of a biological nature are upheld, they would not necessarily diminish the importance of the environment or psychosocial hypotheses. Both are important because, within a psychobiosocial framework, each variable plays a critical role. Nature and nurture cannot exist without the other. In considering biological contributions, we focus on sex hormones and the way sex hormones and experience both alter brain structure and function. In this way, we close the loop depicted in the psychobiosocial model and show how even the brain – presumably a "biological" organ – changes in structure and function in response to experience, thus permanently blurring the distinction between biological and psychosocial influences.

Sex Hormones

Here's a sure bet. Start a discussion about any of the ways males and females differ and within a few minutes, the conversation will turn to sex

hormones. Sex hormones are chemical messengers excreted from the gonads (ovaries in women and testes in men), adrenal glands in women and
men, and other structures such as fat. They travel throughout the blood-
stream, thus affecting many organs, including the brain. The hormone that
is typically associated with being "male" is testosterone; the hormones
that are associated with being "female" are estrogen and progesterone.
This simple distinction can be misleading because both males and females
have estrogen, progesterone, and testosterone, with different levels or concentrations. One of the major biological theories of cognitive differences
between men and women is that sex hormones mediate the differences. Sex
hormones wax and wane in predictable patterns throughout the life span,
making any theory about the importance of sex hormones a developmental
theory. Prenatal hormones are clearly implicated in brain development, so
not unexpectedly, theories of female and male differences in math ability
start with events in prenatal life.

Geschwind's Theory of Prenatal Hormonal Effects

Geschwind (1983, 1984) proposed a "grand theory" of prenatal brain development that tied together several seemingly unrelated topics – dyslexia,
handedness, allergies and other immune system disorders, sexual orientation, and cognition. Not surprisingly, his theory has generated a great deal
of criticism and research, with (some) partial confirmations. He assumed
that prenatal hormones not only determined whether a developing fetus
would be male or female by directing the development of the genitals and
other reproductive organs in either a female or male direction, but also
played a critical role in the formation of the central nervous system. Under
normal development, the developing testes of males secrete testosterone,
which affects the developing nervous system of male fetuses. It is through
this action (greatly simplified for this context) that a "male" brain pattern
is created. The process for creating a "female" brain is similar (but not
directly analogous because the effect of high levels of estrogen on brain
development is not as well established in humans).

There are some clearly demonstrable effects of sex hormones on brain
development during prenatal life. (Interested readers are urged to consult
the original texts because only a sketchy outline of the process is presented
here.) In addition, it is generally acknowledged that the right hemisphere
of the brain develops faster than the left hemisphere in humans; therefore,
the left side of the brain is more vulnerable to any sort of disruption because it takes longer to develop. Advocates of Geschwind's theory claim
that the high levels of (prenatal and perinatal) testosterone in males slow
the development of the left hemisphere, resulting in right brain dominance. One rough index of brain dominance is hand preference (right- or
left-handed). Motor activity is controlled by the contralateral side of the
brain, which means that individuals who are right-handed are commonly

"left brain dominant" for motor control, and those who are left-handed or adept at using both hands are more usually "right brain dominant." Therefore, according to Geschwind's theory, there should be more males who are left-handed because they are exposed to higher levels of testosterone prenatally than females. A large number of studies have confirmed that males are more likely to be left-handed than females (Bryden, 1977; Halpern, Haviland, & Killian, 1998). Also in accord with predictions from Geschwind's theory, females who are exposed to high levels of prenatal testosterone (because of an abnormality in prenatal development) have been shown to have significantly higher proportions of left-handedness than those who are not (Resnick, Berenbaum, Gottesman, & Bouchaard, 1986).

If being left-handed is correlated with higher levels of prenatal testosterone on brain development, then this theory predicts that more males will display cognitive ability patterns that are more closely associated with right hemisphere functioning. Males tend to perform well at (some) mathematical reasoning and spatial tasks, especially on advanced tests like the SAT-M where both skills are required. Both of these cognitive abilities are believed to be under greater control by the right hemisphere, although there is no strict dichotomization of hemispheric functioning as this theory seems to be suggesting. More males than females are also found to have language and reading problems, which are identified with left hemispheric processing under typical development. In addition, being left-handed is correlated with mathematical giftedness (Benbow, 1988). As mentioned, Geschwind's theory is controversial, in part because he attempts to relate a large number of seemingly unrelated phenomena, many of which are controversial in themselves, and he relates them to prenatal environment, which seems to suggest that there is little that can be done to affect cognition (or the other correlates he studied) once the brain is formed. This last inference is obviously wrong. All cognitive abilities improve with education – that is why we teach math and other subjects in school – so it is clearly not a fatalistic theory or one that necessarily diminishes the importance of learning and other experiences. It is possible that some brain organizations are more conducive to some sorts of learning, but none of these biological theories discount or even necessarily diminish the critical importance of psychosocial variables.

Optimal Level of Estradiol: Prenatal and Postnatal Hormones

Nyborg (1983) also proposed a biological explanation based on hormone levels. Nyborg hypothesized that sex hormone levels can account for some portion of the differences in visual-spatial abilities, which in turn have an indirect effect on math abilities because many advanced math problems require spatial visualization for their solution. According to Nyborg, there is a specific range or concentration of hormones that maximizes visual-spatial ability. Androgens (the general term for a class of hormones that includes testosterone) can be chemically transformed (aromatized) into estradiol, which is the hormone that Nyborg believes is most important in determining levels of spatial ability. To further complicate what is already a complex process of hormone and brain interactions, estradiol is a type of estrogen, and females tend to have higher levels of estradiol than males. Therefore, those males with high levels of estradiol (compared with their male peers) will have estradiol levels that are similar to those of females who have low levels of estradiol (in comparison with their female peers). This theory posits that females who are more masculine than most females (low estradiol for females) and males who are more feminine than most males (high estradiol for males) will have estradiol levels that are optimum for the expression of spatial abilities.

There are several studies that report findings that are in accord with Nyborg's prediction about an optimal range of estradiol. Petersen (1976) studied the levels of hormones in males and females at 13, 16, and 18 years of age. In her findings, those males who had high levels of male hormones (hence, lower levels of estradiol) had poor spatial ability, whereas those females who had high levels of male hormones were found to have high spatial ability. Maccoby (1966) also found that males who had high spatial ability were described as more feminine by their classmates. Nyborg's theory has also gained support from studies that investigate the impact of hormones in older women. These women, who tend to have abnormally lower levels of estradiol, improve their spatial and verbal memory when these levels are raised (Resnick, Maki, Galski, Kraut, & Zonderman, 1998). Despite these (and other) positive findings, Nyborg's theory still awaits much more stringent confirmation before it can gain greater acceptance, and even if it had additional empirical support, the relationship to math abilities would hold only for those math problems with a visual-spatial component. Like Geschwind's theory, it is not meant to disprove or discredit psychosocial theories. Many factors work together.

Arguing from Abnormalities

Another approach to better understanding the effects of hormones on cognitive abilities is to examine those individuals who are born with a genetic or other sex-related abnormality. People with abnormal levels of sex hormones can provide a valuable source of data because it is not possible to vary hormone levels in humans intentionally (for obvious ethical reasons). Therefore, researchers have looked to populations that are born with an abnormal trait to learn more about the role of hormones in normal humans, realizing that generalizing from abnormally high or low levels of hormones to normal hormone levels can be misleading.

Most humans have a total of 46 sex chromosomes, but females with Turner's syndrome only have 45. For women with this abnormality, there is either a defective or missing chromosome. They tend to have very low levels of all hormones, thus they are an excellent population for helping us tease apart various types of contributions to female and male abilities. Hines (1982) described women with this syndrome as having normal IQs and verbal ability functioning; however, they specifically have poor visual-spatial abilities, which is a component process in some types of math problems. Numerous studies have been conducted that show that females with this syndrome are similar to normal females in their verbal abilities. However, studies that specifically focused on mathematical abilities showed that females with Turner's syndrome performed very poorly (Rovet, Szekely, & Hockenberry, 1994). Turner's women provide an important clue suggesting that normal hormone levels are important in developing math abilities in women because these women are presumably socialized and have other life experiences that are similar to that of most other females. Of course generalization of findings may be limited by dissimilar social experiences, as well as the relatively small sample sizes used in these studies.

Variance of Cognitive Abilities Over the Menstrual Cycle

This question most likely sent up immediate warning flares, due to its obviously controversial nature. Some critics argue that such a question should not be asked because answers could be used to justify discrimination and increase prejudice against women. We believe that this concern is similar to the argument described earlier that any sex difference in cognition should not be studied because data can be misused. In response, we add that ignoring important questions will not increase understanding or dispel myths. Prejudice and discrimination flourish in the absence of data. There is little to be gained from censorship and ignorance.

In normal cycling females, the major female sex hormones, namely estrogen and progesterone, vary over the menstrual period. At the beginning and end of each cycle, progesterone and estrogen levels are low, with both peaking about midcycle. Thus, if these hormones affect cognition in normal adult females, it would be expected that these fluctuations in hormones may accordingly influence cognitive abilities in a correlated and cyclic fashion. In response to this question, Hampson and Kimura (1988; Hampson, 1990a, 1990b) conducted a series of studies to determine whether these hormone levels were correlated with fluctuations in cognitive abilities, and if so, in what way. One possibility is that during midcycle when estrogen and progesterone levels are high, females will perform well on tasks that are typically female dominant (e.g., verbal fluency). The other possibility is that females will perform well on tasks that are typically male dominant at the time of menstruation when estrogen and progesterone are low. In an investigation of these two possibilities, Hampson and Kimura selected those tasks that show the greatest difference for males and females and assessed performance on these tasks at different times in the menstrual cycle. They found that females performed significantly better on tasks they labeled female dominant, such as speech articulation and fine muscle movements, during midcycle when compared with the time of menstruation. Correspondingly, they also found that women performed better on spatial tasks, such as mental rotation, during the time of menstruation when estrogen and progesterone levels are low. A number of other studies have provided evidence that confirms these results (e.g., Heister, Landis, Regard, & Schroeder-Heister, 1989).

Although these results generated a firestorm of controversy and media attention, it is difficult to determine the importance of the finding that females perform better during midcycle on certain verbal tasks. Rather, the important finding that this research has revealed is that when spatial abilities are high, verbal abilities are low, whereas the opposite also holds true. The reciprocal effects are important because they also support the theory proposed by Nyborg (1983), as described earlier. In fact, Nyborg (1990) used the results of the study by Hampson and Kimura to give credibility to his theory by explaining that because women have more estradiol than men, when their levels are lowest they perform best at spatial tasks. In contrast to this, women do not perform as well on spatial tasks when their levels of estradiol are at their peak during the midcycle of the menstrual period. Although there have been many replications of the periodicity of cognitive performance over the menstrual cycle, the actual size of the differences in task performance was quite small and probably would not be detected outside the laboratory. Therefore, it is difficult to see how these results have much applied value.

An important fact that is often overlooked in the controversy over the correlation of fluctuating hormones and performance on some cognitive tasks is that males also have fluctuating hormone levels and corresponding changes in performance on cognitive tasks. For example, the expression of spatial ability changes with variations in testosterone levels for men. Testosterone levels are higher during the morning in contrast to later in the day, whereas male performance on spatial tasks is better later in the evening (Moffat & Hampson, 1996), and hormone levels fluctuate seasonally for North American men, such that spatial ability is higher in spring and lower in autumn (Kimura & Hampson, 1994). Therefore, we can see that hormone level variation is just as important for males as it is for females. As for women, daily and seasonal hormone fluctuations for males are unlikely to affect performance significantly. Like the other studies reviewed in this section, these results do not provide any evidence that one sex is superior to the other. What they do show is that some spatial and verbal abilities, especially the ones that show the greatest differences between men and women, may be inversely related to each other.

Closing the Loop: Experience Alters Biology and Biology Directs Experience

Research shows that the brain exhibits physical changes in response to the environment. Ungerleider (1995) demonstrated through brain imaging how the brain changes in response to specific experiences. Earlier work by Greenough and his colleagues (Greenough, Black, & Wallace, 1987) provided evidence that intellectually favorable environments promoted neural growth and connectivity. Diamond (1999) conducted important research with rodents, in which she showed that enriching environments have a significant impact on brain structure. Those rats that were given intellectually stimulating "toys" were able to run mazes faster than control rats who were not the fortunate recipients of these stimuli, and they also showed greater brain development, particularly in the cortices. Diamond believes that this research can have a profound impact on our theories of human brain development, which can be enriched by exposure to enriching environments. In addition, hormones can be significantly impacted by certain environmental factors, such as the use of drugs or prolonged stress, and research reviewed in a prior section has shown that hormones also alter brain development. As already stated, biological and environmental influences cannot be teased apart, as each has a reciprocal effect on the other. By extension, experience with math problems and other complex learning experiences can create a brain that is favorable to "doing math" – a theory that is both biological and psychosocial and a far cry from the "sexist" assumptions that many critics in this field worry about.

PSYCHOSOCIAL CONTRIBUTIONS TO THE PSYCHOBIOSOCIAL MODEL

An exciting area of research shows the importance of the unconscious effects of stereotypes on thought and performance. There are many examples of the way an individual's beliefs can alter a wide range a biological systems, including hormone secretions, motor responses, breathing rates, and digestion, just to name a few. Work by Steele (1997, 1998) has extended these principles to explain how beliefs about the cognitive abilities of different groups can cause or contribute to group differences on tests of cognitive abilities. According to Steele, when group membership is made salient at the time a cognitive test is being administered, commonly held beliefs about the performance of one's group are activated. Test-takers are "threatened" by these beliefs out of the concern that they will conform to their group's negative stereotype. Stereotype threat will only affect test performance when the group membership is made salient, the test that is being taken is relevant to one's group (e.g., the stereotype that females are not as good in mathematics as males), test performance is important to the individuals taking the test, and the test is at a level of difficulty that the additional burden of defending against a perceived threat would cause a performance decrement.

In an interesting demonstration of the way different stereotypes can be activated under various conditions, the stereotype that Asians are good at mathematics was pitted against the stereotype that women are not good at mathematics (Shih, Pittinsky, & Ambady, 1999). Researchers found that Asian-American women performed relatively better on an advanced test of mathematics when the positive stereotype (Asians are good at math) was made salient, compared with the condition when the negative stereotype (women are not good at math) was made salient. However, there have also been several failed attempts to find evidence that stereotype threat decreases performance on high-stakes tests. In a series of studies using real-life testing environments, researchers did not find that manipulations of the salience of one's sex or ethnicity had any effect on performance (Stricker, 1998; Stricker & Ward, 1998). Thus, there are still many unknowns about the reliability of stereotype threat and the conditions under which it operates.

Banaji and Hardin (1996) demonstrated that implicit attitudes about women and mathematics can operate at an unconscious level, even among people who believe that they do not believe in sex role stereotypes. They found that participants were slower to make associations between stereo- typically inconsistent concepts (women and being good at mathematics) than between those concepts that were stereotypical (women and being good at literature). Nosek, Banaji, and Greenwald (2002) reported similar findings even when looking at explicit and implicit attitude and identity. The cognitive process underlying these categorizations are assumed to be unconscious and automatic as differences in reaction times were in millisec- onds, too short of a time for conscious processing to influence outcomes. Categorization can be seen as an important component of information processing, especially if every time a member of a category (e.g., being fe- male) also activates the stereotypes associated with category membership (being less good at math). The disturbing implication from this research is that these processes can operate without self-awareness, so we cannot stop them. As the authors note, however, we are free to determine how we act, and prejudice and discrimination are conscious actions that cannot be justified with these findings.

Expectancy × Values Models
Values and expectations play a role in determining the outcome of cog- nitive tasks, such as mathematical problem solving (Eccles, 1987, 1994). Expectancy models begin with the simple premise that individuals will work harder and longer on tasks when they expect to be able to achieve a goal (in this case, solve a math problem) than when they believe that they will not be able to achieve a goal. Thus, when girls and boys believe

that hard work will be rewarded with successful outcomes, they will be persistent. These expectations translate into actual differences in success because participants are obviously more likely to solve a problem if they persist in working on it than if they quit as soon as they encounter difficulty. In this way, positive expectancy leads to better skills and better skills lead to greater confidence, and so on. There is a huge literature on achievement motivation that supports this sort of feedback loop. It is important to remember that math skills are learned – often through persistence and hard work. For readers who are looking for the inevitable connection to biological bases of cognition so that expectancies and values can fit into the psychobiosocial model, we note that stress hormones are reduced when performance is good, neural connections are strengthened with the additional math experience, and girls and boys who are experiencing success will seek additional math experiences, which amplify the effect.

Research shows that boys and girls differ in motivational states when working on mathematical problems. Vermeer, Boekaerts, and Seegers (2000) compared the performance and attitudes of sixth-grade boys and girls on application problems and on computation problems. Although there were no significant sex differences in confidence levels reported overall, boys reported higher levels of confidence than did girls on application problems, a type of problem where differences are often found. For application problems, in comparison to boys, girls attributed their failure to arrive at the correct answer more often to their ability and the difficulty of the questions. For computation problems, there were no significant sex differences in attribution. The authors reported that although confidence was strongly related to task performance, the relationship between confidence and persistence was not as strong, and there was a moderate relationship between persistence and task performance. Taken together, these results show how values and expectancies can influence math achievement.

Trait Complexes

There is a large research literature showing that boys and girls, as well as men and women, have somewhat different interests and because of these interests they engage in a host of systematically different experiences, ranging from what they watch on television, the books they choose to read, if they choose to read, how they spend leisure time, and more. Ackerman and his colleagues (Ackerman et al., 2001) have studied the way complexes of traits (groups of traits – abilities, interests, motivations, and personality variables) differ for females and males. For example, Ackerman reported that among college students, the men scored much higher on a science/math/technology trait and the women scored much higher on a worry/traditionalism/anxiety trait. As he predicted, scores on trait complexes were positively correlated with knowledge in different domains. It is easy to see how a general interest in science and technology and the experiences that go with this interest would provide a stronger cognitive scaffolding for learning and understanding math. In this way, trait complexes can account for female and male discrepancies in mathematical literacy.

Ackerman (2002) tackled some of the more traditional explanations for female and male differences in math achievement. He noted that boys and girls do not differ in the number or type of math courses they take through high school, so the differences found on math tests at the end of high school are not caused by differential course-taking patterns. He also negated the generalized notion that schools are generally hostile to the way girls learn because girls are achieving substantially beyond boys in other subject areas that are learned in school (e.g., foreign languages). In addition to this, girls are, by some measures (e.g., graduation rates from high school, college, and number of master's degrees awarded far exceed the rates of boys), outperforming boys in school-related achievement. Thus, Ackerman turned to differences in trait complexes as a more likely explanation. In line with the psychobiosocial model, he suggested that we develop programs to interest more girls in math/science/technology areas, which will increase confidence, lead to a variety of experiences in these areas, develop neural structures that enhance learning in these areas, and continue a positive feedback loop of achievement.

A somewhat different approach to thinking about the reasons for systematic differences in math performance between males and females is to focus on the stages of cognitive processing that are involved in solving math problems, in the hope of finding the locus of the male–female difference. The cognitive process approach is not in competition with the psychobiosocial model – each is designed to examine a different facet of a broader problem. Even if cognitive psychologists found that differences were greatest in a particular stage of processing, the psychobiosocial model would still be needed to explain how those differences came about and how they were maintained. We turn now to the information processing stages that are engaged in mathematical problem solving.

COGNITIVE PROCESSES THAT UNDERLIE MATHEMATICAL ABILITY

It is common to think about math achievement/ability as a single construct or discipline, where males are more competent and confident than females (Banaji & Hardin, 1996; Hyde, Fennema, Ryan, Frost, & Hopp, 1990). Yet, the construct "mathematics" is composed of multiple types of cognitive processes, depending on the nature of the mathematical problem being solved and type of mathematical procedures required for a correct solution. Consider, for example, a basic "arithmetic fact" such as $2 \times 4 = 8$. Once this "fact" is learned, the cognitive processes that produce the correct solution involve retrieval of a well-learned fact, which is more conceptually similar to the retrieval of a word or overlearned phone number from long-term memory than it is to using numbers to solve a problem. There is a large research literature showing that females, in general, are faster and more accurate at tasks that require retrieval from long-term memory (Birenbaum, Kelly, & Levi-Keren, 1994; Halpern, 2000), and as might be predicted based on the advantage for information retrieval, girls perform better than boys in arithmetic in the early elementary school grades when "mathematics" consists of learning and quickly recalling the facts of arithmetic (Willingham & Cole, 1997). Other possible explanations for the female advantage in arithmetic in elementary school include the fact that girls mature faster than boys, reaching puberty almost two years earlier than boys (Tanner, 1962). The enhanced physical maturity is presumably reflected in cognitive maturity for girls relative to same-age boys. One explanation for the finding that girls are better behaved in elementary school and better able to sit at a desk for long periods of time is that they are benefiting from their advanced maturity. Such explanations are circular, though, because we index maturity with more sedentary behavior and then explain the sedentary behavior by calling it more mature. Explanations like this one have a seductive quality, but the reasoning is tautological and cannot advance our understanding.

Tests of mathematical ability show advantages for girls in the early primary school years when mathematics consists of computational knowledge and speed, then usually show little or no sex difference through the rest of the primary school years, and then show a male advantage when the mathematical concepts are more spatial in nature, such as geometry and topology, which are taught in the higher secondary school grades (Hyde, Fennema, & Lamon, 1990). The finding of sex differences in some tests of quantitative or mathematical ability is robust with the size and direction of the finding, depending on both the content that is measured and the age of the child (Naglieri & Rojahn, 2001). These developmental trends fit into a cognitive processes model if we assume that the female advantage in early grades reflects heavy reliance on encoding and retrieving information from long-term memory – a cognitive process where girls, on average, excel – and the later transfer to an advantage to boys reflects the shift to mathematical problems that are more visual-spatial in nature and require construction and transformation of a visual-spatial representation in working memory – a cognitive process that, on average, shows a male advantage (Loring-Meier & Halpern, 1999).

Let's consider the cognitive processes involved when solving a math problem that is encountered in real life (e.g., how much tile to buy to cover a floor) or on an examination. In this analysis, we assume a modal or standard textbook model of memory with an executive or planning process, a visual-spatial and verbal working memory system, and a long-term memory from which information is retrieved for processing (Matlin, 2002).

1. Verbal abilities are needed to interpret and understand the problem context.
2. Visuo-spatial skills are often needed to represent mathematical concepts and the relationships among concepts and to manipulate visual representations of the problem space.
3. Quantitative competence (numeracy [basic operations, calculations, estimation], reasoning, applying logic, judging accuracy of solution) is needed to reach a solution.
4. Speed of processing is important in timed tests (e.g., national and international normed tests) and in problems where the time demands may cause loss of information from working memory.
5. Self-efficacy/motivation and executive processes that monitor progress toward the solution.

Any cognitive model that attempts to account for individual differences in mathematical ability will need to account for procedural, conceptual, and semantic knowledge, plus the motivational states that need to be incorporated into the model. A cognitive process analysis offers a more fine-grained analysis, so female and male differences in mathematics can be viewed from the perspective of the underlying cognitive processes (Loring-Meier & Halpern, 1999).

THE SHAPE OF ABILITIES DISTRIBUTIONS

At least some of the average difference between males and females on tests of math achievement is attributable to the fact that males are more variable in their academic ability/achievement (Hedges & Nowell, 1995), with more males in both tails of the distribution – both the low-ability and high-ability extremes. This means that more females are near the center or average of the distribution than males. There are statistically more male mathematical geniuses, but also more males who have severe cognitive deficiencies. The reason the shape of a distribution is of primary interest is that the way a study is interpreted has a great deal to do with the portion of the ability distribution being sampled (i.e., average ability levels or extremely high ability levels). According to De Lisi and McGillicuddy-De Lisi (2002), a comprehensive understanding of sex differences in mathematics requires that the researchers look for differences between average scores, as well as differences in variability between any two groups being compared.

Studies with Gifted Youth
One of the greatest differences found between males and females on tests of mathematical ability has been demonstrated on advanced tests for high-

SCHOLASTIC ASSESSMENT TEST-MATHEMATICAL

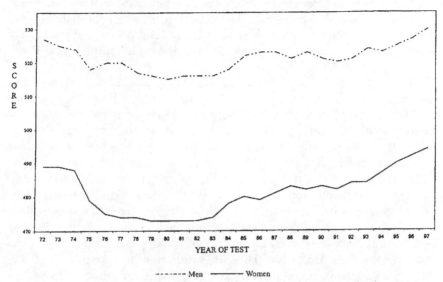

FIGURE 3.3. A comparison of SAT-M scores for females and males over a twenty-five-year-period. Note that the difference has remained relatively stable, while girls have made large gains in the number of advanced math classes they take, have achieved higher grades in school (on average in all classes), and have entered some math-intensive occupations in numbers that equal or exceed that of men.

ability participants, such as the SAT-M, which is taken by students who are planning to attend college. In fact, the gap between males and females on the SAT-M in the United States is about 40 points, favoring males (College Entrance Examination Board, 1997) and has remained relatively stable even as females achieved equity with males in terms of the number and type of advanced math courses taken. Results for females and males on the SAT-M over a 25-year-period are shown in Fig. 3.3. Recall also that females receive higher grades in all courses and have entered math-intensive careers in record numbers. The disparity between classroom achievement in math, which favors girls, and scores on national and international normed tests of mathematics suggests that course grades and normed tests are not tapping the same sets of knowledge and skills.

As large as the male–female difference on the SAT-M is, the size of the difference between females and males grows larger on mathematical tests that are given to those at a higher educational level (i.e., the sample of students who takes the test become more selective). Thus, when we compare male and female scores on the Graduate Record Examination, a test designed for students who are planning for graduate study, the difference increases (Grandy, 1994). This increase is another manifestation of the fact that there are more males in the high ability tail of the math distribution, so as we sample from more extreme regions of the tail, the size of the difference between males and females increases. Differences in tails of distributions become even more important in studies of academically gifted youth and adults who, by definition, are selected from the high-ability tail of distributions.

The Center for Talented Youth at Johns Hopkins University uses the SAT as a tool to select mathematically gifted youth nationwide (Benbow & Stanley, 1983). There are many more males than females who are identified as mathematically gifted. According to their study of preadolescent youth, the ratios of males to females was 2:1 for SAT-M scores greater than 500, 5:1 at greater than 600, and 17:1 at greater than 700. Benbow (1988) documented that these ratios have remained unchanged for over 15 years. Hedges and Nowell (1995) demonstrated that, if one group has slightly higher average scores and is more variable, large group differences will always be found with samples selected from the high- or low-end tail. That is, a small difference in average scores may make a large difference in the outer tails of the distribution. Thus, it is important to take into consideration the portion of the ability distribution one is sampling from and to make a clear distinction between a smaller average difference and a large difference in high- and low-ability groups.

GRADES VS. STANDARDIZED TESTS – HOW TO ASSESS

Mathematics has been described as a "critical filter" that allows only those who know that "math counts" to pass into high-paying jobs with increased status (Sells, 1980). Although males tend to perform better overall on tests of standardized mathematics achievement, such as the SAT-M and GRE-Q, females tend to have better grades in all subjects, including advanced mathematics courses (Astin, 1993). Some argue that this could be due to female conscientiousness and attention to detail, but such explanations seem to denigrate an important measure of math achievement. It is evident, however, that standardized tests such as the SAT or GRE must be overpredicting male performance in school and underpredicting female performance because these tests are designed to predict grades and females achieve both higher grades and lower scores on these tests. Dwyer and Johnson (1997) confirmed the pattern of males getting higher test scores than grades, while the reverse pattern is true for females.

Visual-Spatial Abilities and the Relation to Quantitative Abilities

Depending on the nature of a mathematical problem, there are often several ways that it can be solved, for example, with either a verbal or visual-spatial strategy. However, even when multiple solution paths are possible, one strategy is often easier or faster. For example, when solving calculus and advanced geometry problems, a visual-spatial strategy is more likely to yield mathematical insight than a verbal rule-based strategy. Consider a problem in calculus that requires the problem solver to determine the volume of an object that is created from rotating a two-dimensional line in a three-dimensional plane. An optimal strategy is to visualize the object as the problem solver builds a representation of the problem as a means of identifying the desired solution state. It could be argued that verbal strategies could also work, but a visual-spatial understanding may be easier to grasp. Math problems encountered in a math class or in the course of one's work are more likely to be familiar to the problem solver and therefore less likely to require the construction "from scratch" of a visual representation of the problem. A cognitive process analysis can be used to explain why males perform better on normed math tests that are less closely tied to course content (their better visual-spatial working memory) and females perform better in advanced math classes (their better retrieval and verbal decoding abilities).

Tasks that require maintaining and transforming a visual-spatial image, such as imagining the rotational pattern of the planets, show sex differences that favor boys and men. (See Halpern, 1997, 2000, 2002; Halpern & Collaer, in press for an extensive review.) Differences between girls and boys in visual-spatial working memory can be found in preschool, which may be the earliest threshold that these abilities can be measured. In a systematic investigation of the relationship between visual-spatial and mathematical abilities, Casey et al. (1995) compared the scores on a popular visual-spatial test, the Vandenberg Mental Rotation Test, with SAT-M and SAT-V scores. They reported that for females in all portions of the ability distribution, the spatial test predicted performance on the SAT-M, even when the scores for the SAT-V were statistically controlled. They concluded that the SAT-M and the Vandenberg Mental Rotation Test are tapping the same or related ability patterns, bringing the relationship between mathematics and spatial abilities closer together. It is important to note that, while these studies found a strong connection between spatial and mathematical abilities, other studies yield inconclusive results. Most likely, visual-spatial abilities are important for a subset of math problems, whereas spatial mental representations are important in determining a solution. Numerous other factors are also important, including learning history, the efficacy of verbal and other types of solutions, and familiarity with the problem-solving task.

Problem-Solving Strategies

Another topic that has generated a great deal of interest is whether the methods or strategies used by males and females differ when taking tests of math ability such as the SAT-M or GRE-Q. Gallagher and De Lisi (1994) collected data on problem-solving strategies by observing high-scoring students as they work on SAT-M problems. They found that males outperformed females on novel problems, but females outperformed males on conventional problems – a conclusion that fits well with the fact that females get higher grades in math courses (where the problems are familiar) and males achieve higher scores on standardized tests (where the problems are more likely to be novel). Males used more novel approaches to solve the problems, whereas females more often used an algorithmic approach. Although it makes sense that it would be best to be able to use both approaches to solve problems, depending on which is needed in a particular context, the fact that males and females tend to use different strategies may account for some of their differing performance in math assessments. Differences in the types of solutions that were tried as males and females worked on difficult math problems could be related to the finding that girls are better students than males, in that they use what they learn in the classroom.

THE PSYCHOBIOSOCIAL MODEL REVISITED

How can psychologists and educators explain why females and males show different patterns of performance on many academic/cognitive measures, including math? This question, like its near cousins that ask about racial, ethnic, and socioeconomic differences on academic assessments, is firmly planted in a value-laden context whereby each individual's preferred explanations are in accord with his or her broader network of political beliefs. Every first-year student in a social science class or philosophy of science is familiar with the idea that science can never be value free. Contemporary values are reflected in the types of research questions we ask, the answers we are willing to accept, and how we define appropriate and inappropriate uses of research findings. By definition, people cannot see their own blind spots, but that does not mean that we should shut our eyes and refuse to see anything. The psychobiosocial model that we use to organize causal influences on academic measures is based on a continuous interplay of biological and psychological variables, such that it is meaningless to attempt to quantify their independent contributions because they are not independent variables. We believe this sort of model will move the field ahead so unwinnable battles over "how much" of the variance is attributable to biological or environmental effects are left on the old battlefields in favor of models with multiple and reciprocal influences that can be used to help all students achieve at higher levels in math and other academic areas. The current and future workforce demands more advanced knowledge from a greater number of participants. Doing well in math is not a zero sum game; a psychobiosocial model to understand the development of math achievement can be used to enhance achievement for everyone. If math really is a critical filter that permits access to some of our most important, prestigious, and lucrative occupations, we can identify multiple strategies that "widen the mesh" to allow equal passage through old math barriers.

References

Ackerman, P. L. (2002). Gender differences in intelligence and knowledge: How should we look at achievement score differences? *Issues in Education: Contributions from Educational Psychology.*

Ackerman, P. L., Bowen, K. R., Beier, M., & Kanfer, R. (2001). Determinants of individual differences and gender differences in knowledge. *Journal of Educational Psychology, 93,* 797–825.

American Association of University Women. (1992). *How schools shortchange girls: The AAUW report.* New York: Marlowe.

Astin, A. W. (1993). *What matters in college? Four critical years revisited.* San Francisco: Jossey-Bass.

Banaji, M. R., & Hardin, C. D. (1996). Automatic stereotyping. *Psychological Science, 7,* 136–141.

Baumeister, R. F. (1988). Should we stop studying sex differences altogether? *American Psychologist, 42,* 756–757.

Benbow, C. P. (1988). Sex differences in mathematical reasoning ability in intellectually talented preadolescents: Their nature, effects, and possible causes. *Behavioral and Brain Sciences, 11,* 169–232.

Benbow, C. P., & Stanley, J. C. (1983). Sex differences in mathematical reasoning ability: More facts. *Science, 222,* 1029–1031.

Birenbaum, M., Kelly, A. E., & Levi-Keren, M. (1994). Stimulus features and sex differences in mental rotation test performance. *Intelligence, 19,* 51–64.

Bryden, M. P. (1977). Measuring handedness with questionnaires. *Neuropsychologia, 15,* 617–624.

Casey, M. B., Nuttall, R., Pezaris, E., & Benbow, C. P. (1995). The influence of spatial ability on gender difference in mathematics college entrance test scores across diverse samples. *Developmental Psychology, 31,* 697–705.

College Entrance Examination Board. (1997). *National report on college-bound seniors, various years.* New York: Author.

De Lisi, R., & McGillicuddy-De Lisi, A. (2002). Sex differences in mathematical abilities and achievement. In McGillicuddy-De Lisi, A., & De Lisi, R. (Eds.), *Biology, Society, and Behavior: The development of sex differences in cognition* (pp. 155–181). CT: Ablex Publishing.

Diamond, M. C. (1999). Enrichment response of the brain. In G. Adelman & J. DePasquale (Eds.), *Elsevier's encyclopedia of neuroscience* (pp. 655–657). New York: Elsevier Science.

Dwyer, C. A., & Johnson, L. M. (1997). Grades, accomplishments, and correlates. In Willingham, W. W., & Cole, N. S. (Eds.), *Gender and fair assessment* (pp. 127–156). Mahwah, NJ: Lawrence Erlbaum Associates.

Eagly, A. H. (1990). On the advantages of reporting sex comparisons. *American Psychologist, 45,* 560–562.

Eagly, A. H. (1994). On comparing women and men. *Feminism & Psychology, 4,* 513–522.

Eccles, J. S. (1987). Gender roles and women's achievement-related decisions. *Psychology of Women Quarterly, 11,* 135–172.

Eccles, J. S. (1994). Understanding women's educational and occupational choices: Applying the Eccles et al. model of achievement-related choices. *Psychology of Women Quarterly, 18,* 585–609.

Evelyn, J. (2002, June 28). Community colleges start to ask, where are the men? 151 women receive associate degrees for every 100 men who do. *The Chronicle of Higher Education,* p. A32.

Gallagher, A. M., & De Lisi, R. (1994). Gender differences in scholastic aptitude test mathematics problem solving among high ability students. *Journal of Educational Psychology, 86,* 204–211.

Geschwind, N. (1983). Biological associations of left-handedness. *Annals of Dyslexia, 33,* 29–40.

Geschwind, N. (1984). Cerebral dominance in biological perspective. *Neuropsychologia, 22,* 675–683.

Grandy, J. (1994). *GRE – Trends & profiles: Statistics about general test examinees by sex and ethnicity* (ETS RR-94-1) and *Supplementary tables* (ETS RR-94-1A). Princeton, NJ: Educational Testing Service.

Greenough, W. T., Black, J. E., & Wallace, C. S. (1987). Experience and brain development. *Child Development, 58,* 539–559.

Halpern, D. F. (1997). Sex differences in intelligence: Implications for educations. *American Psychologist, 52,* 1091–1102.

Halpern, D. F. (2000). *Sex differences in cognitive abilities* (3rd ed.). Mahwah, NJ: Lawrence Erlbaum Associates.

Halpern, D. F., & Collaer, M. L. (in press). Sex differences in visuospatial abilities: More than meets the eye. In P. Shah & A. Miyake (Eds.), *Higher-level visuospatial thinking and cognition.* Cambridge, MA: Cambridge University Press.

Halpern, D. F., Haviland, M. G., & Killian, C. D. (1998). Handedness and sex differences in intelligence: Evidence from the Medical College Admission Test. *Brain and Cognition, 38,* 87–101.

Hampson, E. (1990a). Estrogen-related variations in human spatial and articulatory-motor skills. *Psychoneuroendocrinology, 15,* 97–111.

Hampson, E. (1990b). Variations in sex-related cognitive abilities across the menstrual cycle. *Brain and Cognition, 14,* 26–43.

Hampson, E., & Kimura, D. (1988). Reciprocal effects of hormonal fluctuations on human motor and perceptual-spatial skills. *Behavioral Neuroscience, 102,* 456–495.

Hedges, L. V., & Nowell, A. (1995). Sex differences in mental test scores, variability, and numbers of high-scoring individuals. *Science, 269,* 41–45.

Heister, G., Landis, T., Regard, M., & Schroeder-Heister, P. (1989). Shift of functional cerebral asymmetry during the menstrual cycle. *Neuropsychologia, 27,* 871–880.

Hines, M. (1982). Prenatal gonadal hormones and sex differences in human behavior. *Psychological Bulletin, 92,* 56–80.

Hyde, J. S., Fennema, E., & Lamon, S. J. (1990). Gender differences in mathematics performance: A meta-analysis. *Psychological Bulletin, 107*, 139–153.

Hyde, J. S., Fennema, E., Ryan, M., Frost, L. A., & Hopp, C. (1990). Gender comparisons of mathematics attitudes and affect: A meta-analysis. *Psychology of Women Quarterly, 2*, 299–324.

Jacobson, L. (2002, April 24). Poll: Public sees schools as a priority. *Education Week.* Retrieved June 29, 2002, from http://www.edweek.org/ew/newstory.

Kimura, D., & Hampson, E. (1994). Cognitive pattern in men and women is influenced by fluctuations in sex hormones. *Current Directions in Psychological Science, 3*, 57–61.

Loring-Meier, S., & Halpern, D. F. (1999). Sex differences in visuospatial working memory: Components of cognitive processing. *Psychonomic Bulletin & Review, 6*(3), 464–471.

Maccoby, E. E. (1966). Sex differences in intellectual functioning. In E. E. Maccoby (Ed.), *The development of sex differences* (pp. 25–55). Stanford, CA: Stanford University Press.

MacGillis, A. (2001, December 31). Gender gap dogs nation's vet schools: Nearly 75% of students are women, leading some to predict far-reaching changes in the profession. *The Baltimore Sun.* Retrieved June 29, 2002, from http://web.lexis-nexis.com/universe.

Matlin, M. W. (2002). *Cogntion* (5th ed.). Fort Worth: Harcourt College Publishers.

Moffat, S. D., & Hampson, E. (1996). A curvilinear relationship between testosterone and spatial cognition in humans: Possible influence of hand preference. *Psychoneuroendocrinolgy, 21*, 323–337.

Naglieri, J. A., & Rojahn, J. (2001). Gender differences in planning, attention, simultaneous, and successive (PASS) cognitive processes and achievement. *Journal of Educational Psychology, 93*, 430–437.

National Assessment of Educational Progress. (1999). *NAEP trends in academic progress.* U.S. Department of Education.

National Center for Education Statistics (NCES). (1997). *Pursuing excellence: A study of U.S. fourth-grade mathematics and science achievement in international context* (NCES 97-255). Washington, DC: U.S. Government Printing Office.

National Center for Education Statistics (NCES). (1998). *Pursuing excellence: A study of U.S. twelfth-grade mathematics and science achievement in international context* (NCES 98-049). Washington, DC: U.S. Government Printing Office.

National Center for Education Statistics (NCES). (2000). *Pursuing excellence: Comparisons of international eighth-grade mathematics and science achievement from a U.S. perspective, 1995 and 1999* (NCES 2001-028). Washington, DC: U.S. Government Printing Office.

National Center for Education Statistics (NCES). (2002). Outcomes of learning: Results from the 2000 Program for International Student Assessment of 15-year-olds in reading, mathematics, and science literacy (NCES 2002-115). Washington, DC: U.S. Government Printing Office. Retrieved July 5, 2002, from http://nces.ed.gov/quicktables.

Nosek, B. A., Banaji, M. R., & Greenwald, A. G. (2002). *Math = Male, Me = Female, Therefore Math ≠ Me. Journal of Personality and Social Psychology, 83*, 44–59.

Nyborg, H. (1983). Spatial ability in men and women: Review and new theory. *Advances in Behaviour Research and Therapy, 5*, 89–140.

Nyborg, H. (1990). Sex hormones, brain development and spatio-perceptual strategies in Turner syndrome. In D. B. Berch & B. G. Bender (Eds.), *Sex chromosome abnormalities and human behavior* (pp. 100–128). Washington, DC: American Association for the Advancement of Science.

Petersen, A. C. (1976). Physical androgyny and cognitive functioning in adolescence. *Developmental Psychology, 12*, 524–533.

Resnick, S. M., Berenbaum, S. A., Gottesman, I. I., & Bouchard, T. J., Jr. (1986). Early hormonal influences of cognitive functioning in congenital adrenal hyperplasis. *Developmental Psychology, 22*, 191–198.

Resnick, S. M., Maki, P. M., Golski, S., Kraut, M. A., & Zonderman, A. B. (1998). Effects of estrogen replacement therapy on PET cerebral blood flow and neuropsychological performance. *Hormones and Behavior, 34*, 171–182.

Rovet, J., Szekely, C., & Hockenberry, M. (1994). Specific arithmetic calculation deficits in children with Turner syndrome. *Journal of Clinical and Experimental Neuropsychology, 16*, 820–839.

Sells, L. W. (1980). The mathematics filter and the education of women and minorities. In L. H. Fox & D. Tobin (Eds.), *Women and the mathematical mystique* (pp. 66–75). Baltimore: Johns Hopkins University Press.

Shih, M., Pittinsky, T. L., & Ambady, N. (1999). Stereotype susceptibility: Identity salience and shifts in quantitative performance. *Psychological Science, 10*, 80–83.

Sommers, C. (2000). *The war against boys: How misguided feminism is harming our young men.* New York: Simon & Schuster.

Steele, C. M. (1997). A threat in the air: How stereotypes shape intellectual identity and performance. *American Psychologist, 52*, 613–629.

Steele, C. M. (1998). Stereotyping and its threat are real. *American Psychologist, 53*, 680–681.

Stricker, L. J. (1998). *Inquiring about examinees' ethnicity and sex: Effects on AP Calculus AB Examination performance* (Report No. 98-1). New York: The College Board.

Stricker, L. J., & Ward, W. C. (1998). Inquiring about examinees' ethnicity and sex: Effects on computerized placement tests performance (Report No. 98-2). New York: The College Board.

Swainson, G. (2002, January 10). Girls not wired for science, author claims. *Toronto Star.* Retrieved June 29, 2002, from http://web.lexis-nexis.com/universe.

Tanner, J. M. (1962). *Growth and adolescence.* Oxford, England: Blackwell.

Ungerleider, L. G. (1995). Functional brain imaging studies of cortical mechanisms for memory. *Science, 270*, 769–775.

U.S. Bureau of the Census. (2001). Statistical abstract of the United States: 2001 (121st ed.). Washington, DC: Author.

Vermeer, H. J., Boekaerts, M., & Seegers, G. (2000). Motivational and gender differences: sixth-grade students' mathematical problem-solving behavior. *Journal of Educational Psychology, 92*(2), 308–315.

Willingham, W. W., & Cole, N. S. (1997). *Gender and fair assessment.* Hillsdale, NJ: Erlbaum.

4

Gender Differences in Math

Cognitive Processes in an Expanded Framework

James P. Byrnes

Scientists and nonscientists alike construct theories to explain variations in the environment (Byrnes, 2001a). For example, zoologists devise theories to explain observable differences in the physical appearance of species, and developmental scientists create theories to explain changes in performance that occur between early childhood and adulthood. The authors in this book are chiefly concerned with variations in math performance that are evident when one compares boys with girls or men with women. Explaining these gender-based variations is not an easy task because the size and direction of differences change with age, content, measure, and context (Hyde, Fennema, & Lamon, 1990). The purpose of this chapter is to present a comprehensive account of gender differences that explains most of the variations that have been revealed to date. As I will argue later, the primary virtue of such an account is that it could form the basis of highly effective forms of intervention.

The rest of this chapter is organized as follows. In the first section, I provide a brief overview of the pattern of gender differences that have been reported in the literature. This pattern represents the phenomenon that needs to be explained by any theory of gender differences. In the second section, I summarize and critique existing explanations of these findings (including a Cognitive Process approach that my colleagues and I proposed in the mid-1990s). In the third section, I present a new explanatory model that was created to extend and integrate the existing explanations (called the Three Conditions model). In the final section, I consider the theoretical, empirical, and practical implications of the Three Conditions model.

PATTERNS OF GENDER DIFFERENCES IN MATH

Before considering the merits of existing theories of gender differences in math, it is first important to consider the phenomena that these theories are trying to explain. In my view, a theory gains both scientific credibility and practical value to the extent that it can explain an increasing array of related phenomena. For example, consider the following three findings from the literature on gender differences in math:

1. High school males perform much better than high school females on the SAT-math.
2. Prior to high school, gender differences are usually not found on measures of math problem solving.
3. Boys rate their math competence higher than girls in both elementary school and high school (Hyde et al., 1990; Wigfield, Eccles, Yoon, Harold, Arbreton, Freedman-Doan, & Blumenfeld, 1997).

In my view, theories that can explain all three of these findings are preferable to theories that can explain only one or two of them for the following reason: important developmental outcomes are nearly always produced by the confluence of multiple factors that work in concert. If so, then interventions must necessarily target multiple factors to have any hope of being effective. To know which factors to target, however, one must have an accurate and comprehensive theory of the outcome in question. Theories, after all, identify the causal factors responsible for an outcome.

With this argument in mind, we can consider the primary findings in the literature on gender differences in math. For more detailed summaries of these and other findings, see Byrnes (2001a), Halpern (2000), or Hyde et al. (1990):

1. Below the age of 15, girls tend to perform better than boys on tests requiring computational skill (e.g., Green, 1987; Newman, 1984). No differences are found for tests that measure math concepts or math problem solving (e.g., Fennema & Sherman, 1978; Lewis & Hoover, 1987). Among gifted 7th graders, however, a moderate difference favoring boys ($d = 0.41$) appears for overall scores on SAT-like tests (e.g., Benbow & Stanley, 1980). On SAT items that require one to know when one has enough information to provide an answer, however, gifted girls perform better than gifted boys (e.g., Becker, 1990).

2. At around age 15, a small to moderate gender difference appears for problem solving ($d = 0.29$, favoring boys), especially when college-bound students are at issue (Hyde et al., 1990). Moderate differences also emerge on timed standardized tests such as the SAT-math ($d = 0.40$) and the GRE-Quantitative ($d = 0.70$). Both of these findings illustrate how the gender gap is larger in select samples than in the general population.

3. No gender differences emerge for students older than 14 for measures of math concepts or computations, however (Hyde et al., 1990). In addition, male and female 12th graders have obtained nearly identical scores on the last four National Assessments of Educational Progress (NAEPs)

for math (e.g., means of 299 and 303 on the 2000 NAEP). The latter involve large, nationally representative samples ($N > 17,000$) and assess computational and problem-solving skills in algebra, geometry, probability, and arithmetic. Students are given 45 minutes to solve 40 to 60 items.

4. Girls tend to obtain either the same grade as, or higher grades than, boys in mathematics at all grade levels (*d*s ranging from −0.09 to −0.35; Kimball, 1989).

5. Boys tend to give higher ratings of their math ability than girls at all grade levels (Wigfield et al., 1997).

In essence, then, theories of gender differences have to answer questions such as (1) why does the computational advantage of girls exist prior to age 15 but disappear after age 15?; (2) why does the gap in problem solving grow over time (i.e., nonexistent in most ability groups prior to age 15 but apparent after age 15?); (3) why do boys rate their abilities higher than girls even at ages when they fail to demonstrate more ability?; (4) why do girls demonstrate similar or better performance on various indicators of achievement at all grade levels (e.g., grades in courses or scores on the NAEP), whereas boys demonstrate better performance on SAT-like tests mainly after age 15?

EXISTING THEORIES AND THEIR SHORTCOMINGS

Various theories have been proposed over the years to explain some of these findings. In what follows, four representative theories are briefly explained and critiqued in turn. As noted above, more detailed treatments of these theories can be found in sources such as Byrnes (2001a) or Halpern (2000).

Genetic and Other Physiological Views
One way to explain gender differences in math is to appeal to brain-based differences between males and females (e.g., Benbow, 1988). To be consistent with what we currently know about the brain (and to also be sufficiently precise and plausible), this perspective would have to consist of the following component propositions:

1. In the brain, there are specific networks of neural assemblies dedicated to particular cognitive processes (e.g., comparing the magnitude of two numbers). When someone engages in a given cognitive process, the network dedicated to this process tends to be active (around 70% of the time). Networks dedicated to other, unrelated, or uninvolved processes tend not to be active. The locations of various networks can be observed using technologies such as functional magnetic resonance imaging. These technologies show that all major cognitive processes (including

math) activate widely distributed assemblies from all four lobes and both cerebral hemispheres of the brain.

2. There are specific, still-to-be-determined configurations of neural assemblies within these networks that lead to optimum mathematics performance (e.g., problem types are quickly recognized, relevant knowledge is accessed quickly). Other configurations lead to average or below average performance. Presumably, the key differences among these configurations have to do with such things as the total number of neurons (too many or too few can cause problems), the proportion of certain kinds of neurons in the assembly (e.g., inhibitory vs. excitatory), which assemblies are recruited (in what order), and patterns of interconnections within and among neurons and neural assemblies.

3. Each configuration of neural assemblies is the end product of normal processes of brain development (e.g., creating enough cells of different types, cells migrating to the right locations after they are produced, cells growing in size and projecting axons, preprogrammed and experience-based synaptogenesis, cell death).

4. These normal processes of brain development operate somewhat differently in males and females (according to advocates of this perspective). As a result, (a) neural assemblies used during mathematical thinking tend to be configured differently in males and females, and (b) males are more likely than females to acquire the optimal configuration for assemblies dedicated to math.

Whereas most researchers who advocate an important role for brain physiology would probably agree with assertions 1 to 4 above, they often disagree about the mechanisms that are responsible for achieving the presumed differences between male and female brains. For example, some researchers appeal to genetics and suggest that male genes specify a different brain morphology than female genes. Several facts about brain development are consistent with this claim. First, there is good evidence to suggest that processes such as cell proliferation (i.e., creating brain cells), cell migration, cell differentiation, cell growth, and initial, preexperience synaptogenesis are largely determined by genetic instructions (although local signaling among cells also affects these processes; see Byrnes, 2001b). Second, male brains are about 9% larger than female brains, which suggests that cell proliferation and growth operate differently in the two gender groups (e.g., the proliferation phase lasts a little longer in males, giving them more brain cells; cell growth also lasts longer, giving them larger brain cells).

Other researchers agree that genes play a role in the process, but argue that genes mainly contribute to the creation of hormone-producing organs (e.g., gonads) and receptors for sex hormones in brain cells. Research with rats shows that male and female hormones alter the morphology of brain structures such as the hypothalamus and corpus callosum; therefore, some researchers assume that prenatal exposure to sex hormones would probably also affect the growth and development of human brains.

To illustrate one variant of the hormonal perspective, consider the accounts proposed by the research groups of Benbow, Casey, and others to explain gender differences in math (e.g., Benbow, 1988; Casey, Pezaris, & Nuttall, 1992). Researchers in these groups sought a physiological account that would emphasize the right hemisphere because

The right hemisphere is traditionally considered specialized for non-verbal tasks and the left for verbal, although these differences may not be qualitative but quantitative. Mathematical reasoning ability, especially in contrast to computational ability, may be more strongly under the influence of the right hemisphere. (Benbow, 1988, p. 180.)

Some advocates of this perspective found what they needed in the work of the late Norman Geschwind and colleagues on the anatomical basis of dyslexia. Geschwind and Galabura (1985) proposed a model to explain three sets of findings: (1) a higher incidence of language problems in boys than in girls, (2) symmetry or reversed asymmetry in the size of certain brain areas in dyslexic children, and (3) unexpected empirical links between left-handedness, language disorders, and immune disorders. To explain these findings, Geschwind and colleagues proposed that, during prenatal development, testosterone levels affect the growth of the left cerebral hemisphere in such a way that an anomalous form of dominance develops. Instead of being right-handed and having language lateralized in the left hemisphere, affected individuals become left-handed with language lateralized in the right or both hemispheres. This altered physiology, in turn, leads to problems such as developmental dyslexia, impaired language development, and autism. Testosterone levels also affect the thymus, resulting in disorders of the immune system (e.g., allergies, colitis). To explain asymmetries in the size of the left and right hemispheres that are found in most normal individuals, Geschwind and colleagues suggested the testosterone may either retard the growth of the left hemisphere, or interfere with normal reductions in the right. With respect to the latter, note that most children produce many more cells than needed prenatally. If children avoid brain insults postnatally, excess cells are believed to be eliminated through cell death (but this claim is somewhat controversial).

To test these speculations about right hemisphere development, Benbow and colleagues considered whether gifted children were more likely than nongifted children to be left-handed and have immune disorders (e.g., allergies). To assess handedness, Benbow and colleagues gave the Edinburgh Handedness Inventory (Oldfield, 1971) to two kinds of children who were drawn from their sample of more than 100,000 gifted students: (1) an extremely precocious group of seventh-grade children ($N = 303$)

who scored above 700 on the SAT-math or above 630 on the SAT-verbal, and (2) a less precocious group who scored closer to 500 on the SAT-math ($N = 127$). Whereas the norms for Edinburgh Handedness Inventory suggest that 8% of Scottish adults use their left hands occasionally or often to perform everyday tasks, 13% of children who were extremely precocious for math and 10% of the less precocious group were left-handed in this way (Benbow, 1986). Whereas the incidence of left-handedness was found to be significantly higher in the extremely precocious children than in the Scottish adults ($p < 0.04$), two other comparisons revealed no significant differences: (1) less precocious children vs. the Scottish adults, and (2) extremely precocious children vs. less precocious children.

As for gender differences in the extent of left-handedness in extremely precocious students, Benbow (1988) reports that more males (16%) than females (11%) were left-handed in the study ($p < 0.05$, using an unspecified test). The present author, however, applied the standard test for comparing frequencies (i.e., the chi-square test) to Benbow's (1986) data and found that the difference between 16% and 11% is not significant ($p = 0.17$). In addition, the key difference between mathematically precocious males (14%) and mathematically precocious females (6%) was also not significant ($p = 0.33$).

With respect to immune disorders, Benbow (1988) reports that students with extremely high mathematical ability are twice as likely to have allergies as children in the general population (53% vs. 25%). A comparison between extremely precocious males (53%) and females (54%), however, showed no significance difference in the incidence of allergies.

Thus, the preliminary findings based on handedness and allergies were not terribly supportive of the idea of greater right hemisphere involvement in gifted children, in general, and gifted males, in particular. It could be argued, however, that these studies really do not test the right-hemisphere proposal directly because indices such as handedness and allergies are fairly imprecise. A more direct approach would be to look at patterns of activation in the right and left hemisphere using either neuroimaging or gross electrical recording techniques. In their review of the literature using the latter, O'Boyle and Gill (1998) report that gifted adolescents appear to engage their right hemispheres more than nongifted adolescents when they listen to auditory stimuli or process facial expressions. In addition, gifted adolescents show a pattern of resting neural activation that is similar to that of college students and significantly different from nongifted adolescents (i.e., greater activation in the frontal and occipital lobes).

Other studies conducted by Benbow and colleagues revealed gender differences with respect to the involvement of the right hemisphere for the processing of faces and mental rotation (more involvement for males), but not for verbal stimuli. In addition, graphs of data presented in Alexander, O'Boyle, and Benbow (1996) also suggest greater resting activations in the parietal and possibly frontal lobes in gifted males than in gifted females, but these specific comparisons were not reported in the text. The one study that had the potential to consider whether greater right hemisphere involvement was associated with higher SAT-math scores (i.e., O'Boyle & Benbow, 1990) failed to report this correlation because the authors expressed concerns over a restricted range problem with the SAT-math scores (i.e., most students scored over 500). The authors did report a correlation of $r = -0.29$ between laterality scores and total SAT scores (i.e., greater bias to process faces in the right hemisphere corresponded to higher total SAT scores).

Whereas Benbow and colleagues suggested in their earlier work that the right hemisphere is associated with math skill in some unspecified way, Casey and colleagues suggest that the link has to do with spatial ability (Casey, Nuttall, Pezaris, & Benbow, 1995). This idea seemed reasonable because there are rather substantial gender differences in spatial skills such as mental rotation (ds on the order of 0.7 to 1.5). Math is often alleged to require spatial skills (e.g., to imagine solutions), so Casey and colleagues wanted to see if (1) spatial ability would predict performance on the SAT-math (controlling for other factors), and (2) gender differences on the SAT-math would disappear once one controlled for spatial ability. As for the first hypothesis, Casey et al. (1995) found that spatial ability did predict SAT-math scores after one controlled for SAT-verbal scores (an average of 9% of the variance in four female age groups and 8% in four male age groups). However, verbal skills explained two to three times as much variance as spatial skills (26% in females and 15% in males). In another study of 8th graders, spatial ability only predicted math skills for non-right-handed females. It did not predict math skills for right-handed females, right-handed males, or left-handed males (Casey et al., 1992). As for the second prediction, Casey et al. (1995) found that the significant gender difference in SAT-math scores can be eliminated when one controls for spatial ability. However, whereas such an effect was found for college students and high-ability high school students, it was not found for precocious students.

Besides the lack of strong or consistent support in the studies conducted by advocates of the right hemisphere/spatial ability account, several other problems also exist. First, other researchers have not found any correlation between spatial scores and math performance (e.g., Fennema & Sherman, 1977). Second, some have argued that it is not clear that spatial skills would even be required to solve SAT-like items where the gender differences are largest (e.g., Royer, Tronsky, Chan, Jackson, & Marchant, 1999). Third, most neuroscientists assume that the frontal lobes are the sites of higher-order reasoning (Luria, 1973; Waltz et al., 1999). More posterior regions of the right hemisphere could be associated with certain aspects of conceptual knowledge in math or certain types of spatial reasoning (but not all), but these regions are also active when working memory and attention are engaged (Byrnes, 2001b). Thus, even if evidence suddenly did accumulate to suggest that extremely talented mathematicians engage their right hemispheres more than less talented individuals, this difference could reflect the former's greater reliance on math concepts, spatial skills, or working memory. These capacities may relate to the kind of reasoning required to do well on the SAT, but the core processes of problem comprehension and strategic planning are likely to be associated with the frontal lobes.

Fourth, speculations about size differences in the right hemisphere between genders have not been borne out in neuroimaging studies or autopsies (Byrnes, 2001b). Whereas these studies have shown that the average female brain tends to be 9% smaller overall than the average male brain (as noted earlier), the difference is not limited to the right hemisphere. Moreover, researchers have not found gender differences in the degree of asymmetry of the left and right hemispheres.

Fifth, it is not at all clear why a theory designed to account for reading disabilities (i.e., the model of Geschwind and colleagues) would even be appropriate for explaining high levels of math *talent*. If the Geschwind model really did apply, one would expect to find reading disabilities in many of the extremely precocious children or people with high spatial ability. In fact, however, most precocious children have a great deal of verbal ability in addition to having considerable math ability (Benbow, 1986, 1988). Sixth, comprehensive meta-analyses of the literature reveal that there is little evidence in support of the proposals of Geschwind and colleagues, even where it is meant to apply (e.g., Bryden, McManus, & Bulman-Fleming, 1994).

Seventh, many studies have shown that experience can alter brain morphology (Byrnes, 2001b). Experiences can promote the growth of dendrites and also the retraction or pruning of axons. So, if the genders are found someday to differ in cytoarchitecture (number, types, and patterns of connectivity among neurons), this difference could be due to genes, hormones, or experience. Eighth, males and females may have the same morphology but use different strategies when they solve tasks (Byrnes & Takahira, 1993; Halpern, 2000). These strategies might show up in brain scans as different regions of the brain being active when problem solving is underway, but such a difference in activity does not mean that male and female brains are "naturally" more or less lateralized (or better organized, etc.). If all students were taught to use the same strategy, then the same regions of the brain would probably be active in all students (given the correspondence between networks of assemblies and particular tasks).

Finally, perhaps the biggest problem with existing physiological views is that they do not provide a comprehensive story that can account for the *entire pattern* of gender differences reported here. For example, if the right hemisphere account is true, why are gender differences in problem solving more likely to appear in adolescence than in childhood? Why does the computational advantage for females disappear by adolescence? Why do boys hold more positive opinions of their talent even at ages when gender differences in performance are not apparent?

Socialization Accounts

The polar opposite of the genetic/physiological category is the Socialization view. Researchers who adopt this view assume that gender differences in cognitive performance arise from the values inherent in a society or particular culture that are transmitted to students by their family, peers, and teachers (Eccles, 1983; Halpern, 2000). Certain domains (e.g., math and science) are stereotyped as "male" domains and others (e.g., reading and writing) are stereotyped as "female" domains. Such stereotypes are likely to affect the achievement-related beliefs of students in a variety of ways (Nosek, Banaji, & Greenwald, 2002). In the first place, girls would be less likely to find math interesting or important than boys, and would be more likely to form low expectations for how well they will perform in math than boys. In addition, girls would be less likely to (1) try hard in math classes, (2) believe that they have high math ability, (3) volunteer to take part in math talent programs as 7th graders (even if they met the selection criteria), (4) pursue math-related careers, and (5) take the additional math courses required for such careers. Further, gender biases in teachers would prompt teachers to expect more of boys and interact with them more during math class.

Many studies have supported these predictions regardless of whether these beliefs are measured explicitly or implicitly (Eccles, Wigfield, & Schiefele, 1998; Leder, 1992; Nosek et al., 2002). In fact, gender differences in beliefs can be found as early as the first grade. Thus, it is clear that students and teachers do seem to internalize cultural values and these attitudes can affect choices and preferences even at an unconscious level. The question is, however, whether gender differences in beliefs are causally responsible for the gender differences in math achievement.

What is needed to support such an assertion is a comprehensive theory that links beliefs to those behaviors that serve as intermediaries to successful performance on achievement tests. For example, one theory might be that interest promotes active, engaged listening in class (rather than passive listening coupled with "spacing out"). Moreover, prior to taking classroom tests, students who value math and believe that they have talent in math will study harder and more effectively than students who do not. Over time, the former students will gain more expertise in a subject area than the latter students. Then, when students are not forced to take certain classes anymore (e.g., math in high school), only the interested and self-efficacious student will take electives in that domain. These additional classes, in turn, would promote still greater knowledge and skill. With greater knowledge and skill, students can perform quite well on achievement tests.

Such an account could effectively explain many of the gender differences that appear in the literature in various subject areas. Perhaps girls like to read and write more than boys. Perhaps boys like math and science better. All of this sounds reasonable, but it remains to be tested directly. There is, however, indirect evidence than can be gleaned from cross-cultural studies. If the socialization view is right and the genetic view wrong, then there should be a positive correlation between the strength of gender biases in a culture and the size of the gender gap in certain subject areas. For example, in cultures that espouse the idea that math is a male subject, the gender gap in math achievement should be largest. In cultures that take a less biased stance, however, the gender gap in math achievement should be small or nonexistent. One study of math performance in 8th graders in 19 countries showed just such a correlation. If gender differences were entirely genetic, the gap should not vary this way and there should be no countries in which males and females perform the same. In fact, however, Takahira (1995) and Byrnes, Li, and Shaoying (1997) found no gender differences in performance on SAT-math items in Japanese and Chinese high school students, respectively. Interestingly, they used SAT items that produced the largest gender differences in American students in these studies.

Although the foregoing arguments and evidence seem compelling, the Socialization view runs into its own problems. First, it is hard to find a study that demonstrates the longitudinal relations between interest, type of engagement, amount of studying, and so forth described here. Instead, we have only piecemeal, often low (i.e., 0.30) correlations among one or two variables from cross-sectional studies. Second, we have the fact that girls routinely get better grades than boys in subjects such as math and science. Girls think that math is more difficult than boys and value it less (e.g., Wigfield et al., 1997), so why are girls trying so hard to get better grades? If we assume that good grades mean that they are learning something, girls must be acquiring a considerable amount of skill over time, are they not?

Third, studies of mathematically precocious students show no gender differences in the explicit beliefs of these children or in their parents' beliefs, yet 13-year-old precocious boys perform significantly better than 13-year-old precocious girls on the SAT (Benbow, 1988). It could be argued, however, that these results are difficult to interpret given that implicit beliefs (which were not measured) could exert a more powerful influence than explicit beliefs (Nosek et al., 2002) and that students self-select into the talent programs from which precocious children are recruited for studies (a problem of generalizability). Nevertheless, the findings must be reckoned with. Fourth, whereas gender differences in beliefs can be found in the first grade, some gender differences in achievement test performance do not occur until adolescence. Why the long delay?

Fifth, whereas the correlation reported earlier between the degree of stereotyping in a country and math performance holds up when children are in the 8th grade, they do not hold up when children in the same countries are in the 12th grade (Hanna, Kundinger, & Larouche, 1992). Also, in the Third International Mathematics and Science Study conducted in 1995, 12th-grade males outperformed 12th-grade females in 12 out of 16 countries. The pervasiveness of the differences would be difficult to explain from the standpoint of socialization theories (unless one could demonstrate that sexism is greater in Sweden, France, Germany, Canada, Lithuania, Russia, Switzerland, Czech Republic, Austria, United States, and Denmark than it is in Greece, Cyprus, Australia, Italy, and Slovenia). Finally, the socialization view could not easily accommodate the lack of gender differences in math performance found in studies of Japanese or Chinese students because gender biases in beliefs also exist in these countries (Byrnes et al., 1997).

Differential Experience Views
One of the first versions of the Differential Experience view to appear in the literature was the Differential Coursework account that was originally proposed by researchers such as Fennema and Sherman (1977) and Pallas and Alexander (1983). Pallas and Alexander showed that taking courses such as algebra, geometry, and calculus was a good predictor of success on the SAT. This predictive relation makes sense in light of the fact that the SAT requires knowledge of arithmetic, algebra, and geometry (but not calculus). Students have to recruit this knowledge and use it in creative ways to solve SAT problems. In addition, Pallas and Alexander showed that the usual 47-point gender difference in SAT scores could be statistically reduced to 13 points when prior coursework is controlled. In a related vein, Byrnes and Takahira (1993, 1994) found that knowledge of arithmetic, algebra, and geometry topics was a good predictor of success on SAT items. Typically, one gets such knowledge by way of courses.

Despite the empirical support it receives from the studies of Pallas and Alexander and Byrnes and Takahira, however, the Differential Coursework view has its problems. First, gender differences in math achievement appear either just before (i.e., age 13) or right after girls and boys start taking different classes (i.e., age 15). For coursework to have an effect, one would think that several years of different course-taking has to pass. Second, performance on calculus courses predicts success on the SAT, but calculus material is not part of this test. So perhaps course-taking is a proxy variable for math talent or aptitude. Third, gender differences in reading and writing occur from the beginning of schooling, not after boys and girls have taken different courses for years. Why wouldn't the differential coursework theory also be true for reading and writing? Fourth, Linn and Kessel (1996) found that even when boys and girls in a large sample in Maryland took the same courses from the same teachers, an effect size of $d = 0.40$ was still found for the SAT-math. Finally, gifted 13-year-olds who have not yet attended high school still show the usual gender difference in SAT performance.

Of course, one could revise the Differential Coursework view to accommodate many of these problems. Using the category label "Differential Experience" view, for example, one could say that knowledge and skill can be acquired either in school or out of school. Moreover, formal courses may be less important than experiences within specific courses. For example, perhaps boys and girls receive different amounts of reading and writing experiences in the preschool years at home with their parents. Similarly, perhaps gifted children receive more instruction in algebra and geometry in elementary school than the average seventh graders get (which they clearly do and the latter do receive some instruction in algebra and geometry). Finally, perhaps boys and girls have different amounts of informal exposure to math activities in their home lives or different amounts of attention from their teachers. Nevertheless, before the value of the Differential Experience view can be fully assessed, additional studies need to be conducted that carefully document experience differences such as these and trace their effects.

Cognitive Process Views

All the views presented so far have included either "proximal" or "distal" variables in their explanation of gender differences. Proximal means that explanatory variables are closely connected to performance in space or time. Distal means that explanatory variables are somewhat removed from actual performance. For example, in a chain of events such as

Genes → Hormones → Lateralization → Exposure to content

　　　　→ SAT performance,

the variable "genes" would be viewed as somewhat "distal" because they are at least four steps removed from performance and they exert their influence years before students take the SAT. In contrast, the idea of exposure to content in the Differential Coursework view is more proximally related.

The Cognitive Process view emphasizes variables that are even more "proximal" than those of the Differential Coursework view because the former's variables would be inserted between the "exposure to content" and "SAT performance" steps in the chain. Researchers who have adopted the Cognitive Process view have tried to identify the key processes responsible for success on an achievement test. After delineating these processes, they try to determine which processes seem to clearly differentiate the two groups of interest (usually high scorers and low scorers).

To illustrate, Byrnes and Takahira (1993, 1994) used the Cognitive Process approach to explain success on SAT items. They argue that students have to successfully execute the following processes in order to perform well on items from the SAT:

1. *Define the problem* (i.e., determine what the author of the item wants him or her to do).
2. *Access prior knowledge* (i.e., retrieve item-specific concepts and procedures from long-term memory).
3. *Assemble an effective strategy* (i.e., arrange prior concepts and procedures into an effective sequence of problem-solving steps).
4. *Perform computations without error* (i.e., solve for unknowns using arithmetic, geometry, and algebra).
5. Avoid being seduced by *misleading alternatives*.
6. Carry out operations 1 to 5 *quickly enough* that each problem can be solved in one minute or less.

Generally speaking, these six components were assumed in the original proposal to be carried out in the order described here, although it has been subsequently found that the order of operations sometimes varies across individuals and items (e.g., skipping the strategy construction process and examining alternatives to eliminate implausible ones, skipping the computational process by using estimation, and so on; see Gallagher, De Lisi, Holst, McGillicuddy-De Lisi, Morely, & Cahaln, 2000, for examples of these alternative orderings). In the studies conducted by my colleagues and I, however, we have largely disregarded order and given students credit for demonstrating any of the processes in their think-aloud protocols. We then tried to explain performance using these processes within regression analyses or analyses involving conditional probabilities. For example, Byrnes and Takahira (1993) tried to predict performance on SAT items using the following predictors: (1) prior knowledge of item-specific arithmetic, algebra, and geometry concepts and procedures; (2) the strategies subjects used to solve individual problems; (3) their math GPA; and (4) the student's gender. Whereas prior knowledge and strategies were unique and strong predictors of success on the SAT (explaining 50% of the variance), the variable "gender" was not when it was added after prior knowledge and strategies. In other words, success was more a function of a student's knowledge and skill than his or her gender (because some successful students were knowledgeable and strategic females, whereas some unsuccessful students were unknowledgeable and unstrategic males). In follow-up studies, Byrnes and Takahira (1994), Takahira (1995), and Byrnes et al. (1997) found further support for the model in American, Japanese, and Chinese students, respectively.

The value of the Cognitive Process approach is that the findings immediately suggest the causes of failure in the group who is not performing as well (e.g., they are using suboptimal strategies or they lack prior knowledge). Once these causes or shortcomings have been identified, a training program can be implemented to improve performance (e.g., training them to use better strategies).

Similar to the other three approaches, however, the Cognitive Process approach has its problems. One important defect is that it fails to specify why males and females may differ on the processes identified. For example, it does not tell us why females have less knowledge, or use suboptimal strategies, or fall prey to misleading alternatives. Another defect is that it cannot explain all the key findings reported earlier.

SUMMARY. In sum, then, the four main categories of theories have either empirical problems or theoretical shortcomings (or both). The empirical problems include one or more of the following: (1) there is no evidence in support of key claims, (2) the evidence suggests that certain claims seem to be wrong, and (3) the evidence supports the key claims of more than one theory. In effect, there is no clear empirical "winner." The primary theoretical problems include the fact that (1) no one model can explain all the findings for gender differences in math that were listed earlier, and (2) existing models fail to capture the full chronology of events ranging from early childhood to adolescence. Hence, there is a need for a new, comprehensive model that can accommodate the empirical problems of existing models, explain a wider variety of findings, and place events in a broader developmental context. In the next section, I describe such a model.

THE THREE CONDITIONS MODEL OF ACHIEVEMENT

By way of introduction, it is important to note that the Three Conditions (3C) model was originally designed to explain gender differences and many other kinds of group differences as well (e.g., ethnic differences). My work on the 3C model began with the insight that questions about specific group differences (e.g., "Why do males perform better than females on the SAT-math?") are particularized instances of the more general question, "Why are *certain students* more likely than *other students* to demonstrate proficiency in a *given subject area*?" Here, one substitutes the groups of interest and the subject areas of interest for the italicized terms in this general question (e.g., males or white children for *certain students*, females or minority children for *other students*, and math or reading for *given subject area*). I tried to provide answers to this question that would use many of the same constructs to explain ethnic differences, gender differences, and other kinds of differences. The goal was to explain differences within and across subject areas (e.g., the fact that males perform better on the SAT math in high school, whereas females perform better on timed writing assessments at all ages).

A second introductory point is that the 3C model was designed to integrate and extend most of the existing explanations of gender differences. In other words, I tried to answer the question, "how could all the existing theories of gender differences be true (even at some level)?" As noted earlier, there is every reason to think that important developmental outcomes are caused by a host of factors (in this case, the factors identified in prior models). However, it is important to do more than simply include prior claims in an incoherent hodgepodge of assertions. Unprincipled eclecticism cannot provide a basis for effective interventions because the core variables of human development interact in a systemic fashion; as such, we need to know how each variable relates to others (concurrently and over time).

With these introductory points in mind, we can now return to the general question above (with italicized components) and move to the specific case of gender differences in math. The 3C model suggests that the answer to the general question is that children are most likely to acquire high levels of proficiency in a given subject area (e.g., math) if *all three* of the following conditions hold: (1) they *regularly* find themselves in contexts that provide them with *genuine* opportunities to enhance their skills (the exposure condition), (2) they are *willing* to take advantage of these opportunities (the motivation condition), and (3) they are *able* to take advantage of these opportunities (the aptitude condition). Thus, a core assumption of the model is that gender differences in math skills can largely be explained by appealing to different levels of exposure to genuine opportunities to learn, different levels of motivation, or different levels of aptitude in males and females.

To fully understand the implications of the model, however, it is necessary to "unpack" this answer somewhat. Consider first the notion of genuine opportunities to learn. The model assumes that an opportunity to learn is genuine to the extent that (1) teachers do not give preferential treatment to certain students (e.g., males); (2) students engage in learning activities that are challenging, meaningful (to them), arranged in an effective sequence, and promote skills that are required on the measures used to assess achievement levels (e.g., SAT, NAEP); (3) teachers hold high expectations for all students; (4) teachers are effective in managing student behavior; and (5) teachers understand the purpose of classroom activities, ask students to regularly practice skills in meaningful contexts, engage in scaffolding, and use a balance of effective techniques that promote the internalization and self-regulation of skills (Schmidt, 2001; Taylor, Pressley, & Pearson, 2000). Empirically, one would consider whether the exposure condition has been met by determining the frequency with which children are provided with opportunities, as well as the quality of these opportunities. Higher achievement is expected if children are frequently exposed to high-quality opportunities.

To explain gender differences in math proficiency, one would examine whether gender was confounded with one or more of the previous features of genuine opportunities to learn. In the case of preferential treatment, for example, there is evidence that teachers do not always respond to their male and female students in the same way (Leder, 1992). For example, math teachers may wait longer for a boy to provide an answer to a question than they wait for a girl to provide an answer. Similarly, teachers may call on boys more often during math periods, praise them more, or hold higher expectations of them. If teachers show such biases in their classrooms, boys and girls are not really given the same opportunities to learn. As such, one would expect gender differences in proficiency to emerge over time *even though children took the same courses from the same teachers*. To illustrate this claim using a sports analogy, note how we would not expect boys and girls on the same co-ed soccer team to develop skills at the same rate if (1) boys get substantially more playing time during games than girls, and (2) their coach's comments and behaviors imply that the boys who are given extra time are the best players on the team.

If differences could emerge even when boys and girls have the same teachers, it follows that differences would be even larger if gender biases exist in the assignment of boys and girls to math ability groups or programs of study. For example, boys may be selected or nominated more often to take part in gifted and talented programs in mathematics (even when there are no differences in achievement test scores in math). Whereas children in higher-ability groups often get exposed to challenging content and the most talented teachers in the school, those in lower-ability groups tend to get exposed to nonchallenging content or lesser-skilled teachers (Entwisle & Alexander, 1992; Guiton & Oakes, 1995). Then, when students are allowed to choose their own courses in high school, it is likely that students who are exposed to lower-quality environments would tend to take only the minimum number of math courses required. These within-school differences in exposure could, of course, be augmented by differences in out-of-school experiences (e.g., fathers playing math games with sons, but not with daughters; boys figuring out batting averages of their favorite players).

The effects of such differential levels of exposure from the first through 12th grades would be expected to "snowball" over time (Stanovich, 1986), producing an ever-widening gap between lower- and higher-scoring children. Recall that such a pattern of ever-widening differences was one of the key findings that had to be explained by theories of gender differences in math (i.e., in most samples, no gender differences in problem solving prior to age 15 but differences after 15). In essence, then, there is reason to suspect that gender is confounded with the exposure condition of the 3C model.

Turning next to the motivation condition, the methodological strategy is to consider whether there is reason to suspect that gender would be confounded with the willingness to take advantage of opportunities that might be presented to them. The motivation condition is needed to explain situations in which boys and girls seem to have been presented with genuine opportunities to learn, but only boys take advantage of these opportunities. By "take advantage," I mean that boys willingly engage in math activities because they (1) are interested in math, (2) are intrinsically motivated to become more competent in math, (3) are not worried about what others would think of them if they demonstrated math competence, and (4) believe that they will probably perform well. As noted earlier (and in Chapters 12 and 14 of this volume), there are gender differences in children's motivation to be engaged in mathematical activities. Hence, there is reason to think that gender is confounded with both the exposure and motivation conditions of the 3C model.

The need for the third and final condition (the aptitude condition) becomes apparent when one considers the possibility that gender differences could arise even when male and female students are given equal opportunities to learn in a particular classroom and are equally motivated to take advantage of these opportunities. This outcome could occur if males were more advanced in their math skills than girls when they began a shared learning opportunity. The aptitude condition is also needed to explain cases in which a somewhat disinterested but talented student gets more out of a learning opportunity (e.g., a semester-length course) than a highly motivated but underprepared or lesser-skilled student. When two students differ in the amount of aptitude that they bring to a learning opportunity, the student with more aptitude would be expected to get more out of the experience than the student with less aptitude. This claim is easiest to appreciate by considering cases in which course material is advanced and only high-aptitude students seem to grasp the material.

The assertion that aptitude matters has a considerable amount of support in the literature. For example, it has been commonly observed that measures of general aptitude (e.g., IQ) and specific aptitudes (e.g., achievement test scores for the preceding academic year) are very good, if not the best, predictors of the amount of learning that takes place in a given academic year (e.g., Morrison, Griffith, & Alberts, 1997; Smith, Jussim, & Eccles, 1999; Taylor, Frye, & Maruyama, 1990). Measures of specific aptitudes (e.g., Spring 2001 test scores), for example, often explain 40% to 60% of the variance in later achievement (e.g., Spring 2002 test scores). In addition, many studies have shown that the regression weights for prior year scores tend to be at least three times the size of regression weights for all other factors in a given study (e.g., teacher perceptions, self-efficacy beliefs).

However, the question is not whether aptitude is an important factor in predicting achievement. It clearly is. The question for this chapter is whether there is reason to think that gender is confounded with aptitude. In reflecting on the latter question, I have found it necessary to make a distinction between natural and acquired aptitude. By *natural aptitude* I mean long-standing, hard-to-modify constraints on the rate with which existing skills show improvement or new skills are acquired in a specific domain (even when high-quality, intensive training is provided). These constraints, which often become apparent in challenging situations, place an upper limit on a person's "reaction range" (to borrow a term from the field of genetics). Informally, the notion of natural aptitude is what people mean when they say that certain individuals "pick things up quickly" in a domain like music, math, or sports. The idea of upper limit metaphorically relates to the "heights" a person could achieve even in a maximally rich environment. Collectively, these attributes of natural aptitude suggest that the constraints are physical in nature.

In contrast, *acquired aptitude* is more akin to expertise. Expertise is not inborn or something that has an upper limit per se. Rather, it is developed through an average of three or four hours of daily, deliberate practice that is conducted over a period of at least 10 years (Ericsson, 1996). A person may not have an extraordinary level of natural aptitude for a domain (e.g., music or math) but could be far along an expertise continuum due to years of practice. If such a person and a novice were given the same challenging learning opportunity, the expert would be expected to get more out of this experience than the novice.

Although it is possible that there are gender differences in natural aptitude for math, the findings reported earlier suggests otherwise. If the differences were inborn, hard to modify, and primarily evident in challenging situations, why are there typically no differences in higher-level aspects of math in elementary students (e.g., math concepts and problem solving)? Similarly, why would differences only appear on SAT-like tests in adolescence (and not on difficult achievement tests like the NAEP)? If expertise theorists were to take an interest in gender differences in math, they would find it highly significant that large gender differences only start to emerge after average children have been given formal education for ten years (i.e., ages 5 to 15). Many gifted children have reported that they were given informal education in math beginning in their preschool years (e.g., age 3). They too would be expected to show an advantage 10 years later when they are in the 7th grade. However, the issue of whether gender differences are natural or acquired has yet to be resolved in convincing lines of research. Regardless of their origin and nature, moreover, male students would be expected to get more out of a learning opportunity than female students (e.g., a high school math course) if the former enter that experience with more aptitude than the latter.

Thus, there are three important implications of the 3C model for studies that consider whether the size of the gender gap would shrink after one controls for prior coursework. First, as noted earlier in the discussion of the exposure condition, the fact that male and female students took the same courses from the same teachers does not mean that males and females were presented with the same opportunities to learn. Teacher biases could make these courses differentially favorable to male students. Second, if male and female students come to these classrooms with different levels of motivation, the gender gap would be expected to widen further (because interested, self-efficacious male students would get more out of these courses than disinterested, underconfident female students). Third, if older male and female students come to middle school and high school courses with different levels of acquired aptitude (in response to the snowballing effects of the exposure and motivation conditions), the gap would widen still further. Thus, unless one supplements the variable "high school coursework" with indices of genuine opportunities to learn, student motivation, and entering level of skill, gender differences in math achievement would still be observed even when one controls for high school coursework.

Besides indices of the three conditions, however, the 3C model highlights other variables that would be important to include in predictive, longitudinal studies. The present author identified these variables using the "multiple why" technique suggested by Byrnes et al. (1997) in their cross-cultural study. In brief, the technique involves the following recursive steps: (1) asking a "why" question about an outcome of interest (e.g., why do high school males perform better than high school females on the SAT-math?), (2) providing an answer (e.g., males were given more genuine opportunities to learn, were more willing to take advantage of these opportunities, and entered these experiences with more acquired aptitude than females), (3) asking a second "why" question about the answer to the first question (e.g., "why were males presented with more genuine opportunities to learn . . . .?), (4) providing an answer, and so on. Typically, the existing theories presented earlier provide partial answers to many of these questions. Other answers come from various other pockets of research that have relevance. Either way, one works backward in time from the outcome of interest to a chronologically arranged sequence of causal factors.

To illustrate the case of gender differences, let's assume that the original question was, "why are 12th-grade males more likely to demonstrate math proficiency on the SAT-like tests than 12th-grade females?" First, as noted earlier, the 3C model suggests that the answer to this question would be "males were given more genuine opportunities to learn, were more willing to take advantage of these opportunities, and were more equipped to take advantage of these opportunities at the time." If so, then the primary follow-up questions to this answer become:

- *Question 1*: Why are male students more likely than female students to find themselves in contexts that provide them with genuine opportunities to learn?
- *Question 2*: Why are male students more willing to take advantage of these opportunities to learn than female students?
- *Question 3*: Why do male students demonstrate a greater ability to learn what is presented to them in skill-enhancing contexts than female students?

As suggested earlier, plausible answers to Question 1 include the following:

- *Answer 1A*: Throughout their schooling, males were given *preferential treatment* by teachers and administrators (in classroom interactions and in decisions regarding children's placement in academic tracks or gifted programs).
- *Answer 1B*: Males were given greater access to *outside-of-school opportunities to learn* (e.g., activities at home, libraries, museums).
- *Answer 1C*: The parents of male students *pressured school personnel* to provide their children with access to skill-enhancing contexts in school.

Plausible answers to Question 2 (i.e., why male students are more willing . . .) include the following:

- *Answer 2A*: Male students hold more *positive views of their abilities*.
- *Answer 2B*: Male students hold more *positive views of math* (i.e., they believe it involves more than just fact learning, they believe that it is interesting, they believe that it is important to learn, they believe that it is relevant to their goals, they are not concerned about how effort and competence in the area would make them look to their primary peer group or members of the opposite sex).

Plausible answers to Question 3 (i.e., why do male students demonstrate a greater ability . . .) are the following:

- *Answer 3A*: Male students acquire skills in math more readily than female students because they are more likely to have a natural *aptitude* for math.
- *Answer 3B*: Male students acquire skills in math more readily than female students because, at later ages, the former tend to be farther along an *expertise* continuum for math than the latter; they began learning math skills at an earlier age and engaged in larger amounts of *deliberate practice*.

To elaborate the model and provide further clues regarding possible places where intervention efforts might be effective, it is important to ask

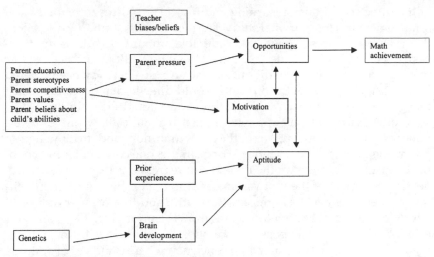

FIGURE 4.1. The three conditions model.

seven additional "why" questions about Answers 1A to 3B. With respect to Answer 1A, for example, one would ask, "why were male students given preferential treatment by teachers?" (Plausible answer: Teachers have unconscious gender biases). For brevity sake, it can be said that these additional questions would implicate variables such as the following: teacher and administrator *biases* (1A), parent and child *stereotypes* about gender and math (1B, 2A, 2B), *parent education* and income (1C), *parent values* about the importance of education or other forms of training (1C, 3B), *parent beliefs* about their children's abilities (1C), parent *competitiveness* (1C), *performance feedback* supplied to children (e.g., report cards, 2A), *instructional techniques* of teachers (2B), content of the *curriculum* (2B), and genetic and epigenetic processes of *brain development* (3A). The overall model is shown in Fig. 4.1.

In essence, then, the 3C model effectively integrates and extends most of the earlier accounts of gender differences. Rather than take a single-factor, dichotomized stance (i.e., differences are mainly due to socialization vs. differences are mainly due to biology), it attempts to explain how the variables implicated by prior accounts would conspire to predict gender differences in some math skills by adolescence. In the next section, I consider how one could test the model in future studies and I also describe the implications of the model for intervention efforts.

IMPLICATIONS OF THE THREE CONDITIONS MODEL

With respect to the empirical implications of the 3C model, several methodological options exist. One promising approach would be to obtain indices of the three conditions of learning and use these indices to predict math achievement in a longitudinal study. The model gains support to the extent that (1) these indices explain a considerable amount of variance in proficiency scores, and (2) gender explains little or no additional variance after the indices of the three conditions of learning have already been entered in regression equations. Such results would directly demonstrate the fact that gender is confounded with the three conditions of learning.

Another virtue of this approach is that it would allow one to determine the relative contributions of the three conditions and thereby suggest promising targets of intervention. For example, one could enter indices of the exposure condition on the first step of regressions (e.g., coursework), next enter indices of the motivation condition (e.g., interest in math, self-reported engagement, self-efficacy for math), and finally enter indices of aptitude (e.g., achievement test scores from the prior year, IQ tests). If, for example, indices of the exposure and motivation conditions are found to explain 60% of the variance in math proficiency, whereas indices of aptitude explain 10%, one could argue that, in an era of limited funds, interventions should attempt to increase the amount of exposure and motivation in girls. Such a conclusion would have to be tempered, though, because indices of aptitude in older students could not be considered to be "pure" in an important sense because they necessarily reflect levels of motivation and exposure in earlier years.

In a study examining ethnic differences in math achievement (Byrnes, 2003), I found that fairly imprecise measures of exposure (i.e., coursework) and motivation (three items) explained 60% of the variance in math proficiency. Ethnicity explained less than 1% of the variance in performance after indices of exposure and motivation had been entered. Hence, I showed that ethnicity was confounded with these two conditions and that it seems not to be confounded with aptitude (because the role of ethnicity was eliminated even without adding indices of aptitude). I suspect that similar findings would emerge in the case of gender differences. Note that imprecise measures attenuate the size of predictive relations. One can only imagine how much additional variance would be explained if one were to use more precise measures.

In addition to conducting more of such investigations, future studies are needed to delineate the precise components of the exposure and aptitude conditions, and also determine the complex interactions among the conditions. Regarding studies of components, for example, researchers need to build on the suggestions of Taylor et al. (2000) to create coding schemes for high-quality learning opportunities. Few developmental scientists could enter classrooms and identify such opportunities within 45-minute class periods. Researchers in the field of educational psychology have been struggling with this vexing measurement issue for more than

40 years (with little success). In addition, more work is needed to delineate the components and nature of aptitude. In our work using the Cognitive Process approach, my colleagues and I proposed a model of aptitude for SAT-math tests. Other kinds of assessments require a similar level of detail. In addition, it is not clear that standardized assessments or existing models of aptitude (e.g., Snow, 1998) really tap into the notion of aptitude as described earlier. Alternatives include measures that directly consider the rate with which particular skills are mastered (e.g., Gettinger, 1984) or the extent to which performance can be modified in a fixed period of time. When such studies are conducted, we will have a much clearer sense of causes of, and solutions to, gender differences in mathematics.

References

Alexander, J. E., O'Boyle, M. W., & Benbow, C. P. (1996). Developmentally advanced EEG alpha power in gifted male and female adolescents. *International Journal of Psychophysiology, 23,* 25–31.

Becker, B. J. (1990). Item characteristics and gender differences on SAT-M for mathematically able youths. *American Educational Research Journal, 27,* 65–87.

Benbow, C. P. (1986). Physiological correlates of extreme intellectual precocity. *Neuropsychologia, 24,* 719–725.

Benbow, C. P. (1988). Sex differences in mathematical reasoning ability in intellectually talented preadolescents: Their nature, effects, and possible causes. *Behavioral and Brain Sciences, 11,* 169–232.

Benbow, C. P., & Stanley, J. C. (1980). Sex differences in mathematical ability: Fact or artifact? *Science, 210,* 1262–1264.

Bryden, M. P., McManus, I. C., & Bulman-Fleming, M. B. (1994). Evaluating the support for the Geschwind-Behan-Galabura model of cerebral lateralization. *Brain and Cognition, 26,* 103–167.

Byrnes, J. P. (2001a). *Cognitive development and learning in instructional contexts* (2nd ed.). Needham Heights, MA: Allyn & Bacon.

Byrnes, J. P. (2001b). *Minds, brains, and learning: Understanding the psychological and educational relevance of neuroscientific research.* New York: Guilford.

Byrnes, J. P. (2003). Factors predictive of mathematics achievement in White, Black, and Hispanic 12th graders. *Journal of Educational Psychology, 95,* 316–326.

Byrnes, J. P., Li, H., & Shaoying, X. (1997). Gender differences on the math subtest of the scholastic aptitude test may be culture-specific. *Educational Studies in Mathematics, 34,* 49–66.

Byrnes, J. P., & Takahira, S. (1993). Explaining gender differences on SAT-math items. *Developmental Psychology, 29,* 805–810.

Byrnes, J. P., & Takahira, S. (1994). Why some students perform well and others perform poorly on SAT-math items. *Contemporary Educational Psychology, 19,* 63–78.

Casey, M. B., Nuttall, R., Pezaris, E., & Benbow, C. P. (1995). The influence of spatial ability on gender differences in mathematics college entrance test scores across diverse samples. *Developmental Psychology, 31,* 697–705.

Casey, M. B., Pezaris, E., & Nuttall, R. L. (1992). Spatial ability as a predictor of math achievement: The importance of sex and handedness patterns. *Neuropsychologia, 30*, 35–45.

Eccles, J. (1983). Expectancies, values, and academic behavior. In J. T. Spence (Ed.), *Achievement and achievement motives: Psychological and sociological approaches* (pp. 77–146). San Francisco: W. H. Freeman.

Eccles, J. S., Wigfield, A., & Schiefele, U. (1998). Motivation to succeed. In W. Damon (Series Ed.), N. Eisenberg (Vol. Ed.), *Handbook of child psychology: Vol. 3. Social, emotional, and personality development* (5th ed., pp. 1018–1095). New York: Wiley.

Entwisle, D. R., & Alexander, K. L. (1992). Summer setback: Race, poverty, school composition, and mathematics achievement in the first two years of school. *American Sociological Review, 57*, 72–84.

Ericsson, K. A. (1996). *The road to excellence: The acquisition of expert performance in the arts, sports, and games.* Mahwah, NJ: Erlbaum.

Fennema, E., & Sherman, J. (1977). Sex-related differences in mathematics achievement, spatial visualization, and affective factors. *American Educational Research Journal, 14*, 51–71.

Fennema, E., & Sherman, J. (1978). Sex-related differences in mathematics achievement and related factors: A further study. *Journal for Research in Mathematics Education, 9*, 189–203.

Gallagher, A. M., De Lisi, R., Holst, P. C., McGillicuddy-De Lisi, A. V., Morely, M., & Cahalan, C. (2000). Gender differences in advanced mathematical problem solving. *Journal of Experimental Child Psychology, 75*, 165–190.

Gettinger, M. (1984). Achievement as a function of time spent in learning and time needed for learning. *American Educational Research Journal, 21*, 617–628.

Geschwind, N., & Galabura, A. M. (1985). Cerebral lateralization: Biological mechanisms, associations, and pathology I: A hypothesis and a program for research. *Archives of Neurology, 42*, 428–459.

Green, D. (1987, August*). Sex differences in item performance on a standardized achievement battery*. Paper presented at the 95th annual meeting of the American Psychological Association, New York.

Guiton, G., & Oakes, J. (1995). Opportunity to learn and conceptions of educational equality. *Educational Evaluation & Policy Analysis, 17*, 323–336.

Halpern, D. F. (2000). *Sex differences in cognitive abilities* (4th ed.). Hillsdale, NJ: Erlbaum.

Hanna, G., Kundinger, E., & Larouche, C. (1992). Mathematical achievement of grade 12 girls from fifteen countries. In L. Burton (Ed.), *Gender and mathematics: An international perspective* (pp. 86–97). London: Cassell.

Hyde, J. S., Fennema, E., & Lamon, S. J. (1990). Gender differences in mathematical performance: A meta-analysis. *Psychological Bulletin, 107*, 139–155.

Kimball, M. M. (1989). A new perspective on women's math achievement. *Psychological Bulletin, 105*, 198–214.

Leder, G. C. (1992). Mathematics and gender: Changing perspectives. In D. A. Grouws (Ed.), *Handbook of research on mathematical teaching and learning* (pp. 597–624). New York: Macmillan.

Lewis, J., & Hoover, H. D. (1987). Differential prediction of academic achievement in elementary and junior high school by sex. *Journal of Early Adolescence, 7,* 107–115.

Linn, M. C., & Kessel, C. (1996). Success in mathematics: Increasing talent and gender diversity among college majors. *CBMS Issues in Mathematics Education, 6,* 101–144.

Luria, A. R. (1973). *The working brain.* New York: Basic Books.

Morrison, F. J., Griffith, E. M., & Alberts, D. M. (1997). Nature–nurture in the classroom: Entrance age, school readiness, and learning in children. *Developmental Psychology, 33,* 254–262.

Newman, R. S. (1984). Children's achievement and self-evaluations in mathematics: A longitudinal study. *Journal of Educational Psychology, 76,* 857–873.

Nosek, B. A., Banaji, M. R., & Greenwald, A. G. (2002). Math = male, me = female, therefore math ≠ me. *Journal of Personality and Social Psychology, 83,* 44–59.

O'Boyle, M. W., & Benbow, C. P. (1990). Enhanced right hemisphere involvement during cognitive processing may relate to intellectual precocity. *Neuropsychologia, 28,* 211–216.

O'Boyle, M. W., & Gill, H. S. (1998). On the relevance of research findings in cognitive neuroscience to educational practice. *Educational Psychology Review, 10,* 397–410.

Oldfield, R. C. (1971). The assessment and analysis of handedness: The Edinburgh inventory. *Neuropsychologia, 9,* 97–113.

Pallas, A. M., & Alexander, K. L. (1983). Sex differences in quantitative SAT performance: New evidence on the differential coursework hypothesis. *American Educational Research Journal, 20,* 165–182.

Royer, J. M., Tronsky, L. N., Chan, Y., Jackson, S. J., & Marchant, H. (1999). Math-fact retrieval and the cognitive mechanism underlying gender differences in math test performance. *Contemporary Educational Psychology, 24,* 181–266.

Schmidt, W. H. (2001). *Why schools matter: A cross-national comparison of curriculum and learning.* San Francisco: Jossey-Bass.

Smith, A. E., Jussim, L., & Eccles, J. E. (1999). Do self-fulfilling prophecies accumulate, dissipate, or remain stable over time? *Journal of Personality & Social Psychology, 77,* 548–565.

Snow, R. E. (1998). Abilities as aptitudes and achievements in learning situations. In J. J. McArdle & R. W. Woodcock (Eds.), *Human cognitive abilities in theory and practice* (pp. 93–112). Mahwah, NJ: Erlbaum.

Stanovich, K. E. (1986). Matthew effects in reading: Some consequences of individual differences in the acquisition of literacy. *Reading Research Quarterly, 21,* 360–407.

Takahira, S. (1995). *Cross-cultural study on variables influencing gender differences in mathematics performance.* Unpublished doctoral dissertation, University of Maryland, College Park.

Taylor, B. M., Frye, B. J., & Maruyama, G. M. (1990). Time spent reading and reading growth. *American Educational Research Journal, 27,* 351–362.

Taylor, B. M., Pressley, M., & Pearson, D. (2000). *Effective Teachers and Schools: Trends across Recent Studies.* Ann Arbor, MI: Center for the Improvement of Early Reading Achievement, Ann Arbor, MI.

Waltz, J. A., Knowlton, B. J., Holyoak, K. J., Boone, K. B., Mishkin, F. S., de Menezes Santos, M., Thomas, C. R., & Miller, B. L. (1999). A system for relational reasoning in human prefrontal cortex. *Psychological Science, 10,* 119–125.

Wigfield, A., Eccles, J. S., Yoon, K. S., Harold, R. D., Arbreton, A. J. A., Freedman-Doan, C., & Blumenfeld, P. C. (1997). Change in children's competence beliefs and subjective task values across the elementary school years: A 3-year study. *Developmental Psychology, 89,* 451–468.

5

Cognitive Contributions to Sex Differences
in Math Performance

James M. Royer and Laura M. Garofoli

This chapter offers an explanation, or a set of explanations, for how sex differences in cognitive abilities result in sex differences in math performance, and particularly differences in performance on high-level math tests. By high-level math tests, we mean tests such as the SAT-M, ACT-M, or GRE-M that are commonly used for competitive selection decisions. Our chapter is not about sex differences in math in general. Therefore, there are interesting differences between males and females in areas such as math self-concept, math anxiety, and so on that we do not discuss. We make this distinction because the general area of sex differences in mathematics is large, unwieldy, contradictory, and ultimately, in our opinion, not explainable by a common set of factors. We do, however, briefly examine some of the areas encompassed under the general topic of sex differences in mathematics because research in those areas serves to constrain explanations for sex differences in high-level math test performance. We now examine some of those areas of research.

GRADES IN MATH CLASSES

Reviews of the literature examining sex differences in math grades indicate that girls generally receive better grades than boys, especially after junior high school (Dwyer & Johnson, 1997; Kimball, 1989). Kimball concluded that junior high and high school girls received better grades than their male peers in specific courses and had a higher overall math grade point average. In addition, at the university level the typical finding has been that there is either not a difference between the sexes in grades, or that females get better grades than their male counterparts (Bridgeman & Lewis, 1996; Dwyer & Johnson, 1997).

One possible explanation of why females get better grades than males is that they take easier courses. However, studies comparing the performance of females and males taking the same classes suggest that the easier course explanation is not supported. For example, Benbow and Stanley (1982) reported a study examining the highly select sample of males and females from the Study of Mathematically Precocious Youth. Males in the study performed significantly higher than females on SAT-M tests, but nonetheless, females had significantly higher math grades than males when both were taking the same demanding math curriculum.

Another way of examining the grade issue is to ask the question of whether males and females taking the same college math class differ in grade performance when matched on an ability index (e.g., SAT-M scores). Bridgeman and Lewis (1996) addressed this question in a study involving a data set of 30,000 students. Males having an SAT-M score of 700 or above received an average grade of 2.94 in calculus classes compared with a grade of 2.98 for females having the same SAT score. Comparisons of other SAT-M matching categories ranging all the way to 500 showed the same pattern of female superiority in grades.

The fact that differences between the sexes in grades are small, and sometimes even favor females, constrains some of the explanations that might be posed for sex differences on high-level math tests. For instance, an explanation that argued for general male superiority in mathematics would be difficult to square with the data on math grades.

SEX DIFFERENCES ON MATH ACHIEVEMENT TESTS ADMINISTERED TO ELEMENTARY AND SECONDARY SCHOOL STUDENTS

The general conclusion in the literature is that sex differences in math tests administered to the general population of elementary and secondary school students are small, and show no clear advantage for either sex. Hyde, Fennema, and Lamon's (1990) meta-analysis of 100 studies (involving more than 3 million participants) indicated that females from the general population had a slight advantage ($d = -0.05$) over their male counterparts ($d = $ *mean of males – mean of females/pooled standard deviation*). Willingham and Cole (1997) reached a similar conclusion of very small sex differences in math test performance after examining a national sample of grade 12 students taking 13 different tests. They reported a slight female advantage on tests of math computation ($d = -0.06$), but a slight male advantage on tests measuring math concepts ($d = 0.11$).

There does appear to be some change in the pattern of general sex differences in math test performance when the data is examined by grade in school. Hyde et al. (1990) reported that girls tended to score higher than boys on math tests administered in elementary school ($d = -0.06$) and middle school ($d = -0.22$), but high school boys performed better than high school girls ($d = 0.20$). Cleary (1992) examined data sets totaling more than 10 million students and reported similar trends where girls at ages 9 to 11 and 12 to 14 performed slightly better than boys on math tests, but boys were slightly better at ages 15 to 18. Willingham and Cole (1997) reported similar trends in National Assessment of Educational Progress (NAEP) data, where there was a larger advantage for boys in grade 12 than there was in grades 8 and 4.

SEX DIFFERENCES IN VARIABILITY

Willingham and Cole (1997) report that males often display more variability of performance on standardized tests than do females. As an instance, they report performance on 15 different content area tests administered to grade 12 students and males had a larger standard deviation on all of the tests, and in 12 of the 15 tests males were more variable by 5% or more. The ratio of male to female standard deviations in math tests was 0.93.

We do not know for certain what the distribution of high-level math scores for males and females looks like, but a figure originally developed by Cleary (1992) and reprinted in Willingham and Cole (1997) suggests that the male distribution has a longer tail at the high score end of the distribution. Cleary (1992) reported her results separately for select students such as those that take the SAT and unselected students, which would include all students at a particular age level. Cleary (1992) reported that the gap between unselected fifteen- 18-year-old boys and girls scoring in the lowest 10th percentile of the distribution was essentially zero, whereas the gap for unselected boys and girls scoring at the 90th percentile was $d = 0.36$ (estimated from her figure). As might be expected from this distribution, when the population consists of select students there is a general shift favoring boys. Cleary (1992) reported that select boys scoring in the bottom 10th percentile on math tests scored higher than their female counterparts ($d = 0.22$), and this advantage widened when the comparison was between boys and girls scoring at the 90th percentile and above ($d = 0.38$).

With these preliminaries completed, we now turn to the research of most interest to this discussion, the comparison between males and females on high-level math tests.

MALE AND FEMALE COMPARISONS ON HIGH-LEVEL MATH TESTS

Males have outperformed females on the SAT-M for at least thirty years. The difference generally has been in the range of about 40 points ($d = 0.39$), but recently has shrunk to 33 points in 2000. Performance on the ACTM has shown a similar trend with a difference of 3.1 points in 1970 shrinking to 1.2 points in 2001 ($d = 0.24$) (Langenfield, 1997; U.S. Office of Education, 2001).

Because boys are more variable test performers, leaving more boys at the high end of the distribution, the discrepancy between male and female test scores becomes more pronounced as the samples become more select

(Benbow & Stanley, 1982; Mills, Ablard, & Stumpf, 1993; Willingham & Cole, 1997). This is of particular interest because it is generally the upper-level students who plan to go to college and who take the SAT or the ACT as a college entrance requirement. Benbow and Stanley (1983) found that the ratio of boys to girls scoring within a particular range on the SAT-M becomes disproportionate as the scores increase, growing from a 2:1 ratio in the 500 score range to 13:1 in the 700 score range.

Interestingly, this selectivity effect is not limited to older children or to standardized test scores. Robinson, Abbott, Beringer, and Busse (1996) found that gifted boys outperform gifted girls on mathematics tasks as early as the preschool and kindergarten years. Further, sex differences in related propensities, such as math fact retrieval (Carr & Davis, 2001; Carr & Jessup, 1997; Carr, Jessup, & Fuller, 1999; Royer, Tronsky, Chan, Jackson, & Marchant, 1999) and spatial processing (Lummis & Stevenson, 1990; Robinson et al., 1996) have been found as early as the first grade and also exhibit a selectivity effect.

EXPLANATIONS FOR SEX DIFFERENCES IN MATH TESTS

Previous explanations for the development of sex differences in mathematics test performance generally come in four forms: social, cognitive, biological, and combinations thereof. Numerous authors have proposed that all three play some role in the emergence and persistence of such differences, with biology seemingly underlying many of the social and cognitive factors involved. Wilder (1997) reached this conclusion in her analysis of the causes of sex differences in mathematics that accompanied the Willingham and Cole (1997) volume. Wilder (1997) wrote:

That both sides of the equation – the biological and the social – are involved in the differences that are reflected in test performance seems beyond question. However, there remain major questions about the ways in which these major categories of influence interact to produce differences that exist. Added to the fact that the differences appear to be changing over time, and that they vary as a function of the way in which they are measured, there is good reason to believe that the antecedents of male-female differences will remain a fertile field for continuing research. (p. 39)

Halpern and LaMay (2000) reached a similar conclusion in an article that argued for a "psychobiosocial" model for sex differences in cognitive abilities. Their psychobiosocial model is based on the idea that some influences on cognitive ability are both biological and social, and cannot be readily classified as one or the other. Wilder's (1997) and Halpern and LaMay's (2000) conclusion regarding the contribution of biological, social, and cognitive factors in *all* the sex differences in math is undoubtedly correct to some degree. However, the problem with the explanation is that it does not specifically identify the social and cognitive mechanisms that underlie sex differences in math performance, it does not identify which specific difference (e.g., test performance, attitudinal differences, affective differences) is impacted by each factor, and it does not provide a process description of how those mechanisms operate to produce sex differences.

Our goal in this chapter is to offer an explanation that identifies the cognitive mechanisms responsible for sex differences in math test performance and to describe a processing description that indicates how those mechanisms become operative. To foreshadow our conclusions, we will suggest that males and females differ in two important cognitive attributes – spatial cognition ability and speed of math fact retrieval. These two abilities impact mathematical problem solving in different ways, with one having a primary impact on the ability to identify and represent the nature of a problem, and the second having an impact on an examinee's ability to correctly solve a problem once a cognitive representation of the problem has been developed.

DIFFERENCES IN SPATIAL COGNITION AS A FACTOR IN SEX DIFFERENCES IN MATH PERFORMANCE

It has long been known that there are sex differences in spatial cognition ability and the hypothesis that these differences are responsible for sex differences in math performance has been the dominant view for many years. Research supporting the connection between spatial cognition ability and mathematical performance has been obtained in studies involving both children and adults. As an example of research involving children, Robinson et al. (1996) reported early sex differences in mathematical functioning and correlations between visuospatial skills and mathematical skills among gifted preschoolers and kindergartners. Likewise, similar differences in spatial tasks have even been reported in elementary school children (Lummis & Stevenson, 1990).

Sex differences among older children and adults have been obtained consistently on spatial rotation tasks (Just & Carpenter, 1985; Masters & Sanders, 1993) and spatial dynamics measures (Law, Pellegrino, & Hunt, 1993), and these differences have been related to differences in math performance (e.g., Geary, 1996). An early view was that the male problem-solving advantage was predominantly evident on problems that can be solved through the use of spatial strategies (e.g., geometric problems, word problems involving set comparisons; Harnisch, Steinkamp, Tsai, & Walberg, 1986; Johnson, 1984; Lewis, 1989; Lewis & Mayer, 1987). Thus, it was generally presumed that mathematical functioning was directly related to spatial functioning, thereby resulting in increased mathematical ability for those with better spatial competence. The problem with this view is that the data does not break down cleanly by test item type. For instance, given the direct spatial strategy view, one would expect to see the largest differences between males and females on geometry items and the smallest difference on word problems, where females can use their sometimes superior verbal abilities to overcome any male advantages in math skills. However, research shows that the difference between male and female performance on geometry items is actually smaller than the difference on word problem items.

A more recent conception of the connection between mathematics and spatial functioning suggests that spatial cognition is not directly related to mathematical functioning; rather, spatial abilities mediate mathematical abilities (Geary, Saults, Liu, & Hoard, 2000). Geary et al. did not offer an explanation of how this might happen, but we suggest a hypothesis as to how this process works later in this chapter.

Until recently, the evidence linking spatial cognition ability and math test performance was strictly correlational. However, several studies provided stronger evidence for the link between spatial abilities and math abilities. Casey, Nuttall, and Pezaris (1997) contrasted two socialization explanations for math sex differences with a spatial cognition explanation. The participants in their study were select males and females who scored 480 or above on the SAT-V. While sophomores, the students took a mental rotation test (on which males performed better) and a test that measured math anxiety and confidence in math performance. Two years after completing these tests, the students' SAT scores were obtained. The results of a path analysis, in which SAT-M was the criterion variable and the remaining variables were predictor variables, found that math anxiety was not related to test performance, but math self-confidence and mental rotation ability were related. A decomposition of the sex/SAT-M relationship into direct and indirect effects indicated that there were no direct effects of sex on SAT-M performance, but there were indirect effects with 36% of the effect being mediated by math self-confidence and the remaining 64% being attributable to mental rotation ability.

Two other studies provided additional evidence for the link between spatial and math abilities. However, because those studies also involve math fact retrieval, a description of the studies is provided after describing the research linking math fact retrieval and math test performance.

DIFFERENCES IN MATH FACT RETRIEVAL AS A FACTOR
IN SEX DIFFERENCES IN MATH TEST PERFORMANCE

Royer et al. (1999) proposed that sex differences in math fact retrieval contributed to sex differences in math test performance. They reported nine studies that examined sex differences in math fact retrieval and the relationship of those differences to performance on math tests. There were more than 1,000 students participating in the nine studies, 127 college students and approximately 900 students enrolled in grades two through eight. Fifty-one of the grade 5 and 6 students were either Chinese American or

Hong Kong Chinese students (divided evenly between males and females) who were recruited via permission slips sent home to parents. The college students participating in the studies were recruited from introductory psychology classes, and the ratio of women to men in the studies was approximately 60/40 (mirroring the sex breakdown in introductory psychology courses). The grade 2 to 8 participants were in intact classrooms (with the exception of the Chinese students) with every student in the classroom participating, except for students with an individualized education plan. The ratio of males to females in the elementary school studies was approximately 50/50. The school system the grade 2 to 8 participants came from did not have a tracking system at lower levels, so the participating students were a representative sample of the school as a whole.

Math fact retrieval in the Royer et al. (1999) studies was measured by presenting (via computer) elementary and middle school students with problems such as "$4 + 5 =$" or problems such as "$5 + 6 + 4 =$" to college students, and then recording the speed and accuracy of performance.

Several of the studies reported by Royer et al. (1999) involved examining the extent to which math fact retrieval performance predicted the math test performance of students in grades 5 to 8, and college students. The math test used in the prediction studies for grades 5, 7, and 8 consisted of 22 complex computational problems (i.e., problems involving multiple digits) and 28 word problems. These problems were patterned after problems from three sources: problems appearing in previous word problem research (Lewis, 1989; Lewis & Mayer, 1987; Riley, Greeno, & Heller, 1983), problems that appear in the grade six Iowa Test of Basic Skills (ITBS) booklet, Form K, Level 12, and problems suggested by the math teachers at the participating school. The math test used for grade 6 was the ITBS test mentioned above. The math performance measure used in the college student prediction study was SAT-M scores obtained from central administration at the college or university. All tests were administered with a set amount of time to complete the tests. Most examinees did not complete all the items on the experimenter-generated math test, and they probably also did not complete all the items on the standardized tests.

To briefly summarize pertinent findings from the large number of results in the Royer et al. (1999) studies, they found that by grade 4 select male students (those scoring in the top half of the speed distribution) were faster at math fact retrieval than select female students and that males and females did not differ in accuracy of performance. The male advantage in speed of math fact retrieval appearing in elementary school persisted through middle school into college. They also found that speed of math fact retrieval was a significant predictor of math test performance in both middle school and college for both males and females.

In addition, Royer et al. (1999) reported that males and females did not differ in speed of performance on a number of nonmath tasks such as letter naming, word naming, sentence understanding, and recognition of simple stimuli (e.g., stars, pluses). The fact that the two sexes were similar on nonmath retrieval tasks would tend to discredit a hypothesis suggesting that males were generally faster than females at retrieval tasks. The fact that males and females did not differ on nonmath retrieval tasks would also suggest that an emotional factor like impulsivity was not responsible for the male advantage in math fact retrieval.

The Relationship of Math Fact Retrieval to Math Test Performance

Royer et al. (1999) proposed that there were two reasons that speed of math fact retrieval might be related to performance on math tests. The first, relatively mundane, reason is associated with limited time to take a test. Several of the studies reported by Royer et al. found that males were sometimes 250 milliseconds faster than females on average time to retrieve a math fact. Given that there may be several hundred facts to retrieve when completing a math test, this could result in the average male having more effective time to complete a test than the average female. Because the difference between a very high score and a high score on a test such as the SAT-M is only a matter of a few more items correct, the added effective completion time could be very advantageous for high-performing males.

The theoretically more interesting reason that speed of math fact retrieval may play a role in math test performance is that fast retrieval may result in additional working memory capacity that can then be used for high resource-consuming activities such as problem representation and solution planning. Problem representation is the process of identifying the nature of a problem, and this typically involves searching memory for previously experienced analogues to the problem under consideration. The theory is that this search process consumes a lot of cognitive capacity, and the problem nature, once it is identified, must be held in working memory while a solution strategy is formulated, and both the representation and the solution strategy must then be held in memory while the problem is being solved. If the examinee is slow at computation, or if the computation must be completed "offline" on a calculator, the representation might fall apart and have to be reconstructed. This again subtracts effective time to complete the test and relatively poor computation ability could produce solution errors.

RESEARCH EXAMINING BOTH SPATIAL COGNITION AND MATH FACT RETRIEVAL AS CONTRIBUTORS TO SEX DIFFERENCES IN MATH TEST PERFORMANCE

The previous two sections report evidence that spatial cognition and speed of math fact retrieval are predictors of math test performance. In this section, we report three studies that examined the influence of both spatial cognition and math fact retrieval in the same prediction study.

Geary et al. (2000) reported a study that pitted the math fact retrieval explanation against the spatial cognition explanation. Geary et al. administered a timed math computation test (an index of fact retrieval speed), a mental rotation spatial cognition test, the Raven's progressive matrices (IQ) test, and an arithmetical reasoning test to 236 college students (113 male, 123 female). The arithmetical reasoning test consisted of four tests from the Educational Testing Service (ETS) kit of factor-referenced tests (Ekstrom, French, & Harmon, 1976). The tests were two forms of the Necessary Arithmetic Operations (NOA) test and two forms of the Arithmetic Aptitude (AA) Test. Five minutes were allowed for the completion of each form of the NOA, and 10 minutes were allowed for completion of each form of the AA.

The Geary et al. (2002) study showed that males and females differed significantly (male advantage) on the fact retrieval test, the spatial cognition test, and the math problem-solving test, but there were no sex differences on the IQ measure. The results of a structural-equation-modeling (SEM) analysis of the Geary et al. (2000) data are reported in Fig. 5.1. All the links in the model are significant (nonsignificant relationships are not shown). It is noteworthy that the link between sex and math performance is not significant, whereas it was significant before the effects of spatial cognition and math fact retrieval were entered into the model.

Geary et al.'s (2000) results are certainly suggestive that both spatial cognition and fact retrieval are implicated in sex differences in math test performance, but the case would be stronger if, in fact, the results were replicated with a test that has been previously shown to produce sex differences in

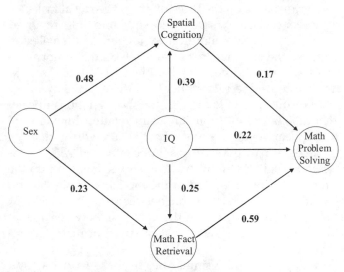

FIGURE 5.1. Results of Geary's research contrasting the influence of IQ, spatial cognition, and math fact retrieval on math problem solving.

performance. A study by Royer, Rath, Tronsky, Marchant, and Jackson (2002) used SAT-M scores as the criterion variable in the study, thereby satisfying the desire for examining a test that had previously produced sex differences in performance. One hundred seventy-five college students (108 females, 67 males) recruited from introductory psychology classes completed tests of spatial cognition and fact retrieval. Their SAT math and verbal scores were then obtained from administration offices. SAT-V scores were used as an index of nonmathematical intellectual ability. The spatial cognition measure was the Vandenberg & Kuse (1978) mental rotation test that was also used in the Geary et al. (2000) study. The math fact retrieval measure was the same measure that was used in the Royer et al. (1999) studies involving college students. It consisted of three kinds of computer-administered (using the Computer-Based Academic Assessment System [CAAS]) math fact retrieval tasks: (1) a subtraction task involving 10 single-digit minus single-digit problems and 10 double-digit minus double-digit problems (digits between 10 and 20), (2) a division task consisting of 10 single-digit divided by single-digit problems and 10 double-digit divided by double-digit or triple-digit divided by double-digit problems (5 of each), and (3) a triple addition task (e.g., $4 + 8 + 9 =$) containing 12 single + single + single-digit problems. The procedure for administering the math fact retrieval task involved the presentation of a problem on the computer screen (thereby initiating the timing sequence), followed by the examinee saying the answer into the microphone (thereby recording the time interval between problem presentation and response) and the examiner then scoring the response as correct or incorrect by pressing a scoring button. The measure used in the analyses was a composite (average z-score) of performance on the three math fact retrieval tasks.

The results of the Royer et al. (2002) study were similar to those reported by Geary et al. (2000). Males scored significantly higher than females on the spatial cognition test, the math fact retrieval test (speed, but not accuracy), and the SAT-M test, but did not differ on the SAT-V test. An SEM analysis of the data also showed results similar to those reported by Geary et al. (2000). The SEM results, presented in Fig. 5.2, show relationships between variables that are significant (nonsignificant relationships are not shown). Similar to the Geary et al. (2000) study, it is noteworthy that sex differences in SAT-M performance were not significant when SAT-V, spatial cognition scores, and math fact retrieval scores were entered into the model. However, the other links reported in the model were significant. Specifically, there was a significant relationship between SAT-V and SAT-M performance (the strongest relationship in the analysis), between spatial cognition and SAT-M performance, and between speed of math fact retrieval and SAT-M performance.

The previous paragraph noted the similarities in the Geary et al. and Royer et al. research, but it is also worthwhile to comment on the differences

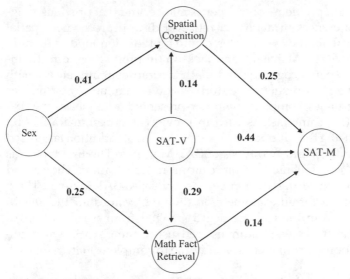

FIGURE 5.2. Results of Royer et al. (2002) contrasting the influence of SAT-V, spatial cognition, and math fact retrieval on math problem solving.

in results. In particular, Geary et al. (2000) found a stronger relationship between math fact retrieval and math problem solving than the relationship between spatial cognition ability and math problem solving. The pattern was the opposite in the Royer et al. (2002) research, where the relationship between spatial cognition and SAT-M was stronger than the relationship between math fact retrieval and SAT-M. These differences are probably associated with the influence of the nonmath ability measure that differed in the two studies. Geary et al. (2000) included the Raven's Progressive matrices as a measure of IQ. Because the test is highly visual in nature, there is a good chance that it captured some of that variance that might otherwise be captured by the spatial cognition measure, thereby lessening the relationship between spatial cognition and math problem solving. In contrast, Royer et al. (2002) used SAT-V as a nonmath ability measure. Performance on the timed SAT-V test probably captures some of the processing efficiency variance that would ordinarily be captured by the math fact retrieval measure, thereby lessening the relationship between math fact retrieval and SAT-M performance.

Identifying How Spatial Cognition and Math Fact Retrieval Influences Math Test Performance

The results of both the Geary et al. (2000) and the Royer et al. (2002) studies indicate that both spatial cognition and math fact retrieval were significant predictors of math problem-solving performance, and that previously significant sex differences in math fact retrieval disappeared when spatial and fact retrieval abilities were entered into a prediction model. A study by Royer, Wing, Rath, Marchant, and Jackson (in press) more directly investigated how spatial cognition and math fact retrieval influenced math problem-solving performance. The study involved having 167 examinees (119 females, 48 males) complete computer-presented tasks measuring spatial cognition (the same task as used in previous studies), math fact retrieval (again, using the subtraction, division, and triple addition tasks used in previous studies), and two types of SAT-M scores. The first type was actual SAT-M scores obtained from central administration. The second type was performance on sixteen previously released SAT-M items. The p (proportion correct for all examinees on the item) values for the SAT-M items (acquired from the College Board) ranged from 0.91 to 0.10. All the experimental tasks were administered using the CAAS, which collected information on both accuracy and time to complete an item for each measure.

An SEM analysis of the form presented in Fig. 5.2 was first completed using SAT-M math scores from central administration as the criterion variable and SAT-V, spatial cognition, and math fact retrieval as predictor variables. The spatial cognition and math fact retrieval scores were average z-scores computed by averaging an examinee's z-score for time to complete items with their z-score for inaccuracy on the items. Inaccuracy, rather than accuracy, was used so low scores on both the time measure and the accuracy measure would be associated with good performance. The results of this analysis, presented in Fig. 5.3, mirrored those found by Geary et al. (2000) and Royer et al. (2002) in that male and female examinees were significantly different (male advantage) on the spatial cognition, math fact retrieval, and SAT-M measures, but did not differ on SAT-V. Sex was not a significant predictor of SAT-M with the other factors entered into the SEM analysis (note that it was significant without those factors), but spatial cognition, math fact retrieval, and SAT-V were significant predictors of total SAT-M performance.

Having established that the results from the new study matched those from previous research, Royer et al. (in press) then proceeded to repeat the SEM analyses using either time to complete the 16 previously released SAT-M items or accuracy of performance on those items as the criterion variable and average z-score (combining time and accuracy) on the spatial cognition and math fact retrieval measures as predictor variables. Again, SAT-V was also included in the analyses. Prior to reviewing the results of this analysis, it should be mentioned that males had a significantly higher percent correct on the 16 released items as indicated by a regression analysis containing SAT-V and student Sex as predictor variables (SAT-V was also a significant predictor). Males were also faster in completing the 16 released

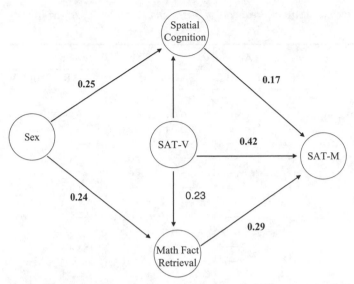

FIGURE 5.3. Results of Royer et al. (in press) contrasting the influence of SAT-V, spatial cognition, and math fact retrieval on math problem solving.

items than were females, although a regression analysis using both SAT-V and student sex as predictor variables showed that neither SAT-V or student sex was a significant predictor of speed of solving the items.

The interesting result that emerged from the separate analyses of accuracy of completing and time to complete the 16 released SAT-M items was that spatial cognition performance was a significant predictor of *time* to complete the SAT-M items, but was not a predictor of *accuracy* of completing the items. In contrast, math fact retrieval performance was a significant predictor of *accuracy* (along with SAT-V) of completing the SAT-M items, but did not predict the *time* to complete the items. This result is depicted in the first line of Table 5.1.

To understand what this differential predictive result might mean, we turn to a theory of mathematical problem solving. Mayer (2003) proposed that mathematical problem solving involves four serially initiated cognitive processes: translating, integrating, planning, and execution. Imagine a problem where the examinee is told that soda can be purchased for 65 cents per bottle at Wal-Mart and 2 cents more per bottle at Big Y Markets. The question is how much more does a person pay for a six pack at Big Y compared with what they would pay at Wal-Mart?

Mayer (2003) suggests that *translating* occurs when a problem solver takes a problem sentence such as "At Wal-Mart soda costs 65 cents per bottle" and converts it into a mental representation such as "Wal-Mart bottle = 0.65". The process of translating depends on the problem solver's

TABLE 5.1. *Significance Level of Predictors of Speed and Accuracy of SAT-M Item Solution*

Item	p Value	Accuracy			Speed		
		Spatial	MFR	SAT-V	Spatial	MFR	SAT-V
All 16 item	0.62 (average)	—	<0.01	<0.01	<0.01	—	—
1	0.75	—	—	<0.05	<0.01	—	<0.01
2	0.70	<0.05	—	—	—	—	—
3	0.51	—	—	—	<0.05	<0.01	—
4	0.87	—	—	—	<0.05	<0.05	<0.05
5	0.35	—	<0.01	—	—	<0.01	<0.01
6	0.89	—	—	—	—	<0.01	<0.05
7	0.77	—	—	<0.05	<0.05	—	<0.05
8	0.59	—	<0.01	<0.05	—	<0.01	—
9	0.50	—	—	—	—	<0.01	—
10	0.45	<0.05	—	—	<0.05	<0.05	—
11	0.1	—	—	—	—	—	—
12	0.75	—	—	<0.01	<0.05	—	—
13	0.91	—	<0.05	—	—	<0.05	—
14	0.53	—	<0.01	—	<0.05	—	—
15	0.71	—	—	—	<0.01	<0.01	—
16	0.61	—	<0.01	—	<0.01	—	—

Source: From Royer et al. (in press).

storehouse of *semantic knowledge* (such as knowing that there are 100 cents in a dollar) and linguistic knowledge (such as knowing the English language).

Integrating occurs when a problem solver builds a mental model of the situation described in the problem or what can be called a *situation model* or *problem model* (Kintsch & Greeno, 1985; Mayer & Hegarty, 1996). For example, in the soda problem, the problem solver must mentally select relevant information and organize it into a coherent mental representation such as a mental number line with Wal-Mart at 65 and Big Y at two units beyond Wal-Mart. The process of integrating depends on *schematic knowledge* (such as knowing that this problems fits the problem type, "total cost = unit cost × number of units").

Planning occurs when a problem solver devises a solution plan, such as first determining the price of a bottle of soda at Big Y by adding 2 to 65, and then determining the total cost of a six-pack by multiplying the result by 6. The process of planning requires *strategic knowledge* (such as knowing how to break a solution plan into component steps). In addition to planning, *monitoring* involves keeping track of the effectiveness of the solution plan, and *reflecting* involves looking back over the cognitive processing involved in producing a completed problem solution.

Executing occurs when a problem solver carries out a solution plan, such as adding 0.02 to 0.65 to get 0.67 and multiplying 6 times 0.67 to get $2.48, making a similar calculation based on the Wal-Mart price, and then subtracting one value from another. The process of executing requires *procedural knowledge* (such as how to carry out arithmetic computations).

We suggest that Mayer's (2003) problem-solving phases can be divided roughly into two stages, one involving developing a *representation* of a problem (consisting of Mayer's translation and integration phases), and one involving *solving the problem* (Mayer's planning and execution) phases. We would also describe the cognitive processes occurring in our representation stage a little different than Mayer described the cognitive processes in his translation and integration phases. We would propose that the primary determiner of whether an examinee successfully represents a problem is whether the examinee is successful in retrieving a memory analogue that bears a structural resemblance to the problem at hand.

We believe that Hummel and Holyoke's (1997) theory of analogical reasoning, which used verbal reasoning as an example, provides a description of the process math problem solvers engage in while attempting to develop a problem representation. Their theory describes how a problem solver breaks down the features of a problem into elements, and then carries out a search and match process that matches features of the problem with features of a memory representation. This process is constrained by a limited-capacity working memory, and can be influenced by a variety of individual difference and motivational factors. We believe that a similar process occurs in math problem solving. To correctly solve an unfamiliar problem, the problem solver must isolate relevant elements of the problem to be solved and then search memory for problems that contain similar structural elements. If the search is successful, the memory analogue is transferred to working memory to serve as a guide for the remainder of the problem-solving process.

We propose as a working hypothesis that the representation phase of problem solving is primarily indexed by the amount of time it takes an examinee to provide an answer to a problem, whereas the problem solution stage is primarily measured by whether the answer is correct or incorrect. Moreover, we propose the hypothesis that spatial cognition ability is the largest contributor to the process of developing the representation for a problem, whereas math fact retrieval is the largest contributor to the process of providing a computational answer to a problem.

If our hypotheses are correct, it would explain why spatial cognition ability is related to the time taken to solve the average problem in our set of sixteen released items, whereas math fact retrieval is related to the accuracy of solving the released items. It should also be noted that both time to solve problems and accuracy in solving problems would contribute to overall number correct on an actual SAT-M test. The contribution of accuracy is obvious, but time also comes into play in actual SAT-M performance. The faster one can solve problems means that one gets the opportunity to attempt a solution to more problems, thereby increasing the opportunity to get a higher score.

The hypotheses offered here provides an explanation of how and why spatial cognition and math fact retrieval might contribute to sex differences on high-level math tests. The explanation is that males have an advantage over females in both spatial cognition ability and math fact retrieval ability, and that these differences result in males having an advantage over females in both the problem representation and solution stages of problem solving.

Examining Patterns of Performance on Individual Items

After examining overall performance on the 16 SAT-M items Royer et al. (in press) examined performance on individual items using the same analysis framework used in the overall analysis. That is, two SEM analyses were completed, one using time to complete an *individual item* as the criterion variable, and the second using accuracy of performance on the item as the criterion variable. In both analyses, the predictor variables were a composite math fact retrieval score, a composite spatial cognition score, and SAT-V performance. There was only a single SAT-M item that did not show a significant relationship with any of the predictor variables. That item had a p value of 0.10. The remaining items showed a mixed bag of significant relationships that are shown in Table 5.1. Simply counting the number of times that each predictor variable significantly predicted speed of SAT-M item solution, Table 5.1 shows that the spatial measure significantly predicted the speed of solution of 9 of the 16 items, MFR also significantly predicted the speed of solution for 9 of the 16 items (although not necessarily the same items predicted by spatial ability), and SAT-V significantly predicted the speed of solution for 4 of the 16 items.

Turning to the prediction of accuracy of solution for the SAT-M items, Table 5.1 shows that the spatial measure significantly predicted the solution accuracy of two of the SAT-M items, math fact retrieval significantly predicted the solution accuracy of five of the SAT-M items, and SAT-V significantly predicted the solution accuracy of three of the SAT-M items.

As the data shows, both spatial ability and math fact retrieval are predictors of both speed and accuracy for some of the items. This contrasts to some degree with the results of the overall analysis involving all the items, where math fact retrieval predicted the accuracy of performance on the total set of items and spatial ability predicted the speed of performance on the total set of items. The reasons for the differences in results between the individual item analyses and the total set analysis are not obvious at this point, although we would note that the division between stages of problem solution and the cognitive processes operative during the stages are not independent of one another. That is, quick computation and quick problem representation will contribute to overall time to reach solution on a problem, and inability to develop a problem representation and inability to maintain that representation (thereby requiring reactivation of the representation) will contribute to accuracy of solving a problem. Thus, both abilities can influence both stages of solution, but our working hypothesis remains that overall performance on a set of items is best characterized by a model that suggests that spatial abilities influence the problem representation stage of problem solving, and math computational competence primarily influences the problem solution stage of problem solving.

WHY SEX DIFFERENCES EXIST IN HIGH-LEVEL TEST PERFORMANCE, BUT NOT MATH GRADE PERFORMANCE

The explanation for sex differences in high-level math test performance that we pose in the previous section also provides a suggestion for why there is not a male advantage in math grades. We noted in the previous section that males were better than females at spatial cognition activities, and we proposed that spatial cognition ability was related to the ability to retrieve structural analogues from memory that could be used to guide math problem solution. The necessity to retrieve a structural analogue for a problem would only occur in circumstances where the problem was unfamiliar. That is, it would occur in circumstances where the nature of the problem and the approach to solving the problem was unfamiliar. These conditions are unlikely to be present in class circumstances where problem solving related to grades typically entails problems that are familiar and that have been the subject of class instruction. Moreover, in many cases, similar problems have been practiced in homework. In these circumstances, abilities related to the retrieval of structural analogues of problems is relatively unimportant, and hence, the cognitive advantage of males in this ability is less important. The ability that is likely to be of importance in this situation is diligence and good study habits, and given that females are often found to excel in these attributes, this may explain why they often get better grades than their male counterparts.

A similar argument can be presented for a lessening of the role of math fact retrieval in course-related performance. The male advantage in math fact retrieval impacts on math performance in two ways. First, faster fact retrieval can result in males having more effective solution time on timed tests. Second, faster retrieval times can help preserve limited cognitive resources by limiting the amount of computational effort associated with math calculations. Both factors are more likely to be important in test-taking activities than they are in course-related activities. Students taking tests administered as part of a math course are allowed ample time to complete the tests, and less strain is placed on working memory because the problem forms are familiar through instruction and homework.

SUMMARY OF REPORTED RESEARCH

At this point, we want to summarize the research literature examined in this chapter:

- Males and females differ in performance on high-level math tests such as SAT-M, ACT-M, or GRE-M, which are used for college or graduate school selection purposes.
- We reviewed evidence from other studies and reported our own evidence showing that both spatial cognition ability and math fact retrieval ability are predictors of math test performance, as indexed for example by an examinee's SAT-M score. We also reviewed evidence and reported additional evidence that males score higher than females on both spatial cognition tests (particularly mental rotation tests) and math fact retrieval tests.
- We reported evidence that spatial cognition ability is a significant predictor of speed of solution for a set of 16 SAT-M items. In contrast, spatial cognition did not predict the accuracy of performance on those items. We hypothesized that the reason for these relationships was that spatial cognition ability is an index of an examinee's ability to create a problem representation that can then be used to develop and guide a solution to a problem. Examinee's who have high spatial cognition ability are faster at this, and possibly more successful at this, than are examinees who have low spatial cognition abilities. Once the problem is represented, however, spatial ability has a lessor role in accurately solving the problem.
- We reported evidence that math fact retrieval is a significant predictor of the accuracy of SAT-M math performance. Math fact retrieval was not, however, a significant predictor of the time it took examinees to complete SAT-M items. We hypothesized that math fact retrieval ability taps into an examinee's ability to correctly carry out the mathematical computations necessary to solve a problem once the problem representation has been developed. This ability to solve problems is, however, independent from an examinee's ability to develop problem representations and, therefore, is a less important factor in the speed of problem solution.
- We suggest that spatial cognition and math fact retrieval will be less important for course-related performance than for test performance, and we further offer the hypothesis that this is the reason why there are male advantages in high-level test performance, but no male advantages in class performance.

DIRECTIONS FOR FUTURE RESEARCH

We provided evidence in this chapter that sex differences in high-level math tests such as the SAT-M are at least partly attributable to sex differences in spatial cognition and math fact retrieval ability. The direct evidence for this comes from the studies conducted by other researchers and from our own studies, which show that significant sex differences in math test performance disappear when math fact retrieval ability and spatial cognition ability are entered into an SEM prediction model.

We also described what we view as surprising evidence that math fact retrieval and spatial cognition may have an impact on different stages of the math problem-solving process. Specifically, we suggested that math problem solving may be roughly divided into a problem representation stage and a solution stage. We also suggested that spatial cognition ability predicts the time it takes an examinee to solve math problems, whereas math fact retrieval ability predicts the accuracy with which an examinee solves the problems. This generalization refers to performance on an entire set of items, and it may be modified on individual items that have particular properties.

We now turn to additional research questions that we believe are important. One that we are particularly interested in has to do with the origins of differences in math fact retrieval and spatial cognition. Royer et al. (1999) traced math fact retrieval differences back to the fourth grade. Other researchers (e.g., Carr & Davis, 2001; Carr & Jessup, 1997) traced the differences to first-grade children. The second author of this chapter has recently completed a PhD dissertation (Garofoli, 2003) that appears to trace the origin of sex differences in math fact retrieval back to kindergarten-age children. She also reports findings that possibly link differences in math fact retrieval to spatial processing differences. This is a line of research we will continue to pursue in our laboratory. One reason that the research is very interesting is that it raises the possibility that the small initial differences between boys and girls in kindergarten and first grade might be ameliorated by instructional intervention, and this in turn might have long-term consequences that lead to a lessening of the gap between adolescent and adult males and females in spatial cognition and math fact retrieval abilities. This possibility raises a further interesting possibility. If an early intervention resulted in the lessening of the sex difference between males and females in spatial ability and math fact retrieval, would this also reduce the gap in high-level math test performance?

Another question that we are interested in is whether there are properties of test items that differentially load on the abilities we have examined in our studies. For example, in Table 5.1 we report that the speed and/or accuracy of solution of items are differentially predicted by spatial cognition and math fact retrieval. Moreover, some of the items are not predicted by either factor. This indicates that it might be possible to identify the properties of items that load on these abilities, and by selecting test items appropriately, reduce or eliminate sex differences in test performance. For instance, imagine that one could identify the properties of construct valid test items that did not load on either spatial ability or math fact retrieval ability. An entire test consisting of such items might be a valid indicator of math ability, but not show sex differences in performance.

Another line of research that we find interesting is to attempt to test our theory that math fact retrieval influences the problem solution part of problem solving, whereas spatial cognition influences the problem representation part of the process. Our plan is to develop experiments that will allow us to determine if the theory has merit. We also anticipate that this line of research will entail the development of measures that more directly assess the ability to retrieve problem analogues from memory. We believe that spatial rotation measures provide only a very indirect means of measuring this ability, and more direct measures should provide indices of performance that are more directly related to mathematical problem solving.

References

Benbow, C. P., & Stanley, J. C. (1982). Consequences in high school and college of sex differences in mathematical reasoning ability: A longitudinal study. *American Educational Research Journal, 19*, 598–622.

Benbow, C. P., & Stanley, J. C. (1983). Sex differences in mathematical reasoning ability: More facts. *Science, 222*, 1029–1031.

Bridgeman, B., & Lewis, C. (1996). Gender differences in college mathematics grades and SAT-M scores: A reanalysis of Wainer and Steinberg. *Journal of Educational Measurement, 33*, 257–270.

Carr, M., & Davis, H. (2001). Gender differences in strategy use: A function of skill and preference. *Contemporary Educational Psychology, 26*, 330–347.

Carr, M., & Jessup, D. L. (1997). Gender differences in first-grade mathematics strategy use: Social and metacognitive influences. *Journal of Educational Psychology, 89*, 318–328.

Carr, M., Jessup, D. L., & Fuller, D. (1999). Gender differences in first-grade mathematics strategy use: Parent and teacher contributions. *Journal for Research in Mathematics Education, 30*, 20–46.

Casey, M. B., Nuttal, R. L., & Pezaris, E. (1997). Mediators of gender differences in mathematics college entrance test scores: A comparison of spatial skills with internalized beliefs and anxieties. *Developmental Psychology, 33*, 669–680.

Cleary, T. A. (1992). Gender differences in aptitude and achievement test scores. In *Sex equity in educational opportunity, achievement and testing: Proceedings of the 1991 ETS invitational conference*. Princeton NJ: Educational Testing Service.

Dwyer, C. A., & Johnson, L. M. (1997). Grades, accomplishments and correlates. In W. A. Willingham & and N. S. Cole (Eds.), *Gender and fair assessment* (pp. 127–156). Mahwah, NJ: Erlbaum Associates.

Garofoli, L. M. (2003). *Early gender differences in arithmetic strategy proficiency. Unpublished Ph.D. Dissertation.* Amherst, MA: University of Massachusetts.

Geary, D. C. (1996). Sexual selection and sex differences in mathematical abilities. *Behavioral and Brain Sciences, 19,* 229–247.

Geary, D., Saults, S. J., Liu, F., & Hoard, M. K. (2000). Sex differences in spatial cognition, computational fluency and arithmetical reasoning. *Journal of Experimental Child Psychology, 77,* 337–353.

Halpern, D. E., & LaMay, M. L. (2000). The smarter sex: A critical review of sex differences in intelligence. *Educational Psychology Review, 12,* 229–246.

Harnisch, D. L., Steinkamp, M. W., Tsai, S. L., & Walberg, H. J. (1986). Cross-national differences in mathematics attitude and achievement among seventeen-year-olds. *International Journal of Educational Development, 6,* 233–244.

Hummel, J. E., & Holyoke, K. J. (1997). Distributed representations of structure: A theory of analogical access and mapping. *Psychological Review, 104,* 427–466.

Hyde, J. S., Fennema, E., & Lamon, S. J. (1990). Gender differences in mathematics performance: A meta-analysis. *Psychological Bulletin, 107,* 139–155.

Johnson, E. S. (1984). Sex differences in problem solving. *Journal of Educational Psychology, 76,* 1359–1371.

Just, M. A., & Carpenter, P. A. (1985). Cognitive coordinate systems: Accounts of mental rotation and individual differences in spatial ability. *Psychological Review, 92,* 137–172.

Kimball, M. M. (1989). A new perspective on women's math achievement. *Psychological Bulletin, 105,* 198–214.

Kintsch, W., & Greeno, J. G. (1985). Understanding and solving word problems. *Psychological Review, 92,* 109–129.

Langenfield, T. E. (1997). Test fairness: Internal and external investigations of gender bias in mathematics testing. *Educational Measurement: Issues and Practice, 16,* 20–26.

Law, D. J., Pellegrino, J. W., & Hunt, E. B. (1993). Comparing the tortoise and the hare: Gender differences and experience in dynamic spatial reasoning tasks. *Psychological Science, 4,* 35–40.

Lewis, A. B. (1989). Training students to represent arithmetic word problems. *Journal of Educational Psychology, 81,* 521–531.

Lewis, A. B., & Mayer, R. E. (1987). Students' miscomprehension of relational statements in arithmetic word problems. *Journal of Educational Psychology, 79,* 363–371.

Lummis, M., & Stevenson, H. W. (1990). Gender differences in beliefs and achievement: A cross-cultural study. *Developmental Psychology, 26,* 254–263.

Masters, M. S., & Sanders, B. (1993). Is the gender difference in mental rotation disappearing? *Behavior Genetics, 23,* 337–341.

Mayer, R. E. (2003). Mathematical problem solving. In J. M. Royer (Ed.), *Mathematical cognition* (pp. 69–92). Greenwich, CT: Infoage Publishing.

Mayer, R. E., & Hegarty, M. (1996). The process of understanding mathematics problems. In R. J. Sternberg & T. Ben-Zeev (Eds.), *The nature of mathematical thinking* (pp. 29–53). Hillsdale, NJ: Erlbaum.

Mills, C. J., Ablard, K. E., & Stumpf, H. (1993). Gender differences in academically talented young students' mathematical reasoning: Patterns across age and subskills. *Journal of Educational Psychology, 85,* 340–346.

Riley, M. S., Greeno, J. G., & Heller, J. I. (1983). Development of children's problem-solving ability in arithmetic. In H. P. Ginsburg (Ed.), *The development of mathematical thinking* (pp. 153–196). New York: Academic Press.

Robinson, N. M., Abbott, R. D., Beringer, V. W., & Busse, J. (1996). The structure of abilities in math-precocious young children: Gender similarities and differences. *Journal of Educational Psychology, 88*, 341–352.

Royer, J. M., Rath, K., Tronsky, L. N., Marchant, H., & Jackson, S. (2002). *Spatial cognition and math fact retrieval as the causes of sex differences in math test performance.* Paper presented at the annual meeting of the American Educational Research Association, New Orleans, LA.

Royer, J. M., Tronsky, L. N., Chan, Y., Jackson, S. J., & Marchant, H. (1999). Math-fact retrieval as the cognitive mechanism underlying gender differences in math test performance. *Contemporary Educational Psychology, 24*, 181–266.

Royer, J. M., Wing, R. E., Rath, K., Jackson, S., & Marchant, H. (in press). Spatial cognition and math fact retrieval affect different stages on the math problem solving process.

U.S. Office of Education. (2001). *The digest of education statistics (2001).*http://www.ed.gov/.

Vandenberg, S. G., & Kuse, A. R. (1978). Mental rotation, a group test of Three-dimensional spatial visualization. *Perceptual and motos skills, 47*, 599–604.

Wilder, G. Z. (1997). Antecedents of gender differences. In W. W. Willingham & L. M. Johnson (Eds.), *Supplement to gender and fair assessment.* Princeton, NJ: Educational Testing Service.

Willingham, W. W., & Cole, N. S. (1997). *Gender and fair assessment.* Mahwah, NJ: Erlbaum.

6

Spatial Ability as a Mediator of Gender Differences on Mathematics Tests

A Biological–Environmental Framework

Ronald L. Nuttall, M. Beth Casey, and Elizabeth Pezaris

It is well known that there is a gender difference on a number of standardized mathematics tests, with males outperforming females (Hyde, Fennema, & Lamon, 1990; Willingham & Cole, 1997). In addition, a relationship has been found between spatial abilities and mathematics test scores (Burnett, Lane, & Dratt, 1979; Casey, Nuttall, Pezaris, & Benbow, 1995; Casey, Nuttall, & Pezaris, 1997; Geary, Saults, Liu, & Hoard, 2000; Robinson, Abbott, Berninger, & Busse, 1996). This relationship may be key for understanding gender differences in mathematics because one of the best-known and largest gender differences is the male advantage on some types of spatial skills (Linn & Petersen, 1985). In fact, evidence has begun to accumulate that shows a connection between gender differences in mathematics achievement and gender differences in spatial skills (Casey et al., 1995; Casey et al., 1997; Casey, Nuttall, & Pezaris, 2001).

In this chapter, we review our research findings, which were designed to address a series of questions to better understand gender differences in math achievement. We propose that gender differences in spatial skills are the key to understanding gender differences in math achievement. After presenting findings on this connection, the conclusion of the chapter provides a biological/environmental framework to help understand how variations in spatial abilities might arise.

GENDER DIFFERENCES IN MATH ACHIEVEMENT

The observed gender differences in mathematics performance are not universal (Hedges & Nowell, 1995; Hyde et al., 1990). During the elementary years of schooling, up to early adolescence, females have a slight advantage over males in terms of computational ability as assessed by achievement tests. However, Robinson, Abbott, Berninger, Busse, & Mukhopadhyay (1997) followed mathematically precocious kindergartners and first graders longitudinally, and found that boys gained more than girls on both quantitative and visual-spatial measures. As the math competencies shift in high school, males have a slight advantage over females, especially in problem solving and geometry (Hyde et al., 1990; Marshall & Smith, 1987). When math grades are analyzed instead of achievement tests, females often outperform males (Kimball, 1989). There are little or no gender differences on math achievement tests for those samples that include individuals with low or average abilities, and in low-ability samples, females excel over males (Hedges & Nowell, 1995). Overall, the general trend is for gender differences favoring males on achievement tests to occur primarily among high-ability students of middle school or older ages (Hyde et al., 1990).

SPATIAL SKILLS AND GENDER DIFFERENCES

Spatial skills involve the ability to think and reason using mental pictures rather than words. Both verbal and spatial strategies can be applied to mathematics problem solving (Battista, 1990). There are many mathematics problems that can be solved either by drawing a diagram of the solution, which is a spatial solution, or by laying out the step-by-step algorithmic solution, a verbal, logical-deductive approach (Casey, 2003). Individuals in many fields depend on spatial thinking. In particular, mathematicians often visualize mathematical relations, whereas physical scientists visualize and reason about the models of the physical world (Clements & Battista, 1992; Hershkowitz, Parzysz, & Van Dormolen, 1996). Spatial reasoning can be an important component in solving many types of mathematics problems. This includes (1) the use of diagrams and drawings, (2) solving algebraic word problems, (3) searching for numerical patterns, (4) considering how fractions can be broken down into geometric regions, (5) graphing, and (6) conceptualizing mathematical functions (Casey, 2003; Geary et al., 2000; Wheatley, 1990).

There are a variety of different types of spatial skills (e.g., spatial visualization and spatial perception). Because there are some spatial tasks that do not show gender differences (e.g., spatial visualization tasks), one must carefully select the spatial measures to be used in this type of research, focusing on the measures that show gender differences (Halpern, 2000; Linn & Petersen, 1985, 1986). We have focused our research on mental rotation ability, the water levels test (WLT), mechanical reasoning, and block-building constructional skills because these measures have some of the largest gender differences (Bassi, 2000; Casey et al., 2001; Halpern, 2000).

Mental rotation involves the ability to look at a picture of an object and visualize what it might look like when rotated in three-dimensional space. This skill has been most commonly measured by the Vandenberg Mental Rotation Test (Linn & Petersen, 1985). It is related to the ability to mentally transform and manipulate images, which is useful in a variety of tasks, such as carpentry, architecture, map reading, engineering, sports involving ball throwing, and measurement estimations, such as how to rotate a table through a doorway.

Mental rotation ability shows a substantial cognitive gender difference with an effect size of 0.94 (Linn & Petersen, 1986) (close to one standard deviation) with males outperforming females (Linn & Petersen, 1985). The large gender effect on this type of task has been further supported in other studies (Masters & Sanders, 1993; Voyer, Voyer, & Bryden, 1995). Thus, although some cognitive gender differences have shown a reduction in recent years (Feingold, 1988; Hyde et al., 1990), gender differences in mental rotation ability have remained constant over many years (Linn & Petersen, 1985; Voyer et al., 1995).

Gender differences on the WLT are moderate in strength. Wittig and Allen (1984) found that 40% of female college students, as compared with only 17% of male students, failed the WLT. The Piagetian-based WLT, a spatial perception task, measures the ability to predict the location of a water surface in tilted bottles that are half filled. The respondent draws a line representing the water level in several drawings of containers tilted at various angles. In this task, the participant has to generate an image of a half-full bottle of water and *mentally rotate it to a different angle* (Sholl, 1989). In his component-skills analysis, Kalichman (1988) reduced the WLT to four subabilities: visual-perceptual skills, mental imagery and rotation skills, utilization of spatial coordinate systems, and recall of relevant information. According to Piaget, competence on the WLT is related to spatial competence involving the ability to use an Euclidean system of reference to organize spatial experience (Li, Nuttall, & Zhao, 1999; Liben & Golbeck, 1984).

Mechanical reasoning is typically assessed using the Mechanical Reasoning subtest of the Differential Aptitude Test (Bennett, Seashore, & Wesman, 1990). These items test basic knowledge of mechanical principles and knowledge of the effects of common physical forces, such as gravity. The student examines a picture showing mechanical devices, such as gears, levers, wheels, and pulleys, and has to make deductions, often by visualizing what the effect would be on the devices pictured, if they were manipulated (Casey et al., 2001). Thus, this task also depends on spatial thinking and the ability to manipulate images. This is supported by the fact that spatial and mechanical skills have been shown to load on the same factor (Hamilton, Nussbaum, Kupermintz, Kerkoven, & Snow, 1995; Humphreys, Lubinski, & Yao, 1993).

The Mechanical Reasoning subtest has the greatest gender effect of any of the Differential Aptitude Tests (0.98 of a standard deviation in the United States and 0.82 of a standard deviation in Britain) (Hedges & Nowell, 1995; Lynn, 1992). There is also evidence for gender differences on composite spatial-mechanical measures. In a national study of science achievement, a spatial-mechanical factor was strongly related to gender ($r = 0.48$) at the tenth-grade level (Hamilton et al., 1995). Furthermore, in another study, large gender effects for a spatial-mechanical composite were found, and this composite measure was also useful in predicting group membership in mathematics-science fields at the undergraduate and graduate levels as well as in career choices (Casey et al., 2001; Humphreys et al., 1993).

The fourth skill we have examined in our research is block building. One of the most dramatic and early examples of gender differences in spatial play is in the amount of interest and time spent building with blocks (Connor & Serbin, 1977). Almost any preschool teacher will tell you what a striking difference there is between boys and girls in their fascination with block play. They have to work hard to have gender equity in the block area because the boys will fight to go there and many girls seem to have little interest in this type of activity.

In Erikson's (1951) seminal study, which used a combination of toys and blocks as props, 468 adolescent students were individually asked to build "an exciting scene out of an imaginary moving picture." A key finding was that a higher percentage of 12- and 13-year-old boys, when compared to girls, built towers that were at least twice as high as they were wide and had at least half its height above the rest of the construction. The girls, however, were more likely to build enclosed scenes of everyday life, often using only the nonblock props, such as furniture, to create inside enclosures (Erikson, 1951). Many subsequent researchers dismissed Erikson's findings mainly because of the Freudian interpretation by which he explained his results.

Prompted by Erikson's findings (although not his interpretation), we investigated the hypothesis that boys do build structures that are significantly higher than girls. However, rather than attributing this height difference to Freudian notions of "inner space" and genital morphology, we proposed that boys may be focusing more on the structural property of the constructions when compared with their female counterparts. According to this theory, one could argue that the boys in Erikson's study created higher structures, in part, because of the tendency for boys to use more sophisticated structural elements of balance in their block play than do girls.

Thus, we decided to study the ability to construct a tall, well-balanced, architecturally complex structure out of blocks. We reasoned that children who work at building high and complex structures will have mastered spatial problem solving related to principles of balance, by finding ways to stabilize their tall constructions through both mental and physical manipulation and rotation of blocks. This spatial activity involves visualization, spatial planning, and spatial manipulation of images.

The decision was made to study block building in older students. By this point in the children's development, there is little block-building activity;

therefore, the behavior patterns in terms of block play are relatively stable. In the initial research, we explored gender differences in the structures built by boys and girls at age 13. Some interesting patterns emerged from this study of 13-year-olds (Pezaris, Casey, Nuttall, Bassi, Trzynski, Averna, & Galluccio, 1998) and were supported in a later study of high-ability seniors in high school (Bassi, 2000). Students were asked to "build something interesting" using wooden blocks, thereby assessing preference in "style" of block building. It was hypothesized that males would build higher structures overall than females and incorporate more sophisticated principles of balance into their block constructions. These predictions were supported. Thus, even among older middle school and high school students, gender differences in block building occurs.

Furthermore, in her study on high school students, Bassi (2000) added a second task in which students were again asked to build, but this time were given instructions designed to maximize their height and balance scores. The purpose of the second task was to determine whether a gender difference in the balance score would still be found, even when both the boys and the girls were given specific instructions on how to build. In fact, the instructions did not eliminate the gender gap in terms of spatial performance. Males outperformed females on the balance measure during both the open-ended and instructed phases of the study.

SKILL AT MENTAL ROTATION AND ITS RELATION TO MATH ACHIEVEMENT IN FEMALES

Once it has been established that gender differences are strong on these different types of spatial abilities, the next critical question is whether these abilities have any practical applications, particularly in relation to math achievement in females. Much of our research has focused on the relationship between mental rotation ability and the SAT-M. We examined this relationship in 760 students across four diverse samples: a college sample, a self-selected sample of mathematically talented youth drawn from the top 1% nationally, and college-bound high school students divided into high- and low-ability groups, based on their verbal scholastic aptitude scores (SAT-V) (Casey et al., 1995). We found that for all four samples, the females showed a significant relationship between mental rotation skills and the SAT-M (with correlations between 0.35 and 0.38 across the four samples). We also found that this relationship remained even when scores on a measure of their verbal ability (SAT-V) were statistically controlled. This finding tells us that mental rotation is important for girls' performance on the math SATs. Those girls who are effective at figuring out how to mentally rotate the shapes on the Vandenberg are also effective at figuring out how to solve the math problems on the SATs. (Note: This relationship is not as consistent for the male students because it varied as a function of sample [Casey et al., 1995].)

THE CONTRIBUTION OF GENDER DIFFERENCES IN MENTAL ROTATION ABILITY TO GENDER DIFFERENCES IN MATH ACHIEVEMENT

The next question we asked in this study (Casey et al., 1995), was "do gender differences in mental rotation ability account for the gender difference in math achievement?" First, we established that there was a gender difference favoring males for both mental rotation and the math SATs. We found that this effect occurred for the college students and the high SAT-V college-bound students, but not for the low SAT-V college-bound students. Thus, we focused on the college and high-ability, college-bound groups and asked, "when mental rotation ability is statistically controlled, do the boys still show significantly higher math achievement?" The answer was no, for both groups of students. The previously significant gender differences in SAT-M were eliminated when scores were adjusted for the ability to mentally rotate images for these groups. These findings suggest that mental rotation ability is a critical factor contributing to gender differences on the math SATs among higher-ability high school and college students.

THE IMPORTANCE OF MENTAL ROTATION ABILITY AS A CONTRIBUTOR TO GENDER DIFFERENCES ON THE SAT-M

Once we had established that skill at mental rotation contributed to gender differences on the SAT-M, a new question arose. Specifically, we asked, "is mental rotation a stronger mediator of gender differences in math than socioemotional factors?" Thus, we compared mental rotation ability with attitudes toward math and math anxiety as potential mediators of gender differences on the SAT-M (Casey et al., 1997). The self-confidence measure was taken from a questionnaire cited in Parsons, Adler, Futterman, Goff, Kaczala, Meece, and Midgley (1980), including items such as the following: (1) "How good are you at math?" and (2) "If you were to order all the students in your math class from the worst to the best in math, where would you put yourself?" The items on math anxiety were taken from a questionnaire cited in Wigfield and Meece (1988). Examples included the following: (1) "How much do you worry about how well you are doing in math?" and (2) "Do math tests scare you?" We studied a high-ability, college-bound sample (scoring at or above 480 on the SAT-V, and consisting of 51 females and 43 males who had taken at least 4 math courses). Using path analytic techniques, we found that differences in mental rotation skills were *more important* in accounting for gender differences on the SAT-M than *either* math self-confidence or math anxiety (Casey et al., 1997).

The path analysis indicated that the male advantage in SAT-M is an indirect effect of two factors. On average, it is first mediated through the better mental rotation ability of males compared with females and is mediated second through the increased self-confidence that males have when doing these math problems on the SAT-M. These effects occurred even when statistically controlling for verbal aptitude (SAT-V). In contrast to these two mediators, internalized feelings of anxiety in regard to math did not serve as a mediator. The path analysis showed that the gender difference in math anxiety (although significant) had no significant effect on SAT-M performance. Furthermore, the results indicate that mental rotation skill is almost twice as influential a mediator of gender differences in SAT-M, as was the measure of math self-confidence.

THE CONTRIBUTION OF SPATIAL SKILL TO GENDER DIFFERENCES ON THE TYPES OF MATH ITEMS AT WHICH MALES TYPICALLY EXCEL

Our next set of questions focused on specific types of math items showing a significant male advantage, rather than on total math scores. The eighth-grade Third International Mathematics and Science Study (TIMSS; Beaton, Mullis, Martin, Gonzalez, Kelly, & Smith, 1996) was ideal for our purposes because this carefully researched test provided information on gender differences for each item in the test. We created a mathematics subtest from items on the TIMSS, comprised of the items that showed the largest male advantage in the U.S. sample. Our goal was to study what factors mediated gender differences on these types of math items. To this end, we compared spatial-mechanical skills with mathematics self-confidence (Parsons et al., 1980) as mediators of gender differences on these math items. The 8th-grade sample in this study consisted of 187 students (96 females, 91 males) (Casey et al., 2001). The Vandenberg Mental Rotation Test (Vandenberg & Kuse, 1978), the WLT (Sholl, 1989), and the Mechanical Reasoning Test (Bennett et al., 1990) were combined into a composite spatial-mechanical measure because the three spatial measures were highly intercorrelated with each other.

This study gave us a window into what factors might predict for females' lower performance on the types of math items at which males typically excel. For our sample, we chose an age prior to the point at which gender differences favoring males start to emerge in overall math performance. Using path analytic techniques, we found that the spatial-mechanical composite measure was almost three times as influential a mediator of gender differences on the TIMSS-male items as was the measure of math self-confidence. (It should be noted that the same mediational effects were found for all three spatial measures separately as well as for the composite spatial measure.) Thus, we found that by 8th grade, it is girls' relatively poorer spatial-mechanical skills that make a strong contribution to their lower scores on the types of math items at which boys show the greatest success. Our next goal was to begin to understand the precursors of these gender differences in terms of the types of experiences that boys may be extensively exposed to that may contribute to these gender differences in spatial thinking.

THE RELATIONSHIP BETWEEN BLOCK-BUILDING SKILLS AND MATH ACHIEVEMENT

The ultimate goal of our program of research is to trace the origins of gender differences in spatial and mathematical skills. One salient difference in the early behavior of boys and girls is the amount of time they spend constructing with three-dimensional objects using wooden blocks in preschool and kindergarten (Connor & Serbin, 1977). Research on both preschoolers and early primary students has shown that skill at block play was related to spatial skills for both boys and girls (Brosnan, 1998; Caldera, Culp, O'Brian, Truglio, Alvarez, & Huston, 1999).

A series of studies (Bassi, 2000; Pezaris et al., 1998) was designed to examine (1) gender differences in the block structures created by middle and high school students, and (2) the relationship between style of block building and math achievement in high-ability seniors in high school. As indicated earlier, evidence for gender difference in block building is present as late as eighth grade, and for a sample of high-ability seniors, in high school as well. Thus, the spatial learning achieved in block play is one potential factor influencing later math skills (Connor & Serbin, 1977). In her dissertation, Bassi (2000) investigated the relationship between skill at block building and math SATs in high-ability seniors (43 males and 57 females). She found that when the students were given specific instructions on how to build, a positive relationship was found between the task and SAT-M ($r = 0.30$). However, the picture is not totally clear because there was no evidence that skill at block building contributed to male/female differences in SAT-M performance. Nevertheless, these findings indicate a possible link between early block-building activities and later math skills. A longitudinal study supports this hypothesis (Wolfgang, Stannard, & Jones, 2001). Children's block-building skills were assessed in preschool, and their later math performance was followed up both in terms of grades and achievement. No relationship was found in elementary school. Yet, at the beginning of middle school and in high school, a positive correlation emerged between their early block performance and their later mathematics achievement.

SUMMARY OF RESEARCH FINDINGS ON SPATIAL ABILITY AND MATHEMATICS

- Among high-ability students, males excel relative to females on mental rotation ability, mechanical reasoning, the WLT, and the application of balance principles in building block constructions (even when specific instructions are given to build tall and architecturally complex structures).

- Mental rotation ability is a stronger mediator of the gender difference on the math SATs than is math self-confidence as measured by Parsons et al. (1980) and math anxiety as measured by Wigfield and Meese (1988).
- TIMSS items that had previously shown large gender differences (favoring males) in performance were examined. It was found that mechanical/spatial skills were a stronger contributor to gender differences on these items than math self-confidence.
- When given building instructions, those high-ability seniors who built architecturally complex block constructions tended to score higher on the SAT-M.

A FRAMEWORK FOR UNDERSTANDING INDIVIDUAL DIFFERENCES IN SPATIAL SKILLS

Combined, the body of work discussed so far in this chapter, suggests that spatial skills are pivotal in performance on mathematics tests, especially among high-ability females (Casey et al., 1995). Understanding the basis of individual differences in these skills among females is an important first step toward improving the spatial skills of girls, and, thereby, closing the gap in performance. Therefore, we chose to study the characteristics that contribute to the success of the females who excel at mental rotation ability; in other words, to study the females who represent the exception to the male advantage on mental rotation tasks (Casey & Brabeck, 1989).

Typically, hypotheses about the origin of gender differences in spatial skills are developed from either a genetic or an environmental perspective (Burnett, 1986; Caplan, MacPherson, & Tobin, 1985), with researchers positioning themselves on only one side of this argument. The possibility of an interaction between heredity and environmental effects is acknowledged, but little theory or research has actually been done to develop this interactionist position (Casey, 2002).

Halpern (1992) suggested that in order to understand the nature of cognitive sex differences, it is necessary to develop theories that incorporate the independent and joint effects of biology and environment. She recommended focusing on research that jointly investigates such biologically based measures as handedness and laterality, and such environmentally based measures as parents' endorsement of sex role stereotypes and academic background and attitudes. This is the direction that we have taken in our program of research. In this section, we present a model of how differences in patterns of brain organization might interact with spatial experiences to produce individual differences in mental rotation ability within females. We then describe findings from our program of research designed to examine predictions based on this model.

THE "BENT TWIG" INTERACTION ANALYSIS OF INDIVIDUAL DIFFERENCES IN SPATIAL ABILITY

In our research, we have used a "bent twig" model (Sherman, 1978) to account for individual differences within females in spatial ability. The theory is based on the old saying, "As the twig is bent, so grows the tree." The crux of our particular version of the "bent twig" theory is to consider how females with different patterns of brain organization might differ in their ability to capitalize on spatial experiences. We call this theory the "bent twig" interaction model. Thus, depending on their pattern of brain organization, subgroups of females would react differently to spatial experiences, even when they had equivalent exposure to them.

We considered spatial experiences gained through activities such as carpentry and math/science courses to have a positive impact on the development of spatial skills. Girls who inherit a pattern of brain organization that fosters the development of spatial skills and who have been exposed to these types of spatial experiences should excel in spatial ability relative to those females with the same amount of exposure, but who do not have this potential. In addition, girls who are similar in pattern of brain organization, but who lack the appropriate experiences, will also not develop as effective spatial skills.

Biological Influences

We selected a theory of brain organization that fits effectively within the framework of a "bent twig" interaction analysis, incorporating a well-known theory of individual differences in pattern of brain organization (Annett, 1985, 1995a), as a basis for identifying the females with the initial predisposition to excel in this area. Then we identified possible environmental experiences that might be critical in further developing this propensity among females.

Annett's theory (1985, 1995a) provides the underlying theoretical rationale for the genetic component of the "bent twig" interaction model. According to this theory, individual differences in patterns of handedness are expressions of individual differences in brain organizations (Bishop, 1990; Geschwind & Galaburda, 1987; Springer & Deutsch, 1989). According to Annett, most people inherit a right-shift factor, which predisposes them to be right-handed and left-hemisphere dominant for language, with females showing this effect more strongly. The subset of individuals who do not carry the right-shift factor (i.e., who are *recessive* for the right-shift gene) are likely to be left-handers or ambidextrous right-handers (able to use the left hand to perform a variety of tasks, even though they use their right hand for writing). These individuals (particularly males) are more prone to be at risk for language problems due to their atypical pattern of brain organization. With no right-shift factor, this group is highly variable in the development of pattern of brain organization. Thus, it includes both those who excel spatially and those who may have deficits in this and other areas of cognitive functioning, making it difficult to predict their level of spatial performance.

Right-handers with all right-handed close relatives are likely to be *homozygotic* for the right-shift factor, receiving this gene from both parents (Annett, 1995b). They are more likely to be strongly left-hemisphere dominant for language (particularly females), to prefer verbal strategies for solving problems and to be at risk for poor spatial ability. In contrast, right-handers with nonright-handed relatives are more likely to be *heterozygotic* for this gene (Annett, 1995b). Because they have immediate relatives who are left-handed or ambidextrous, these right-handers are likely to carry the recessive as well as the dominant allele for the right-shift factor.

Within genetics, there is a concept referred to as the heterozygotic advantage. Individuals who carry both the dominant and recessive alleles fare better than those who are homozygotic for the gene. This concept of the heterozygotic advantage is what makes Annett's theory of brain organization so useful to the "bent twig" interaction model in terms of understanding individual differences in females. She argues that females show the right-shift effect more strongly than males, due to their earlier development of the left hemisphere. Thus, the right-shift gene carries greater costs for poor spatial ability among females, particularly those right-handers who have all right-handed, first-degree relatives. In contrast, right-handed females with nonright-handed relatives (females likely to have the heterozygotic advantage) are not as strongly left-hemisphere dominant for language, are less dependent on purely verbal strategies for solving problems, and therefore, have the potential for good spatial ability.

According to Annett (1985), a large percentage of females carry the heterozygotic advantage for the right-shift factor (about 50% of the population). Thus, according to her theory, these females have inherited a pattern of brain organization that should enable them to develop effective spatial skills. Yet, given the large gender differences found for some spatial skills, it appears that relatively few of these females are, in fact, capitalizing on their potential.

Environmental Influences

In the development of our "bent twig" individual differences model, we selected spatial and math/science experiences as key environmental factors for the development of spatial ability (Casey & Brabeck, 1989, 1990; Casey, 1996, 2002). This choice was based on the literature. Baenninger and Newcombe (1989) found a weak but reliable relation between spatial activity participation and spatial ability. Furthermore, Burnett and Lane (1971) found that women in math-science programs showed greater improvements in mental rotation performance from the beginning to the end of their programs than women in social sciences and humanities.

Biological/Environmental Interactions

The key aspect of our "bent twig" interaction model is the prediction that not all females should benefit equally from these types of spatial experiences. We proposed to examine how individuals likely to inherit different patterns of brain organization might differentially respond to these types of spatial experiences. Based on a synthesis of Annett's theory and our review of research on environmental variables, we hypothesized that females who excel spatially will be those who (1) have the heterozygotic advantage in relation to the right-shift factor, and (2) have had the appropriate spatial or math/science experiences.

A PROGRAM OF RESEARCH THAT EXAMINES OUR "BENT TWIG" INTERACTION MODEL

Applications of the Model to Mental Rotation Ability

The next question we asked was how we could identify the particular group of women with the heterozygotic advantage (Annett, 1985) who *also* had had the opportunity to capitalize on their genetic potential through experience. In an article in *Neuropsychologia* (Casey & Brabeck, 1989), we investigated family handedness as a way of identifying the women with the biological bent to excel spatially. Family handedness refers here to handedness of immediate relatives. Right-handers with all right-handed close relatives (parents and siblings) were compared with both right-handers with at least one left-handed or ambidextrous close relative and nonright-handers. Any of the right-handed subjects in the study who had a sibling or a parent who was left-handed or ambidextrous was considered to be a right-hander with nonright-handed relatives. If they had *only* right-handed parents or siblings, then they were labeled as a right-hander with right-handed relatives. If they were left-handed or ambidextrous, they were identified as a nonright-hander.

Math/Science Major as Our Environmental Measure

We used math or science major as a way of identifying the college women likely to be exposed to spatial experiences (Burnett & Lane, 1971). We predicted that those right-handed women with nonright-handed relatives

TABLE 6.1. *Mental Rotation Scores as a Function of Choice of Major and Handedness in a Female College Sample*

Handedness Group	Mean	SD	N
Female math-science majors			
RH/FRNH[a]	26.69[d]	7.39	39
RH/FRH[b]	20.70	9.80	61
NRH[c]	21.42	8.83	41
Female nonmath-science majors			
RH/FRNH[a]	19.01	7.34	70
RH/FRH[b]	19.67	9.32	64
NRH[c]	16.26	5.91	39

[a] RH/FNRH = right-handers with at least one nonright-handed relative.
[b] RH/FRH = right-handers with all right-handed relatives.
[c] NRH = nonright-handers.
[d] This target group of math-science females outperformed the other two groups of female math-science majors, $p < 0.05$.

who also majored in math and science would excel in mental rotation ability (outperforming the other women in the study, and performing closer to the level of the males).

We investigated 433 male and female students across three samples (see Table 6.1). Participants were selected based on their major, and then administered the Vandenberg Test of Mental Rotation Ability (Vandenberg & Kuse, 1978), the Edinburgh Handedness Inventory (Oldfield, 1971), and a family handedness inventory (Casey & Brabeck, 1989). Using an analysis of variance design, a significant three-way interaction was obtained. Simple effect analyses showed no effects for males. However, for females there was a significant interaction between family handedness and major. The right-handers with nonright-handed relatives were labeled the target group because we identified them as having the heterozygotic advantage. We looked at the nonmath/science women first and found no significant effect of family handedness (see Table 6.1).

Then we looked within the math/science majors and found that the target group, the right-handers with nonright-handed relatives, excelled relative to the other two groups of women. In addition, this target group of math/science majors performed at the level of the males on the Vandenberg (see Table 6.1). The effect held up over three samples, and the results remained when parents' educational level and math and verbal aptitude scores were statistically partialled out. Thus, we concluded that biologically based individual differences interacted with environmental factors to influence level of mental rotation skill in females.

Although we argued for a biological/environmental *interaction* explanation of these data, we do recognize that there may be an active biological/environmental *correlation* involved in choice of major. Biological-environmental correlations and interactions do not happen in isolation and can occur simultaneously or in tandem (Wachs, 1992, p. 158). Individual selection of math/science majors is probably influenced both by prior spatial skills and by spatial experiences. Thus, college major is not a "pure" environmental variable. Nevertheless, in this research we have controlled the self-selection process to some extent because we included females who self-selected into math and science across *all the handedness* subtypes, not just the target group. Yet, it was only the target group of math/science majors who excelled spatially.

Using Self-Ratings of Spatial Experience as Our Environmental Measure

In a 1990 article in *Brain and Cognition* (Casey & Brabeck, 1990), we investigated the environmental component of the "bent twig" interaction model more directly in the college population. We had raters identify those items in Newcombe's spatial activities questionnaire, which require mental visualizations of two-dimensional and three-dimensional objects in space. These included carpentry, electrical circuits, sketching house plans, constructing go-carts and model airplanes, and glass blowing. We found that the target handedness group who also rated themselves as having extensive spatial experiences on at least one of these types of spatial activities excelled over the other right-handed women (see Table 6.2). Thus, these results suggest more directly that the combination of genetic potential and spatial experiences may be critical for development of mental rotation ability in women.

TABLE 6.2. *Mental Rotation Scores as a Function of Spatial Experience and Familial Handedness in a Right-Handed Female College Sample*

Handedness Group	Mean	SD	N
High levels of spatial experience			
RH/FRNH[a]	22.30[c]	8.59	30
RH/FRH[b]	16.86	9.50	36
Low levels of spatial experience			
RH/FRNH[a]	17.44[d]	7.07	32
RH/FRH[b]	17.46	8.68	46

[a] RH/FNRH = right-handers with at least one nonright-handed relative.
[b] RH/FRH = right-handers with all right-handed relatives.
[c] This target group of women was significantly different from all other groups of women, using planned comparisons, $p < 0.05$.

TABLE 6.3. *Mental Rotation Scores for Eighth Graders Who Have Brothers in Their Families as a Function of Familial Handedness and Shared Spatial Activities with Brothers*

Family Handedness	Mean	SD	N
High levels of shared spatial activities with brothers			
From all right-handed families[a]	15.06	6.27	16
From families with mixed handedness[b]	22.04[c]	9.98	45
Low levels of shared spatial activities with brothers			
From all right-handed families[a]	17.40	9.34	15
From families with mixed handedness[b]	14.94	8.54	36

[a] All right-handed families = all right-handed first-degree family members.

[b] Families with mixed handedness = at least one left-handed or ambidextrous first-degree family member.

[c] Among students with high levels of spatial experience with their brothers, this group of children from families with mixed handedness outperformed the group of children from families with all right-handers: $p < 0.05$.

Spatial Experiences with Brothers as Our Environmental Measure

In another follow-up of our research on the "bent twig" interaction model in *Developmental Psychology* (Casey, Nuttall, & Pezaris, 1999), we explored within the family unit to determine how spatial experiences with a male sibling interacted with family handedness. Those eighth graders who had at least one brother in their family reported the degree of shared spatial experiences with their brothers. Individuals from families with all right-handed first-degree family members were compared with individuals from families with mixed-handedness (both right-handers and nonright-handers). Their performance on the Vandenberg Mental Rotation Test was assessed. No differences were found for the family handedness groups reporting few spatial experiences with their brothers. However, for both boys and girls reporting extensive spatial experiences with their brothers, family handedness made a difference (see Table 6.3). Children who came from families with mixed-handedness performed significantly higher on the mental rotation test than those who came from families with all right-handed members. This effect was found across gender. Thus, the girls and boys from families with only right-handers were not able to use their spatial experiences with their brothers to increase their mental rotation skills.

EDUCATIONAL IMPLICATIONS

In our view, the modifications of standardized math tests or changes in the entry process into math-science fields (Gallagher, DeLisi, Holst, McGillicuddy-DeLisi, Morely, & Cahalan, 2000) are not the most effective "routes to go" in addressing gender differences in math test scores. Instead, there should be a major focus on developing educational intervention programs specifically designed to facilitate spatial skills. Changing the achievement test items will not eliminate the advantage that males have using spatial strategies for solving mathematical problems (an advantage that has implications for later success in math/science/and technical careers). Several studies have compared the spatial skills of males and females in different types of occupations and majors. When males and females from occupations and majors requiring spatial skills were examined, little or no gender effects were found on spatial tasks (Govier & Feldman, 1999; Quaiser-Pohl & Lehmann, 2002). Furthermore, experiential factors showed a relationship to mental rotation performance only for females (Quaiser-Pohl & Lehmann, 2002). Thus, a key focus should be on developing educational tools to enable girls, particularly the substantial group with biological potential, to develop their spatial thinking strategies. This approach may eventually lead to the entry of more females into technical and spatially based fields.

Much of the past intervention research on gender has focused on changing gender-based classroom dynamics or math attitudes in girls (e.g., see books by American Association of University Women, 1992; Burton, 1986; Secada, Fennema, & Adajian, 1995).

There are a number of potential strategies that should be considered when revising teaching methods used in the teaching of mathematics at the elementary and high school levels. One issue relates to content. Many elementary mathematics curricula concentrate on number sense and barely touch on geometry (Clements & Battista, 1992; Fuys & Liebow, 1993). Even when geometry is addressed in the mathematics curriculum in the elementary and middle school years, it typically focuses on shape naming, formulas, and rules, rather than on spatial reasoning, and on two-dimensional rather than on three-dimensional geometric ideas. Math activities requiring the transformation or manipulation of mental images are rarely required for successful math performance. However, just increasing geometry content in the curriculum may not be sufficient. Another implication of the present findings is that teachers should require greater use of spatial strategies in mathematics content *throughout* the mathematics curriculum. To have long-term and significant effects, this process should start at the kindergarten level or earlier. As recommended by the principals and standards of the National Council of Teachers of Mathematics (2000), the goal should be to provide mathematics content in which spatial as well as number sense is taught in a systematic way (Casey, 2003).

A second issue is the method of presentation of the math content. In a review of cross-cultural mathematics teaching methods, Stigler and Hiebert (1999) point out that in the United States, "Teachers present definitions of terms and demonstrate procedures for solving specific problems. Students are then asked to memorize the definitions and practice the procedures" (p. 27). Furthermore, the procedures taught almost exclusively depend on analytical rather than spatial reasoning (Clements & Battista, 1992). Thus, one change in teaching mathematics might be to provide in-class modeling of procedures using spatial solutions as well as analytical solutions to the same problem, and to also require both types of solutions for homework problems. Textbooks should also reflect this shift, with the spatial solutions presented alongside algorithmic approaches to the problems (Casey et al., 2001).

However, the modeling of spatial strategies in class may not be sufficient to develop gender equity. In-class grades are not likely to be changed substantially when specific spatial procedures are modeled in class, as females already outperform males in terms of math grades (Kimball, 1989). Yet, the effect of this spatial strategy modeling approach may still not be sufficient to improve females' performance on standardized tests, which frequently have items requiring unconventional solutions to math problems. Therefore, a focus on independent, high-level, problem-solving skills that require spatial strategies should also be encouraged in classrooms. Gallagher et al. (2000) found that use of spatial strategies on unconventional problems was one of the factors differentiating males from females on the Graduate Record Exam – Quantitative, with males excelling overall. There were fewer gender differences on problems requiring verbal skills or mastery of classroom-based content.

Thus, students should not be asked just to reproduce the spatial strategies modeled by the teacher when solving problems spatially in class or in homework. In addition, students should be expected to transfer their spatial thinking to higher-level problems that require complex solutions. The expectation on homework problems should be that they invent new spatial solutions as well as reproduce the spatial strategies provided by the teachers and students in class, particularly among talented students who may eventually be seeking careers in math or science (Casey et al., 2001).

The educational implications of these findings cannot be directly inferred until researchers conduct a long-term educational intervention in which spatial skills are specifically taught. In fact, the research findings presented here have led to the development of a supplementary mathematics program for prekindergarten through second grade that focuses on spatial reasoning and spatial content throughout mathematics (Casey, 2002). This program was funded by a National Science Foundation Grant and is called 'Round the Rug Math: Adventures in Problem Solving (for more information on the series, see Casey, 2003). It consists of a six-book series that covers the spatial content of block building and spatial relations (Casey, Paugh, & Ballard, 2002), shape attributes (Casey, Goodrow, Schiro, & Anderson, 2002), part-whole relations (Schiro, Casey, & Anderson, 2002), measurement (Anderson, Casey, & Schiro, 2002), patterning (Casey, Schiro, & Anderson, 2002), and data analysis and graphing (Casey, Napoleon, Schiro, & Anderson, 2002). To be interesting to a wider range of girls, the spatial concepts in this program are taught within the context of oral storytelling using people-oriented adventure stories and puppets. Boys also benefit from these materials. The hands-on, interactive, and spatial nature of the adventure stories make math lessons more compelling to highly active boys who have difficulty with seat-based, paper-and-pencil instruction. Because many early childhood teachers are not familiar with how to teach spatial thinking, this program carefully lays out: (1) the rationale for teaching the spatial concepts, (2) the sequences of activities to build these concepts, and (3) the specific kinds of questioning and interventions that the teacher should use to develop these ideas.

Now that the spatially based math materials have been developed, our next step is to evaluate the effectiveness of this math program on the spatial and mathematical skills of both girls and boys. We would predict that all students would benefit from this educational program. However, our "bent twig" interaction model would further predict that among the girls, it is the target group carrying the heterozygotic advantage who would be able to profit most from this educational intervention (e.g., right-handers from nonright-handed families). Because Annett (1985, 1995a) considers this group to include approximately half the population, the gender gap should narrow, but not necessarily be eliminated.

References

American Association of University Women. (1992). *How schools shortchange girls: A study of major findings on girls in education*. Washington, DC: Author.

Anderson, K., Casey, B., & Kerrigan, M. (2002). *Froglets do the measuring*. Chicago: The Wright Group/McGraw-Hill.

Annett, M. (1985). *Left, right, hand, and brain: The right shift theory*. London: Erlbaum.

Annett, M. (1995a). The right shift theory of a genetic balanced polymorphism for cerebral dominance and cognitive processing. *Cahiers de Psychologie Cognitive, 14,* 427–480.

Annett, M. (1995b). The fertility of the right shift theory. *Cahiers de Psychologie Cognitive, 14,* 623–650.

Baenninger, M., & Newcombe, N. (1989). The role of experience in spatial test performance: A meta-analysis. *Sex Roles, 20,* 327–344.

Bassi, J. (2000). *Block play: Exposing gender differences and predicting for math achievement*. Unpublished doctoral dissertation, Northeastern University, Boston.

Battista, M. T. (1990). Spatial visualization and gender differences in high school geometry. *Journal for Research in Mathematics Education, 21,* 47–60.

Beaton, A. E., Mullis, I. V. S., Martin, M. O., Gonzalez, E. J., Kelly, D. L., & Smith, T. A. (1996). *Mathematics achievement in the middle school years: IEA's Third International Mathematics and Science Study*. Chestnut Hill, MA: TIMSS International Study Center, Boston College.

Bennett, G. K., Seashore, H. G., & Wesman, A. G. (1990). *Differential aptitude tests* (5th ed.). San Antonio, TX: The Psychological Corporation.

Bishop, D. V. M. (1990). *Handedness and developmental disorder*. Philadelphia: MacKeith Press.

Brosnan, M. J. (1998). Spatial ability in children's play with lego blocks. *Perceptual and Motor Skills, 87*, 19–28.

Burnett, S. A. (1986). Sex-related differences in spatial ability: Are they trivial? *American Psychologist, 41*, 1012–1014.

Burnett, S. A., & Lane, D. M. (1971). Effects of academic instruction on spatial visualization. *Intelligence, 4*, 233–242.

Burnett, S. A., Lane, D. L., & Dratt, L. M. (1979). Spatial visualization and sex differences in quantitative ability. *Intelligence, 3*, 345–354.

Burton, L. (Ed.). (1986). *Girls into maths can go*. London: Holt, Rinehart & Winston.

Caldera, Y. M., Culp, A. M., O'Brien, M., Truglio, R. T., Alvarez, M., & Huston, A. C. (1999). Children's play preferences, construction play with blocks, and visual-spatial skills: Are they related? *International Journal of Behavioral Development, 23*, 855–872.

Caplan, P. J., MacPherson, G. M., & Tobin, P. (1985). Do sex-related differences in spatial abilities exist? A multilevel critique with new data. *American Psychologist, 40*, 786–799.

Casey, B. (2003). Mathematics problem-solving adventures: A language-arts based supplementary series for early childhood that focuses on spatial sense. In D. Clements, J. Sarama, & M. A. DiBaise (Eds.), *Engaging young children in mathematics: Results of the conference on standards for pre-school and kindergarten mathematics education*. Mahwah, NJ: Erlbaum Associates.

Casey, B., Anderson, K., & Schiro, M. (2002). *Layla finds secret patterns*. Chicago: The Wright Group/McGraw-Hill.

Casey, B., Goodrow, A., Schiro, M., & Anderson, K. (2002). *Teeny goes to Shapeland*. Chicago: The Wright Group/McGraw-Hill.

Casey, B., Napoleon, I., Schiro, M., & Anderson, K. (2002). *Seeking Mathapotamus*. Chicago: The Wright Group/McGraw-Hill.

Casey, B., Paugh, P., & Ballard, N. (2002). *Sneeze the Dragon builds a castle*. Chicago: The Wright Group/McGraw-Hill.

Casey, M. B. (1996). Understanding individual differences in spatial ability within females: A nature/nurture interactionist framework. *Developmental Review, 16*, 241–260.

Casey, M. B. (2002). Developmental perspectives on gender. In S. G. Kornstein & A. H. Clayton (Eds.), *Women's mental health*. New York: Guilford Press.

Casey, M. B., & Brabeck, M. M. (1989). Exceptions to the male advantage on a spatial task: Family handedness and college major as a factor identifying women who excel. *Neuropsychologia, 27*, 689–696.

Casey, M. B., & Brabeck, M. M. (1990). Women who excel on a spatial task: Proposed genetic and environmental factors. *Brain and Cognition, 12*, 73–84.

Casey, M. B., Nuttall, R., Pezaris, E., & Benbow, C. P. (1995). The influence of spatial ability on gender differences in mathematics college entrance test scores across diverse samples. *Developmental Psychology, 31*, 697–705.

Casey, M. B., Nuttall, R. L., & Pezaris, E. (1997). Mediators of gender differences in mathematics college entrance test scores: A comparison of spatial skills with internalized beliefs and anxieties. *Developmental Psychology, 33*, 669–680.

Casey, M. B., Nuttall, R. L., & Pezaris, E. (1999). Evidence in support of a model that predicts how biological and environmental factors interact to influence spatial skills. *Developmental Psychology, 35*, 1237–1247.

Casey, M. B., Nuttall, R. L., & Pezaris, E. (2001). Spatial-mechanical reasoning skills versus mathematics self-confidence as mediators of gender differences on mathematics subtests using cross-national gender-based items. *Journal for Reseach in Mathematics Education, 32,* 28–57.

Clements, D. H., & Battista, M. T. (1992). Geometry and spatial reasoning. In D. A. Grouws (Ed.), *Handbook of research on mathematics teaching and learning* (pp. 420–464). New York: Macmillan.

Connor, J. M., & Serbin, L. A. (1977). Behaviorally based masculine- and feminine-activity-preference scales for preschoolers: Correlations with other classroom behaviors and cognitive tests. *Child Development, 48,* 1411–1416.

Erikson, E. H. (1951). Sex differences in the play configurations of preadolescents. *American Journal of Orthopsychiatry, 21,* 667–692.

Feingold, A. (1988). Cognitive gender differences are disappearing. *American Psychologist, 43,* 95–103.

Fuys, D. J., & Liebow, A. K. (1993). Geometry and spatial sense. In R. J. Jensen & S. Wagner (Eds.), *Research ideas for the classroom: Early childhood mathematics* (pp. 45–62). New York: Macmillan.

Gallagher, A. M., DeLisi, R., Holst, P. C., McGillicuddy-DeLisi, Morely, M., & Cahalan, C. (2000). Gender differences in advanced mathematical problem solving. *Journal of Experimental Child Psychology, 78,* 165–190.

Geary, D. C., Saults, S. J., Liu, F., & Hoard, M. K. (2000). Sex differences in spatial cognition, computational fluency, and arithmetical reasoning. *Journal of Experimental Child Psychology, 77,* 337–353.

Geschwind, N., & Galaburda, A. M. (1987). *Cerebral lateralization.* Cambridge, MA: Bradford Books/MIT Press.

Govier, E., & Feldman, J. (1999). Occupational choice and patterns of cognitive abilities. *British Journal of Psychology, 90,* 99–108.

Halpern, D. F. (1992). *Sex differences in cognitive abilities* (2nd ed.). Hillsdale, NJ: Lawrence Erlbaum.

Halpern, D. F. (2000). *Sex differences in cognitive abilities* (3rd ed.). Hillsdale, NJ: Lawrence Erlbaum.

Hamilton, L. S., Nussbaum, E. M., Kupermintz, H., Kerkoven, J. I. M., & Snow, R. E. (1995). Enhancing the validity and usefulness of large-scale educational assessments: II. NELS:88 science achievement. *American Educational Research Journal, 32,* 555–581.

Hedges, L. V., & Nowell, A. (1995). Sex differences in mental test scores, variability, and numbers of high-scoring individuals. *Science, 269,* 41–45.

Hershkowitz, R., Parzysz, B., & Van Dormolen, J. (1996). In A. Bishop, K. Clements, C. Keitel, J. Kilpatrick, & C. Labore (Eds.), *International Handbook of Mathematics Education.* Norwell, MA: Kluwer Academic Publishers.

Humphreys, L. G., Lubinski, D., & Yao, G. (1993). Utility of predicting group membership and the role of spatial visualization in becoming an engineer, physical scientist, or artist. *Journal of Applied Psychology, 78,* 250–261.

Hyde, J. S., Fennema, E., & Lamon, S. J. (1990). Gender differences in mathematics performance: A meta-analysis. *Psychological Bulletin, 107,* 139–155.

Kalichman, S. C. (1988). Individual differences in water-level task performance: A component-skills analysis. *Developmental Review, 88,* 273–295.

Kimball, M. M. (1989). A new perspective on women's math achievement. *Psychological Bulletin, 105,* 198–214.

Li, C., Nuttall, R. L., & Zhao, S. (1999). The effect of writing Chinese characters on success on the water-level task. *Journal of Cross-Cultural Psychology, 30,* 91–105.

Liben, L. S., & Golbeck, S. L. (1984). Performance on Piagetian horizontality and verticality tasks: Sex-related difference in knowledge of relevant physical phenomena. *Developmental Psychology, 20,* 595–606.

Linn, M. C., & Petersen, A. C. (1985). Emergence and characterization of sex differences in spatial ability: A meta-analysis. *Child Development, 56,* 1479–1498.

Linn, M. C., & Petersen, A. C. (1986). A meta-analysis of gender differences in spatial ability: Implications for mathematics and science achievement. In J. S. Hyde & M. C. Linn (Eds.), *The psychology of gender: Advances through meta-analysis* (pp. 67–101). Baltimore: The Johns Hopkins University Press.

Lynn, R. (1992). Sex differences on the Differential Aptitude Test in British and American adolescents. *Educational Psychology, 12,* 101–106.

Marshall, S. P., & Smith, J. D. (1987). Sex differences in learning mathematics: A longitudinal study with item and error analyses. *Journal of Educational Psychology, 79,* 372–383.

Masters, M. S., & Sanders, B. (1993). Is the gender difference in mental rotation disappearing? *Behavior Genetics, 23,* 337–341.

National Council of Teachers of Mathematics. (2000). *Principles and standards for school mathematics.* Reston, VA: National Council of Teachers of Mathematics.

Oldfield, R. C. (1971). The assessment and analysis of handedness: the Edinburgh Handedness Inventory. *Neuropsychologia, 9,* 97–113.

Parsons, J. S., Adler, T. F., Futterman, R., Goff, S. R., Kaczala, C. M., Meece, J. L., & Midgley, C. (1980). *Self-perceptions, task perceptions, and academic choice: origins and change.* Washington, DC: Final Report to the National Institute of Education.

Pezaris, E., Casey, M. B., Nuttall, R. L., Bassi, J. C., Trzynski, M., Averna, S., & Galluccio, L. (1998). *Style of block building in boys and girls and its relationship to their spatial and mathematical skills.* Paper presented at the twenty-first annual mid-year meeting of the International Neuropsychological Society, Budapest, Hungary.

Quaiser-Pohl, C., & Lehmann, W. (2002). Girls' spatial abilities: Charting the contributions of experiences and attitudes in different academic groups. *British Journal of Educational Psychology, 72,* 245–260.

Robinson, N. M., Abbott, R. D., Berninger, V. W., & Busse, J. (1996). The structure of abilities in math-precocious young children: Gender similarities and differences. *Journal of Educational Psychology, 88,* 341–352.

Robinson, N. M., Abbott, R. D., Berninger, V. W., Busse, J., & Mukhopadhyay, S. (1997). Developmental changes in mathematically precocious young children: Longitudinal and gender effects. *Gifted Child Quarterly, 41,* 145–159.

Schiro, M., Casey, B., & Anderson, K. (2002). *Tan and the Shape Changer.* Chicago: The Wright Group/McGraw-Hill.

Secada, W. G., Fennema, E., & Adajian, L. B. (Eds.). (1995). *New directions for equity in mathematics education.* New York: Cambridge University Press.

Sherman, J. A. (1978). *Sex-related cognitive differences.* Springfield, IL: Charles C. Thomas.

Sholl, M. J. (1989). The relation between horizontality and rod-and-frame and vestibular navigational performance. *Journal of Experimental Psychology: Learning, Memory, and Cognition, 15,* 110–125.

Springer, S. P., & Deutsch, G. (1989). *Left brain, right brain.* New York: W. H. Freeman.

Stigler, J. W., & Hiebert, J. (1999). *The teaching gap: Best ideas from the world's teachers for improving education in the classroom.* New York: The Free Press.

Vandenberg, S. G., & Kuse, A. R. (1978). Mental rotations, a group test of three dimensional spatial visualization. *Perceptual and Motor Skills, 48,* 599–604.

Voyer, D., Voyer, S., & Bryden, M. P. (1995). Magnitude of sex differences in spatial abilities: A meta-analysis and consideration of critical variables. *Psychological Bulletin, 117,* 250–270.

Wachs, T. D. (1992). *The nature of nurture.* Newbury Park, CA: Sage.

Wheatley, G. H. (1990). Spatial sense and mathematics learning. *Arithmetic Teacher, 37,* 10–11.

Wigfield, A., & Meece, J. (1988). Math anxiety in elementary and secondary school students. *Journal of Educational Psychology, 80,* 210–216.

Willingham, W. W., & Cole, N. S. (1997). *Gender and fair assessment.* Mahwah, NJ: Erlbaum.

Wittig, M. A., & Allen, M. J. (1984). Measurement of adult performance on Piaget's water horizontality task. *Intelligence, 8,* 305–313.

Wolfgang, C. H., Stannard, L. L., & Jones, I. (2001). Block performance among preschoolers as a predictor of later school achievement in mathematics. *Journal of Research in Childhood Education, 15,* 173–181.

7

Examining Gender-Related Differential Item Functioning Using Insights From Psychometric and Multicontext Theory

Allan S. Cohen and Robert A. Ibarra

Why do men and women tend to perform differently on analytical portions of standardized tests? Psycho/social research often speculates that women's performance "might be more affected by such variables as role expectations or unjustified fears of incompetence" (Basinger, 1997, p. 2; see also Sternberg & Williams, 1997). This "unjustified fear" is similar to what Steele and Aronson (1995) call "stereotype threat" found among African American test takers. With a small number of subjects, and in laboratory conditions, Steele and Aronson found significant differences in test scores when they made only small changes in the directions for taking the test and in the explanations given to their subjects. Their research showed that, when African American college-level students were asked to take a test that had no direct consequence for them, their performance was equal to or better than that of majority test takers in the same group. However, when similar groups were told the outcomes of the same tests would affect them academically, performance levels among African American test takers dropped dramatically. According to Steele and Aronson, the perceived stereotypes associated with testing and other lab or classroom performances of women and minorities created this effect. Their findings suggest that hidden variables in the testing environment may have long-term effects on women and minority test takers.

Steele and Aronson's work clearly points to the impact of hidden variables such as these on test scores. The presence of these variables obviously represents unwanted sources of variation in the test scores, that is, variation unrelated to the purpose of the test, and can lead to potentially serious errors in estimation of examinees' abilities. The presence of one or more unwanted or nuisance dimensions is assumed to cause what is known as differential item functioning (DIF; Ackerman, 1992; Roussos & Stout, 1996). DIF is also sometimes known as item bias and arises when examinees of the same ability have different probabilities of responding correctly to a given question on a test (Pine, 1977). DIF is typically observed when nuisance dimensions are in some way associated with manifest examinee characteristics such as gender or ethnicity.

Psychometric efforts to examine gender-based DIF on mathematics items have focused largely on examination of differences as a function of membership in a manifest group such as gender or ethnicity (e.g., Carlton & Harris, 1989; Scheuneman & Gerritz, 1990; Wild & McPeek, 1986). This approach has been widely used to locate potentially biased items with an eye toward either removing them from the test or correcting the part(s) of the item that may be causing the bias. Some form of DIF analysis is generally used by most testing companies as part of the process of screening items, particularly during the item analysis stage. Unfortunately, knowing that examinees are members of a particular manifest group (e.g., male or female, or African American, Anglo,[1] or Hispanic/Latino) has not led to an understanding of why DIF occurs. In this chapter, we explore two approaches to examining differences in performance on test items, one developed from work on analysis of structural features of items and their relation to gender DIF taken from sociocultural theory and a second based in psychometric work on item response theory. The intent of this chapter is to illustrate how approaches such as these may lead to a more direct understanding of the causes of DIF.

We begin by considering some recent work using an approach to predicting DIF based on an analysis of structural characteristics of items. In the example, we focus on a model that considers responses to be a function of culturally based expectations embedded in item format and content (Ibarra & Cohen, 1999). Next, we consider an approach to detection of DIF based on consistencies in patterns of responses. These consistencies can be used to identify patterns of responses associated with groups that are latent in the data. Such latent groups are assumed to reflect differences in response strategies (Mislevy & Verhelst, 1990). Finally, we contrast this approach with the standard approach to DIF detection based on manifest group characteristics such as gender.

DIF as a Function of Item Characteristics

Much of the work on detection of DIF focuses on identification of differences in response patterns as a function of membership in a manifest group such as gender or ethnicity. An alternative to the standard approach of studying DIF based on manifest or latent groups is to examine DIF as a function of structural characteristics of items. This approach examines response tendencies as a function of cultural expectations embedded in structural characteristics of the items on the test. We begin by reviewing

---

[1] The term *Anglo*, according to the tenth edition of *Merriam Webster's Collegiate Dictionary*, is a shortened version of *Anglo-American* and refers to "a white inhabitant of the U.S. of non-Hispanic descent." In this chapter, the term is used as a synonym for *majority* and *white*.

work specifically based on the multicontext theory (Ibarra, 2001). Then we illustrate the use of the multicontext theory to predict gender DIF based on item characteristics.

Multicontext Theory

Multicontext theory (Ibarra, 2001) provides an explanation of ethnic and gender group differences in test and item performance as a function of differences in cognitive strategies (Ramírez, 1983, 1991, 1998, 1999; Ramírez & Castañeda, 1974) associated with a construct called *cultural context* (Hall, 1966, 1977). According to this explanation, DIF may be a result of a culture-based conflict between cultural context found in organizational cultures, the cultural context of ethnic and gender groups, and their respective cognitive expectations. The cultural context considered in this model includes the topics of the items and the format of the items. This conflict has been found to be associated with lower retention rates and poorer academic performance of Latinos in graduate education (Ibarra, 1996, 2001). The cultural conflict explanation has been useful in explaining some gender DIF (Ibarra & Cohen, 1999; Li, 2001).

Culture is described by Ibarra (2001) as the set of learned patterns of group behavior and values imprinted on individuals. As such, culture is not a single entity but a complex set of associated and interlinked systems that mold and shape individuals within groups (in ways that are not unlike imprinting), and this process begins at birth (Hall, 1974, 1993). Thus, people raised in different cultures live in different sensory worlds often unaware of how these worlds differ (Hall, 1959).

These patterns play an important role in people's learning, thinking, and communication. Hall (1959, 1966, 1977, 1984, 1992, 1993) identified high-context cultures existing in the United States as consisting predominantly of females and certain ethnic minorities, and low-context cultures as predominantly from northern European ethnic groups and majority males. Individuals from high-context cultures tend to focus on streams of information surrounding an event, situation, or social interaction in order to extract meaning from the context in which it occurs. Individuals from low-context cultures, in contrast, tend to focus on words and objective facts rather than the conditions surrounding an event, situation, or interaction. In high-context cultures, nonverbal signals are used frequently, communication is indirect, messages are implicit, and personal commitment to people is high. In low-context cultures, however, messages tend to be carried more by words than by nonverbal cues, communication is generally more direct, messages more explicit, and personal commitment to people is somewhat lower.

According to multicontext theory, people from different culture contexts have culturally different ways of learning and thinking. The process of learning a culture helps shape how people are expected to think and behave within a specific cultural (e.g., ethnic or gender) group. Another framework is a function of social transactions, relationships, activities, or emotional interactions between various people both inside and outside a group. A culturally coherent group will tend to manifest a discernible set of cognitive and cultural expectations that can be identified as high or low context. For individuals from high-context cultures, for example, knowledge is a gestalt; facts are embedded in situations and integrated in structures not easily separated for analysis. High-context individuals usually prefer to work in groups for shared learning and problem solving. In contrast, for individuals from low-context cultures, knowledge is less socially based and more rational; facts are derived by objective analysis. Reality is elemental, fragmented, compartmentalized, and easier to analyze. Low-context individuals usually prefer to approach tasks and learning individually. Ibarra (2001) suggested that the conflict between the cultural context represented in an item and the cultural expectations of the examinee may be a cause of DIF on standardized tests.

Unique Characteristics of Multicontext Theory

Multicontext theory is clearly a departure from current assumptions about ethnic and gender diversity associated with standardized testing. A brief comparison of these perspectives is relevant to our analysis. Most current explanations of ethnic and gender DIF are based on affirmative action principals and multicultural concepts. An implicit assumption underlying such initiatives is that social systems are inherently discriminatory toward underrepresented populations. Removing those barriers helps to diminish or eliminate institutional racism, the implied origin of stereotype threats (Steel & Aronson, 1995). The assumption is that, in time, the academic performance gaps among specific ethnic or gender groups should also diminish.

A longitudinal study by Bowen & Bok (1998) on the benefits of affirmative action on undergraduates attending Ivy League schools questions these assumptions. Results from Bowen & Bok show that ethnic minorities, particularly African Americans, have benefited greatly from race-sensitive admissions policies since 1968. However, the data on average cumulative grade point average (GPA) by groups also show that even after controlling for variables such as gender, ethnicity, socioeconomic status, standardized test scores, and high school grades, African Americans' and Hispanic/Latinos' GPAs were lower relative to their college graduating class, compared with majority students (Bowen & Bok, 1998). In essence, the study showed that among ethnically diverse undergraduate populations with similar socioeconomic profiles, traditionally underrepresented populations continued to "underperform" despite the benefits provided them by affirmative action initiatives.

Multicontext theory suggests that such gaps in academic performance may be the result of less obvious variables in academic culture. The theory does not assume that self defined or other-defined groups (e.g., governmentally defined ethnic categories) are the appropriate populations to be examined for explaining the cause and effects associated with academic underperformance or differential item functioning on standardized tests. Rather, other variables related to cultural context and cognition may have equal, if not greater, importance on academic performance outcomes. The theory proposes that among test taker populations of significant size, there are latent groups of high- and low-context populations that include all categories of examinees, including women, minorities, and even Anglo males. The groups of high-context populations that tend to do less well on standardized tests, also tend to be comprised largely, although not entirely of traditionally underrepresented ethnic and gender populations. Thus, structural features of tests or test items that reflect low-context culture will also negatively affect these same underrepresented groups. According to multicontext theory, the conflicts generating academic performance gaps and differential testing outcomes is related to differences between a relatively static low-context academic culture and the more fluid high-context cultures. The stress generated by high-stakes testing situations and the conflict between academic and individual cultural contexts may be important variables for explaining the results found in stereotype threat research.

Detection of DIF

Li (2001) described an attempt to use the multicontext model for identifying characteristic features of mathematics test items that were likely to be associated with gender DIF. Li began by first using a standard approach to DIF detection using the likelihood ratio test (Thissen, Steinberg, & Wainer, 1988, 1993). Data from the 1998 form of a university mathematics placement test were first examined for gender DIF. Estimates of item parameters for the three-parameter logistic model were computed using the computer program MULTILOG (Thissen, 1991). The placement test was designed to measure entering freshmen's competence in high school mathematics in order to provide university instructors with information about students' preparation. The full test consisted of Sections A, B, and C. Section A had 32 operational items and measured preparation in arithmetic, basic algebra, and intuitive geometry. Section B consisted of 32 operational items and measured algebra, advanced algebra, geometry, and statistics. Section C was not used but consisted of 36 operational items and measured advanced algebra, analytic geometry, trigonometry, and geometry. All items were multiple choice.

Items found to function differentially between gender groups were next examined and a post hoc coding scheme was developed based on the multicontext model. The resulting coding scheme (described in Table 7.1) consisted of two components, a social-cultural component, and a mathematical

TABLE 7.1. *Coding Scheme Based on Multicontext Theory*

Coding Categories	Cultural Context Involved
I. Social cultural domain	
The nature of the topic 1. Is it a female-oriented topic? 2. Is it a male-oriented topic?	In general, females/males are more likely to do better on problems that involve topics that are of interest to them (e.g., females may do better on topics such as the cost of a dress on sale). If the topic of the problem is of interest to both females and males, or is a combination of female topic and male topic, then it does not necessarily favor a particular gender group.	a) **Information:** For low-context (LC) individuals, information can be separated from context. For high-context (HC) individuals, information without context is meaningless and unreliable. b) **Association:** Personal commitment to people, and community is high for HC people, and commitment is low to people and community for LC people.
Real world application 3. Is the problem one with a real world content or context? 4. Is the problem one with practical application?	Problems that have a real world content or context, or have practical applications, are less likely to be biased against females.	a) **Academic systems:** Scientific thinking is emphasized for LC individuals. They value examining ideas rather than broad comprehension of real world applications. Practical thinking is valued among HC individuals. They value application of knowledge in real world events. b) **Learning:** LC prefer analytical thinking using the inductive reasoning process. They focus on compiling details. HC prefer comprehensive thinking using deductive reasoning. They use expanded thinking ("big picture" actions, ideas, and/or complex forms).
Spatial reasoning 5. Does the question involve an object? (if not, go to #8)	If the item involves an object (e.g., a graph) and the object is one that is commonly found in the real world or has practical application, it is less likely to be biased against females.	**Information:** LC separated from context, HC meaningless when separated from context and real world application.

6. Is the object one commonly found in the real world?
7. Is the object one has practical application?

II. Mathematic problem domain

Algebra or geometry
8. Is the problem a geometry question?
9. Is the problem an algebra question?
10. Can the problem be solved by geometry?
11. Can the problem be solved by algebra?

Definition-based question
12. Is the problem a definition-based question?

In general, males are more likely to do better on geometry problems, and females are more likely to do better on algebra problems. However, some other characteristics of the questions could change that outcome. Therefore, we needed to first classify the question either as geometry or algebra or both. Next, we coded the question on the following categories:

Definition-based questions are questions that can only be solved based on some definitions. Definition-based questions tend to favor LC individuals and do not favor HC people because HC people do not learn using the same strategies used by LC individuals.

a) **Learning:** LC learn best by following directions. They assemble or combine facts according to rules they memorize. HC people learn best by demonstration. They learn by hands-on methods, observing and mimicking others, practicing mentally and physically, and demonstrating to others.

b) **Association:** LC people are task oriented. Things get done when everyone follows policies and procedures, and pays attention to a goal. HC people are more process oriented. Getting things done depends on one's relationship with people and attention to the group process.

(continued)

TABLE 7.1. (*continued*)

Coding Categories	Cultural Context Involved
Indefinite answer question 13. Is a definite answer given in the item?	If the item involves an indefinite answer, females are less likely to do well. Indefinite answers would include choices such as "none of the above" or choices that ask the examinee to give a possible value for a mathematics problem.
Symbol problems 14. Does the item contain unfamiliar or confusing symbols?	HC people are more likely to do better on items containing some unfamiliar symbols. This could happen if a problem contained inconsistent references to unknowns, such as mixing up x, y, and z and also a, b, c, and d in the same item.
Mathematical reasoning 15. Does the question focus on reasoning?	Females are less likely to do better on items in which mathematical reasoning is involved. This is because HC people focus on application of knowledge in real world events rather than analytical thinking.
	Learning: HC people gain knowledge by gestalt model. Facts are perceived as complete units embedded in the context of situations. When the problem involves some ambiguity, it is difficult for the HC people to analyze the information.
	Learning: HC people focus on expanded thinking ("big picture" ideas or complex forms). They have few problems in translating messages symbolically.
	a) Academics: LC people values examining ideas rather than broad comprehension of real world applications. HC people values application of knowledge in real world events. **b) Learning:** LC people prefer analytical thinking using the inductive reasoning process. They focus on compiling details. HC prefer comprehensive thinking using deductive reasoning. They use expanded thinking ("big picture" actions, ideas, and/or complex forms).

Congruity

16. Is there a congruity between the question and the answer?

An incongruity arises when the answer choices do not follow logically from the question. In an item with an incongruity, the choices do not seem to have anything to do with the problem given in the stem, and the answers in the choices do not lead directly from the stem (e.g., an item includes a real world context in the stem, but the choices are complex mathematical statements that would not be a common answer in the real world context presented in the stem). HC people are less likely to do better if there is an incongruity between the question and the answer.

Temporality: For HC people, synchrony (congruity) is important. Body movement while interacting with others is consciously or unconsciously synchronized (kinesics). (Physical synchronicity carries over into physical presentation of items and answer choices.) For LC people, synchrony (congruity) is not important. They are less likely to consciously or unconsciously synchronize body movements while interacting with others.

Connection between answers and solutions

17. Does the answer choice indicate how the solution was obtained?

Females (and HC individuals in general) are more likely to do better on mathematical problems if the answer choices indicate how the solution was obtained (e.g., the perimeter of a figure composed of rectilinear and semicircular parts can be found by adding the perimeters of the two parts together, and this is indicated by the answer choices).

Learning: HC gain knowledge by gestalt model. Facts are perceived as complete units (gestalts) embedded in the context of situations or experiences.

problem component. In the social-cultural component, the following three features of the item were considered:

1. *The Nature of the Topic.* Females are more likely to do better on problems that involve topics that are of interest to females (e.g., the cost of a dress on sale), and males are more likely to do better on problems that involve topics that are of interest to males (e.g., race cars). If the topic of the problem is of interest to both females and males, or is a combination of female topic and male topic, then it does not necessarily favor a particular gender group.

2. *Real-World Applicability.* Females are less likely to function differentially on an item if it contains a practical application or is posed in a real-world content or context.

3. *Spatial Reasoning.* An item that involves an object, such as a graph, which is also commonly found in the real world, or if there is a practical application posed in the problem, the item is less likely to be biased against females.

In the mathematical problem component, there were seven features of the item that were considered:

1. *Algebra or Geometry.* Females are more likely to perform better on algebra problems, and males are more likely to do better on geometry problems. This feature can be mitigated, however, by other characteristics of the item.

2. *Definition-Based Question.* Questions that are definition based are ones that need to be solved by reference to a definition. Males are generally favored by this type of item.

3. *Indefinite Answer Questions.* Females are less likely to do well if the item involves an indefinite answer. Indefinite answers would include choices such as "none of the above" or choices that ask the examinee to give a possible value for a mathematics problem.

4. *Symbol Problems.* Females are more likely to do better on items containing some unfamiliar symbols. This could happen in a problem that contained inconsistent references to unknowns, such as mixing up x, y, and z and also a, b, c, and d in the same item.

5. *Mathematical Reasoning.* Females are less likely to do better on items in which pure mathematical reasoning is involved. This is because high-context individuals tend to focus on application of knowledge in real-world situations rather than on strictly analytical problems.

6. *Congruity.* An incongruity arises in an item when the answer choices do not follow logically or directly from the stem (e.g., an item includes a real world context in the stem, but the choices are complex mathematical statements that would not be a common answer or response in the real world context presented in the stem). Females and high-context individuals

are less likely to do better if there is an incongruity between the question and the answer.

7. *Connection Between Answers and Solutions*. Females (and high-context individuals in general) are more likely to do better on mathematical problems if the answer choices indicate how the solution was obtained (e.g., the perimeter of a figure composed of rectilinear and semicircular parts can be found by adding the perimeters of the two parts together, and this is indicated by the answer choices).

Li then applied the coding scheme in Table 7.1 to a different form of the test administered to a different sample of examinees and used the results to predict gender DIF. Items for this second part of the Li study came from the Spring 2000 administration of the placement test and item response data for a sample of 2,000 examinees (1,000 males and 1,000 females) were randomly drawn from the sample of approximately 11,350 students who took Sections A and B of this test. Interrater agreement between the two raters was 0.94.

The likelihood ratio test for DIF detected 26 DIF items, 15 on Section A and 11 on Section B (see Table 7.2). Comparisons between the difficulty parameters indicated that 15 items favored males (7 on Section A and 7 on Section B) and 9 items favored females (8 on Section A and 4 on Section B). DIF items favoring females measured basic algebra (e.g., multiplication and factoring, formulas and expressions, positive integer exponents, linear equations) and algebra (e.g., factoring quadratics, rational expressions). One female DIF arithmetic item measured ratio, proportion, and percent. The 15 male DIF items measured intuitive geometry (e.g., perimeters of polygons and circles, areas of polygons and circles, measuring solids, basic vocabulary, sum of angles in a triangle), advanced algebra (e.g., absolute value, systems of linear equations and verbal problem set up, solution and interpretation), and geometry (e.g., properties of circles, Pythagorean relationships, incidental properties). In addition, two male DIF items measured arithmetic (fractions) and algebra (graphs).

A measure of the effect size of DIF was calculated based on the Mantel-Haenszel D-DIF (MH D-DIF) index (Holland, 1985; Holland & Thayer, 1988). This index is calculated as MH D-DIF $= -2.35 \log(\hat{\alpha}_{MH})$ where $\hat{\alpha}_{MH}$ is the Mantel-Haenszel (adjusted) odds-ratio estimator. An index of 0 indicates absence of DIF, positive values indicate the item favors the focal group (females were the focal group in this analysis), and negative values indicate the item favors the reference group. The MH D-DIF indices for all items are given in Table 7.2 along with the multicontext scores. Zieky (1993) describes the following MH D-DIF classification rules used at Educational Testing Service: Category A DIF, negligible DIF for MH D-DIF not different from zero and values of less than 1.0; Category B DIF, MH D-DIF different from zero and an absolute value of at least 1 and either less

TABLE 7.2. *DIF Results for Li (2002)*

Item No.	Cultural Context Score	MH D DIF Index	Item No.	Cultural Context Score	MH D DIF Index
A1	8.00	−0.35	B1	10.00	−0.53
A2	12.00	0.24	B2	10.00	0.40
A3	10.00	0.08	B3	9.00	−1.61
A4	4.00	−1.13	B4	10.00	−0.06
A5	10.00	0.11	B5	7.00	−1.05
A6	8.00	−0.25	B6	8.00	−0.37
A7	12.00	1.08	B7	4.00	−1.11
A8	5.00	−0.75	B8	11.00	0.32
A9	5.00	−0.27	B9	9.00	0.24
A11	12.00	0.91	B11	9.50	−0.08
A12	11.00	0.61	B12	10.00	0.02
A13	10.00	0.22	B13	11.00	−0.07
A14	4.50	−1.68	B14	5.00	−0.68
A15	12.00	0.85	B15	10.00	0.18
A16	8.00	−0.11	B16	11.00	0.76
A17	10.00	0.18	B17	8.00	0.22
A18	4.50	−0.70	B18	10.00	0.39
A19	9.50	−0.32	B19	11.00	0.48
A21	10.00	0.39	B21	9.50	0.20
A22	5.00	−0.42	B22	11.00	0.59
A23	9.00	0.76	B23	10.00	0.43
A24	11.50	0.36	B24	11.00	0.79
A25	4.50	−0.72	B25	3.50	−0.86
A26	11.00	−0.01	B26	10.00	0.34
A27	9.00	−0.69	B27	9.00	0.32
A28	12.00	0.72	B28	11.00	0.50
A29	6.50	−0.39	B29	7.00	−0.99
A31	8.00	0.14	B31	10.00	−0.04
A32	10.00	0.31	B32	10.00	−0.04
A33	11.00	0.71	B33	10.00	0.02
A34	4.50	−0.51	B34	9.00	0.50
A35	11.00	0.16	B35	10.00	0.15

than 1.5 or not significantly greater than 1.0; and Category C MH D-DIF, significantly greater than 1.0 and absolute value of 1.5 or higher.

Multicontext scores for all 64 items ranged from 3.5 to 12 (M = 8.95, SD = 2.41). According to multicontext theory, items with high multicontext scores are likely to favor females, and items with low cultural context scores are likely to favor males. In this study, Li used one standard deviation above the mean or higher (11.36 or higher) to predict female DIF, and one standard deviation below the mean or lower (6.54 or lower) to predict male DIF. Using these cut-off scores, 6 female DIF items and 12 male DIF items were predicted.

TABLE 7.3. *Comparison of DIF Predictions by Multicontext Method and DIF Detections by Likelihood Ratio Test*

	Detected DIF			
Predicted DIF	**Male DIF**	**No DIF**	**Female DIF**	**Total**
Male DIF	10	6	0	16
No DIF	2	34	2	38
Female DIF	0	6	4	10
Total	12	46	6	64

Comparisons of DIF, predicted by the multicontext coding scheme and DIF detected by the likelihood ratio test are shown in Table 7.3. The multicontext coding scheme was correct in 76% of the predictions of male DIF, female DIF, or no DIF. MH D-DIF indices for items detected as DIF were all above 0.40.

Characteristics of Items That Were Correctly Predicted to Function Differentially

Items A4, A8, A14, A18, A22, A25, A34, B7, B14, and B25 were detected as DIF items favoring males and were correctly predicted to have male DIF. Items A8, A14, B7, B14, and B25 were predicted to have male DIF and had one or more of the following characteristics: contained an object, required multiple solutions or shortcuts, required mathematical reasoning, included a definition-based question, or involved conversion of a word problem to a spatial representation. In addition, item A4 also contained an indefinite answer, items A18, A22, and A25 required definition-based solutions, and item A34 required mathematical reasoning.

Items A7, A11, A15, and A28 were detected as DIF favoring females and were correctly predicted as having female DIF. These items had one or more of the following characteristics: included a female-oriented topic, was a typical textbook question, contained confusing symbols, required reading mathematics, consisted of pure algebraic manipulation, or the answer choice indicated how the solution was obtained. Items A11 and A28 both measured basic algebra, involved reading mathematics, contained possibly confusing symbols, and had answer choices that indicated how the solution was obtained. Items A7 and A15 both contained symbols that could be considered confusing and had answer choices that indicated how the solution was obtained.

Items A27, B3, and B5 were detected as male DIF but were missed by the multicontext coding scheme. These items were phrased as textbook-like questions. Items A27 and B3 required processing verbal information. Item B3 also required multiple steps, accuracy, and a systematic approach to arriving at the correct solution. Item B5 was one for which a quick solution could be insightful and one for which good test-taking skills could contribute to a faster solution. It also contained an object, had more than one solution path to the correct answer, and the choices did not provide a definite answer.

Items A12, A23, A33, B16, B22, B24, and B28 were detected as female DIF but were missed by the coding scheme. These items were also typical textbook questions. In addition, item A33 involved reading mathematics, consisted of multiple steps, and required accuracy and a systematic approach to arrive at the correct solution, item B16 involved reading mathematics and pure algebraic manipulation, and item B24 involved pure algebraic manipulation.

Items A9 and A29 were predicted as male DIF but were not detected as DIF by the likelihood ratio test. Item A9 was a geometry item, phrased as a typical textbook-like question, and contained an object not commonly found in the real world. Item A29 was also a geometry item, was phrased as a typical textbook-like question, and involved conversion of a word problem to an algebraic expression. Items A2 and A24 were predicted as female DIF, but were not detected as DIF by the likelihood ratio test. Item A2 was an algebra question, phrased as a typical textbook question, required accuracy and a systematic approach with multiple steps, and the answer choice indicated how the solution was obtained. Item A24 was an algebra word problem, phrased as a typical textbook question, contained information likely to be more familiar to females, had a real world, practical application, and there was congruity between the question and the answer choices.

Conclusion

The results of Li's study were consistent with previous work by Ibarra & Cohen (1999) on a reading comprehension test. Structural features of items appear to be useful markers for predicting gender DIF. Similar results are reported by Gierl, Bisanz, Bisanz, & Boughton (2002) using coding schemes developed from work from a cognitive processing perspective used to study gender differences developed by Gallagher and her colleagues (Gallagher, 1998; Gallagher & DeLisi, 1994; Gallagher, Morley, & Levin, 1999). For example, Gallagher & DeLisi (1994) report that males and females tend to use different strategies to solve mathematics problems. Females were more likely to use conventional strategies, and males were more likely to use unconventional strategies to solve problems. Problems classified as conventional were similar to routine textbook problems, could be solved with straightforward use of an algorithm, and were more likely to be solved by females. Problems classified as unconventional either required an unusual use of a familiar algorithm or use of some type of estimation or insight. Solution strategies were also categorized as conventional, if they were the same as or closely similar to strategies taught in mathematics class, and as unconventional otherwise. Although Gallagher's work focuses on gender differences and not gender DIF, it still offers clearly useful insights as to what may be causing gender DIF.

Detection of Differences in Cognitive Response Strategies

Psychometric work designed to explain the occurrence of gender DIF has suggested that some DIF may be associated with differences in use of response strategies (Cohen & Bolt, in press). These differences are assumed to reflect the presence of some unwanted source of variation intruding on the assessment of the intended ability. When examinees use different response strategies to solve the same items, standard unidimensional item response theory (IRT) models do not accurately describe the relationship between propensity to give a particular response and underlying ability (Mislevy & Verhelst, 1990). The result is that the underlying ability being measured is confounded with differences in response strategies.

Mixture IRT models assume that, although a general IRT model holds for an entire population of respondents, different parameter values may apply for different latent classes of examinees in that population. Examinees are thus characterized in a mixture model by both a latent ability parameter and by a parameter indicating latent group membership. The discrete nature of the latent groups identified by these models makes it easier to interpret why differences in responses might have occurred. Below, we describe some characteristics of mixture models and then illustrate their use in two contexts, a speededness context, and a gender DIF context.

Mixture IRT Models

Mixture IRT models have been found to be useful for helping to identify latent groups of examinees such that local independence holds within groups (Bolt, 1999). These models also have been found to be useful for understanding item performance when latent groups are defined as a function of cognitive strategies (Mislevy & Verhelst, 1990) or demonstrate different skills needed to solve test items (Rost, 1990). Mixture models have also been suggested for use in investigating how qualitative examinee differences, such as use of different problem-solving strategies, may lead to differences in responses to test items (Embretson & Reise, 2000). In addition, work with a mixture nominal response model has demonstrated that it is possible to detect different latent classes in multiple-choice data and to obtain diagnostic information about examinees based on their class membership (Bolt, Cohen, & Wollack, 2002). Mixture IRT models enable us to discretize examinees along one or more secondary (usually nuisance) dimensions. Within each latent group, the underlying ability is no longer determined by a combination of the ability being measured and the secondary dimension(s).

Mixture Model Analysis of Test Speededness

Below, we present an illustration of the use of a simple mixture model, the mixture Rasch model (MRM; Rost, 1990), to identify examinees for whom the time limits of a test may present a problem. We motivate this illustration by the following: when tests are administered under timed conditions, examinees' performances can sometimes be affected by speededness. For some examinees, the effect of the change in response strategy is that they do more poorly at the end of the test, where speededness is most likely to affect their responses (Yamamoto & Everson, 1997). The impact of this kind of speededness is to change the response strategies these examinees use for selecting their responses. The result is that the estimates of the difficulties of item parameters, particularly those in speeded locations, such as near the end of the test, are affected (Oshima, 1994). The nuisance dimension in this case is associated with the change in response strategy due to the speededness of the test. Bolt, Cohen, & Wollack (2002) describe a strategy using a MRM for reducing the impact of speededness on item parameter estimates. The Bolt et al. (2002) approach used a MRM to identify examinees for whom the test is speeded and those for whom it is not.

Mixture Rasch Model

The MRM considers an examinee population that is assumed to be composed of a fixed number of discrete latent classes of examinees. A Rasch model is assumed to hold within each class, but each class has different item difficulty parameters. Members of a class may also differ in ability. The MRM describes each examinee with a class membership parameter, g, which determines the relative difficulty ordering of the items for that examinee, and a continuous latent ability parameter in class g, θ_g which affects the number of items the examinee is expected to answer correctly.

Modeling Speededness with Ordinal Constraints

Bolt et al. (2002) describe a two-class MRM in which ordinal constraints were used to identify two classes of examinees: a speeded class, consisting of examinees whose performance on the test declined at the end of the test, and a nonspeeded class, composed of examinees for whom no change in performance occurred. Constraints on the MRM were set so that 18 items near the beginning of the test, in positions considered as nonspeeded, were equal in difficulty for both the speeded and the nonspeeded group, and eight items at the end of the test, in positions considered to be speeded, were more difficult for examinees in the speeded group. The percentages of examinees in both classes were estimated, along with the difficulties of the items in the speeded locations.

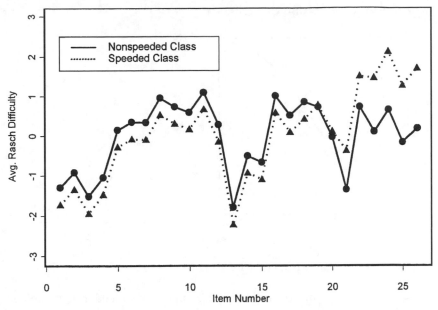

FIGURE 7.1. Plot of difficulties for twenty-six items on Form A.

Responses of 1,000 examinees to 26 precalculus items on Form A of the test were analyzed using this constrained MRM. Results indicated that about 24% of the examinees fell into the speeded group and the remaining 76% fell into the nonspeeded group. There was a significant relationship between membership in the speeded or nonspeeded class and ethnicity but not gender. That is, no gender differences were found between latent groups. The proportion of Anglo examinees, however, was greater in the nonspeeded group than minority examinees.

The nonspeeded group had an average ability of −0.35 compared with the average ability of 0.12 for the speeded group. The difficulties of the 26 items on Form A are plotted in Fig. 7.1. Note that the difficulties for the first 18 items in the speeded and nonspeeded groups differ by 0.47. This is the difference in average ability between the speeded and nonspeeded groups. The higher difficulties for the eight end-of-test items reflect this same difference in ability, as well as the speededness effect.

Six of the eight items at the end of the test appeared earlier, in non-speeded locations, on Form B of the test (see Fig. 7.2). A second sample of 1,000 was randomly drawn from those examinees who had taken Form B. The test characteristic curves (TCCs) for these six items are computed from item parameters estimated for the speeded and nonspeeded

Average Across Samples

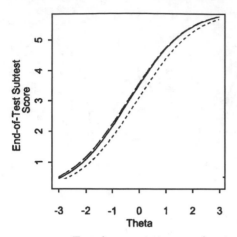

FIGURE 7.2. Test characteristic curve for six end-of-test items.

groups on Form A and for the same six items in nonspeeded locations on Form B.

The TCC for the speeded group taking Form A is clearly lower than for the other two groups, the nonspeeded group taking Form A and the group taking Form B. Although the TCCs for the nonspeeded group taking Form A and the group taking Form B are not completely overlapping, they are very close and indicate the improvement in item parameter estimation that resulted from this kind of analysis.

Characteristics of Examinees in Speeded and Nonspeeded Groups

An important feature of mixture model analysis is that once examinees have been classed into discrete latent groups, these groups are now manifest so we can then directly examine the characteristics of the different groups. With this in mind, the same MRM used by Bolt et al. (2002) was used by Cohen, Wollack, Bolt, & Mroch (2002) to first identify speeded and nonspeeded groups, and then to study academic and background characteristics of individuals in each class on two precalculus forms of a mathematics placement test. The focus of this analysis was on examining characteristics of examinees in the nonspeeded and speeded groups rather than solely on improving estimation of item difficulty parameters.

Two different samples of data were analyzed using the two-group MRM: one sample consisted of 3,000 randomly selected examinees from a total sample of 13,102 who took Form A and a second consisted of 3,000 randomly selected examinees from the 7,073 examinees who had taken Form B during the same test administration. Eight items at the end of Form A were

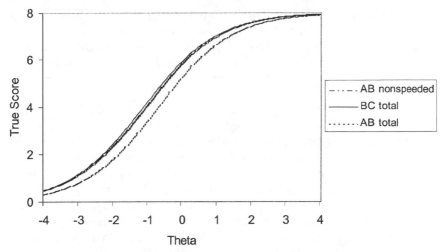

FIGURE 7.3. Sample English usage test items.

constrained to be harder for the members of the speeded group. On Form B, however, these same eight items were located in nonspeeded locations on the test and so were constrained to be equal for members of the speeded and nonspeeded groups.

Results were consistent with those from Bolt et al. (2002). The TCC for the eight items computed for the nonspeeded examinees at the end of Form A were similar to the TCC for the same eight items for all examinees taking Form B (see Fig. 7.3). Item difficulty estimates from the nonspeeded group taking Form A were similar to estimates from the group taking Form B. The TCCs in Fig. 7.3 for the nonspeeded group taking Form A and for the group taking Form B nearly overlap. Although the item difficulties were not exactly the same, the TCCs in Fig. 7.3 illustrate how close the resulting scores based on these difficulty estimates actually were in the three groups.

Classification of the remaining 10,102 examinees taking Form A and the remaining 4,073 examinees taking Form B were done using the model parameters estimated above, from the two-group MRM analyses. The results were consistent with results from Bolt et al. (2002). No gender differences in class membership were present for the 13,102 examinees taking Form A; however, there was a tendency for females taking Form B to be in the nonspeeded group and for males to be in the speeded group ($p < 0.05$).

Some differences were also noted in ability between the latent groups. In Tables 7.4 A and 7.4 B, results are presented for comparisons between males and females and between speeded and nonspeeded groups. All differences in Tables 7.4 A and 7.4 B were significant at $p < 0.01$ although effect sizes were generally small. Still, the results in these tables were consistent with previous research on gender differences. Females tend to do better than males on measures of verbal ability, such as the ACT-English test and a university English placement test, and less well than males on tests of mathematics ability, such as the ACT-Mathematics test. Females tend to do better, however, on indicators of academic achievement than males, such as grade point average (GPA), number of degree credits earned, and even mathematics GPA.

In addition, there were consistent differences, albeit generally small ones between the speeded and nonspeeded groups. On both Forms A and B, examinees in the speeded class performed better on the test as a whole, although not on the speeded items. They also scored higher on their university entrance examinations and placement tests, performed better in their university courses, and made faster progress toward their degrees. These results, which are somewhat more pronounced on Form B (see Table 7.4B), indicate that, although examinees in the speeded group were of higher ability and had higher levels of course-related achievement than examinees in the nonspeeded group, they did not demonstrate this on end-of-test items.

Gender differences were not found between latent speeded and nonspeeded groups. Efforts to study gender differences in the context of DIF revealed some surprising results. Next, we explore the use of mixture models to study gender DIF.

Mixture Model Analysis of Gender DIF

Once a DIF item has been identified, little is known about the examinees for whom the item functions differentially. This is because DIF is typically defined based on manifest group characteristics (e.g., as defined by characteristics such as ethnic group or gender) that are associated with, but do not explain why, examinees respond differentially to items. Mixture IRT models provide us with a mechanism for modeling DIF so it is possible to determine which examinees are actually favored by a DIF item and which are not. Cohen and Bolt (in press) present two approaches to studying DIF using mixture IRT models. In the first approach, the standard DIF approach used to analyze response patterns on a mathematics placement test were for gender DIF. Ordinal constraints were then imposed in a mixture model similar to the constraints in the two speededness studies discussed above, only this time using the pattern of DIF and non-DIF items. In the second approach, an alternative to the standard DIF assessment was described that first defines the dimension according to which DIF occurs and then looks at examinee characteristics associated with that dimension in an attempt to understand the occurrence of DIF.

Standard DIF Assessment
Responses from two samples of 1,000 examinees, each consisting of 500 males and 500 females, were randomly drawn from a sample of 5,249 students who took a 32-item arithmetic and elementary algebra section

TABLE 7.4.A. *Demographic and Achievement-Related Characteristics of Latent Groups for Form A*

| | Gender | | | | | | Latent Group | | | | | |
| | Male | | Female | | Effect | | Speeded | | Non-Speeded | | Effect |
Variable	Mean (SD)	N	Mean (SD)	N	Size		Mean (SD)	N	Mean (SD)	N	Size
High school variables											
Foreign language units	3.12 (1.13)	535	3.41 (1.15)	1,060	0.25						
College entrance examination & placement test scores											
ACT – English	23.73 (3.89)	422	24.95 (3.73)	916	0.32						
ACT – Mathematics	23.97 (3.57)	422	22.93 (3.27)	916	0.31						
English Placement Test	615.47 (84.47)	475	639.07 (81.89)	936	0.29						
College achievement data											
First semester GPA[a]	2.64 (0.76)	527	2.82 (0.77)	1,054	0.24						
Cumulative GPA	2.72 (0.74)	535	2.97 (0.68)	1,062	0.36		2.98 (0.65)	314	2.87 (0.73)	1,283	0.15
Degree credits	95.62 (37.47)	535	103.13 (36.83)	1,062	0.20		106.06 (31.44)	314	99.28 (38.37)	1,283	0.18
Transfer credits	7.73 (12.18)	535	10.21 (12.29)	1,062	0.20						
Failure credits	1.19 (2.93)	535	0.56 (2.11)	1,062	0.26						
Mathematics GPA	2.09 (0.99)	426	2.38 (1.00)	750	0.29		2.42 (0.96)	229	2.24 (1.01)	947	0.18

[a] GPA = Grade point average.

TABLE 7.4.B. *Demographic and Achievement-Related Characteristics of Latent Groups for Form B*

	Gender						Latent Group			
	Male		Female				Speeded		Nonspeeded		
Variable	Mean (SD)	N	Mean (SD)	N	Effect Size	Mean (SD)	N	Mean (SD)	N	Effect Size
High school variables										
Rank in class	39.96 (46.52)	1,534	32.56 (40.53)	1,289	0.17					
Biology units	1.35 (0.58)	1,536	1.47 (0.66)	1,290	0.20					
Chemistry units	1.28 (0.50)	434	1.21 (0.50)	2,392	0.13					
Physics units	0.99 (0.45)	1,536	0.83 (0.48)	1,290	0.34					
Foreign language units	3.42 (1.09)	1,535	3.69 (1.03)	1,287	0.25					
College entrance examination & placement test scores										
ACT – Composite	28.17 (2.81)	398	26.95 (3.29)	2,237	0.38					
ACT – English	25.84 (3.78)	1,417	26.48 (3.79)	1,218	0.17	26.96 (3.53)	398	25.99 (3.83)	2,237	0.26
ACT – Mathematics	28.30 (3.47)	1,417	26.68 (3.57)	1,218	0.46	28.88 (2.91)	398	27.31 (3.67)	2,237	0.44
ACT – Reading	28.25 (4.68)	398	27.24 (4.83)	2,237	0.21					
SAT – Mathematics	667.27 (64.73)	433	624.49 (73.84)	341	0.62	677.50 (58.92)	144	641.78 (73.16)	630	0.50
English Placement Test	656.97 (84.21)	1,385	673.88 (87.80)	1,178	0.20	684.19 (85.17)	387	661.28 (86.03)	2,176	0.27
French Placement Test	485.92 (112.65)	141	538.65 (117.28)	213	0.46					
College Algebra Test	707.74 (96.43)	1,536	673.38 (94.32)	1,290	0.36	735.52 (76.06)	434	684.17 (98.28)	2,392	0.54
Trigonometry Test	715.31 (96.66)	1,536	675.53 (101.66)	1,290	0.40	727.00 (86.67)	434	691.74 (102.38)	2,392	0.35
Coollege achievement data										
First semester GPA	2.99 (0.75)	1,534	3.11 (0.70)	1,283	0.17					
Cumulative GPA	2.97 (0.69)	1,536	3.16 (0.66)	1,290	0.27					
Transfer credits	9.70 (11.07)	1,536	12.67 (12.08)	1,290	0.26					
Failure credits	0.87 (2.81)	1,536	0.34 (1.79)	1,290	0.22					
Mathematics GPA	2.58 (0.96)	1,375	2.73 (0.93)	1,000	0.16	2.77 (0.90)	374	2.62 (0.96)	2,001	0.16

[a] GPA = Grade point average.

of a university mathematics placement test during the 1998 school year. Responses from one sample were used for DIF detection, using a likelihood ratio test for DIF (Thissen et al., 1988, 1993), and estimation of item parameters for a 3-parameter logistic model (3PL). Five DIF items were identified, four items favored males and one item favored females. DIF items favoring males measured geometry (one item), arithmetic (one item), and elementary algebra (two items). The item favoring females measured elementary algebra.

This pattern of DIF was used to constrain a mixture three-parameter logistic model (M3plM) such that the four DIF items favoring males were modeled to be more difficult for females and the one DIF item that favored females was constrained to be harder for males. The remaining 27 items were constrained to be of equal difficulty for both males and females.

The M3plM is an extension of a mixture Rasch model (Rost, 1990), in which a population of examinees is assumed to be composed of a fixed number of discrete latent groups and the 3PL holds for each latent group. As with the MRM, item parameters differ for the different groups. Each examinee is similarly parameterized in the M3plM by both a group membership parameter and a within-group ability parameter.

This mixture model was used to analyze the responses from the second sample of 500 males and 500 females. The results presented in Table 7.5 illustrate how the manifest characteristic associated with DIF often has a weak relationship with the groups actually being advantaged or disadvantaged by the item(s). The sample used for this analysis consisted of 500 males and 500 females. The resulting latent groups identified using the M3plM indicated that 566 examinees responded consistent with the pattern of DIF for males (male-DIF group) and 434 examinees responded with a pattern consistent with the DIF for females (female-DIF group). More interesting was the finding that 312 male examinees were classed into the male-DIF group, but so were 254 females. In other words, slightly more than half the females were put into the male-DIF group. Likewise, 188 males were classed into the female-DIF group, along with 246 females.

Males and females differed along the same lines as shown in Table 7.4. Females performed better on tests of verbal achievement (e.g., ACT-English Test and English Mechanics Placement Test) and better on

TABLE 7.5. *Group Assignment by Gender*

Latent Group	Gender		Total Sample
	Male	Female	
Male-DIF	312	254	566
Female-DIF	188	246	434
Total	500	500	1,000

achievement in their college careers, and males did better on tests of quantitative achievement (see Table 7.3). What is most interesting about the results reported in Table 7.6, however, is the lack of any significant differences between examinees in the male-DIF and female-DIF groups. In other words, examinees whose patterns of responding were consistent with the male pattern of DIF did not exhibit the same achievement or test results observed for males and females. This again reinforces the assertion that gender DIF is only loosely associated with gender and tells us little about those examinees for whom the items actually function differentially.

Results from this first analysis of DIF indicate that the usual approach to studying DIF does not contribute much to understanding the causes of DIF. The use of manifest gender categories to identify those affected by gender DIF, in other words, is most likely misleading. Those examinees for whom items were functioning differentially were not accurately characterized by their gender, despite the fact that the latent groups were defined according to a gender-based DIF analysis. Some males' responses were more consistent with the female-DIF group in their interactions with the mathematics items and some females' responses were more consistent with the male-DIF group.

Analysis of DIF as a Nuisance Dimension

A final approach demonstrates an assessment of DIF in which the nuisance dimensions that cause DIF are first identified, and then manifest examinee characteristics associated with those dimensions are examined as a way of leading to a more informative DIF analysis (Cohen & Bolt, in press). Although this approach examined English placement test data, it also illustrates how mixture IRT models can be used to analyze response patterns of examinees in an effort to identify nuisance dimensions. These results may also have important implications for test development. Distractors on multiple-choice tests can potentially be designed to be attractive to individuals using certain types of problem-solving strategies (Mislevy & Verhelst, 1990) or using particular types of erroneous operational rules (Tatsuoka, 1985). The creation of specially designed distractors and the detection of response patterns associated with use of these distractors may possibly be used to better understand why certain examinees may have responded as they did. Results from Cohen & Bolt suggest that information in such distractors can be useful in understanding why DIF may have occurred.

DISCUSSION

The standard approach to detection of gender DIF focuses on comparison of responses to test questions between males and females who are of the same ability. DIF arises when nuisance variation occurs due to differences

TABLE 7.6. *Achievement-Related Characteristics of Gender and Gender-Like Groups in Total Sample*

| | Gender | | | | | Latent Group | | | | |
| | Male | | Female | | Effect | Male-like | | Female-like | | Effect |
Variable	Mean (SD)	N	Mean (SD)	N	Size	Mean (SD)	N	Mean (SD)	N	Size
High school units										
History units	3.58 (1.30)	481	3.39 (1.31)	900	0.15					
Physics units	0.63 (0.53)	481	0.53 (0.52)	900	0.19					
College Entrance examination & placement test scores										
ACT – English	24.05 (4.37)	401	25.17 (3.79)	798	−0.28					
ACT – Mathematics	25.28 (3.92)	401	23.89 (3.48)	798	0.38					
SAT – Quantitative	591.92 (87.74)	120	554.16 (71.05)	154	0.48					
English Mechanics Test	618.59 (82.38)	423	635.58 (78.71)	760	−0.21					
Elementary Algebra	565.27 (102.16)	447	543.98 (91.40)	815	0.22					
Intermediate College Algebra	566.61 (99.77)	447	542.67 (85.24)	815	0.26					
College achievement data[a]										
First semester GPA	2.70 (0.82)	467	2.88 (0.78)	872	−0.23					
Cumulative GPA	2.68 (0.77)	481	2.91 (0.72)	900	−0.31					
Degree credits			54.76 (20.16)	900	−0.31					
Transfer credits	7.23 (12.99)	481	10.56 (14.80)	900	−0.23					
F credits	1.23 (2.94)	481	0.62 (2.07)	900	0.25					

[a] First 2.5 years of college.

in response strategies that are unrelated to the focus of the examination. The standard approach to DIF detection does not accurately identify those examinees for or against whom a test item functions differentially. Neither does knowing that examinees are members of a particular manifest group (e.g., male or female; African American, Anglo, or Latino) lead to an understanding of why DIF occurs. In this chapter, we illustrate two psychometric approaches to examining differences in performance on test items, one developed from work on analysis of structural features of items and their relation to gender DIF and a second based on work on mixture IRT models. These approaches are illustrative of alternative approaches that may lead to better understanding the causes of DIF.

Findings from the Li (2001) study were interesting because they illustrate an approach to the study of DIF based on structural characteristics of items. The importance of structural features of items for prediction of gender DIF is becoming increasingly clear. The Li study demonstrates the impact of structural features of test items on examinees' test performance. Use of a theoretical framework such as the multicontext model should enable us to develop meaningful hypotheses about the nature of latent groups embedded in populations of examinees. This kind of approach could help guide future research on diversity in examinee populations. Gierl et al. (2002) also noted this same impact using a cognitive processing perspective developed by Gallagher and her colleagues (Gallagher, 1998; Gallagher & DeLisi, 1994; Gallagher et al., 1999). The multicontext theory-based coding scheme (Li, 2001) and the coding schemes developed by Li (2001) and by Gierl et al. (2002) from Gallagher's work, all provide important insights into ways of attempting to understand the causes of gender DIF.

Research with mixture IRT models is beginning to demonstrate their utility for examining characteristics of groups that are latent in the data (e.g., Embretson & Reise, 2000; Mislevy & Verhelst, 1990; Rost, 1990). These types of models also have been found to be useful for detection of specific latent groups (Bolt et al., 2002; Cohen & Bolt, in press). This latter use was illustrated in two contexts: a speededness context and a DIF detection context. In the speededness context, differences in responses from a speeded group and a nonspeeded group were detected using mixture Rasch models and characteristics of examinees in both groups examined. This approach is useful for identifying latent groups and then studying characteristics of individuals in each group. The method by Bolt et al. (2002) has utility beyond the speededness context and should be particularly useful for identification of groups that use different response strategies. This is central to the task of identifying examinees that respond differentially on an item due to the intrusion of one or more nuisance dimension(s) on the measurement process. The second illustration of this method was for gender DIF detection beginning with a standard DIF detection approach to first identify the DIF items and then using the mixture IRT model to identify examinees for which the item functioned differentially. Also illustrated in this example was the use of the mixture model approach described in Bolt, Cohen, and Wollack (2001) for finding general nuisance dimension(s) that cause examinees to respond differentially to particular test items.

These examples illustrate departures from the standard study of DIF and point to some possible promising avenues for the study of DIF. In particular, subsequent research examining examinee reactions during actual tests – such as using a talk-aloud protocols, common to studies in cognitive psychology, during the test – might be useful additions to the methodologies used to study gender DIF.

References

Ackerman, T. A. (1992). A didactic explanation of item bias, item impact, and itemalidity from a multidimensional perspective. *Journal of Educational Measurement*, 29(1), 67–91.

Basinger, J. (1997). Graduate Record Exam is poor predictor of success in psychology. *Academe Today*, web site of the *Chronicle of Higher Education*, August 6 <http://www.chronicle.com/chedata/news.dir/dailarch.dir/9708.dir97080603. htm>(8/6/97).

Bolt, D. M. (1999). *Psychometric methods for diagnostic assessment and dimensionality representation*. Unpublished Ph.D. dissertation. Urbana: University of Illinois.

Bolt, D. M., Cohen, A. S., & Wollack, J. A. (2001). A mixture item response model for multiple-choice data. *Journal of Educational and Behavioral Statistics*, 26(4), 381–409.

Bolt, D. M., Cohen, A. S., & Wollack, J. A. (2002). Item parameter estimation under conditions of test speededness: Application of a mixture Rasch model with ordinal constraints. *Journal of Educational Measurement*, 39(4), 331–348.

Bowen, W. G., & Bok, D. (1998). *The shape of the river: Long-term consequences of considering race in college and university admissions*. Princeton, NJ: Princeton University Press.

Carlton, S. T., & Harris, A. M. (1989). *Female/male performance differences on the SAT: Causes and correlates*. Paper presented at the annual meeting of the American Educational Research Association, San Francisco.

Cohen, A. S., & Bolt, D. M. (in press). A mixture model analysis of differential item functioning. *Journal of Educational Measurement*.

Cohen, A. S., Wollack, J. A., Bolt, D. M., & Mroch, A. A. (2002). *A Mixture Rasch Model Analysis of Test Speededness*. Paper presented at the annual conference of the American Educational Research Association, New Orleans, LA.

Embretson, S. E., & Reise, S. P. (2000). *Item response theory for psychologists*. Mawhah, NJ: Lawrence Erlbaum.

Gallagher, A. (1998). Gender and antecedents of performance in mathematics testing. *Teachers College Record*. 100, 297–314.

Gallagher, A., Morley, M. E., & Levin, J. (1999). Cognitive patterns of gender differences on mathematics admissions tests. *Graduate Record Examinations FAME Report*, 4–11, Princeton, NJ: Author.

Gallagher, A. M., & DeLisi, R. (1994). Gender differences in scholastic aptitude test – mathematics problem solving among high ability students. *Journal of Educational Psychology, 86,* 204–211.

Gallagher, A., Morley, M. E., & Levin, J. (1999). Cognitive patterns of gender differences on mathematics admissions tests. *Graduate Record Examinations FAME Report,* 4–11, Princeton, NJ: Author.

Gierl, M. J., Bisanz, J., Bisanz, G. L., & Boughton, K. A. (2002, April). *Identifying content and cognitive skills that produce gender differences in mathematics: A demonstration of the DIF analysis framework.* Paper presented at the annual conference of the National Council on Measurement in Education, New Orleans, LA.

Hall, E. T. (1959). *The silent language.* Greenwich, CT: Fawcett.

Hall, E. T. (1966). *The hidden dimension* (2nd ed.). New York: Anchor.

Hall, E. T. (1974). *Handbook for proxemic research.* Washington, DC: Society for the Anthropology of Visual Communication.

Hall, E. T. (1984). *The Dance of Life: The Other Dimension of Time* (2nd ed.). Garden City, NY: Anchor Books.

Hall, E. T. (1993). *An Anthropology of everyday life* (2nd ed.). New York: Anchor.

Holland, P. W. (1985). *On the study of differential item performance without IRT.* Proceedings of the 27th annual conference of the Military Testing Association (Vol. 1, pp. 282–287); San Diego.

Holland, P. W., & Thayer, D. T. (1988). Differential item performance and the Mantel-Haenszel procedure. In H. Wainer & H. Braun (Eds.), *Test validity* (pp. 129–145). Hillsdale, NJ: Lawrence Erlbaum Associates.

Ibarra, R. A. (1996). *Latino experiences in graduate education: Implications for change.* Enhancing the Minority Presence in Graduate Education, no. 7. Washington, DC: Council of Graduate Schools.

Ibarra, R. A. (2001). *Beyond affirmative action: Reframing the context of higher education.* Madison: University of Wisconsin Press.

Ibarra, R. A., & Cohen, A. S. (1999, February). *Multicontextuality: A hidden dimension in testing and assessment.* Paper presented at the ETS Invitational Conference on Fairness, Access, Multiculturalism, and Equity (FAME), Princeton, NJ.

Li, Y. (2001). *Detecting differences in item response as a function of item characteristics.* Unpublished masters thesis, Department of Educational Psychology, Madison: University of Wisconsin.

Mislevy, R. J., & Verhelst, N. (1990). Modeling item responses when different subjects employ different solution strategies. *Psychometrika, 55,* 195–215.

Oshima, T. C. (1994). The effect of speededness on parameter estimation in item response theory. *Journal of Educational Measurement, 31,* 200–219.

Pine, S. M. (1977). Application of item characteristic curve theory to the problem of test bias. In D. J. Weiss (Ed.), *Application of computerized adaptive testing: Proceedings of a symposium presented at the 18th annual convention of the Military Testing Association* (Research Rep. No. 77–1, pp. 37–43). Minneapolis: University of Minnesota, Department of Psychology, Psychometric Methods Program.

Ramírez, M., III. (1983). *Psychology of the Americas: Mestizo perspectives on personality and mental health.* New York: Pergamon.

Ramírez, M., III. (1991). *Psychotherapy and counseling with minorities: a cognitive approach to individual and cultural differences.* New York: Pergamon.

Ramírez, M., III. (1998). *Multicultural/multiracial psychology: mestizo perspectives in personality and mental health*. Northvale, NJ: Jason Aronson.

Ramírez, M., III. (1999). *Multicultural psychology: an approach to individual and cultural differences* (2nd ed.). Needham Heights, MA: Allyn and Bacon.

Ramírez, M., III, & Castañeda, A. (1974). *Cultural democracy, bicognitive development, and education*. New York: Academic Press.

Rost, J. (1990). Rasch models in latent classes: An integration of two approaches to item analysis. *Applied Psychological Measurement, 14*, 271–282.

Roussos, L., & Stout, W. (1996). A multidimensionality-based DIF analysis paradigm. *Applied Psychological Measurement, 20*, 355–371.

Scheuneman, J. D., & Gerritz, K. (1990). Using differential item functioning procedures to explore sources of item difficulty and group performance characteristics. *Journal of Educational Measurement, 27*, 109–131.

Steele, C. M., & Aronson, J. (1995). Stereotype threat and the intellectual test performance of African Americans. *Journal of Personality and Social Psychology, 69*(5), 797–811.

Sternberg, R. J., & Williams, W. M. (1997, June). Does the graduate record examination predict meaningful success in the graduate training of psychologists? A case study. *American Psychologist, 52*(6), 630–41.

Tatsuoka, K. K. (1985). A probabilistic model for diagnosing misconceptions by the pattern classification approach. *Journal of Educational Statistics, 10*, 55–73.

Thissen, D. (1991). *MULTILOG* [computer program]. Chicago: Scientific Software.

Thissen, D., Steinberg, L., & Wainer, H. (1988). Use of item response theory in the study of group differences in trace lines. In H. Wainer & H. I. Braun (Eds.), *Test validity* (pp. 147–169). Hillsdale, NJ: Erlbaum.

Thissen, D., Steinberg, L., & Wainer, H. (1993). Detection of differential item functioning using the parameters of item response models. In P. W. Holland & H. Wainer (Eds.), *Differential item functioning* (pp. 67–113). Hillsdale, NJ: Erlbaum.

Wild, C. L., & McPeek, W. M. (1986). *Performance of the Mantel-Haenszel statistic in a variety of situations*. Paper presented at the annual meeting of the American Educational Research Association, San Francisco.

Yamamoto, K., & Everson, H. (1997). Modeling the effects of test length and test time on parameter estimation using the HYBRID model. In J. Rost & R. Langenheine (Eds.), *Applications of latent trait and latent class models in the social sciences*. New York:

Zieky, M. (1993). Practical questions in the use of DIF statistics in test development. In P. W. Holland & H. Wainer (Eds.), *Differential item functioning* (pp. 337–347). Hillsdale, NJ: Erlbaum.

8

The Gender-Gap Artifact

Women's Underperformance in Quantitative Domains Through the Lens of Stereotype Threat

Paul G. Davies and Steven J. Spencer

Women in the traditionally masculine field of mathematics must contend with stereotypes that allege a sex-based math inability. The threat of being personally reduced to these gender stereotypes can evoke a disruptive state that undermines women's math performance – a situational predicament termed "stereotype threat." Women are susceptible to stereotype threat whenever they risk fulfilling, or being judged by, a negative gender stereotype that provides a plausible explanation for their behavior in a given domain. This chapter examines the insidious effects that stereotype threat can have on women's performance and aspirations in all quantitative fields.

Picture in your mind the typical computer scientist. Now picture the typical librarian. Is the librarian shy and the computer scientist socially awkward? Do they both wear glasses? Are they both inept at sports? Is the computer scientist a male and the librarian a female? Most people can clearly articulate the content of stereotypes targeted at various groups in our society, and gender stereotypes are no exception. As Brown and Josephs (1999) suggest, stereotypes regarding gender differences in math and science ability still pervade contemporary Western thought. In fact, if you assumed that the direction of those gender differences benefited men, you have just displayed personal knowledge of some of the negative stereotypes targeted at women in our culture. This is not meant to imply that you personally endorse those stereotypes – research has shown no relationship between personal beliefs and knowledge of stereotypes (Devine, 1989; Devine & Elliot, 1995). With stereotypic portrayals of stigmatized groups permeating our mass media culture, the stigmatized themselves become acutely aware of the negative accusations conveyed in those stereotypes (Crocker, Major, & Steele, 1998). Thus, women are well aware that stereotypes portray them as being inferior to men in mathematics and its related disciplines (Crocker et al., 1998; Spencer, Steele, & Quinn, 1999).

Overt gender stereotyping may be waning, but the beliefs underlying those negative stereotypes still linger. Research confirms that even parents and teachers have distorted perceptions of girls' and boys' competency in various stereotypic domains (Eccles, 1994). With respect to traditionally masculine domains such as math and science, the parents and teachers of equally gifted children underestimate girls' talent and overestimate boys' talent (Yee & Eccles, 1988). These lingering beliefs may contribute to the striking gender disparity that continues in achievement-related choices involving mathematics. For instance, women who are as equally skilled and experienced in mathematics as their male counterparts still avoid college majors involving moderate or high levels of mathematics (Lefevre, Kulak, & Heymans, 1992). Lefevre and her colleagues (1992) found that among these equally gifted students, men are four and a half times more likely than women to select college majors considered high in math content (e.g., computer science, engineering, mathematics). In addition, the college dropout rate for women is two and a half times that of men in the physical sciences, engineering, and mathematics (Hewitt & Seymour, 1991). As a consequence, the gender gap only worsens at the graduate level of education, where women are scarcely represented in math-related domains (Aronson, Quinn, & Spencer, 1998).

Considering the above, it should come as no surprise that most women choose occupations that involve less than moderate amounts of mathematics (Fitzgerald & Crites, 1980; Stangor & Sechrist, 1998). Despite a concerted effort to attract young women to careers in the scientific and mathematical fields, striking gender differences continue in the selection of these occupations (Eccles, 1994). Again, this disparity is most evident in the fields of math, engineering, and the physical sciences – where women only occupy 10% of the jobs and earn just 75% of what their male counterparts earn (Crocker et al., 1998; Hewitt & Seymour, 1991).

Few would question the far-reaching implications of the math-inferiority stereotype targeted at women, but the debate gets heated when discussing whether that stereotype stems from *actual* gender differences in math ability. There is no argument over the reliable finding that women underperform compared with men on standardized tests of mathematics (e.g., AP-Calculus, SAT-Mathematics, GRE-Quantitative); rather, the debate is over the cause of that gender disparity. As demonstrated by the various chapters in this book, explanations for this gender gap run the gamut. For instance, some researchers contend that genetic differences can account for the gender gap in math performance (e.g., Benbow & Stanley, 1980, 1983), while others suggest that gender differences in math performance and its affiliated achievement stems from gender role socialization (e.g., Eagly, 1987; Eccles, 1994). Although appreciating that gender differences in math performance and achievement-related choices is a complex issue, the present chapter focuses on a situational predicament that we believe provides a critical piece to the gender gap puzzle – stereotype threat (Steele, 1992, 1997).

STEREOTYPE THREAT

When members of a stigmatized group find themselves in a situation where stereotypes provide a plausible explanation for their behavior, the risk of being judged by, or treated in terms of, those negative stereotypes can evoke a disruptive state. That is, having to contend with the risk of being personally reduced to a negative stereotype can elicit an extra psychological burden among the stigmatized in targeted domains – a situational predicament that Claude Steele and colleagues have termed stereotype threat (Spencer et al., 1999; Steele, 1997; Steele & Aronson, 1995). Steele maintains that this situational predicament can undermine an individual's performance and aspirations in any alleged stereotype-relevant domain (Steele, 1997). Members of any stigmatized group are susceptible to stereotype threat when the negative stereotypes directed at their group provide a framework for interpreting their behavior in that given domain (Steele & Aronson, 1995). Because we all belong to groups that are stigmatized in certain situations, stereotype threat is a pervasive situational predicament.

A detailed knowledge of relevant stereotypes and their domains of applicability are required to experience stereotype threat, but stigmatized individuals need not have any internal doubts about their ability or their group's ability (Crocker et al., 1998; Steele, 1997). In fact, the negative consequences of stereotype threat may be most striking for individuals who are highly invested and skilled in the targeted domain, or those individuals who at least care about the social consequences of being judged incompetent in that domain (Aronson et al., 1999; Steele, 1997). For these individuals, being personally reduced to a negative stereotype in that domain threatens something that is central to their self-image (Aronson et al., 1998; Steele, 1997).

Stereotypes regarding gender-related aptitudes have historically questioned women's ability to succeed in any traditionally masculine domain. As a result, women in masculine fields face the extra psychological burden of negative stereotypes alleging a sex-based inability. Therefore, women face stereotype threat in any domain that stereotypes target as being inherently masculine – such as mathematics and its related disciplines. Imagine taking a difficult math test that is at the upper limits of your ability. If you are a male and you find yourself having difficulty, you may begin to worry about failing the test. If you are a female, however, any difficulty you have with the test elicits a cloud of suspicion regarding the math inferiority stereotype. Struggling with the test becomes doubly threatening, as you begin to worry not only about failing the test, but also about fulfilling a negative stereotype targeted at your gender (Kunda, 1999). This added psychological burden of having to contend with negative stereotypes during demanding tasks can potentially undermine the performance and aspirations of women in all quantitative domains. There is room for optimism, however. If stereotype threat is responsible for the underperformance of women in quantitative domains, removing stereotype threat from those situations should eliminate women's performance deficit.

STEREOTYPE THREAT IN THE LABORATORY

Spencer and colleagues (1999) directly tested this promising hypothesis by manipulating the level of stereotype threat that participants experienced during a difficult math test. Male and female participants were selected who were highly skilled and invested in mathematics. Half the participants were given instructions designed to eliminate any threat of confirming the math inferiority stereotype (i.e., told the math test had revealed "no gender differences" in the past). It is important to note that these instructions did not question the overall validity of the math inferiority stereotype; rather, they simply informed participants that the stereotype was not applicable to that specific testing situation. Participants in the control condition were provided with no information about the relative past performance of men and women on the math test, which simulated a normal testing situation. Spencer and colleagues reasoned that taking this difficult math test under normal testing conditions would elicit stereotype threat among the female participants and consequently undermine their performance, which is exactly what happened. Replicating the well-documented gender gap in math performance, women in the control condition underperformed compared with men. In contrast, the women's performance deficit was completely eliminated in the no-gender-difference condition (Spencer et al., 1999). A simple modification to the testing situation alerted women that their performance would not be viewed through a stereotypic lens, which alleviated the extra burden of stereotype threat and allowed the women to perform to their full potential. We followed up this seminal work by replacing the no-gender-difference instructions with "nondiagnostic" instructions. Replicating the Spencer et al. (1999) findings, telling women that the difficult math test was nondiagnostic of their mathematical ability completely eliminated women's underperformance (Davies, Spencer, Quinn, & Gerhardstein, 2002).

Further research by Spencer and his colleagues (1999) sheds light on the finding that women's performance deficits are generally limited to timed tests that involve higher levels of mathematics (Hyde, Fennema, & Lamon, 1990). Again, Spencer et al. recruited male and female undergraduates who were highly skilled and invested in mathematics. This time, however, participants were not provided with information regarding the past performance of men and women on the test. Instead, they were randomly assigned to take a difficult math test or a relatively easy math test. The difficult math test was composed of questions taken directly from the GRE-Mathematics subject test, which is designed for students applying to

do graduate work in mathematics. The comparatively easy test was composed of questions taken directly from the quantitative section of the GRE
general exam, which should be well within the ability of math-identified
undergraduates. Spencer and colleagues (1999) reasoned that the disruptive pressures associated with stereotype threat should only interfere with
performance on tests that push the upper limits of cognitive ability. Therefore, women taking the easy math test should overcome the added psychological burden and perform to their full potential. That is, once female
participants realize the exam is within their ability, their performance itself should discredit the math inability stereotype and diminish the disruptive state of stereotype threat. Results confirmed that women taking
the difficult math test revealed the noxious effects of stereotype threat –
underperforming on the test compared with men – whereas women taking
the relatively easy math test performed as well as the men (Spencer et al.,
1999).

The above research reveals that when stereotype-relevant tasks are well
within one's ability, success with the task can eliminate vulnerability to
stereotype threat, allowing stigmatized individuals to perform to their full
potential (Spencer et al., 1999). This helps to explain the curious discovery
that the gender gap revealed on standardized math tests is not replicated
in classroom grades. Even in high-level mathematics courses, women's
grades tend to be as good, if not better, than men's grades (e.g., Kessel &
Linn, 1996; Kimball, 1989). We believe this finding may result from women
being less susceptible to stereotype threat during coursework than during standardized testing. Once a female student has experienced some
success with the assignments and tests given during a math course, stereotype threat within that particular course should diminish. In comparison,
women are well aware of the gender gap on standardized math tests, thus
any difficulty they may experience during testing will certainly elicit stereotype threat and its corresponding underperformance. But how does this
added psychological burden of having to contend with negative stereotypes undermine the math performance of women?

Research by Quinn and Spencer (2001) investigated whether the disruptive pressures elicited by stereotype threat could undermine women's
math performance by interfering with their ability to formulate problem-
solving strategies. Male and female participants, who were equally skilled
and invested in mathematics, were randomly assigned to take the same
difficult math test in either high or low stereotype threat conditions. In
the high stereotype threat condition, an instruction sheet informed participants that they were about to work on a set of math problems specifically
developed for the SAT. Instructions in the low stereotype threat condition, made no reference to the SAT and informed participants that men
and women performed equally well on the test. All participants were instructed to indicate their problem-solving strategies while taking the test,

which were subsequently coded for effectiveness. Results confirmed that women who were told the math problems were developed for the SAT were less able to formulate effective problem-solving strategies. Consequently, although women in the low stereotype threat condition performed equally with men, women in the high stereotype threat condition underperformed on the difficult math test.

Inzlicht and Ben-Zeev (2000) also investigated the problem-solving performance of women compared with men; however, these researchers manipulated the level of stereotype threat experienced by their participants by simply varying the proportion of women to men in the testing situation. In a series of studies employing three-person groups, Inzlicht and Ben-Zeev (2000) found that female's underperformance on the math test was proportional to the number of males in their testing group. The women's math performance dropped incrementally with the addition of each male to the group. Presumably, the presence of males reminded women that their gender identity provided a framework for interpreting their performance on the math test, and thus exposed them to the detrimental effects of stereotype threat.

People have numerous coexisting social identities; in fact, each person likely embodies a unique combination of these social identities. Moreover, a social identity that is critical to an individual in one setting may become meaningless to that individual in a different setting. To illustrate, a single female could identify with being an American, a woman, an Asian, a student, an athlete, a musician, or a daughter, depending on the given situation. As Inzlicht and Ben-Zeev (2000) so eloquently demonstrated, even subtle cues can evoke different social identities. But what happens in a math testing situation if one of our social identities is linked to math inferiority (e.g., being a woman), while another is linked to math superiority (e.g., being Asian)? Shih, Pittinsky, and Ambady (1999) sought to answer this question by priming different identities among Asian American females prior to them taking a difficult math test. Shih and colleagues hypothesized that participants primed to think about their gender identity would underperform on the math test compared with participants primed to think about their ethnic identity. So prior to taking the math test, the researchers instructed participants to complete a questionnaire that primed either their ethnic identity (e.g., How many generations of your family have lived in America?) or their gender identity (e.g., Is your dormitory coed or single sex?). In relation to a control group that had neither identity primed, Asian American females primed with their ethnic identity performed better on the math test, while those primed with their gender identity underperformed on the math test.

This research by Shih and her colleagues (1999) established that priming a valued social identity can actually improve performance in situations where stereotypes question the ability of other social identities. Would this finding generalize to nonstigmatized individuals who find themselves in a testing situation with individuals whose identity is impugned in that setting? For example, what happens to men's performance on a difficult math test when in the presence of women? Walton and Cohen (2003), in a meta-analytic review of numerous studies, discovered a reliable performance boost among nonstigmatized participants aware of negative stereotypes targeted at stigmatized others, a phenomenon they termed "stereotype lift." That is, the performance of nonstigmatized groups actually improves when stereotypes targeting the ability of outgroups are made salient in a given situation. Walton and Cohen (2003) argue convincingly that stereotype lift is a psychological advantage that stems from an assumption of relative superiority to stigmatized others in testing situations.

STEREOTYPE THREAT IN THE REAL WORLD

A critique of stereotype threat theory questions whether these research findings would generalize to the real world (see Steele, Spencer, & Aronson, 2002). Of course, the laboratory affords us the ability to construct the meaning and gender relevance of tests (e.g., nondiagnostic, no gender differences) in a manner that would be impossible in a real-life situation. For instance, convincing a female student that the SAT she is about to take is nondiagnostic of ability, or reveals no gender differences, would not be possible. Students taking the AP, SAT, or GRE are well aware of their diagnostic ability and their long history of gender differences. In short, real world settings have real world constraints that don't exist in the laboratory. Despite these significant hurdles, researchers at the Educational Testing Service (ETS) conducted a series of studies to determine if stereotype threat could undermine women's performance on an actual standardized math test with real-life consequences. For example, Stricker (1998) had students indicate their gender either before or after taking the advanced placement (AP) Calculus exam. Stricker reasoned that indicating their gender prior to the test should remind women that a negative stereotype targeted at their gender is relevant to their performance, which should evoke stereotype threat during the test. Therefore, if stereotype threat is capable of undermining women's performance in real-life situations, women who indicate their gender prior to the test should underperform compared with women who indicate their gender following the test.

It is crucial to note, however, that stereotype threat research has consistently shown that women *normally* experience stereotype threat during a standardized math test. That is, there is no need to prime women with their gender identity prior to a standardized math test. In the absence of any such prime women still experience stereotype threat and its ensuing underperformance (Davies et al., 2002; Spencer et al., 1999). The knowledge that items were developed for, or taken from, a standardized math test is sufficient to elicit stereotype threat among women (e.g., Quinn & Spencer, 2001). Thus, the women who indicated their gender *following* the AP-Calculus exam in Stricker's design would also experience stereotype threat during testing. Consequently, the most that Stricker could expect from his design is that the women who indicated their gender prior to the test would experience slightly more stereotype threat than women who indicated their gender after the test.

Remarkably, in spite of this extremely conservative test of stereotype threat, Stricker's hypothesis was confirmed. Women who indicated their gender before the test scored significantly lower on the AP-Calculus exam than women who indicated their gender following the test. Moreover, social psychologist Christian Crandall determined from the Stricker (1998) data set that simply having students indicating their gender following the AP-Calculus exam would result in as many as 2,837 additional women per year starting college with advanced credit for calculus (see Steele, Spencer, & Aronson, 2002). Stricker's (1998) research provides powerful support for the insidious effects of stereotype threat in the real world, especially when one considers the conservative design that the ETS was required to run because of real world constraints.

CONSEQUENCES OF STEREOTYPE THREAT

Susceptibility to stereotype threat has consequences for women that reach far beyond this troubling underperformance in mathematics. Women who risk being personally reduced to a negative stereotype may withdraw from targeted domains in an attempt to cope with the disruptive state they can elicit. This defensive detachment may not only undermine women's short-term performance in traditionally masculine domains, but also undermine their long-term aspirations and accomplishments in those domains (Crocker et al., 1998; Major, Spencer, Schmader, Wolfe, & Crocker, 1998; Steele, 1997). Stereotype threat vulnerability can lead women to withdraw from traditional masculine domains, while seeking domains in which they are immune to stereotype threat (Davies et al., 2002).

Stereotypes accuse women of having inferior math skills, but no such stereotypes allege inferior verbal skills; therefore, women are not vulnerable to stereotype threat in verbal domains. As Steele (1997) succinctly put it, "women may reduce their stereotype threat substantially by moving across the hall from math to English class" (p. 618). Consequently, we investigated whether stereotype threat could persuade women to leave quantitative domains in favor of verbal domains (Davies et al., 2002). To test this hypothesis, we designed a study to explicitly prime the female stereotype among participants prior to a nondiagnostic aptitude test (Davies et al., 2002). Because stereotype threat requires the broad dissemination of stereotypes, it seemed appropriate to prime the female stereotype via exposure to actual gender-stereotypic television commercials. So prior to taking the nondiagnostic aptitude test, which was composed of both math and verbal questions taken from the GRE, male and female participants were exposed to either gender-stereotypic commercials or to neutral commercials (Davies et al., 2002). Although the stereotypic commercials portrayed women in a less than inspirational light (e.g., woman bounces on bed with joy over the introduction of a new acne product), they made no reference to math ability or its related skills. Results confirmed that women who watched the stereotypic commercials attempted significantly fewer math questions, and significantly more verbal questions, than women who watched the neutral commercials or men in either condition. Replicating our previous stereotype threat findings, only women exposed to the stereotypic commercials underperformed on the math items they attempted – this underperformance did not generalize to the verbal items (Davies et al., 2002).

Encouraged by these findings, we expanded our paradigm to test whether stereotype threat could also influence women's educational and vocational aspirations (Davies et al., 2002). As Stangor and Sechrist (1998) suggest, individuals make educational and vocational choices "on the basis of their perceptions about their likely success in a domain, the extent to which the domain seems appropriate and interesting to them, as well as the perceived likelihood of being stereotyped by others in the domain" (p. 106). The above aptitude test was replaced with a survey in which participants indicated their current interest in a range of college majors and careers (Davies et al., 2002). As expected, women exposed to gender-stereotypic commercials subsequently indicated less interest in both academic and professional domains in which they are vulnerable to stereotype threat (e.g., engineering, computer science, mathematics), and more interest in domains in which stereotypes do not allege a sex-based inability (e.g., linguistics, journalism, communications). This research highlighted a preemptive strategy that women can employ to effectively sidestep the spotlight of stereotype threat – avoiding those domains in which they risk being personally reduced to a negative stereotype.

POTENTIAL MEDIATORS OF STEREOTYPE THREAT

Stereotype threat is a complex interaction between an individual and a situation. As such, the mediational paths of stereotype threat are likely to vary, depending on the given stereotype, individual, and situation (see Steele, Spencer, & Aronson, 2002). Despite these complexities, progress has been made mapping potential mediators (e.g., effort, expectancies, domain identification, evaluation apprehension, anxiety, working memory), of which anxiety has received the most attention. Some researchers found strong evidence for the mediational role of anxiety, whereas others reported that anxiety did not significantly mediate their effects (e.g., Leyens,

Désert, Croizet, & Darcis, 2000; Osborne, 2001; Spencer et al., 1999; Stangor, Carr, & Kiang, 1998; Stone, Lynch, Sjomeling, & Darley, 1999). The reliability of anxiety as a mediator may have been undercut by researchers who failed to recognize that anxiety is only a potential mediator when people are actually experiencing, or at least contemplating, a threatening domain. Confusion surrounding the role of this potential mediator has also been fueled by the use of self-reported measures of anxiety. Research has confirmed that people may not always be willing or able to accurately report their own level of anxiety. Blascovich, Spencer, Quinn, and Steele (2001) collected both self-reported and physiological indicators of anxiety (i.e., blood pressure) in a stereotype threat paradigm. Although the physiological measures confirmed their stereotype threat effects were accompanied by a significant increase in anxiety, the self-reported measures completely failed to reveal this finding. Clearly, both the timing and sensitivity of measures are critical when testing the potential mediational role of anxiety in stereotype threat paradigms.

Steele and Aronson (1995), while investigating the role that stereotype threat plays in the academic underperformance of African American students, discovered another potential mediator of stereotype threat – activation level of relevant stereotypes. Employing an implicit measure of stereotype activation (i.e., word-stem completion task), Steele and Aronson found that simply anticipating taking a diagnostic test activated the racial stereotype among African American participants. "Clearly the diagnostic instructions caused these participants to experience a strong apprehension, a distinct sense of stereotype threat" (p. 805). Steele and Aronson established that African American participants only underperformed on tests described as being diagnostic of intellectual ability. When told the test was nondiagnostic of ability, African American and white participants performed equally well on a difficult test. The researchers then examined whether priming African American participants to think about their ethnic identity would expose them to the detrimental effects of stereotype threat even on a nondiagnostic test. Steele and Aronson confirmed that making race salient, which elicits a sense of being judged in terms of racial stereotypes, undermined the African American students' performance even on a nondiagnostic verbal test.

Steele and Aronson (1995) established that a specific psychological state is directly associated with stereotype threat – the cognitive activation of relevant stereotypes. Consequently, we believe that the experience of stereotype threat involves confronting activated self-relevant stereotypes and realizing that one risks being personally reduced to those stereotypes in targeted domains. In other words, given the right situation, activation level of self-relevant stereotypes should reliably mediate the effects of stereotype threat. It should be made clear, however, that stereotype activation does not necessitate stereotype threat. For stereotype activation to lead to stereotype threat, the individual must be experiencing, or at least contemplating, situations in which stereotypes allege a group-based inability. For example, if Steele and Aronson had primed African American participants to think about their race prior to a test of artistic ability, the participants would have activated racial stereotypes without subsequently experiencing stereotype threat – because stereotypes do not accuse African Americans of having inferior artistic ability. Replace the test of artistic ability with a test of academic ability, and a situation is created that has been shown to elicit stereotype threat (Steele & Aronson, 1995).

To further examine the mediational role of stereotype activation, we again employed the television commercial paradigm discussed earlier in this chapter (Davies et al., 2002). Prior to taking a nondiagnostic math test, male and female participants were exposed to gender-stereotypic television commercials designed to elicit the female stereotype. Only participants for whom the activated stereotype was self-relevant (i.e., women) were expected to underperform on the subsequent math test. Furthermore, level of stereotype activation among those women, as measured by a lexical decision task, should mediate the performance-inhibiting effects of those commercials. To test this mediational hypothesis, activation of the female stereotype was measured following exposure to the commercials, but prior to the math test. This design allowed us to test whether exposure to the commercials activated the female stereotype, and whether the resulting level of stereotype activation mediated the effects of those commercials. Results confirmed that exposure to the stereotypic commercials resulted in activation of the female stereotype among both men and women. Only women, however, underperformed on the subsequent nondiagnostic math test. More important, it was established that level of stereotype activation among the female participants mediated the performance-inhibiting effects of those television commercials (Davies et al., 2002).

STEREOTYPE THREAT CAN LEAD TO DISIDENTIFICATION

Stereotype threat research has reliably demonstrated that women who risk being personally reduced to the math inferiority stereotype underperform on math tests compared with similarly qualified men. Unfortunately, women's defensive reactions to stereotype threat can lead to more far-reaching consequences than just performance deficits. Our research revealed a short-term defensive strategy that women can employ to effectively sidestep the spotlight of stereotype threat – avoiding domains in which they risk being personally reduced to a negative stereotype (Davies et al., 2002). Women's reaction to stereotype threat can range from these preemptive strategies (e.g., domain avoidance) to even more troubling permanent strategies (e.g., domain disidentification). For instance, one way women can cope with stereotype threat is to psychologically disengage their self-esteem from the targeted domain in an effort to keep feelings of self-worth independent of performance in that domain (Major et al., 1998). Psychological disengagement is considered a defensive strategy of maintaining self-esteem by divesting the self from a domain where success is difficult, or the pursuit of success is believed to be too unpleasant (Aronson et al., 1998; Crocker et al., 1998; Major et al., 1998). Therefore, the stereotype threat that some women experience in quantitative domains may lead them to avoid or drop those domains as a basis of self-evaluation in an attempt to cope with the self-evaluative threat they can impose (Major et al., 1998; Steele, 1997).

Like stereotype threat, psychological disengagement can be a temporary state that is situationally specific, but it normally occurs in situations where poor performance is either experienced or anticipated (Major et al., 1998). If women chronically experience stereotype threat in a given domain, however, the temporary strategy of psychological disengagement may be replaced with the permanent strategy of domain disidentification. Disidentification is a defensive strategy of eliminating a domain as a long-term basis of self-evaluation. Obviously, this permanent strategy can lead to a systematic gender gap in math-related achievement and aspirations as women divest themselves from targeted domains. Some members of our society suggest the resulting gender gap accurately reflects sex-based abilities, but we believe this gender gap is simply the byproduct of a defensive effort by women to cope with a self-evaluative threat imposed on them by their own culture.

GENERALIZABILITY OF STEREOTYPE THREAT

Throughout this chapter, we discuss the effects of stereotype threat on women's performance and aspirations in math-related domains. It is important to keep in mind, however, that the insidious effects of stereotype threat are not limited to women or the domain of mathematics. Rather, members of any stigmatized group are susceptible to stereotype threat when they find themselves in a situation where negative stereotypes provide a framework for interpreting their behavior. For instance, we examined the insidious effects that stereotype threat can have on women's leadership aspirations – a domain in which women are stereotyped as lacking ability (Davies & Spencer, 2002). Women exposed to gender-stereotypic television commercials subsequently avoided traditionally masculine leadership roles in favor of nonthreatening subordinate roles. We discovered that stereotype threat could be removed from the leadership role, however, by informing participants the leadership task had revealed no gender differences in the past. That is, making the leadership inability stereotype irrelevant to the task restored women's interest in leadership, even after they had been exposed to the gender-stereotypic commercials. Replicating our previous research (Davies et al., 2002), results confirmed that level of stereotype activation mediated the effect of the commercials on women's leadership aspirations. Level of stereotype activation, however, only predicted women's leadership aspirations for stereotype-relevant tasks. Varying the stereotype relevance of the leadership task *moderated* whether level of stereotype activation *mediated* the coercive effects of the commercials on women's aspirations (Davies & Spencer, 2002).

As noted earlier, Steele and Aronson (1995) documented the undermining effects that stereotype threat can have on African Americans' performance on standardized aptitude tests. This seminal work has been conceptually replicated with numerous other stigmatized groups, such as Latino students (Gonzales, Blanton, & Williams, 2002) and lower socioeconomic status students in France (Croizet & Claire, 1998). Because we all belong to groups that are stigmatized in certain situations, we are all susceptible to stereotype threat given the right situation. This was clearly demonstrated by Aronson and his colleagues (1999) who were able to elicit stereotype threat among white males taking a difficult math test. Because white males are not normally stigmatized as having poor math skills, how was it possible for these researchers to create a threatening environment? It was accomplished by simply informing the white participants that the study was investigating the superior math skills of Asians compared with whites. With the Asian math superiority stereotype primed, white males were exposed the insidious effects of stereotype threat and underperformed on the math test. As this research illustrates, a group need not normally live in the shadow of a negative stereotype to experience the noxious effects of stereotype threat (see Steele, Spencer, Davies, Harber, & Nisbett, 2002).

REAL WORLD SOLUTIONS TO STEREOTYPE THREAT

As discussed earlier, the laboratory enables us to construct the meaning and relevance of tests and situations as a means to eliminate stereotype threat, a strategy that is less viable in real-life situations. This is not meant to imply, however, that the negative effects of stereotype threat cannot be reduced in the real world. In fact, we have reason to believe that intervention programs can successfully reduce the level of stereotype threat experienced by stigmatized groups in both educational and occupational environments. This optimistic view led to the development of a dormitory-based program designed to reduce stereotype threat in a university setting (Steele et al., 2002). The program's goal was to assure minority students at the University of Michigan that they would not be viewed through the lens of negative stereotypes on that campus. In conjunction with their regular course work, undergraduate participants were required to attend seminars, discussion groups, and workshops designed to convey to the minority students that the University of Michigan believed in their academic potential. These extracurricular activities involved challenging schoolwork, direct affirmation of the students' potential, and the fostering of comfortable interracial relationships. African Americans who participated in this intervention significantly outperformed both African Americans in the control group and in the general student body. In fact, the academic performance of the African American participants equaled that of white students in the general student body. Moreover, the African Americans who participated in the program were significantly more likely to stay in university than African Americans in the control group or in the general student body. Why was this program so successful? Analysis of the longitudinal data revealed that participation in the program led to a decrease in level of stereotype threat experienced at the university, which in turn led to an increase in academic performance and retention (see Steele, Spencer, Davies et al., 2002). Thus, it is possible to diminish the harmful effects of stereotype threat in the real world.

This chapter began with an illustration of the vast knowledge of stereotypes that members of our society have no difficulty tapping into. As long as these stereotypes targeting the social identity of various groups permeate our society, all members of such groups will be susceptible to the insidious effects of stereotype threat. Unfortunately, trying to eliminate all negative stereotypes from our culture would likely be a futile exercise, but the research presented throughout this chapter has confirmed that it is possible to create environments that effectively reduce the risk of experiencing stereotype threat – both in the laboratory and the real world. Therefore, the realistic challenge confronting our society is to create environments in which stigmatized individuals can work and study without the threat of being personally reduced to a negative stereotype. Within these identity-safe environments, the viscious cycle of stereotype threat will be eliminated, which will allow all individuals to achieve their full potential.

AUTHORS' NOTE

We are grateful to Claude Steele, Teceta Thomas, and Leanne Isaak for their helpful comments throughout the writing of this chapter.

Correspondence concerning this chapter should be addressed to Paul G. Davies, Department of Psychology, Jordan Hall, Bldg. 420, Stanford University, Stanford, California 94305-2130. Electronic mail may be sent to pgdavies@psych.stanford.edu.

References

Aronson, J., Lustina, M., Good, C., Keough, K., Steele, C., & Brown, J. (1999). When white men can't do math: Necessary and sufficient factors in stereotype threat. *Journal of Experimental Social Psychology, 35,* 29–46.

Aronson, J., Quinn, D., & Spencer, S. (1998). Stereotype threat and the academic underperformance of minorities and women. In J. K. Swim & C. Stangor (Eds.), *Prejudice: The target's perspective* (pp. 83–103). San Diego, CA: Academic Press.

Benbow, C. P., & Stanley, J. C. (1980). Sex differences in mathematical ability: Fact or artifact? *Science, 210,* 1262–1264.

Benbow, C. P., & Stanley, J. C. (1983). Sex differences in mathematical reasoning ability: More facts. *Science, 222,* 1029–1031.

Blascovich, J., Spencer, S. J., Quinn, D. M., & Steele, C. M. (2001). Stereotype threat and the cardiovascular reactivity of African-Americans. *Psychological Science, 12,* 225–229.

Brown, R. P., & Josephs, R. A. (1999). A burden of proof: Stereotype relevance and gender differences in math performance. *Journal of Personality and Social Psychology, 76,* 246–257.

Crocker, J., Major, B., & Steele, C. M. (1998). Social stigma. In D. Gilbert, S. T. Fiske, & G. Lindzey (Eds.), *Handbook of social psychology* (4th ed.) (pp. 504–553). Boston: McGraw Hill.

Croizet, J. C., & Claire, T. (1998). Extending the concept of stereotype threat to social class: The intellectual underperformance of students from low socioeconomic backgrounds. *Personality and Social Psychology Bulletin, 24,* 588–594.

Davies, P. G., & Spencer, S. J. (2002). *Reinforcing the glass ceiling via stereotype threat: Gender-stereotypic media images persuade women to avoid leadership positions.* Unpublished manuscript, Stanford University.

Davies, P. G., Spencer, S. J., Quinn, D. M., & Gerhardstein, R. (2002). Consuming images: How television commercials that elicit stereotype threat can restrain women academically and professionally. *Personality and Social Psychology Bulletin, 28,* 1615–1628.

Devine, P. G. (1989). Stereotypes and prejudice: Their automatic and controlled components. *Journal of Personality and Social Psychology, 56,* 5–18.

Devine, P. G., & Elliot, A. J. (1995). Are racial stereotypes really fading? The Princeton trilogy revisited. *Personality and Social Psychology Bulletin, 21,* 1139–1150.

Eagly, A. H. (1987). *Sex differences in social behavior: A social role interpretation.* Hillsdale, NJ: Erlbaum.

Eccles, J. S. (1994). Understanding women's educational and occupational choices. *Psychology of Women Quarterly, 18,* 585–609.

Fitzgerald, L. F., & Crites, J. O. (1980). Toward a career psychology of women: What do we know? What do we need to know? *Journal of Counseling Psychology, 27,* 44–62.

Gonzales, P. M., Blanton, H., & Williams, K. J. (2002). The effects of stereotype threat and double-minority status on the test performance of Latino women. *Personality and Social Psychology Bulletin, 28,* 659–670.

Hewitt, N. M., & Seymour, E. (1991). *Factors contributing to high attrition rates among science and engineering undergraduate majors.* A report submitted to the Alfred P. Sloan Foundation.

Hyde, J. S., Fennema, E., & Lamon, S. J. (1990). Gender differences in mathematical performance: A meta-analysis. *Psychological Bulletin, 107,* 139–155.

Inzlicht, M., & Ben-Zeev, T. (2000). A threatening intellectual environment: Why females are susceptible to experiencing problem-solving deficits in the presence of males. *Psychological Science, 11,* 365–371.

Kessel, C., & Linn, M. C. (1996). Grades or scores: Predicting future college mathematics performance. *Educational Measurement: Issues and Practice, 15*, 10–14.

Kimball, M. M. (1989). A new perspective on women's math achievement. *Psychological Bulletin, 105*, 198–214.

Kunda, Z. (1999). *Social cognition: Making sense of people.* Cambridge, MA: The MIT Press.

Lefevre, J., Kulak, A., & Heymans, S. (1992). Factors influencing the selection of university majors varying in mathematical content. *Canadian Journal of Behavioral Sciences, 24*, 276–289.

Leyens, J. P., Désert, M., Croizet, J. C., & Darcis, C. (2000). Stereotype threat: Are lower status and history of stigmatization preconditions of stereotype threat? *Personality and Social Psychology Bulletin, 26*, 1189–1199.

Major, B., Spencer, S., Schmader, T., Wolfe, C., & Crocker, J. (1998). Coping with negative stereotypes about intellectual performance: The role of psychological disengagement. *Personality and Social Psychology Bulletin, 24*(1), 34–50.

Osborne, J. W. (2001). Testing stereotype threat: Does anxiety explain race and sex differences in achievement? *Contemporary Educational Psychology, 26*, 291–310.

Quinn, D. M., & Spencer, S. J. (2001). The interference of stereotype threat with women's generation of mathematical problem-solving strategies. *Journal of Social Issues, 57*, 55–71.

Shih, M., Pittinsky, T. L., & Ambady, N. (1999). Stereotype susceptibility: Identity salience and shifts in quantitative performance. *Psychological Science, 10*, 80–83.

Spencer, S. J., Steele, C. M., & Quinn, D. M. (1999). Stereotype threat and women's math performance. *Journal of Experimental Social Psychology, 35*, 4–28.

Stangor, C., Carr, C., & Kiang, L. (1998). Activating stereotypes undermines task performance expectations. *Journal of Personality and Social Psychology, 75*, 1191–1197.

Stangor, C., & Sechrist, G. B. (1998). Conceptualizing the determinants of academic choice and task performance across social groups. In J. K. Swim & C. Stangor (Eds.) *Prejudice: The target's perspective* (pp. 105–124). San Diego, CA: Academic Press.

Steele, C. M. (1992, April). Race and the schooling of Black Americans. *The Atlantic Monthly*, 68–78.

Steele, C. M. (1997). A threat in the air: How stereotypes shape intellectual identity and performance. *American Psychologist, 52*, 613–629.

Steele, C. M., & Aronson, J. (1995). Stereotype threat and the intellectual test performance of African Americans. *Journal of Personality and Social Psychology, 69*, 797–811.

Steele, C. M., Spencer, S. J., & Aronson, J. (2002). Contending with group image: The psychology of stereotype and social identity threat. In M. P. Zanna (Ed.), *Advances in Experimental Social Psychology* (Vol. 34) (pp. 379–440). San Francisco: Academic Press.

Steele, C. M., Spencer, S. J., Davies, P. G., Harber, K., & Nisbett, R. E. (2002). *African American college achievement: A "wise" intervention.* Unpublished manuscript, Stanford University.

Stone, J., Lynch, C. I., Sjomeling, M., & Darley, J. M. (1999). Stereotype threat effects on Black and White athletic performance. *Journal of Personality and Social Psychology, 77*, 1213–1227.

Stricker, L. J. (1998). *Inquiring about examinees' ethnicity and sex: Effects on AP calculus AB examination performance.* (College Board Rep. 98-1;l ETS Research Rep. No. 98-5). New York: College Entrance Examination Board.

Walton, G. M., & Cohen, G. L. (2003). *Stereotype lift. Journal of Experimental Social Psychology, 39,* 456–467.

Yee, D. K., & Eccles, J. S. (1988). Parent perceptions and attributions for children's math achievement. *Sex Roles, 19,* 317–333.

9

"Math is hard!" (Barbie™, 1994)

Responses of Threat vs. Challenge-Mediated Arousal to Stereotypes Alleging Intellectual Inferiority

Talia Ben-Zeev, Cristina M. Carrasquillo, Alison M. L. Ching, Tattiya J. Kliengklom, Kristen L. McDonald, Daniel C. Newhall, Gillian E. Patton, Tiffany D. Stewart, Tonya Stoddard, Michael Inzlicht, and Steven Fein

In 1994, Mattel created a Barbie™ doll that said, "Math is hard." *The Barbie Liberation Organization*, a group composed of activists and media personalities, among others, protested against Barbie's perpetuation of gender-based stereotyping. The media publicized the case and discussions on gender stereotyping in children's toys ensued on and off the air, leading Mattel to withdraw the "math is hard" Barbie from the market.

However, did Barbie's frustration with math represent a reality in which girls and women, more than boys and men, find math to be hard? Benbow and Stanley (1980, 1983) found gender differences in performance on the mathematical section of the SAT (SAT-M) in boys and girls under the age of fourteen who were high in math achievement. The boys outperformed the girls by about half a standard deviation and were overrepresented by a ratio of 13:1 among students who scored above 700. Similarly, in a meta-analysis involving over three million participants, Hyde, Fennema, and Lamon (1990) found a gender difference favoring males that emerged from high school ($d = 0.29$) through college ($d = 0.41$), and into adulthood ($d = 0.59$). Finally, Brown and Josephs (1999) reported that the two most widely used standardized tests of mathematics in the United States, the SAT-M and the quantitative portion of the GRE (GRE-Q), revealed a gender difference in the order of half a standard deviation.

This gender difference can also be seen in the types of activities that females vs. males tend to pursue. Young girls are less likely than boys to be interested in playing with scientific toys, participating in mathematical games, and reading mathematical books (Eccles & Jacobs, 1987). In advanced high school math courses, males outnumber females by a margin of 2:1 (see Geary, 1996, for a review). As far as higher education is concerned, in a 20-year follow up to their research on mathematically gifted students, Benbow and her colleagues (Benbow, Lubinski, Shea, & Eftekhari-Sanjani, 2000) found that males were about twice as likely as their female counterparts to attain a bachelor's degree in math or in the physical sciences, and twice as likely to gain employment in such fields.

It is disheartening that even females with strong math backgrounds and interests tend to underperform relative to equally prepared males in the math domain. In this chapter, we explore how *stereotype threat* – a situational phenomenon that occurs when individuals who are targets of stereotypes alleging intellectual inferiority are reminded of the possibility of confirming these stereotypes – may be an explanatory framework for understanding why females and other stigmatized students succumb to this underperformance (e.g., Aronson, Lustina, Good, Keough, Steele, & Brown, 1999; Aronson, Quinn, & Spencer, 1998; Shih, Pittinsky, & Ambady, 1999; Spencer, Steele, & Quinn, 1999; Steele, 1997; Steele & Aronson, 1995).

STEREOTYPE THREAT

The social context has been strongly implicated in creating, perpetuating, or eliminating the underperformance that has hindered stigmatized groups, such as females in math. In particular, stereotype threat has been hypothesized to occur as a result of a distress that an individual feels when she faces the possibility of confirming a negative stereotype about her group. It is the fear that her behaviors may substantiate disparaging stereotypes (Aronson et al., 1999; Aronson et al., 1998; Spencer et al., 1999; Steele 1997; Steele & Aronson, 1995). This situational distress can then hinder intellectual performance. For example, Spencer et al. (1999) showed that female college students performed significantly worse than males on a standardized math test when the stereotype about their math ability was made relevant (by informing the students that males performed better than females on this test in the past), but that this gender gap was eliminated simply by changing the wording used for introducing the test so the stereotype would seem to be inapplicable in this situation (by informing the students that males and females have performed equally well on this test in the past).

A counterintuitive finding is that only individuals who are *highly identified* with success and achievement in given stereotyped domains are the ones who show performance deficits under threat (Steele, 1997). Thus, it is the people in the vanguard of their group who are the most vulnerable to situations in which stereotypes become salient.

Spencer et al. (1999) had highly math-identified males and females take a difficult math test. Half was told that the math test had shown sex differences in the past, whereas the other half was told that it there had never been sex-differences on the test. Results showed that females and males did equally well on the test in the latter, stereotype removed condition, whereas in the former condition in which the stereotype was made relevant, females performed significantly worse than males.

Steele and Aronson (1995) examined the effects of negative stereotypes about intelligence on the academic performance of African Americans. African American and white undergraduates took a difficult test of verbal ability. Half was told that that the test was diagnostic of intelligence, whereas the other half was told that the test was nondiagnostic of intelligence. Although every participant took the same test, African American participants performed as well as white participants in the nondiagnostic condition, but performed more poorly than whites in the diagnostic condition.

Stereotype threat can be triggered in even subtler and yet frequently experienced ways, such as by the composition of the individuals in the immediate setting. Inzlicht and Ben-Zeev (2000) found that females' math performance could be undermined significantly simply by being outnumbered by males in the room as they take a math test. Inzlicht and Ben-Zeev demonstrated that undergraduate females who took portions of a GRE-math test with two males in the room performed more poorly than females who took the same test with two other females present. Furthermore, females' deficits were proportional to the number of males in their environment. Even females who were placed in a testing environment with more females than males experienced moderate but significant problem-solving deficits. (For a discussion of the properties of an intellectually threatening environment, see Inzlicht, 2001.)

Does the explicit or implicit reminder of a stereotype cause a desire to disconfirm it? Steele and Aronson (1995) had African American and white participants take a verbal test that was described as either diagnostic or nondiagnostic of intelligence. Before taking the test, however, participants were asked to complete measures of stereotype activation and stereotype avoidance. The stereotype activation measure consisted of eighty word fragments, eleven of which could be completed with, among other words, words associated with African American stereotypes (e.g., _ _ C E [RACE], B R _ _ _ _ _ [BROTHER], or W E L _ _ _ _ [WELFARE]). On the stereotype avoidance measure, participants were asked to rate their preferences on various things, including music and sports, some of which were associated with African American life or culture (e.g., hip-hop music or basketball). If describing a test as diagnostic of intelligence introduces stereotype threat, then racial stereotypes should be activated in the minds of African American participants. Moreover, African American participants should be motivated to disconfirm them.

Results showed that after controlling for self-reported SAT scores, African American participants in the diagnostic condition resolved more word fragments with stereotype-related words and exhibited lower preferences for things related to African American culture than African Americans in the nondiagnostic condition. White participants' responses did not vary across test description.

Stereotype threat generalizes to any individual belonging to an ability-stereotyped group. Croizet and Claire (1998), for example, found that students of low socioeconomic status (SES) attained lower accuracy, raw, and adjusted scores than high SES students when a GRE verbal test was framed as a test of intelligence. When the test was framed as a test of attention, however, low SES students performed just as well as high SES students. Similarly, Aronson and Salinas (1997) found that highly identified Latino students received lower scores than whites on a GRE verbal test, but only when the stereotype about Latinos' alleged lower intelligence was made salient.

Stereotype threat is a situational predicament that can affect a member of any group targeted by specific negative stereotypes – disadvantaged minority group or otherwise (Aronson et al., 1999). Thus, even advantaged white males may be susceptible to stereotype threat effects. Aronson et al. tested this hypothesis by giving highly math-identified white males a difficult math test. Half was told that the purpose was to gauge their math ability, whereas the other half was told that the purpose was to better understand why Asians outperformed whites in math tests. As in studies looking at other groups, the participants confronted with the white inferiority stereotype performed worse than other participants. Similarly, Stone, Lynch, Sjomeling, and Darley (1999) found that white participants underperformed on a golf task when they were reminded of the African American athletic superiority stereotype. Likewise, Leyens, Desert, Croizet, and Darcis (2000) found that males made more commission mistakes on an affective processing task when they were prompted with the stereotype that men are less sensitive to emotions than women. Negative stereotypes, then, appear to undermine performance of individuals belonging to any group about which negative stereotypes exist, even if the group is not generally disadvantaged in society.

Despite the enthusiasm that stereotype threat research has triggered, little is known about the specific mechanisms that underlie the effects of stereotype threat. Identifying these mechanisms would be informative with respect to theories of how stereotypes about problem-solving ability affect the intellectual processing of stigmatized high-achieving individuals and to educational practice.

POSSIBLE MEDIATORS OF STEREOTYPE THREAT

Steele and Aronson (1995) offered several mediators for the phenomenon of stereotype threat (also see Baumeister & Showers, 1986). The first is distraction due to evaluation apprehension. Instead of focusing on the task, a stigmatized person may become concerned with others' judgment of his or her ability. A second mediator is lowered self-efficacy, which in turn may moderate performance expectations and effort. Stangor, Carr, and Kiang (1998), for example, suggested that the activation of negative stereotypes lowers task performance expectations, which then undermine initial task confidence. Lowered expectations can undermine motivation and effort (Pyszczynski & Greenberg, 1983), which may then result in lower performance. Hence, negative stereotypes may lead to lower performance because they may undermine confidence and self-efficacy, which, in turn, can lead to a withdrawal of effort.

Empirical research, however, has found little evidence in support of the distraction or expectation mechanisms. For example, in an ambitious study, Spencer et al. (study 3; 1999) examined the potential mediation of both distraction (performance evaluation) and expectation (confidence and self-efficacy). As in previous studies, highly math-identified men and women were instructed to take a math test that was either described as showing gender differences in the past (threat condition) or not (no threat condition). Once all the participants read the test instructions, they filled out a questionnaire assessing evaluation apprehension (e.g., "people will think I have less ability if I do not do well on this test") and self-efficacy (e.g., "I am concerned about whether I have enough mathematical ability to do well on the test"). After filling out this questionnaire, all participants were asked to complete a difficult math test.

Results replicated the basic stereotype threat effect. Women attained lower scores than men in the threat condition, but performed equally to men in the no threat condition. Again, when stereotypes were relevant to performance, women underperformed. Mediation of this effect was tested through a series of mediational analyses for each potential mechanism (Baron & Kenny, 1986), but neither self-efficacy nor evaluation apprehension mediated stereotype threat. Self-efficacy was both unrelated to the stereotype threat manipulation and to test performance, and evaluation apprehension did not appear to mediate the relationship between stereotype threat and performance. Although evaluation apprehension was related to test performance, it was not related to the stereotype threat manipulation, nor did it reduce the direct relationship between the manipulation and performance (Spencer et al., 1999).

Aronson and his colleagues (1999) also investigated the cause of threat, but were unable to reach any definite conclusions. As in previous studies, they found that highly identified white students who were faced with the Asian math superiority stereotype attained fewer number correct than white students who were not made aware of the stereotype. The stereotyped participants also wondered more often what the experimenter would think of them in the threat condition than in the control condition. That is, threatened participants experienced evaluative worries that may have distracted their performance. However, when this evaluation apprehension was partialed out, the relationship between threat and performance was unchanged. Therefore, worries about being negatively evaluated did not seem to cause threat-induced performance deficits.

Finally, Brown and Steele (1999, as reported in Marx, Brown, & Steele, 1999) directly explored the role of performance expectations. As in previous experiments, white and African American undergraduates took a difficult GRE test of verbal ability. Half of the participants were informed that the test was diagnostic of ability (threat condition), whereas the other half were told that it was diagnostic, but racially fair (no threat condition). Prior to taking the main GRE test, participants took either an easy or difficult verbal task that resulted in complete success or clear failure. The idea was that performance on this task would set either high or low performance expectations for the second task. Brown and Steele, however, only assumed that performance expectations were manipulated. That is, they assumed that prior success or failure without feedback was capable of manipulating expectations, but did not explicitly measure them. Nonetheless, results demonstrated that African American participants performed worse than their white peers, even when they presumably had high performance expectations. Because high performance expectations could not overcome the hindering qualities of racial stereotypes, the authors concluded that stereotype threat was not mediated by expectations.

A factor that has not been examined sufficiently thus far but that has the potential to be an important mediator is physiological arousal (e.g., Steele & Aronson, 1995).

AROUSAL AS A SUGGESTED MEDIATOR OF STEREOTYPE THREAT

According to the classic Yerkes and Dodson (1908) law of physiological arousal, performance is optimal at intermediate levels of arousal and decreases when arousal is either low or high, resulting in an inverted U-shaped function. The data that were the basis for this finding came from a study of animal behavior. Yerkes and Dodson had white mice perform a learning task of finding compartments. During learning, the mice were given electric shocks of low, medium, or high intensity. The results showed that medium-intensity shocks were the most efficient in promoting learning as compared with low- and high-intensity shocks. This finding implies that cognitive processes, such as learning and memory, are executed most efficiently under conditions of medium than of low or high arousal.

More recent neurophysiological research has corroborated and expanded on the classic findings of the Yerkes-Dodson law in animals and in humans. For example, Lupien and McEwen (1997) provided evidence for an inverted U-shaped relationship between level of corticosteroids (hormones that get released as a result of high arousal) and cognitive processes in a variety of animal and human studies.

We hypothesize that high-achieving individuals in stigmatized domains approach a problem-solving task in the given domains with an optimal level of arousal for performing well (a medium level of arousal conducive to performance). An exposure to a situation of stereotype threat may interfere with these individuals' performance by leading to arousal that exceeds an optimal level, causing performance deficits (also see O'Brien, Crandall, 2001).

Mathematical problem solving relies heavily on controlled (vs. automatic) processing, which operates serially, requires attention, and is capacity (resource) limited (e.g., Shiffrin & Schneider, 1977). Increased levels of arousal have been shown to interfere with the ability to allocate mental resources during controlled processing (e.g., Kahneman, 1973). Therefore, if the activation of stereotypes results in levels of arousal that exceed the intermediate levels necessary for optimal performance, then the controlled processing required for successful problem solving will be hindered.

What cognitive factors may mediate heightened arousal? The literature points to the cognitive appraisals of threat vs. challenge.

EFFECTS OF COGNITIVE APPRAISAL, THREAT VS. CHALLENGE, ON AROUSAL AND PERFORMANCE

The interpretation of an event as either posing a potential threat to the well-being of a person or as a challenge that can lead to a positive growth experience has differential effects on physiological arousal and, in turn, on intellectual performance. When an environment is perceived as a threatening one, animals and humans show an increase in pituitary-adrenal-corticol arousal, in which the pituitary gland releases adrenocorticotropin (ACTH), which in turn, stimulates the release of the glucocorticoid, cortisol. When an environment is perceived as a challenging one, the hypothalamus, acting through the sympathetic nervous system, tends to stimulate adrenaline release from the medullae (Dienstbier, 1989).

Increased arousal is associated with cognitive and behavioral changes. For example, Ursin, Baade, & Levine (1978) found that Norweigian Army paratroopers with increased adrenaline levels had better success in jumps from airplanes than did paratroopers with increased cortisol levels. The latter also tended to show an increased defensiveness. In animal studies, using a range of subjects, from rats to primates, exposure to stressful stimuli that the animal has no control over (e.g., separating an infant from its mother) tends to result in elevation of cortisol.

The main construct that emerges, psychologically, is that of having perceived resources available to cope with situational demands. The situation becomes challenging when there is a perception of adequate resources, such as sufficient skills or a chance to practice the task at hand. In contrast, situations are appraised as threatening when the resources are perceived to be insufficient (Folkman & Lazarus, 1986). Therefore, situational beliefs about intellectual resources to perform well enough on a math test could play an important role in whether the test is interpreted as a challenge or as a threat.

OUR WORKING STEREOTYPE THREAT MODEL

Our working model of stereotype threat is based on cognitively mediated arousal as the main causal factor (Fig. 9.1).

Spencer et al. (1999) showed that, although generalized arousal (as measured explicitly by asking participants to rate their degree of nervousness and anxiety) was related to both performance and threat, arousal did not significantly reduce the direct relationship between threat and test performance. Nonetheless, these results do not rule out arousal as a mediator of stereotype threat. As Spencer et al. noted, the number of participants in their study was too small to perform an adequate factor analysis. In addition, because the measures of arousal were overt and self-reported, participants' ratings of arousal may have been unreliable or affected by demand characteristics.

To avoid the pitfalls of self-report, correlational analysis, and some of the ecological validity concerns related to directly measuring arousal, we carried out a study to examine the role of arousal using indirect measures (Ben-Zeev, Inzlicht, & Fein, in press). In Experiment 1, high math-identified female college students were divided randomly into two conditions. The experimental group was placed under stereotype threat condition

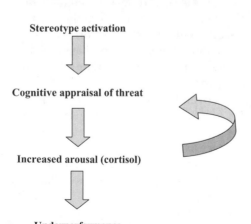

FIGURE 9.1. Performance deficits mediated by threat appraisal and heightened cortisol.

(i.e., they were told that in the past, females have performed more poorly on the math test than males). Participants in the no threat condition were told that males and females have performed equally well on this test. All participants then completed a low-arousal easy task (typing their name forward as many times as they could in a given time frame) and a high-arousal difficult task (typing their name backward as many times as they could in a given time frame) (following the procedure used by Schmitt, Gilovitch, Goore, & Joseph, 1986).

We predicted that if arousal plays an important role in stereotype threat, then the individuals subjected to stereotype threat should do *better* on the easy task but *worse* on the difficult task in comparison to the individuals in the no threat condition. This prediction follows from the arousal and social facilitation literature, which shows that individuals who experience high levels of arousal do better on easy than on difficult tasks (Schmitt et al., 1986; Zajonc, 1965). The data confirmed this prediction. Females in the threat group performed significantly better on the easy ($M = 8.72$) than on the hard task ($M = 5.2$), whereas females in the nonthreat condition performed significantly better on the difficult ($M = 8.2$) than on the hard task ($M = 6.2$), As predicted, the analysis of variance (ANOVA) yielded no significant main effects (both $Fs < 1$), but the interaction was significant, $F(1, 15) = 5.96, p < 0.03$.

A second experiment was done to examine whether arousal is implicated in stereotype threat by using a misattribution paradigm. The stereotype threat manipulation consisted of assigning female college students randomly to either same-sex (one female student with two female confederates) or minority (one female student with two male confederates) conditions. We then carried out an indirect assessment of arousal by using a misattribution manipulation. As part of a general cover story about examining performance on standardized tests, participants were told that one of the factors being studied was the effects of subliminal noise on test performance. All participants were seated in front of a large machine that was introduced as the subliminal noise generator. To illustrate how the audio generator worked, participants were exposed to a series of audible tones that increased in frequency, culminating in a subliminal tone of 20,000 Hz – a "silent tone" well beyond the range of human hearing. Participants were then informed that they would be exposed to this tone for the duration of the math test. Participants in the *control* group were told that the subliminal noise would have no discernible physical effects on them. In contrast, those in the *misattribution* condition were told that the noise was associated with a number of side effects, and that previous participants had noted an increase in arousal, nervousness, and heart rate. They were told not to be alarmed if they felt these side effects and were assured that the any such side effects would be temporary. Next, all participants were given a difficult math test with GRE items to solve.

If the environment leads to performance deficits through the process of arousal, then giving stereotype threatened female students the chance to misattribute their arousal to the subliminal noise should have spared them the performance deficits triggered by stereotype threat. The performance deficit for females in the minority (threat) condition should be attenuated for females in the misattribution condition. The results of the pilot study supported the arousal prediction. A 2×2 analysis of covariance (ANCOVA) was performed on the number of math problems answered correctly, using SAT scores as a covariate, and revealed a significant interaction between the manipulations of sex composition and misattribution, F (1, 31) = 6.06, $p < 0.02$. Simple effects analyses revealed that among women not given the misattribution information, the typical stereotype threat effects emerged. Females in the minority group did significantly worse ($M = 6.34$, $SD = 2.43$) than did females in the same-sex group ($M = 8.82$, $SD = 2.40$), F (1, 31) = 5.44, $p < 0.03$. This constitutes a large effect size, Cohen's $d = 1.03$. In contrast, there were no significant differences between minority participants ($M = 7.97$, $SD = 2.33$) and same-sex participants ($M = 6.61$, $SD = 2.43$) in the misattribution condition, F (1, 31) = 1.44, *ns*, and no other effects approached significance.

The results of this study are consistent with the hypothesis that the activation of stereotype threat may cause arousal to exceed an optimal level, resulting in performance deficits (i.e., controls in the minority condition performed worse than controls in the same-sex condition). However, performance deficits were eliminated when high-achieving females in the threat condition were given an opportunity to misattribute their elevated state of arousal to a benign external source. Females in the misattribution condition who were in the minority performed as well as controls in the same-sex condition. Thus, it appears that the misattribution manipulation may have reduced arousal closer to optimal levels.

Blascovich, Spencer, Quinn, and Steele (2001) found that, when African Americans experienced stereotype threat on a cognitive task, their blood pressure rose faster and reached a higher level than it did in Caucasians. This heightened blood pressure continued even during a five-minute rest period and during an additional task. When stereotype threat was reduced, however, this effect was not apparent. These results, together with the arousal studies by Ben-Zeev et al. (in press), support the view that physiological arousal has a central role in stereotype threat.

We are currently in the process of examining arousal levels by assessing whether individuals under threat secrete higher levels of the corticosteroid cortisol, which has been implicated in a variety of cognitive and health deficits (e.g., Dienstbier, 1989). These findings would imply that intellectual and health risks might become associated with frequent experience of stereotype threat.

We postulate that in order to uncover how stereotype threat is mediated, we must examine the physiological arousal associated with threat as the cause of performance deficits in women's math performance. If a stress response (i.e., cortisol) inhibits cognitive performance, could it be that the physiological response of stress an individual feels under stereotype threat conditions is the mechanism that causes their underperformance? It is our hypothesis that when under stereotype threat, high math-identifying females will perform more poorly than when they are not under threat as a result of this physiological response. A heightened state of arousal due to the stress of possibly confirming the negative stereotype about their group will lead to physiological effects of stress on cognition, namely, subpar performance. Furthermore, women who do not identify strongly with math and/or math-oriented domains (e.g., "low identifiers") will initially exhibit low arousal due to their initial state of apathy toward taking a math test and will subsequently perform better on a difficult math test when under stereotype threat due to an increase in arousal that positively correlates with cognitive functioning. The mediation of physiological arousal, we conjecture, is based on the cognitive appraisals of challenge vs. threat. As can be seen in Fig. 9.1 (as well as in Fig. 9.2), the hypothesized relation between appraisals and arousal is bidirectional. That is, an appraisal can cause a physiological reaction, which, in turn, can affect further appraisals.

PERFORMANCE DEFICITS AND BOOSTS INTERPRETED THROUGH THE LENS OF THREAT VS. CHALLENGE AROUSAL

Traditionally, stereotype threat work has focused on how the activation of stereotypes alleging inferior abilities can cause performance deficits in the given domain. However, it appears that the social context can prime particular aspects of one's self-identity, which, in turn, may hinder or *facilitate* intellectual performance. A particularly compelling illustration of this reality comes from the work of Shih et al. (1999), who examined the effects of stereotype activation on Asian American females' math performance. In the experimental conditions, participants were primed with being Asian American or were primed with being female before taking a difficult math test. The priming was conducted by using pretest questionnaires, which asked participants to answer questions regarding their ethnicity or their gender. A control group of Asian American females was asked to take the math test without completing any demographic questionnaire. Shih et al. found that participants in the Asian American identity priming condition scored significantly higher on the standardized math test than controls, whereas participants in the female identity priming condition scored lower than controls. These results are striking, given that a subtle priming of one aspect of identity (ethnicity) vs. another (gender) was sufficient for either enhancing or undermining performance.

These results conform to our cognitive appraisal framework. More specifically, we hypothesize that the Asian American females who were primed as females engaged in a threat appraisal, which led them to evaluate themselves as having insufficient resources (i.e., math ability) to successfully complete the math test. In contrast, the Asian American females in the Asian priming condition engaged in a challenge appraisal, which helped them to trust that they had the ability to complete the task successfully despite acknowledging that the task was difficult.

Another effect is the tendency of males to perform better on a math test when they are reminded of the stereotype regarding female inferiority in math *or* to "worsen" in performance when the stereotype threat condition is removed. Our challenge vs. threat appraisal framework is also useful for examining this trend over different studies. Spencer et al. (1999) were the first to report males' tendency to perform better in math under female threat conditions than under nonthreat conditions. Spencer et al. speculated that the (nonsignificantly) enhanced performance across multiple studies could be explained in one of two ways. First, males exhibit their baseline math performance under female threat conditions because stereotypes alleging math inferiority for females are present in most real world environments. Thus, it is the nonthreat situation that hinders males' performance. Second, males perform at baseline in the reduced stereotype or no threat condition, whereas the introduction of the threat gives men a "boost" because men are reminded indirectly of the stereotype that they are superior to females in math. Whatever the explanation may be, the trend for males to enhance their math performance under threat can be seen across multiple studies (e.g., Inzlicht & Ben-Zeev, 2000; Walsh, Hickey, & Duffy, 1999).

If our arousal model is correct, then high math-identified males and females experience near peak levels of arousal before being asked to take a math test. Under the female threat conditions, females would be more likely to engage in threat appraisal followed by elevated cortisol levels leading to underperformance, whereas males under the female threat condition may engage in a challenge response that would boost their performance. We expect the magnitude of this "boost" to be small because males would already be performing near ceiling.

The challenge that a nonstigmatized person may feel under threat to a stigmatized person may be captured by the following model (see Fig. 9.2):

The male boost in performance that occurs under female threat is not limited to math domains; it can also be found in the domain of negotiation (e.g., Kray, Thompson, & Galinsky, 2001) and for white males, under African American threat (Steele & Aronson, 1995). This boost in performance for the nonstigmatized population under conditions that elicit the alleged inferiority of stigmatized populations is apparent in the majority

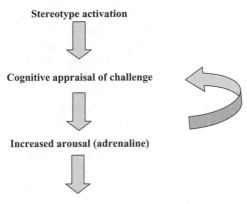

Stereotype activation

Cognitive appraisal of challenge

Increased arousal (adrenaline)

Optimal performance

FIGURE 9.2. Facilitation effects of nonstigmatized individuals mediated by challenge and heightened cathecolamines.

of research on stereotype threat[1] and can provide a fruitful area of investigation for understanding stereotype threat better.

DISCUSSION AND FUTURE DIRECTIONS

In this chapter, we propose a new framework for examining stereotype threat-induced underperformance, in which stigmatized people's responses to stereotypes alleging their intellectual inferiority engage in a threat appraisal that heightens cortisol levels and hurts intellectual performance. A further prediction is that if people learn to adopt a challenge appraisal instead of a threat appraisal, then performance deficits may be averted.

Wheeler and Petty (2001) propose an alternative account to a cognitive appraisal-mediated arousal for explaining stereotype-threat phenomena. They propose that stereotypes may result from an automatic activation of a network of associations that may hurt performance without the elicitation of higher-level cognitive processing, such as cognitive appraisals. For example, ideomotor theory (e.g., Bargh, Chen, & Burrows, 1996) suggests that particular cues in the environment can automatically affect motivation and performance, without conscious awareness. As an example, a woman entering a room in which a television set is playing an advertisement related to cleaning products might automatically shift into an associated

---

[1] Usually, the nonstigmatized population is not the focus of such research in stereotype threat because this population tends to always perform better than the stigmatized population. However, when data are reported on the nonstigmatized population, the trend of the nonsignificant difference becomes apparent across different studies.

motivational state where domestic activities are a priority and other tasks, such as academic or career-oriented tasks, are deemed less important.

The problem with ideomotor theory as an explanation for stereotype threat is its inability to account for the fact that low-domain identifiers do not show performance deficits. Identification with the threatened domain (the degree to which one's self-concept is linked to a domain) is central to stereotype threat theory. The more a person cares about being successful in the domain, the more he or she is predicted to be affected by stereotypes alleging a lack of ability in that domain (Steele, 1997). Research by Aronson et al. (1998) indicates that the stereotype threat manipulation disrupts only the performance of the high identifiers. Thus, people who are at risk from stereotype threat are those stigmatized individuals who are at the vanguard of their group in a given domain.

Wheeler and Petty (2001) also discuss other potential mediators of stereotype threat that are in agreement with our model. For example, they propose that stereotype activation changes people's perceptions of their environment, including aspects of other people in it. They discuss a study done by Herr (1986), which showed that participants primed with hostility cues began perceiving their neutral partner as hostile, and behaved more competitively, than those primed with nonhostile cues. This explanation is consistent with the idea that if people engage in threat vs. challenge appraisals, then they focus on potential failure rather than on potential success.

Wheeler and Petty (2001) argued that another explanatory variable may be found in literature on multiple selves. For example, Ruvolo and Markus (1992) asked participants to imagine their own futures as being successful or unsuccessful. Those who imagined positive visions of their future selves showed greater effort and persistence in the task that followed. Perhaps the types of primes that have been used in stereotype threat research, such as an Asian prime or a female prime, could also be activating possible selves. A person could go through an automatic shift, into a particular "self," as well as engage in a more conscious, cognitive appraisal of threat or challenge at the same time.

Another question is, what are the roles of beliefs in producing threat? As we discuss in the section on alternative mediators to arousal, self-efficacy does not appear to mediate stereotype threat. Instead, based on previous evidence that only high achievers are vulnerable to the debilitating effects of threat (e.g., Steele, 1997), it follows that a high-domain self-efficacy may be a *moderator* of stereotype threat. That is, stigmatized individuals with a high domain self-efficacy would be most prone to experiencing problem-solving deficits in threatening environments.

Situationally, after the activation of a stereotype, and as a possible result of threat, people may endorse maladaptive beliefs. Schoenfeld (1983) found that students who thought less of their mathematical abilities were more likely to attribute their successes to luck and their failures to lack of mathematical ability, whereas students who thought of themselves as high in math ability were more likely to attribute their successes to ability. It would be informative to examine whether, under threat, stigmatized students who identify highly with ability and success in a domain would nevertheless tend to rate themselves lower on ability as a result of experiencing threat situationally.

For example, beliefs about the malleability of intelligence may be implicated in stereotype threat. Dweck and colleagues (Dweck, 1999; Dweck & Leggett, 1988) found that individuals' implicit theories about intelligence have a direct impact on how they think and feel about – as well as approach and engage in – performance tasks. Individuals who believe intelligence to be a malleable and dynamic process ("incremental" theorists) often approach cognitive and performance tasks with a "mastery-oriented" style, which leads them to successful outcomes, whereas those who believe that intelligence is more of a fixed, innate quality ("entity" theorists) are more vulnerable to a "helpless" attitude toward problem solving, which renders them prone to disengage from tasks and to underperform, even in domains in which they have achieved success and enjoy (Dweck, 1999).

However, Dweck (1999) also found that these same, apparently embedded beliefs about intelligence can be changed (if only temporarily) when exposed to different models of intelligence. Notably, when given a lecture on the incremental theory of intelligence, college students who had done poorly on a test were more apt to express interest in taking a tutorial to improve their score, whereas students who had been lectured on an entity theory of intelligence (Hong et al., 1999, in Dweck, 1999) were not.

In addition, Aronson, Fried and Good (2002) found that using an incremental framework of intelligence helped to reduce the impact of stereotype threat among college students. In other words, teaching students that intelligence is not a fixed entity, but is something that can be improved upon both with sustained effort and by varying one's problem-solving strategies, can effectively lessen students' vulnerability to stereotype threat (because stereotypes are based on the idea of innate, fixed traits) and subsequently improve their performance (Dweck, 1999). These findings are encouraging because they give credence to the idea that an individual's abilities may not be predetermined and that stereotype threat (as well as stereotypes themselves) can be diminished with appropriate and meaningful interventions.

The reality of stereotype threat is disconcerting. Students who suffer from stereotypes about their intellectual abilities are vulnerable to situational cues, which activate negative stereotypes and cause performance deficits. We hypothesize that the priming of a stereotype results in threat appraisal that causes heightened arousal and results in more algorithmic rather than meaningful problem solving. By trying to uncover the role of physiological arousal in mediating stereotype threat and the cognitive nature of the resultant deficits, we hope to contribute to the mitigation of stereotype threat. Thus, our work is designed to help understand the the-oretical underpinnings of stereotype threat, as well as to help stigmatized students overcome its effects by enhancing resilience to stereotypes and turning threat into challenge.

AUTHORS' NOTE

The writing of this chapter and some of the research described in it was enabled, in part, by a National Science Foundation ROLE grant, Award # 0207946, given to Talia Ben-Zeev and Steven Fein in September 2002.

We thank Elissa Epel and James Greeno for their invaluable insights. Correspondence concerning this chapter should be addressed to Talia Ben-Zeev, Department of Psychology, 1600 Holloway Ave., San Francisco, California 94132; E-mail: tbenzeev@sfsu.edu.

References

Aronson, J., Fried, C. B., & Good, C. (2002). Reducing the effects of stereotype threat on African American college students by shaping theories of intelligence. *Journal of Experimental Social Psychology, 38*, 113–125.

Aronson, J., Lustina, M. J., Good, C., Keough, K., Steele, C. M., & Brown, J. (1999). When white men can't do math: Necessary and sufficient factors in stereotype threat. *Journal of Experimental Social Psychology, 35*, 29–46.

Aronson, J., Quinn, D. M., & Spencer, S. J. (1998). Stereotype threat and the academic underperformance of minorities and women. In J. K. Swim & C. Stangor (Eds.), *Prejudice: The target's perspective* (pp. 83–103). San Diego, CA: Academic Press.

Aronson, J., & Salinas, M. F. (1997). *Stereotype threat, attributional ambiguity, and Latino underperformance*. Unpublished manuscript, University of Texas.

Bargh, J. A., Chen, M., & Burrows, L. (1996). Automaticity of social behavior: Direct effects of trait construct and stereotype activation on action. *Journal of Personality & Social Psychology, 71*, 230–244.

Baron, R. M., & Kenny, D. A. (1986). The moderator-mediator variable distinction in social psychological research: Conceptual, strategic and statistical considera-tions. *Journal of Personality and Social Psychology, 51*, 1173–1182.

Baumeister, R. F., & Showers, C. J. (1986). A review of paradoxical performance effects: Choking under pressure in sports and mental tests. *European Journal of Social Psychology, 16*, 361–383.

Benbow, C. P., Lubinski, D., Shea, D. L., & Eftekhari-Sanjani, H. (2000). Sex dif-ferences in mathematical reasoning ability at age 13: Their status 20 years later. *Psychological Science, 11*, 474–479.

Benbow, C. P., & Stanley, J. C. (1980). Sex differences in mathematical ability: Fact or artifact? *Science, 210*, 1262–1264.

Benbow, C. P., & Stanley, J. C. (1983). Sex differences in mathematical reasoning ability: More facts. *Science, 222*, 1029–1031.

Ben-Zeev, T., Fein, S., & Inzlicht, M. (in press). Arousal and stereotype threat. *Journal of Experimental Social Psychology.*

Blascovich, J., Spencer, S. J., Quinn, D., & Steele, C. (2001). African Americans and high blood pressure: The role of stereotype threat. *Psychological Science, 12,* 225–229.

Brown, R. P., & Josephs, R. A. (1999). Stereotype relevance and gender differences in math performance. *Journal of Personality and Social Psychology, 76,* 246–257.

Croizet, J. C., & Claire, T. (1998). Extending the concept of stereotype threat to social class: The intellectual underperformance of students from low socioeconomic backgrounds. *Personality and Social Psychology Bulletin, 24,* 588–594.

Dienstbier, R. A. (1989). Arousal and physiological toughness: Implications for mental and physical health. *Psychological Review, 96,* 84–100.

Dweck, C. S. (1999). *Self-Theories: Their role in motivation, personality and development.* Philadelphia: Psychology Press.

Dweck, C. S., & Leggett, E. L. (1988). A social-cognitive approach to motivation and personality. *Psychological Review, 95,* 256–273.

Eccles, J. S., & Jacobs, J. E. (1987). In M. R. Walsh (Ed.), *The Psychology of Women* (question 10, pp. 333–354). New Haven, CT: Yale University Press.

Folkman, S., & Lazarus, R. (1986). Stress process and depressive symptomatology. *Journal of Abnormal Psychology, 95,* 107–113.

Geary, D. C. (1996). Sexual selection and sex differences in mathematical abilities. *Behavioral and Brain Sciences, 19,* 229–284.

Hong, Y., Chiu, C., & Dweck, C. S. (1999). Implicit theories, attributions, and coping: A meaning system approach. *Journal of Personality & Social Psychology, 77,* 588–599.

Hyde, J. S., Fennema, E., & Lamon, S. J. (1990). Gender differences in mathematics performance: A meta analysis. *Psychological Bulletin, 107,* 139–155.

Inzlicht, M. (2001). *Threatening intellectual environments: When and why females perform worse in the presence of males.* Unpublished doctoral dissertation, Brown University.

Inzlicht, M., & Ben-Zeev, T. (2000). A threatening intellectual environment: Why females are susceptible to experiencing problem-solving deficits in the presence of males. *Psychological Science, 11,* 365–371.

Kahneman, D. (1973). *Attention and effort.* Englewood Cliffs, NJ: Prentice-Hall.

Kray, L. J., Thompson, L., & Galinsky, A. (2001). Battle of the sexes: Gender stereotype confirmation and reactance in negotiations. *Journal of Personality & Social Psychology, 80,* 942–958.

Leyens, J. P., Desert, M., Croizet, J. C., & Darcis, C. (2000). Stereotype threat: Are lower status and history of stigmatization preconditions of stereotype threat? *Personality and Social Psychology Bulletin, 26,* 1189–1199.

Lupien, S. J., & McEwen, B. S. (1997). The acute effects of corticosteroids on cognition: Integration of animal and human model studies. *Brain Research Reviews, 24,* 1–27.

Marx, D. M., Brown, J. L., & Steele, C. M. (1999). Allport's legacy and the situational press of stereotypes. *Journal of Social Issues, 55,* 491–502.

O'Brien, L. T., & Crandall, C. S. (2001). *Stereotype threat and arousal: Effects on women's math performance.* Manuscript submitted for publication.

Pyszczynski, T., & Greenberg, J. (1983). Determinants of reduction in effort as a strategy for coping with anticipated failure. *Journal of Research in Personality, 17,* 412–422.

Ruvolo, A. P., & Markus, H. R. (1992). Possible selves and performance: The power of self-relevant imagery. *Social Cognition, 10,* 95–124.

Schmitt, B. H., Gilovitch, T., Goore, N., & Joseph, L. (1986). Mere presence and social facilitation: One more time. *Journal of Experimental Social Psychology, 22,* 242–248.

Schoenfeld, A. H. (1983). Beyond the purely cognitive: Belief systems, social cognitions, and metacognitions as driving forces in intellectual performance. *Cognitive Science, 7,* 329–363.

Shiffrin, R. M., & Schneider, W. (1977). Controlled and automatic human information processing: I. Detection, search, and attention. *Psychological Review, 84,* 1–66.

Shih, M., Pittinsky, T. L., & Ambady, N. (1999). Stereotype susceptibility: Identity salience and shifts in quantitative performance. *Psychological Science, 10,* 80–83.

Spencer, S. J., Steele, C. M., & Quinn, D. (1999). Stereotype threat and women's math performance. *Journal of Experimental Social Psychology, 35,* 4–28.

Stangor, C., Carr, C., & Kiang, L. (1998). Activating stereotypes undermines task performance expectations. *Journal of Personality and Social Psychology, 75,* 1191–1197.

Steele, C. M. (1997). A threat in the air: How stereotypes shape intellectual identity and performance. *American Psychologist, 52,* 613–629.

Steele, C. M., & Aronson, J. (1995). Stereotype threat and the intellectual test performance of African Americans. *Journal of Personality and Social Psychology, 69,* 797–811.

Steele, C. M., Spencer, S. J., & Lynch, M. (1993). Self-image resilience and dissonance: The role of affirmational resources. *Journal of Personality and Social Psychology, 64,* 885–896.

Stone, J., Lynch, C. I., Sjomeling, M., & Darley, J. M. (1999). Stereotype threat effects on Black and White athletic performance. *Journal of Personality and Social Psychology, 77,* 1213–1227.

Ursin, H., Baade, E., & Levine, S. (Eds.). (1978). *Psychobiology of stress: A study of coping men.* New York: Academic Press.

Walsh, M., Hickey, C., & Duffy, J. (1999). Influence of item content and stereotype situation on gender differences in mathematical problem solving. *Sex Roles, 41,* 219–240.

Wheeler, S. C., & Petty, R. E. (2001). The effects of stereotype activation on behavior: A review of possible mechanisms. *Psychological Bulletin, 127,* 797–826.

Yerkes, R. M., & Dodson, J. D. (1908). The relationship of strength of stimulus to rapidity of habit-formation. *Journal of Comparative Neurology of Psychology, 18,* 459–482.

Zajonc, R. B. (1965). Social facilitation. *Science, 149,* 269–274.

10

The Role of Ethnicity on the Gender Gap in Mathematics

Alyssa M. Walters and Lisa M. Brown

Researchers have devoted a great deal of attention to gender differences in math perceptions and performance. Although the gap has closed at some levels, important differences persist and have been addressed in detail in previous chapters. However, when one throws ethnicity into the mix, the picture becomes far more complicated.

While gender differences are a primary focus within the mathematics domain, ethnicity differences are a concern across a wide range of educational areas. This ethnicity gap has been decreasing over the past few decades, however, African American and Latino/Latina students consistently receive lower scores than do European American students across a wide range of high-stakes standardized tests (Camara & Schmidt, 1999; Jencks & Phillips, 1998). Moreover, African American and Latino/Latina high school students have lower average grades and class rank than their European American and Asian American counterparts (National Task Force on Minority High Achievement, 1999). In contrast, on most tests, the performance of Asian American test takers is similar to that of European American students. The one exception to this pattern is the Quantitative Test of the Graduate Record Examination where Asian American students score higher than European American students (Camara & Schmidt, 1999).[1]

Given these gender and ethnic differences, then, some researchers suggested that women of color should be most disadvantaged group in a math context because they suffer from a double bind: they are ostensibly victims of additive effects related to both gender and ethnicity. This makes intuitive sense, but is it true? To fully understand the influence of gender and ethnicity on math performance, the following questions need to be addressed: Do observed gender differences generalize to all groups of color? Are there

---

[1] However, the variance among scores of Asian American students is generally larger than it is for any other ethnic group in the United States; these students receive some of the highest as well as some of the lowest scores on standardized tests (Tsang, 1988).

differences within gender and ethnic groups that affect ways in which students identify with, value, and pursue the math domain? Do stereotypes for gender and ethnicity interact or function independently with respect to performance? It is our hope that through this chapter we will illuminate some of these questions.

It is beyond the scope of this chapter to discuss the performance gap related to ethnicity in appropriate detail. Instead, we focus on major performance trends as they relate to gender differences in math. Also, we limit our discussion to the experiences of European American, African American, Latino/Latina, and Asian American students, groups for which the most data are currently available.

In general, there is a marked absence of research related to more than one dimension of identity. Hurtado (1997) argues that ignoring the interaction between gender and ethnicity has greatly limited our understanding of the experiences of different ethnic groups across time. In this chapter, we aim to provide the fullest possible account of the current understanding of the interaction between ethnicity and gender in mathematics performance by drawing from summary reports of scores on standardized assessments, by describing the few studies that have addressed the gender and ethnicity interaction directly, and by making inferences from studies that have looked at both factors separately.

Gender Differences in Math Performance Across Ethnicity

In a recent summary report of scores on standardized math assessments, Coley (2001) highlighted performance differences across gender within ethnicity. His overview revealed that gender differences are relatively consistent across ethnic groups, however, he noted several differences across age cohorts. For instance, the National Assessment of Educational Progress (NAEP) includes an assessment of math knowledge and ability and is administered to students in the 4th, 8th, and 12th grades. Recent data reveals that 4th-grade males outscored females only among the European American students, and this gender difference disappeared by the 8th grade. Although 12th-grade European American and African American males outscored their female counterparts in previous years, this gap was no longer present by 1996. However, ethnic differences on NAEP mathematics have remained stable, favoring European American and Asian American students at each grade level (approximately two-fifths of a standard deviation in 2000) (National Center for Educational Statistics, 2002).

The mathematics section of the Scholastic Aptitude Test I (SAT-M) produces a somewhat different pattern. On this test, the gender gap is present across all ethnic groups, but it varies considerably in size (Coley, 2001). The gap is largest among Latino/Latina test takers (about one-half a standard deviation or 55 points), and the smallest difference is found among African Americans (about one-fifth of a standard deviation or 19 points). Similarly, on the quantitative portion of the Graduate Record Examination (GRE-Q), men outscore women across all four ethnic groups. However, the largest differences (about seven-tenths of a standard deviation or 70 points) are found among European American test takers (rather than Latino/Latina test takers). And again, the smallest differences are found among African American test takers (about two-fifths of a standard deviation or 43 points).

For both the SAT-M and the GRE-Q, then, the magnitude of gender differences varies across ethnicity groups (Coley, 2001). However, for both tests, the differences across ethnicity are generally more pronounced than gender differences (Camara & Schmidt, 1999; Graduate Record Examination, 2001). For instance, on the SAT-M the difference between scores of European American and African American test takers is approximately 100 points (about one standard deviation), and on the GRE-Q, the difference is approximately 125 points.

We can also explore the gender and ethnicity gap by examining empirical studies that have included both ethnicity and gender as predictor variables of math performance. An overview of several studies reveals a pattern similar to that of the summary reports of standardized test scores – the gender effect varies across ethnicity and is smaller than the effect for ethnicity. For instance, in a large-scale study of social and environmental factors related to GRE General test scores, Walters, Lee, and Trapani (2004) found that gender predicted GRE-Q scores among European American, Latino/Latina, and Asian American test takers, but not among African American test takers. Other research has explored the relative contribution of gender and ethnicity on math performance. Gibbins and Bickel (1991) investigated the advantage of public vs. private high schools in promoting SAT scores. They found that while gender and race (here being African American or not) predicted SAT math scores, the effect of race ($\beta = -68.13$) was much larger than the effect of gender ($\beta = 35.64$). (The public/private status of the school did not have a consistent effect.)

DeMars (2000) investigated math and science scores on the Michigan High School Proficiency Test for more than 11,000 high school students and also found the ethnicity effect on test scores to be larger than the gender effect. In fact, the gender effect in math was not significant, whereas the ethnicity effect (favoring European American students) was highly significant. There was no interaction between gender and ethnicity on the math scores. (Note there was an interaction between gender and ethnicity in *science* exam scores in which the gender difference existed among European Americans, but was virtually nonexistent among African Americans.)

Hall, Davis, Bolen & Chia (1999) studied math performance on the California Achievement Test among middle school students. They found no gender effects on math achievement; however, they did find that African American students scored lower than European American students. Hauck and Finch (1993) found the same results in their analysis of middle school students using the math component of the Stanford Achievement Test and the math assessment used by the South Carolina Basic Skills Assessment Program. Catsambis (1994) similarly found no consistent gender differences in math achievement among middle and high school students. However, she did find that European American students outperformed African American and Latino students.

All these studies found that ethnicity had a strong effect favoring European Americans across several age cohorts, but those examining interactions between ethnicity and gender (DeMars, 2000; Hall et al., 1999) found none. We suspect that the absence of an interaction is due to both the large main effect for ethnicity and the minimal effects for gender. Overall, research studies and test score data reveal that ethnic differences in math performance may appear earlier and are larger than gender differences. Also, gender differences favoring males tend to be smallest among African Americans and largest among European American and Latino/Latina students.

Math-Related Interests, Attitudes, and Self-Efficacy

These gender and ethnic differences in math performance may be closely related to the degree to which students identify with, feel capable in, and value the math domain. To explore these issues, Catsambis (1994) conducted an analysis of students' attitudes toward math using males and females across different ethnicities and age cohorts. She found that, across all ethnicities, middle school males relative to females were more likely to have positive attitudes toward math, be active in math-related clubs, look forward to math class, and be low in anxiety regarding asking questions in class. She also reports that these differences were most pronounced among Latinos/Latinas, and often nonexistent among African Americans.

Among high school students, females were more likely than males to report that they took math classes because they are required. This effect was again weakest among African Americans and strongest among Latinos/Latinas (Catsambis, 1994). Latinas were particularly likely to report low confidence in their math performance relative to males, and were also less likely to aspire to math-related careers. Interestingly, although this work found few gender differences in math-related attitudes among African American high school students, African American females were also unlikely to report aspirations for a career in math (European American boys are most likely to have these aspirations). Catsambis's work suggests that Latinas may be particularly unlikely to identify with the mathematics domain.

Such attitudes toward math may guide students' decisions to take math courses. A review of course-taking patterns among college-bound high school seniors revealed that females across all ethnic groups are closing the gender gap in math preparation (Coley, 2001). By 1999, European

American, African American, and Asian American women equaled males in number of math courses taken. Only Latinas continued to take fewer math courses than males. This may help to explain why the gender gap in SAT-M scores for Latinas/Latinos is larger than in other groups.

However, some work suggests that by college, math-related attitudes among African American students may begin to diverge. Among African American undergraduates, males were found to report more self-efficacy in math (Gainor & Lent, 1998) and a greater interest in pursuing a math-related career (Post, Stewart, & Smith, 1991) than their female counterparts. For males, both self-efficacy and interests predicted consideration of a math-related career. However, for African American females, only interest, and not self-efficacy, predicted consideration of a math-related career (Post, Stewart, & Smith, 1991).

Overall, we see the most pronounced gender differences in students' attitudes toward math among Latinos/Latinas, and these attitudes may relate to low enrollment in math courses. The smallest gender differences appear among African American students, although these attitudes may grow more dissimilar in college. Interestingly, lack of interest appears to play a pivotal role in African American women's decisions about participation in mathematics, while both lack of confidence and interest appear to contribute to lower participation by Latinas.

So far, we have identified attitudes that may relate to decisions among some women of color to abstain from math-related coursework and careers. However, the next step is to explore the influence of gender and ethnicity for students who have chosen to pursue math-related careers. We presume that such students enter programs perceiving themselves to be capable in mathematics and having developed a real interest in the area. Thus, they have at some level come to integrate math performance into their identity.

To explore the experiences of women of color within the mathematics field, we can review the results of Seymour and Hewitt's (1997) in-depth analysis of attitudes related to persistence in college-level science, math, and engineering (SME) degree programs. One finding of this interview and survey data is that these disciplines often represent a white, male-oriented tradition, emphasizing values such as independence and competition. Women and students of color (African American, Latino/Latina, and Asian American students) reported that this environment often conflicts with their own cultural values and socialization experiences. As a result, many of these students simply opt to switch into other disciplines or to leave college entirely. Indeed, women of all ethnicities and male students of color are disproportionately more likely than European American men to leave mathematics programs (Astin & Astin, 1993; *Science* editorial, 1992; Seymour & Hewitt, 1997; Strenta, Elliot, Matier, Scott, & Adair, 1994).

Seymour and Hewitt (1997) also report that these environments may eventually erode women's perceptions of their quantitative abilities (independent of their actual performance), and this loss of confidence may be due to changes in external support structures. Women of color were particularly likely to attribute their decisions to enroll in SME programs to having been encouraged by educators and other members of their community. Yet, once they are enrolled in a SME program this support may no longer be present. The researchers suggest that a noncollegial environment paired with the abrupt withdrawal of this external support and validation is likely to diminish confidence.

However, as was the case at the precollege level, women's reactions to college-level math environments varied across ethnicity. African American women were less likely than women of all other ethnicities to decide to leave SME programs because of a lack of confidence (Seymour & Hewitt, 1997). Instead, African American women expressed greater confidence with regard to quantitative-oriented education, and adapted more easily to the independent study style than did women in other groups. This is consistent with findings from a survey of occupational interests among college men and women of different ethnicities (Tomlinson & Evans-Hughes, 1991). Responses to the Strong-Campbell Interest Inventory revealed that of all groups, African American women had the strongest preference for environments in which they could work alone. In this way, African American women may not experience conflict with the values required for success in SME programs (e.g., noncollegial working environment) to the same extent as for others.

We can think of several possible explanations for this finding. African American women who have succeeded in math to the extent that they have pursued it in college have possibly done so *because* they have learned to work independently. Having often been the solo representative of their gender and/or ethnic group in high school math courses may have fostered less reliance on peer support and greater need to hone this skill of working independently. In a survey of minority women in SME programs, Brown (1994) found African American women often lamented being not only the sole student of color in their classes, but often also the only woman. Another explanation may be related to the central role that interests play in African American females' decisions to pursue a math degree. Interest in the field has been shown to be an important predictor of persistence in higher education (e.g., Swanson & Hansen, 1985).

Overall, we begin to see several patterns emerge. First, a lack of interest rather than confidence may be key to the low participation of African American women in math-related fields. Among African American women who do opt to select math fields, they appear to be less adversely affected by the seemingly "male-dominated" environments. In contrast, Latinas may avoid math-related fields out of a lack of both confidence and interest, and their confidence may be further diminished within college-level math environments.

We seem to know less about the experiences of Asian American women in math fields. However, we suspect that in this case, attitudes and performance may involve a more complex interplay between gender and Asian American identity. Next, we address the role of stereotypes about math abilities across gender and ethnicity.

Multiple Group Identities and Math-Related Stereotypes

Cultural stereotypes about math ability may be another key influence on math performance for women of color in higher education. A growing body of research reveals that environments where a negative ability stereotype is salient can undermine the performance of targets of the stereotype (Steele & Aronson, 1995). Described as *stereotype threat*, this effect is limited to people who value and, consequently, identify with the performance domain (Aronson et al., 1999). Davies and Spencer (in this volume) discuss in detail the research that has been conducted on women and stereotype threat. In short, women who identify with mathematics as a field underperformed on math tests when they were reminded of the stereotype that women typically perform worse than men on tests of quantitative ability (Spencer et al., 1999). This threat can apply to anyone who belongs to a group to which an ability-related stereotype applies (see Aronson & Salinas, 1997; Steele & Aronson, 1995).

Math performance, however, can be linked to multiple group identities. For instance, women, Latino/Latinas and African Americans are typically negatively stereotyped with regard to mathematical ability (Benbow, 1988; Niemann et al., 1994), whereas Asian Americans are more often positively stereotyped, leading to the label of "model minority" (Kao, 1995; Steen, 1987).

For this reason, researchers have begun to investigate the influence of multiple group stereotypes on math performance. In one such investigation of Asian American women, Shih, Pittinsky, and Ambady (1999) found that the stereotypes related to the identity that is most salient (either gender or ethnicity) exerts the greatest influence on performance. Specifically, when ethnicity was made salient, and presumably the stereotype of high math ability was evoked, women performed well on a math test. However, when gender was made salient, reminding subjects of the stereotype of low math ability, they performed poorly on the test.

These findings suggest that women who belong to a group to which a positive stereotype applies may experience a "performance boost" under certain circumstances, and that performance will vary with environmental cues that make salient different aspects of their identities. However, others have argued that there is more to the story for women who belong to groups labeled as "model minorities"; even positive stereotypes may be deleterious to math performance. Specifically, Asian American women's performances suffered when their ethnic identity was evoked in a way that reminded them of others' high expectations for their performance (Cheryan & Bodenhausen, 2000). Therefore, when positive stereotypes serve to heighten concern about failing to meet the high expectations associated with the stereotype, performance may decline. Women who are defined as "model minorities," then, are susceptible to choking under the implicit pressures of that positive label.

Priming one identity over another may not only affect women's math performances, but it may also relate to others' perceptions of their ability. Pittinsky, Shih, and Ambady (1999) found that when participants were asked to evaluate a female Asian American college applicant, reminding them of her ethnicity resulted in their recalling a higher SAT-M score for her. Conversely, priming her gender resulted in their recalling a significantly lower score.

Together, these studies highlight the influence of cues in the social environment on math performance, and groups that are subject to both positive and negative stereotypes may be affected differently, depending on the types of social cues that are present. So far, the most salient identity appears to exert the greatest influence, and both positive and negative stereotypes can harm performance.

In the case of Asian American women, however, the stereotype of their ethnicity suggests a positive math performance. What is the case for women whose ethnicity bears a negative math-related stereotype – such as African American women or Latinas? It is possible that the effects of each identity will have an independent and equivalent influence on performance as was found among Asian American women. However, in the case where multiple group identities are associated with negative stereotypes, researchers have found that the stereotypes interact to simultaneously affect performance.

In an effort to examine the consequences of activating two negative stereotypes simultaneously, Gonzales, Blanton, and Williams (2002) examined math performances of European American and Latino/Latina students under stereotype-threatening conditions. Findings revealed both a gender-based and an ethnicity-based stereotype threat effect, with an interaction between the gender and the ethnicity effect. Specifically, all women experienced a greater performance decline in response to the gender-based manipulation than did men, and Latinos/Latinas performed worse than did European Americans in response to the ethnicity-based manipulation. However, in the case of the ethnicity-based manipulation, Latinas experienced a greater performance decline than did Latino men. The researchers concluded that being Latina seems to sensitize a woman to stereotypes associated with her gender, but that gender does not appear to sensitize her to Latino-based stereotypes. The authors speculate that it is the distinctiveness of belonging to a non-European American ethnic group that makes students of color chronically aware of that identity. This distinctiveness, in turn, creates a general awareness of stereotypes such as gender, which alone do not incite such a generalization. However, given prior research on attitudes and math performance across ethnicity, it is unclear whether these effects will generalize to African American women.

These studies reveal that the influence of stereotypes and the social environment on math performance is a complex one. Environmental cues can impede or boost performance, depending on whether they evoke stereotypes relevant to the target's gender or ethnicity, and the expectations of an evaluative audience. Moreover, the activation of stereotypes will also influence others' perceptions of the target's math ability.

SUMMARY AND DISCUSSION

We sought to address three questions pertaining to the role of ethnicity on the gender gap in math performance: (1) do existing gender differences generalize to all groups of color?, (2) are there differences within gender and ethnic groups that affect ways in which students identify with, value, and pursue the math domain?, and (3) do stereotypes for gender and ethnicity interact or function independently with respect to math performance? We presented evidence from two sources: summary reports of math standardized test scores, and empirical studies that have included both gender and ethnicity in their analyses of math performance. Thus, we have drawn certain conclusions based on cross-sections of students from different ages and contexts, and clearly have not captured the full range of math-related experiences and perceptions of all female students of color. However, we believe this is a starting point.

With regard to our first question, we see that on each measure of math performance that tends to show gender differences, the magnitude of the difference varies across ethnic groups. Gender differences tend to be largest among Latino/Latina and European American students, and smallest for African American students, with Asian American students falling somewhere in the middle. However, in general, ethnic differences in math performance tend to appear earlier and be more pronounced than gender differences.

Regarding the second question of whether attitudes toward math vary across gender and ethnicity, we found several patterns of differences. Generally, the differences between males and females are similar to the patterns of performance – they are largest among Latinos/Latinas, intermediate among European Americans, and smallest and often nonexistent among African Americans. Moreover, African American women's decisions to participate in math-related fields appear to more closely relate to their interest in the field rather than to a lack of confidence in their math ability. However, for Latinas, a lack of confidence may be a primary reason for their low participation.

It is feasible that these gender differences in math-related attitudes and performances relate to different socialization experiences. One possibility is that socialization in many Latino homes is from a patriarchal framework, so distinct gender roles may be an important part of the Latino/Latina identity. For instance, although females are generally encouraged to pursue their education, Gandara (1995) found that Latino/Latina parents are more likely to encourage their sons than their daughters to pursue higher education. Such messages may hinder their identification with traditionally male domains such as math. Also, within low-income Latino/Latina homes, Laosa (1978) found that mothers were less likely to convey to their children messages that foster the independent problem-solving strategies that are required in American classrooms. (Latina mothers from middle-class homes did not differ from European American mothers.) As we saw previously, independence appears to be a key factor in sustaining students through math programs in higher education.

In contrast, African American females may receive socialization messages that foster a high level of confidence and resilience when confronted with negative ability-related stereotypes in the math field. Crocker and Major (1989) suggest several mechanisms by which people of color can buffer their self-views from negative ability-related stereotypes. Specifically, they propose that stereotyped people may (1) attribute negative evaluations to prejudice on the part of the evaluator, (2) devalue domains in which their group tends to do poorly, and (3) limit self–other comparisons to ingroup members. African American women may have been taught to use these mechanisms with regard to mathematics to a greater extent than have Latinas. Indeed, among adolescents, African American females have higher self-esteem than do African American males and European American girls (Eccles, Barber, Jozefowicz, Malenchuk & Vida, 1999.

Next, we look at research on the role of the social environment and math performance to address our third question: do stereotypes for multiple group identities interact or function independently with respect to math performance? We see that among Asian American women, a group to which both positive and negative math-related stereotypes apply, performance depends on the identity that is most salient; women perform well when their ethnicity is salient, and worse when their gender is salient. Thus, for Asian American women, the two group identities function independently. Among Latinas to whom two negative math-related stereotypes apply, however, we see an interactive effect – making ethnicity salient seems to prime negative stereotypes about gender. This evidence might also contribute to the consistently large gender gap among Latino/Latinas in math performance. It remains to be seen whether a similar, additive effect occurs for African American women.

When considering efforts to retain girls and women of color in mathematics programs, we should understand that one size does not fit all. Different factors relate to their participation and retention in these programs, depending on their age and ethnic group membership. Future research can continue to investigate various sources of resiliency that certain girls and women have. Once research delineates these factors, specific policies and practices can be implemented into mathematics programs. However, at this juncture there is still a need for research that investigates the intersection of gender and ethnicity, as well as other factors like socioeconomic status and nativity, as they relate to mathematics participation and performance. It is our hope that this topic will be a fruitful line of work that brings insight into the complex array of experiences that girls and women have in the mathematics context.

References

Aronson, J., Lusting, M., Good, C., Keogh, K., Steele, C., & Brown, J. (1999). When White men can't do math: Necessary and sufficient conditions for stereotype threat. *Journal of Experimental Social Psychology, 35,* 29–46.

Aronson, J., & Salinas, M. F. (1997, April). *Stereotype threat: Is low performance the price of self-esteem for Mexican Americans?* Paper presented to the Western Psychological Association Conference, Seattle, Washington.

Astin, A. W., & Astin, H. S. (1993). *Undergraduate science education: The impact of different college environments on the educational pipeline in the sciences.* Los Angeles: Higher Education Research Institute, UCLA.

Benbow, C. P. (1988). Sex differences in mathematical reasoning ability among the intellectually talented: Their characterization, consequences, and possible explanations. *Behavioral and Brain Sciences, 11,* 169–183.

Brown, S. V. (1994). *Under-represented minority women in science and engineering education.* Princeton, NJ: Educational Testing Service.

Camara, W., & Schmidt, A. E. (1999). *Group differences in standardized testing and social stratification.* (College Board Rep. No. 99–5). New York: College Board.

Catsambis, S. (1994). The Path to Math: Gender and Racial-Ethnic Differences in Mathematics Participation from Middle School to High School, *Sociology of Education, 67*(3), 199–215. [Reprinted in L. A. Pepleau, S. Chapman DeBro, R. C. Veniegas, & P. L. Taylor (Eds.). (1998). *Gender, Culture and Ethnicity.* Mayfield Publishing, pp. 102–119.]

Cheryan, S., & Bodenhausen, G. (2000). When positive stereotypes threaten intellectual performance: The psychological hazards of "model minority" status. *Psychological Science, 11,* 399–402.

Coley, R. J. (2001). *Differences in the gender gap: Comparisons across racial/ethnic groups in education and work.* Princeton, NJ: Education Testing Service.

Crocker, J., & Major, B. (1989). Social stigma and self-esteem: The self-protective properties of stigma. *Psychological Review, 96,* 608–630.

DeMars, C. E. (2000). Test stakes and item format interactions. *Applied Measurement in Education, 13*(1), 55–77.

Eccles, J., Barber, B., Jozefowicz, D., Malenchuk, O., & Vida, M. (1999). Self-evaluations of competence, task values, and self-esteem. In N. G. Johnson, M. C. Roberts, & J. Worell (Eds.), *Beyond appearance: A new look at adolescent girls* (pp. 53–88). Washington, DC: American Psychological Association.

Gainor, K. A., & Lent, R. W. (1998). Social cognitive expectations and racial identity attitudes in predicting the math choice intentions of Black college students. *Journal of Counseling Psychology, 45*(4), 403–413.

Gandara, P. (1995). *Over the Ivy Walls: The educational mobility of low-income Chicanos (Suny Series, Social Context of Education)*. Albany: State University of New York Press.

Gibbins, N., & Bickel, R. (1991). Comparing public and private high schools using three SAT data sets. *Urban Review, 23*(2), 101–115.

Gonzales, P. M., Blanton, H., & Williams, K. J. (2002). The effects of stereotype threat and double-minority status on the test performance of Latino women. *Personality & Social Psychology Bulletin, 28*, 659–670.

Graduate Record Examination. (2001). Sex, race, ethnicity, and performance on the GRE General Test 2001–2002: A companion to the GRE Guide to the Use of Scores. Retrieved June 30, 2002, from Graduate Record Examinations Web site: http://www.gre.org/code1st.html.

Hall, C. W., Davis, N. B., Bolen, L. M., & Chia, R. (1999). Gender and racial differences in mathematical performance. *Journal of Social Psychology, 136*(6), 677–689.

Hauck, A. L., & Finch, A. J., Jr. (1993). The effect of relative age on achievement in middle school. *Psychology in the Schools, 30*(1), 74–79.

Hurtado, A. (1997). Understanding multiple group identities: Inserting women into the cultural transformations. *Journal of Social Issues, 53*, 299–328.

Jencks, C., & Phillips, M. (Eds.). (1998). *The black-white test score gap*. Washington, DC: Brooking Institution Press.

Kao, G. (1995). Asian Americans as model minorities? A look at their academic performance. *American Journal of Education, 103*, 121–159.

Laosa, L. (1978). Maternal teaching strategies in Chicano families of varied educational and socioeconomic levels. *Child Development, 49*, 1129–1135.

Morgan, R., & Maneckshana, B. (1996). *The psychometric perspective: Lessons learned from 40 years of constructed response testing in the Advanced Placement Program*. Paper presented at the annual meeting of the National Council of Measurement in Education in New York.

National Center for Educational Statistics. (2002). Retrieved June 30, 2002, from http://nces.ed.gov/nationsreportcard/naepdata/.

National Task Force on Minority High Achievement. (1999). *Reaching the top: A report of the National Task Force on Minority High Achievement*. New York: College Board.

Niemann, Y. F., Jennings, L., Rozelle, R. M., & Baxter, J. C. (1994). Use of free responses and cluster analysis to determine the stereotypes of eight groups. *Personality & Social Psychology Bulletin, 20*, 379–390.

Pittinsky, T. L., Shih, M., & Ambady, N. (1999) Identity adaptiveness: Affect across multiple identities. *Journal of Social Issues, 55*(3), 503–518.

Post, P., Stewart, M., & Smith, P. (1991). Self-efficacy, interest, and consideration of math/science and non-math/science occupations among Black freshmen. *Journal of Vocational Behavior, 38*(2), 179–186.

Science editorial. (1992). Minorities in science: The pipeline problem. *Science, 258.*

Seymour, E., & Hewitt, N. M. (1997). *Talking about leaving.* Boulder, CO: Westview Press.

Shih, M., Pittinsky, T. L., & Ambady, N. (1999). Stereotype susceptibility: Identity salience and shifts in quantitative performance. *Psychological Science, 10,* 80–83.

Spencer, S., Steele, C., & Quinn, D. (1999). Stereotype threat and women's math performance. *Journal of Experimental Social Psychology, 35,* 4–28.

Steele, C., & Aronson, J. (1995). Stereotype threat and the intellectual performance of African Americans. *Journal of Personality and Social Psychology, 69,* 797–811.

Steen, L. A. (1987). Mathematics education: A predictor of scientific competitiveness. *Science, 237,* 251–253.

Strenta, C. R., Elliot, M., Matier, M., Scott, J., & Adair, R. (1994). "Choosing and leaving science in highly selective institutions," *Research in Higher Education, 35*(5), 513–547.

Swanson, J. L., & Hansen, J. C. (1985). The relationship of the construct of academic comfort to educational level, performance, aspirations, and prediction of college major choices. *Journal of Vocational Behavior, 26,* 1–12.

Tomlinson, S. M., & Evans-Hughes, G. (1991). Gender, ethnicity, and students' responses to the Strong-Campbell Interest Inventory. *Journal of Counseling and Development, 70,* 151–155.

Tsang, S. L. (1988). The mathematics achievement characteristics of Asian-American students. In Rodney R. Cocking & Jose P. Mestre (Eds.), *Linguistic and cultural influences on learning mathematics. The psychology of education and instruction* (pp. 123–135). Hillsdale, NJ: Lawrence Erlbaum Associates, Inc.

Walters, A. M., Lee, S., & Trapani, C. (2004). *Stereotype threat, the test center environment, and performances on the GRE general test* (GRE Board Research Report). Princeton, NJ: Educational Testing Service.

11

The Gender Gap in Mathematics

Merely a Step Function?

Sophia Catsambis

INTRODUCING THE PROBLEM

The gender gap in mathematics and science has been an issue of national concern since the mid-1970s because it is a matter of educational equity with far-reaching consequences for the lives of women and their families. As world economies rely increasingly on science and technological innovation, women's limited participation in mathematics and science can adversely affect their employment and economic opportunities.

To conceptualize the relationship between gender and mathematics performance, I turn to the field of mathematics and its terminology. At first glance, the mathematics gender gap appears to be like a mere step function, with male students performing better than females. However, for social scientists, this relationship is better expressed by a complex mathematics equation that includes a constellation of social, psychological, and biological factors. Research evidence from national and cross-national studies showing that the gender gap in mathematics has narrowed over the years and varies across countries, supports social scientists' assertion that this gender gap is rooted in a complex array of social-environmental factors (American Association of University Women [AAUW], 1998; Baker & Jones, 1993; Friedman, 1989; Oakes, 1990). This chapter reviews the contributions that sociological research has made toward understanding the complexity of the gender gap in mathematics.

In a literature review that put together decades of relevant sociological research, Oakes (1990) identified that the gender gap in mathematics test performance involves differences in three domains: opportunity, achievement, and choice. She concluded that gender role socialization limits girls' learning opportunities in mathematics and science, resulting in their lower mathematics test scores and their limited interest in this subject, compared with equally able males. As a result of their relatively low levels of achievement and interest in mathematics, only a few women choose careers in scientific and technical fields.

For sociologists, learning opportunities and educational choices remain key factors explaining differences in achievement (the term they most often use for performance in standardized tests). The sections that follow synthesize current knowledge of the social factors linked to gender differences in mathematics opportunities, achievements, and choices from the early elementary grades to the last years of high school and beyond. The chapter begins with a presentation of the current gender gap in mathematics and continues with a discussion of how the social domains of family, community, and school can influence students' performance and participation in mathematics. It concludes by taking stock of the scientific knowledge base that links social factors to the gender gap in mathematics performance and participation.

THE GENDER GAP IN MATHEMATICS: WHERE WE STAND NOW

Concerns over women's underrepresentation in mathematics and science were first raised during the 1960s. Research evidence at that time provided a fairly consistent picture of gender differences in academic achievement favoring male students in mathematics. Differences in mathematics test scores were accompanied by gender-stereotyped differences in attitudes toward this subject, academic self-concept, and course work selection (AAUW, 1992; Maccoby, 1966). For decades, research showed that few women considered mathematics performance to be relevant to their lives and future social roles. Female students were less confident of their abilities in mathematics and science, tended to attribute their success to good luck rather than ability, and were less likely to enroll in advanced math coursework during high school (AAUW, 1992; Brophy, 1985; Chipman, Brush, & Wilson, 1985; Eccles, 1987; Eccles & Blumenfeld, 1985; Meece, Parsons, Kazcala, Goff, & Futterman, 1982; Oakes, 1990; Sadker, Sadker, & Klein, 1991). The pattern of these gender differences in elementary and secondary education led to the well-documented underrepresentation of women in scientific and technical occupations (National Science Foundation, 1988; Oakes, 1990; Sadker et al., 1991).

Concern over women's underrepresentation in mathematics and science rose again in the early 1990s due to projections that the nation was soon to be faced with a critical shortage of scientific and technical personnel. Educators, women's advocates, and policy makers argued that women's underrepresentation in these fields not only threatened the well being of women and their families, but also the strength of the U.S. economy. Numerous research publications, including the highly publicized report, *How Schools Shortchange Girls* (AAUW, 1992) attracted national attention to the gender gap in mathematics and science. Governmental agencies, private foundations, and universities mobilized to support the development of educational equity programs promoting women's achievement and interest in mathematics and science. The degree to which such programs were successful is not clear, but the national attention on the "mathematics gender gap" was followed by a significant decline in its magnitude.

In fact, the gender gap in mathematics achievement has been declining steadily since the early 1960s (AAUW, 1998; Friedman, 1989). National data sources reveal that among elementary and secondary school students, the gender gap in mathematics test scores is now either negligible, or has completely disappeared (AAUW, 1998; Catsambis, 1994; Willingham, Cole, Lewis, & Leung, 1997). The gender gap favoring males in the mathematics portion of the SAT has also considerably narrowed, from 44 points in 1985 to 35 points in 2000 (National Center for Education Statistics [NCES], 2002). These changes in test scores may be part of an overall trend, whereby gender differences in areas traditionally favoring boys are diminishing or shifting to favor girls, whereas gender differences in areas traditionally favoring girls, such as reading and writing, are increasing (Marsh & Yeung, 1998). This trend is also reflected in students' grades. Female students in all ethnic groups and across different ages earn higher grades in school than males in almost all subjects, including mathematics and science (Dwyer & Johnson, 1997). Gender differences in grades have also disappeared in high-level mathematics and science courses (Bridgeman & Wendler, 1991; Kessel & Linn, 1996). To some scholars, these trends signal the end of the mathematics gender gap; to others, there is still considerable cause for concern. Gender differences still persist among subgroups of students as well as in different aspects of the mathematics experience, beyond that of test scores and grades. Recall that according to Oakes (1990) it is not only achievement, but also learning opportunities and student choices that define the mathematics gender gap.

Although a gender gap in mathematics achievement no longer exists for the majority of middle school and high school students, it persists for some race and ethnic groups (Catsambis, 1994), and among the high-performing students who constitute the nation's mathematics and science talent pool. Males are still ahead in receiving mathematics and science honors, such as awards in the prestigious Westinghouse Science Talent Search competition (Science Service, 1998). Women and men continue to score differently on the SAT test, with women scoring lower on the mathematics portion of the SAT (AAUW, 1998; NCES, 2002). Similar gender differences are found in the ACT tests and the Advanced Placement (AP) mathematics and science exams (AAUW, 1998).

Despite substantial gains, women continue to trail men in their opportunities to learn mathematics, possibly explaining the persistent gender gap in test scores among high achievers. Women's ability to score high on mathematics and science achievement tests depends on their opportunities to take advanced courses during high school. If they do not take such courses, they will eventually drop out of the mathematics and science talent pool, foregoing future studies, scholarships, and high-paying careers (AAUW, 1998). In the 1980s, female high school students were far less likely than their male classmates to take science and math classes, but by 1994, this gap had closed, with male and female students taking a comparable number of mathematics courses in high school (AAUW, 1998; NCES, 2002). However, gender differences still persist in the types of courses in which high school students enroll. Female students are more likely to end their high school mathematics coursework with Algebra II, and not to continue in the more advanced courses that would place them in the mathematics and science talent pool (AAUW, 1998). To be sure, female students have increased their participation in mathematics and science AP courses; the proportion of women taking AP examinations in these subjects has gone up, from 37% in 1982–3 to 43% in 1992–3 (Willingham, Cole, Lewis, & Leung, 1997). Men, however, are still overrepresented in advanced courses in math and science, and they still do better than women in AP tests (AAUW, 1998; NCES, 2002).

Narrowing of the gender gap in general mathematics coursework and tests may have less to do with female students' own choices than with a nationwide trend to strengthen the academic requirements for high school graduation. In fact, gender differences related to mathematics choices continue to exist (AAUW, 1998). Nationally, female students still show less interest in mathematics, even when their achievement levels are comparable to those of their male classmates. They are also less confident of their mathematics abilities than equally achieving male students (Catsambis, 1994). Gender differences related to mathematics choice appear as early as the middle grades and continue into higher education (Catsambis, 1994; Seymour & Hewitt, 1997).

Women (and especially minority women) have made enormous strides in college attendance and in obtaining professional degrees. In most colleges, women now constitute the majority (about 56%) of the student population. They have greatly increased their portion of the professional degrees, receiving 45% of the law degrees and 42% of the medicine degrees in 1998 (NCES, 2002). Again though, despite the narrowing of the gender gap in many aspects of higher education, women still trail men in the mathematics and science disciplines, earning only a fraction of the doctorate degrees (25% in 1998) in mathematics and physical sciences (NCES, 2002). Ambitious women are not seeking mathematics- and science-related careers in accordance to their abilities. Unfortunately, closing this gender gap may not be simply a matter of time. National and cross-national studies reveal that women's participation in mathematics, science, and technical fields has remained fairly stable over the years (Bradley, 2000; Charles & Bradley, 2002; Jacobs, 1995). For this reason, the gap between women and men in mathematics and the natural sciences continues to be cause for concern and scholars from a variety of disciplines continue to search for its roots. Various social scientists have weighed differently the role of societal factors in producing this gender gap, but existing research evidence shows their influence to be indisputable (Gallagher, 1998).

SOCIAL INFLUENCES ON THE GENDER GAP IN MATHEMATICS

Social scientists have long established that societal influences play a defining role in children's academic success and their future life chances (Coleman et al., 1966; Sewell, Haller, & Portes, 1969). Society exerts its influence on student performance primarily through three overlapping spheres: family, school, and community (Epstein, 2001). All three social domains can reinforce gender-stereotyped socialization patterns through a variety of practices that define boys' and girls' opportunities, achievements, and choices. The sections that follow synthesize current knowledge on how family, community, and school affect students' mathematics experiences in ways that lead to gender differences in test performance.

Family and Social Background Influences on the Gender Gap in Mathematics

The strong influence that the family exerts on students' academic success is well established (Coleman et al., 1966). Family background characteristics and family life create a social matrix that define the achievement of children in all academic subjects. Socioeconomic status is by far the most important background characteristic predicting students' success in most academic subjects. It is especially related to mathematics achievement. National and international studies show that high socioeconomic status (SES) is associated with high mathematics test scores (AAUW, 1992; Papanastasiou, 2000).

Parental characteristics indicative of high SES tend to influence the achievement of both male and female students. Research on the determinants of cognitive ability by Parcel and Menaghan (1994a, 1994b) showed that the most important predictors of the Peabody Individual Achievement Test, in addition to the personal characteristics of students, were maternal cognitive ability and spouse's education. Highly educated and economically advantaged parents are able to provide more learning opportunities for their children at home, as well as in school. They are able to secure better learning opportunities for their children at school because they tend to have more information on how the school works and are more comfortable in communicating with the school personnel (Hoover-Dempsey & Sandler, 1995; Lareau, 1989). For example, research by Useem (1992) showed that parents of higher SES were able to negotiate with school personnel about the mathematics placement of their children, placing them in higher-ability groups than they were originally assigned. This research, however, did not examine whether these parents were more proactive in the mathematics education of their sons rather than their daughters.

The pattern of gender differences in achievement suggests that learning opportunities in mathematics may not be equally distributed among boys and girls of different social backgrounds. The gender gap is smallest among students from professional family origins and often nonexistent among middle-class students (Lamb, 1996; Papanastasiou, 2000). Researchers conclude that social class cuts across gender differences by providing middle-class girls with more access to learning opportunities in mathematics than working-class girls. Among students of high SES, however, males continue to maintain an advantage in mathematics performance over females (AAUW, 1992).

The direction of the gender gap in mathematics achievement reverses among economically disadvantaged students (AAUW, 1992). Economically disadvantaged males and African American males are the students who are doing least well in all academic coursework, including mathematics (AAUW, 1998; Walker, 2001).

The reasons for these variations in the mathematics gender gap among different social groups are not clear and call for more research that clarifies whether these trends are due to gender differences in the allocation of learning opportunities, or in the interests and cultural expectations of students from different social backgrounds (AAUW, 1992). Scholars are only now beginning to unravel the patterns of these gender differences and have not yet developed a comprehensive theory explaining the influences of social class or race/ethnicity. So far, sociologists have focused on explaining why disadvantaged boys are underachieving in practically all subjects. Although not without controversy, the most commonly held explanation refers to antischool peer cultures that prevail among socially disadvantaged boys and young men (Ogbu & Simons, 1998). These subcultures influence young men's interests and choices, steering them away from academic pursuits (Fordam & Ogbu, 1986; Ogbu & Simons, 1998; Weis, 1990; Willis, 1977). Still, those explanations leave many unanswered questions because the mathematics gender gap among disadvantaged groups does not always favor girls. For example, among Latinos, males tend to outperform females in mathematics (Catsambis, 1994).

In addition to social background, other characteristics of the family play an important role in the mathematics experiences of male and female students. Regardless of the child's gender and his or her social background, parents' involvement in childrens' education is crucial in influencing student achievement in mathematics. Parental support, encouragement, and interest in the child's schoolwork contribute to mathematics achievement and to later choice of mathematics- and science-related majors (Maple & Stage, 1991; Muller, 1998; Wang & Wildman, 1995).

Parent's attitudes and orientations, though, may also contribute to the mathematics gender gap, influencing their son's and daughters' achievements, self-perceptions, and academic choices. If parents hold different expectations for their daughters and sons, then their expectations can lead to the gender gap in mathematics in two distinct ways: (1) by affecting student's learning opportunities, and (2) by influencing their social-psychological attributes related to mathematics achievement. A number of research studies indicate that both students' perception of their family support and their perception of mathematics as a male domain are important influences on their mathematics achievement (Ma & Kishor, 1997). Research by Eccles (1994) indicates that parents who hold traditional views on gender roles tend to evaluate their children's competencies according to these stereotypes and provide them with different learning opportunities. For example, parents provide their sons with more opportunities to engage in sports and computing, whereas they provide their daughters with more opportunities to read and interact with their peers. Boys' mothers were also found more likely than girls' mothers to intervene to influence students' placement in mathematics courses (Baker & Stevenson, 1986).

The above findings indicating that parents' actions contribute to the gender gap in mathematics are not uncontested. Analyzing national data of secondary school students, Muller (1998) found no evidence that parental practices reinforced gender stereotypes in mathematics achievement and concluded that parents may contribute to a narrowing of the gender gap in mathematics learning opportunities. She did, however, report that different parent activities were associated with gains in the mathematics test scores of male and female students. Young men's gains in test scores between grades 10 and 12 were more strongly associated with parental guidance and social control, whereas young women's test score gains were more strongly related to parental verbal communication and support.

As previously noted, young women's attitudes and mathematics self-concepts begin to wane by the eighth grade. Thus, even though young women are equally competent in mathematics with their male classmates, they are less confident in their abilities and show less interest in pursuing mathematics-related careers than young men (AAUW, 1998; Catsambis, 1994). Some research evidence indicates that parents may not serve as an equalizing force in this domain. Research by Jacobs (1991) on secondary school students and their parents revealed that parent's expectations of their daughters and sons were affected by whether they considered mathematics to be a male domain. Parental expectations play a major role on student's attitudes toward school and plans for the future. Unlike parental influence on test scores, which weakens during students' high school years (Catsambis, 2001; Muller, 1998), parental influence on attitudes and future plans continues till their last year of high school (Catsambis & Suazo-Garcia, 1999). The gender-stereotyped messages that parents may transmit to their children can undermine girls' confidence in their mathematics abilities and limit their interest in further pursuing mathematics education. In Jacobs' study (1991), students' confidence in their mathematics abilities was more closely related to parental expectations than to their actual performance in mathematics. Although we do not have recent studies, past research showed that more males than females received parental support for taking advanced math and science courses (Clewell & Anderson, 1991).

The connection between parental support and gender-stereotyped perceptions regarding mathematics is also evident by the role that maternal occupation seems to play on the mathematics success of female students. Researchers have found that mothers being employed and the nature of their work can have an influence on their daughter's pursuit of mathematics-related careers (Seymour & Hewitt, 1997). Support by significant others, in general, is particularly important for women's mathematics attitudes and career choices (Clewell & Anderson, 1991; Seymour & Hewitt, 1997). In-depth interviews with women in mathematics-related careers reveal that one of the most important factors enhancing their mathematics self-efficacy and sustaining their career decisions was that significant others had confidence in their abilities, and that this confidence was clearly expressed to them (Zeldin & Pajares, 2000). Therefore, data from various sources indicate that women's mathematics achievement and participation is especially vulnerable to societal pressures that identify mathematics as a male domain. Parental support and encouragement for nontraditional pursuits may be paramount for talented young women to sustain their high mathematics performance and to persist as members of the national mathematics and science talent pool.

School Influences on the Gender Gap in Mathematics

Although family plays a crucial role in shaping children's attitudes and orientations, the school environment is also an equally important sphere of influence. The gender gap in mathematics first appears in students' attitudes during the middle grades (Catsambis, 1994). Changes in mathematics-related attitudes are associated with developmental changes in gender identity. During early adolescence, girls begin to firmly establish their feminine identity and become susceptible to social pressures that undermine their self-confidence and performance in male-dominated fields, such as mathematics and science. Some scholars suggest that the new learning environment that students face when they enter middle school or junior high school may interact with adolescent developmental changes in ways that result in a mathematics and science gender gap (Steincamp & Maehr, 1984). In the middle grades, students become exposed to a greater number of male teachers and to more competitive and unstructured learning environments, which may place girls at a disadvantage.

Numerous research studies have tried to identify aspects of schooling that contribute to the gender gaps in mathematics performance and participation. Existing research has concentrated on three general features of the schooling experience: organizational characteristics of schools and classrooms, social interactions within the school (between students and school personnel, or among students themselves), and methods of assessment and curriculum content. Organizational features and social interactions tend to be the main focus of sociological research. This section therefore discusses how the social organization of schools, as well as the social interactions that occur within schools and classrooms, contribute to the gender gap in mathematics.

Overall, researchers have mostly focused on social influences within the classroom and have paid less attention to how school structure and organization can lead to gender differences in education. A few organizational features, however, have attracted considerable attention among researchers and the public at large. Specifically, the relative merits of public vs. private, and single-sex vs. coeducational schools have been extensively debated. Researchers analyzing nationally representative data of high school students in the United States reported that students in Catholic schools had higher test scores in core academic subjects, including mathematics, than students in public schools (Coleman, Hoffer, & Kilgore, 1982; Bryk, Lee, & Holland, 1993). Within the Catholic school sector, students in single-sex schools had higher test scores in subjects such as mathematics than those in coeducational schools. The differences in academic performance between students attending these two types of Catholic schools were stronger for females than males. Female students in single-sex Catholic schools did more homework, took more mathematics courses, and scored higher in mathematics test scores than their counterparts in coeducational Catholic schools (Lee & Bryk, 1986; Riordan, 1990).

Studies from other countries, most notably from Australia, also reported that female student's performance in stereotypically male subjects is higher in single-sex than coeducational schools (Mael, 1998). At the postsecondary level, graduates of women's colleges were more accomplished and pursued mathematics- and science-related careers more often than women graduates of coeducational colleges and universities (Tidball, 1980). Thus, single-sex education is seemingly associated with a smaller gender gap in mathematics achievement, opportunities, and choices. Proponents of single-sex schools argue that they may promote gender equity because they offer female students more opportunities to learn, more female teachers in traditionally male subjects who can serve as role models and mentors, and an environment that is free of competition with male classmates. Moreover, the absence of male peers in single-sex schools may decrease the pressure for female students to conform to traditional gender expectations.

Overall, the above findings suggest that schools' use of tracking may affect the gender gap in mathematics through its influence on the self-concept and the educational interests of male and female students. Although it may narrow the gender gap, it may not do so in a desirable way (it affects high-achieving males negatively). The importance of these findings lie not only in unveiling effects of ability grouping that were not previously considered, but also in indicating that classroom organization may influence the mathematics gender gap. As for the mechanisms through which tracking may confer these differential effects, they are not clear at this time. The authors of the above research speculate that it may affect teachers' expectations as well as the types of peer groups against which students judge their own competencies (comparing themselves with equally able students in tracked classes, or with students of varying abilities in nontracked classes) (Catsambis et al., 2001; Mulkey et al., 2002). The potential influence of both teachers and peers on the mathematics gender gap is discussed separately below.

Besides single-sex schooling and tracking, the possibility that other school programs affect gender equity in mathematics is not well researched. An Australian study reported that schools with more flexible policies regarding access to different curricula had narrower gender gaps than schools adhering to more traditional practices of student management and curriculum organization (Lamb, 1996). Overall, a positive school environment that encourages women's achievements in nontraditional fields may be most important in closing the mathematics gender gap. A study of students attending summer programs for mathematics- and science-talented youth indicates that girls' mathematics-related choices and academic self-concepts are more vulnerable to the social climate of their school than boys'. Findings from this research indicate that high-achieving young women are more likely to maintain a commitment and interest in relevant fields if their mathematics and science activities entail supportive and meaningful social relationships (Lee, 2002). Having a supportive educational environment is important for women at all levels of education, including college, where the female talent loss from the mathematics and science talent pool continues to be substantial (Seymour & Hewitt, 1997). Many women pursuing such majors encounter a "chilly climate" in college classrooms, making it hard to sustain their educational performance and their career commitments in these male-dominated fields. (Hall & Sandler, 1982; Seymour & Hewitt, 1997).

Characteristics of the school personnel is an aspect of school organization that has concerned advocates of gender equity in education for many years. Gender disparities exist in school authority structures and teaching fields. They exist even in elementary and secondary education, which were traditionally considered as "women's fields." Women are concentrated in teaching positions, especially in the elementary grades. Fewer women than men are found in authority positions such as principals, superintendents, and school board members, and also fewer women than men teach mathematics, science, and technical subjects in high school (AAUW, 1992; Oakes, 1990; Sadker et al., 1991). Women's advocates argued that their under-representation in school administration and in mathematics and science teaching does not only reflect inequities in employment, it also affects female students negatively. It affects female students' efforts to excel in mathematics and their interest in the field because they lack appropriate role models and same-sex mentors that will encourage their pursuits in non-traditional fields. Not much research, however, exists on whether gender segregation of the teaching and administrative force affects students. Most researchers investigating the influence of teachers on young women's opportunities, achievements, and choices focused on the effects of counselors' and teachers' attitudes rather than their gender.

Counselors' traditional gender orientations could influence the course-taking patterns and career paths of students during high school. Teachers' orientations could influence students as soon as they enter school. Observational studies revealed gender differences in teacher–student interactions that could adversely affect girls' problem-solving skills and interests in mathematics and science careers (AAUW, 1998). Male students tend to receive both more positive and more negative attention from teachers, and teachers tend to encourage male students to rethink incorrect answers and arrive at correct answers. In contrast, female students tend to receive less encouragement and more questions with yes/no answers (AAUW, 1992; Sadker et al., 1991; Sadker & Sadker, 1995). Eccles and Blumenfeld (1985) reported that males and females tend to receive different negative feedback from teachers. Feedback to males focused on procedural violations, whereas feedback to females focused on academic performance. According to the authors, negative feedback for academic performance might lower female students' confidence in their ability to perform well on future math tasks. Moreover, teachers' stereotypic behaviors may reinforce gender differences in mathematical competence. Research on teacher–student interactions revealed that due to gender-stereotyped expectations (girls are expected to be compliant and boys to be independent and resistant to rules) teachers may unintentionally encourage boys and girls to employ different problem-solving techniques in mathematics (Hyde & Jaffee, 1998).

Together with the support of significant others, teachers' encouragement may be particularly important for girls' development of positive attitudes toward mathematics and toward their own competence in the field. In interviewing women who were successful in mathematics and science careers, Zeldin and Pajares (2000) found that almost all of them spoke about the influence of supportive teachers. Teacher's gender was not important, but rather, what was most important was that these young women perceived their teachers as being supportive of their mathematics pursuits. Some evidence exists that gender-stereotyped expectations by others may even affect female students' test performance directly. Spencer (1999) reported that high-achieving females who were informed prior to taking a standardized mathematics test that the test generally did not produce gender differences performed equally well as high-achieving males, but those who were informed that the test generally produced gender differences, performed worse.

In addition to teachers' own attitudes, the abstract character of math instruction and conventional teaching practices such as whole classroom instruction, competitive reward structure, cross-sex teaming, and reliance on voluntary participation in mathematics and science demonstrations may place girls at a disadvantage (Lockheed, Thorpe, Brooks-Gun, Casserly, & McAloon, 1985; Oakes, 1990; Sadker et al., 1991). Female students tend to be more comfortable and to do better in cooperative rather than competitive classroom environments and in hands-on activities (AAUW, 1998; Sadker et al., 1991). Teaching practices in elementary school may interact with young girls' competencies and orientations in ways that do not provide them with the skills for high-level mathematical problem solving that they will need later in their educational careers (Fennema, Carpenter, Jacobs, Franke, & Levi, 1998).

Both teachers' attitudes and practices may contribute to gender differences in skills, such as problem solving, that may be critical for high achievement in advanced mathematics, where the gender gap persists. Males and females tend to employ different strategies in solving mathematical problems (Fenemma et al., 1998; Gallagher & DeLisi, 1994). Males become autonomous learners in mathematics, persisting in solving complex tasks, more often than females. They tend to exert independence and to be inventive when they solve mathematics problems, whereas females tend to follow standard problem-solving procedures. These gender differences in problem-solving strategies may lead to even stronger gender differences in later years and could possibly explain why the gender gap in mathematics performance persists among high-achieving students. Male students' abstract and inventive problem solving allows them to master more advanced mathematics (Fennema et al., 1998).

Teacher training in schools of education could both alert teachers of any gender-stereotyped biases in their interactions with students and equip young teachers with more equitable teaching practices. Unfortunately, teachers receive little or no training in gender equity from schools of education or faculty development programs and are unprepared to confront the issue of gender equity in their classrooms (AAUW, 1998; Sadker & Sadker, 1995).

Social interactions within the school do not only occur between students and the school personnel, but also among students themselves. Indeed peer groups are an important source of gender role socialization in the schools since the early elementary grades. Studies of elementary school children show that their play activities are segregated by sex and that they adhere to rather rigid gender roles (Sadker & Sadker, 1995; Thorne, 1986). Although peer influences may contribute to the gender socialization of boys and girls from an early age, they begin to affect students' mathematics-related interests and performance from the middle grades on. It is at this time that adolescents become vulnerable to peer pressures that often reinforce gender stereotypical behaviors. At this age, young women begin to lose their self-esteem, and to become overly concerned with their physical appearance and their popularity (AAUW, 1992; Sadker & Sadker, 1995). Young women's social-psychological make-up is particularly vulnerable to sexual harassment by peers, which according to an AAUW survey, is widespread in American secondary schools (AAUW, 1993). Their sharp drop in self-esteem in early adolescence is accompanied by a weakening in their confidence for success in male-dominated fields, such as mathematics and science (AAUW, 1992; Ornstein, 1994). Having supportive peers and friends – especially friends who are interested and engaged in mathematics and science studies themselves – at this age, is especially important for young women's commitment to mathematics-related achievements and choices (Zeldin & Pajares, 2000).

Extracurricular activities provide opportunities for children and adolescents to interact with other like-minded peers and to increase their learning opportunities in different academic fields. Mathematics and science extracurricular activities are important for maintaining students' interests in these fields. Unfortunately, talented young women are less likely than their male classmates to participate in extracurricular activities related to mathematics and science (Catsambis, 1994; Clewell & Anderson, 1991; Oakes, 1990). Young women's achievements and choices in mathematics and science can also benefit from participation in other nontraditional activities, such as sports (Hanson & Kraus, 1998). Excelling in male-dominated activities may offer an additional boost to young women's confidence, allowing them to choose nontraditional paths related to high performance in mathematics.

Opportunities to participate in extracurricular activities that foster supportive peer relationships are not only affected by the school, but also by the larger community. The following section discusses how factors in the wider social environment can affect male and female students' opportunities, achievements, and choices in mathematics.

Community Influences on the Gender Gap in Mathematics

A number of factors of the wider social environment can affect the education of children from an early age. These influences begin to intensify when children reach adolescence and begin to assert their independence and spend more time outside the home (Steinberg, 1998).

Scholars have proposed a number of mechanisms through which neighborhoods may exert their influence on children, especially adolescents. Disadvantaged neighborhoods may affect adolescents because of their high incidence of undesirable behaviors, which may produce "peer-based epidemics" and antischool peer cultures (Crane, 1991; Ogbu & Simons, 1998), low quality or scarcity of organizations such as schools and recreation centers (Bryk et al., 1993; Mayer & Jencks, 1989; McLaughlin, Irby, & Langman, 1994), or low levels of social control (Bursik & Grasmik, 1993). Therefore, the social context of many poor, inner-city neighborhoods may constitute a source of behavioral risk and an educational disadvantage for adolescents.

Disadvantaged neighborhoods may also pose constraints on parents' effectiveness with their children (Brooks-Gunn, Duncan, & Aber, 1997; Catsambis & Beveridge, 2001; Sampson, 2000). These neighborhoods tend to have high concentrations of adolescents engaging in "at-risk" behaviors who may create antischool peer cultures. The peer cultures and the less cohesive social climate of many disadvantaged neighborhoods could undermine the effectiveness of positive parental practices on students' academic performance (Catsambis & Beveridge, 2001). In contrast to inner-city poor neighborhoods, socially advantaged neighborhoods benefit students because of their readily available positive adult role models, peers with high educational aspirations, and neighborhood or community organizations, including high-quality schools (Brooks-Gunn et al., 1997).

Minority children are particularly vulnerable to neighborhood disadvantages because they are more often segregated in high-risk neighborhoods than white groups (Dornbush, Ritter, & Steinberg, 1991; Massey & Denton, 1993; Slaughter & Epps, 1987). For example, a study of African American adolescents in Seattle, Washington, revealed significant interrelationships between neighborhood characteristics, parental practices, and peer relationships. For adolescents living in low-risk neighborhoods, supportive relationships with both mothers and peers were associated with higher school grades. For those living in high-risk neighborhoods, only restrictive parental control was linked to higher grades in school. The authors concluded that the social climate of high-risk neighborhoods where many African American adolescents live undermines the positive effects of parent–child and peer relationships on students' achievement (Gonzales, Cauce, Friedman, & Mason, 1996).

So far, researchers have linked social characteristics of disadvantaged, especially urban, neighborhoods to negative adolescent behaviors such as delinquency, teen pregnancy, and dropping out of school. Another study shows that neighborhood characteristics are also linked to students' performance in standardized mathematics tests (Catsambis & Beveridge, 2001). The study was based on the National Educational Longitudinal Study, a large-scale survey of middle school students, their parents, and schools that was sponsored by the U.S. Department of Education. It compared the mathematics test scores of eighth-grade students who lived in neighborhoods with different social characteristics. Results showed that students in racially segregated and disadvantaged neighborhoods had lower mathematics test scores than similar students who lived in more socially advantaged or less racially segregated neighborhoods.

This study also revealed that neighborhood characteristics mediated the relationship between parental involvement in children's education and students' mathematics achievement. The relationship between parents' educational practices and their children's mathematics achievement was found to be weaker for those who lived in disadvantaged neighborhoods. Despite this overall trend, the link between students' mathematics achievement and some specific parental practices was stronger for students in disadvantaged neighborhoods than for similar students who lived in neighborhoods with fewer social and educational risks. These parental practices included maintaining frequent communication with children, closely monitoring children's activities, and providing them with extra learning opportunities (Catsambis & Beveridge, 2001). Although these data are not conclusive, they suggest that complex interrelationships exist between neighborhood characteristics, family life, and children's academic success.

This research did not investigate whether the relationship between neighborhood characteristics and mathematics performance is similar for male and female students. Unfortunately, research on the possible effects of communities and neighborhoods on the gender gap in mathematics is practically nonexistent. A study by Entwisle, Alexander, and Olson (1994), however, does indicate that neighborhood characteristics may affect gender differences in mathematics performance. In their study of Baltimore City youth, these researchers found that the gender gap in mathematics achievement widened over the summer school break. Although they did not investigate neighborhood effects directly, the researchers suggested that this gender gap may be due to parents encouraging their sons more than their daughters to explore and take advantage of neighborhood resources and learning opportunities.

Overall, though, the empirical evidence on the effects of neighborhoods on students' family life and academic achievement tends to be weak. Quantitative research is most important in this respect because studies need to compare students from a wide variety of neighborhood, family, and school configurations. So far, these types of studies have not produced definitive results due to methodological limitations and data constraints (existing data sources do not identify students' residential locations, do not include information from both neighborhoods and schools, or do not include adequate numbers of students within neighborhoods and schools). The most important weakness of existing research in this area is the failure to adequately control for school characteristics. Because schools may constitute an important source of variation affecting academic achievement, most of the research on neighborhood effects has been criticized as being subject to omitted variable bias (Arum, 2000). Methodological advances in the analysis of hierarchically nested data, paired with existing national longitudinal studies hold the promise of identifying neighborhood effects that are independent of the effects of students' families and schools.

Future quantitative research employing the new methodologies together with qualitative studies can shed light on whether and how neighborhoods also affect the mathematics gender gap. Although research on this topic is sparse, there is reason to believe that neighborhoods may indeed affect differently boys' and girls' mathematics learning opportunities and interests. Gender role norms typically allow boys and young men to explore their surrounding environment and spend time outside the home more often than young women. Therefore, neighborhoods may have a stronger affect on boys than girls, but this may not always work to the benefit of boys. Whether exposure to the neighborhood environment offers advantages or disadvantages to boys over girls would depend on the social climate and learning resources of neighborhoods, as well as on the ways that neighborhoods affect family life and parents' influence on their children.

Employment opportunities and the overall gender stratification in communities and society as a whole is a final social influence on the mathematics gender gap that should not be ignored. The attitudes and aspirations of young women and men can be shaped by the examples of occupational opportunities that they see in their families and communities (Cunningham, 2001; Jacobs, Finken, Griffin, & Wright, 1998). At the national level, gender ideologies provide the framework for gender equity laws and women's social opportunities. Cross-national studies indicate that gender stratification in occupations and in postsecondary education is related to the gender gap in mathematics achievement (Baker & Jones, 1993). Patterns of gender stratification that young women observe around them guide their future aspirations. They may get discouraged from sustaining their efforts to do well in mathematics if they are confronted with traditional gender ideologies or with the prospect of limited opportunities for successful employment in mathematics related occupations. Under these social conditions, parents and other actors may also be less inclined to encourage or help female students to engage in math and science-related activities (Baker & Jones, 1992). Adopting a legal system that promotes gender equity, providing employment opportunities in mathematics- and science-related fields, and espousing gender egalitarian ideologies may be necessary conditions for societies to eliminate sex segregation in educational and career choices (Charles & Bradely, 2002). Although they are still a handful, cross-national studies highlight the breadth of social factors that influence individuals' opportunities, achievements, and choices related to mathematics.

TAKING STOCK OF CURRENT KNOWLEDGE AND DIRECTIONS
FOR FUTURE RESEARCH

This chapter began by making an analogy between the gender gap in mathematics performance and the mathematical expression of a "step function." The past twenty years witnessed a flurry of research on the gender gap in mathematics and revealed the complexity of its roots. Therefore, the mathematics performance of women and men can no longer be considered as a mere "step function" of being male or female. Rather, as social scientists contend, it is an outcome of social interactions that better resembles a complex matrix equation. This chapter highlighted some important social factors leading to the gender gap in mathematics achievement and linked it to students' learning opportunities, educational interests, and career choices. Over the years, the gender gap in these domains has considerably narrowed. Women have made remarkable gains in access to learning opportunities and in mathematics test scores. However, lingering inequalities, especially among high-achieving students, leave cause for concern. Beginning in the middle grades, young women are less confident of their mathematics abilities and show less interest in mathematics careers than equally talented young men. The achievement gap among mathematically talented youth, paired with gender gaps in students' interests and choices, is likely to produce future inequalities in mathematics, science, and technical fields. In an era of rapid technological innovation and change, these trends may limit women's economic opportunities.

Cause for concern also exists for the employment opportunities of minority and working-class men who lag behind their more advantaged classmates in mathematics achievement. In fact, the patterns of the mathematics gender gap have shifted in such a way that female students are not always the disadvantaged group. For example, the mathematics achievements of African American women far outpace those of African American men. Researchers have begun to tackle the mathematics gender gaps among different social groups, and the social factors that lie behind them.

There are numerous social factors within family, school, and community that contribute to gender differences in mathematics opportunities, achievements, and choices, as discussed in this chapter. Various aspects of this sociological knowledge base have been used to develop educational programs aimed at producing gender equity in mathematics. Yet, the contributions of educational programs to the recent movement toward gender equity in mathematics are not clear. The increased focus on gender equity in schools has coincided with other educational reforms and societal changes in gender ideologies, gender equity laws, and employment opportunities for women. Therefore, it is difficult to attribute the changes in the mathematics gender gap to any one social factor. Because the above social realms are interconnected, the specific social forces driving gender equity in mathematics and science remain elusive. The previous sections of this chapter identified specific weaknesses in the existing sociological knowledge base, where more, or better, research is needed. Overall, most research focused on discovering aspects of students' experiences within the school that lead to the gender gap in mathematics performance. Much less is known regarding the effects of the wider social environment at the family, local, and national levels. For example, research has not established whether influences at the level of the family, community, or school are cumulative, or whether social forces in one of these spheres can overcome inequalities that are found in the others. Little is known of the processes that produce differences in the magnitude and direction of the gender gap in mathematics performance by social class or race and ethnicity. Finally, research is only beginning to emerge on the apparent paradox of gender equity trends. Women have made impressive gains in educational achievement and participation in higher education, while they continue to opt out of the traditionally male-dominated fields of mathematics and science.

The lack of knowledge concerning these wider social forces can have important consequences for school programs that seek to promote gender equity in mathematics achievement. Social forces that students encounter outside the school may actually undermine the effectiveness of these programs.

New conceptualizations of the schooling experience can spark research that will address limitations of the existing knowledge base and strengthen the effectiveness of educational interventions. Social researchers have increasingly turned their attention to theoretical work that views students as actors who are embedded into multiple social contexts that are inherently interconnected (Bronfenbrenner, 1979; Epstein, 2001). According to Epstein (1987), students' academic performance is highest in social environments where family, community, and school share similar goals for students' success and conduct various practices together as partners. Such conceptualizations of overlapping social spheres have prompted researchers to simultaneously consider different aspects of students' lives (see Epstein, 2001, for a review). More research is needed to investigate how the different aspects of schooling discussed in this chapter interact with students' cultural backgrounds, social conditions, or family configurations. Research is only beginning to emerge on the types of parental practices and the specific family, school, and community partnerships that are most effective for the academic performance of students who live under different social conditions. Yet another line of emerging research investigates how interrelationships between gender ideologies and educational and occupational opportunities affect the gender gap in mathematics participation and achievement. Moreover, interdisciplinary research is much needed to uncover how students' social characteristics interact with psychological processes and biological traits. Although these emerging "multilevel" lines of research are methodologically and conceptually challenging, they are the key to understanding the gender gap in mathematics and to developing educational programs that can close it.

References

Alexander, K. L., & Cook, M. A. (1982). Curricula and coursework: A surprise ending to a familiar story. *American Sociological Review, 47,* 626–640.

American Association of University Women (AAUW). (1992). *How schools shortchange girls.* Washington, DC: American Association of University Women Educational Foundation.

American Association of University Women (AAUW). (1993). *Hostile hallways: The AAUW survey on sexual harassment in America's schools.* Washington, DC: American Association of University Women Educational Foundation.

American Association of University Women (AAUW). (1998). *Gender gaps: Where schools still fail our children.* Washington, DC: American Association of University Women Educational Foundation.

Arum, R. (2000). Schools and communities: Ecological and institutional dimensions. *Annual Review of Sociology, 26,* 395–418.

Baker, D. P., & Jones, D. (1992). Gender stratification in the science pipeline: A comparative analysis of seven countries. In J. Wrigley (Ed.), *Education and Gender.* London: Falmer Press.

Baker, D. P., & Jones, D. (1993). Creating gender equity: Cross-national gender stratification and mathematics performance. *Sociology of Education, 66,* 91–103.

Baker, D. P., & Stevenson, D. L. (1986). Mothers' strategies for school achievement: Managing the transition to high school. *Sociology of Education, 59,* 156–67.

Bradley, K. (2000). The incorporation of women into higher education: Paradoxical outcomes? *Sociology of Education, 73,* 1–18.

Bridgeman, B., & Wendler, C. (1991). Gender differences in predictors of college mathematics performance. *Journal of Educational Psychology 83*(2), 275–284.

Bronfenbrenner, U. (1979). *The ecology of human development.* Cambridge, MA: Harvard University Press.

Brooks-Gunn, J., Duncan, G. J., & Aber, L. J. (Eds.). (1997). *Neighborhood poverty. Volume I: Context and consequences for children.* New York: Russell Sage Foundation.

Brophy, J. (1985). Interactions of male and female students with their male and female teachers. In L. C. Wilkinson & C. B. Marrett (Eds.), *Gender influences in classroom interaction* (pp. 115–142). New York: Academic Press.

Bryk, A., Lee, V. E., & Holland, P. B. (1993). *Catholic schools and the common good.* Cambridge, MA: Harvard University Press.

Bursik, R. J., & Grasmik, H. G. (1993). *Neighborhoods and crime: Dimensions of effective community control* (1st ed.). New York: Lexington Books.

Catsambis, S. (1994). The path to math: Gender and racial-ethnic differences in mathematics participation from middle school to high school. *Sociology of Education, 67,* 199–215.

Catsambis, S. (2001). Expanding knowledge of parental involvement in children's secondary education: Connections with high school seniors' academic success. *Social Psychology of Education, 5*(2), 149–177.

Catsambis, S., & Beveridge, A. (2001). Does neighborhood matter? Family, neighborhood and school influences on eighth-grade mathematics achievement. *Sociological Focus, 43*(4), 435–457.

Catsambis, S., Mulkey, L. M., & Crain, R. L. (2001). For better or for worse? A nationwide study of the social psychological affects of gender and ability grouping in mathematics. *Social Psychology of Education, 5*(1), 83–115.

Catsambis, S., & Suazo-Garcia, B. (1999). *Parents matter: Parent influences on high school seniors' school-related behaviors, plans and expectations.* Paper presented at the American Sociological Association, Chicago, IL.

Charles, M., & Bradley, K. (2002). Equal but separate? A cross-national study of sex segregation in higher education. *American Sociological Review, 67,* 573–599.

Chipman, S. F., Brush, L. R., & Wilson, D. M. (1985). *Women and mathematics: Balancing the equation* (pp. 59–94). Hillsdale, NJ: Erlbaum.

Clewell, B. C., & Anderson, B. (1991). *Women of color in mathematics, science & engineering.* Washington, DC: Center for Women Policy Studies.

Coleman, J., Campbell, E., Hobson, C., McPartland, J., Mood, A., Winfield, F., & York, R. (1966). *Equality of educational opportunity report.* Washington, DC: U.S. Government Printing Office.

Coleman, J. C., Hoffer, T., & Kilgore, S. (1982). *High school achievement: Public, Catholic and private schools compared.* New York: Basic Books.

Crane, J. (1991). The epidemic theory of ghettos and neighborhood effects on dropping out and teenage childbearing. *American Journal of Sociology, 96*(5), 1226–1259.

Cunningham, M. (2001). The influence of parental attitudes and behaviors on children's attitudes toward gender and household labor in early adulthood. *Journal of Marriage and the Family, 63*(1), 111–122.

Dornbush, S. M., Ritter, P. L., & Steinberg, L. (1991). Community influences on the relation of family practices to adolescent school performance: Differences between African Americans and Non-Hispanic Whites. *American Journal of Education, 543–567.*

Dwyer, C. A., &. Johnson, L. M. (1997). Grades, accomplishments and correlates. In W. W. Willingham & N. S. Cole (Eds.), *Gender and fair assessment* (pp. 127–156). Mahwah, NJ: Lawrence Erlbaum Associates.

Eccles, J. S. (1987). Gender roles and achievement patterns: An expectancy value perspective. In J. M. Reinisch, L. A. Rosenblum, & A. A. Sanders (Eds.), *Masculinity/femininity: Basic perspectives* (pp. 240–280). New York: Oxford University Press.

Eccles, J. S. (1994). Understanding women's educational and occupational choices. *Psychology of Women's Quarterly, 18,* 585–609.

Eccles, J. S., & Blumenfeld, P. (1985). Classroom experiences and student gender: Are there differences and do they matter. In L. C. Wilkinson & C. B. Marrett (Eds.), *Gender influences in classroom interaction* (pp. 79–114). Hillsdale, NJ: Erlbaum.

Entwisle, D. R., Alexander, K. L., & Olson, L. S. (1994). The gender gap in math: Its possible origins in neighborhood effects. *American Sociological Review, 59*, 822–838.

Epstein, J. L. (1987). Toward a theory of family-school connections: Teacher practices and parent involvement. In K. Hurrelman, X. Kaufmann, & F. Losel (Eds.), *Social intervention: Potential and constraints*. Berlin: Walter de Gruyter.

Epstein, J. L. (2001). *School, family, and community partnerships*. Boulder, CO: Westview Press.

Fennema, E., & Peterson, P. L. (1985). Autonomous learning behavior: A possible explanation of gender-related differences in mathematics. In L. C. Wilkinson & C. B. Marrett (Eds.), *Gender-related differences in classroom interactions* (pp. 111–125). New York: Random House.

Fennema, E., Carpenter, T. P., Jacobs, V. R., Franke, M. L., & Levi, L. W. (1998). A longitudinal study of gender differences in young children's mathematical thinking. *Educational Researcher, 27*(5), 6–11.

Fordam, S., & Ogbu, J. (1986). Black students' school success: Coping with the burden of acting white. *Urban Review, 18*(3), 176–206.

Friedman, L. (1989). Mathematics and the gender gap: A meta-analysis of recent studies of sex differences in mathematical tasks. *Review of Educational Research, 59*(2), 185–213.

Gallagher, A. M. (1998). Gender and antecedents of performance in mathematics testing. *Teachers College Record, 100*(2), 297–314.

Gallagher, A. M., & DeLisi, R. (1994). Gender differences in scholastic aptitude test mathematics problem solving among high ability students. *Journal of Educational Psychology, 86*(2), 204–211.

Gamoran, A., & Mare, R. D. (1989). Secondary school tracking and educational inequality: Compensation, reinforcement or neutrality? *American Journal of Sociology 94*, 1146–1183.

Gonzales, N. A., Cauce, A. M., Friedman, R. J., & Mason, C. A. (1996). Family, peer, and neighborhood influences on academic achievement among African-American adolescents: One-year prospective effects. *American Journal of Community Psychology, 24*(3), 365–388.

Hall, R., & Sandler, B. (1982). *The classroom climate: A chilly one for women?* Project for the Status and Education of Women. Washington, DC: Association of American Colleges.

Hallinan, M. T., & Sorenson, A. B. (1987). Ability grouping and sex differences in mathematics achievement. *Sociology of Education, 60*, 63–72.

Hanson, S. L., & Kraus, R. S. (1998). Women, sports and science: Do female athletes have an advantage? *Sociology of Education, 71*(2), 93–110.

Hoover-Dempsey, K. V., & Sandler, H. M. (1995). Parental involvement in children's education: Why does it make a difference? *Teachers College Record, 97*(2), 310–331.

Hyde, J. S., & Jaffee, S. (1998). Perspectives from social and feminist psychology. *Educational Researcher, 27*(5), 14–16.

Jacobs, J. E. (1991). Influence of gender stereotypes on parent and child mathematics attitudes. *Journal of Educational Psychology, 83*(4), 518–527.

Jacobs, J. A. (1995). Gender and academic specialties: Trends among recipients of college degrees in the 1980's. *Sociology of Education, 68*, 81–98.

Jacobs, J. E., Finken, L. L., Griffin, N. L., & Wright, J. D. (1998). The career plans of science-talented rural adolescent girls. *American Educational Research Journal,* 35(4), 477–496.

Kessel, C., & Linn, M. C. (1996). Grades or scores: Predicting future college mathematics performance. *Educational Measurement: Issues and Practice,* 15(4), 10–14.

Lamb, S. (1996). Gender differences in mathematics participation in Australian schools: Some relationships with social class and school policy. *British Educational Research Journal,* 22(4), 223–240.

Lareau, A. (1989). *Home advantage: Social class and parental intervention in elementary educaation.* London: Falmer Press.

Lee, J. D. (2002). More than ability: Gender and personal relationships influences science and technology involvement. *Sociology of Education,* 75(4), 349–373.

Lee, V. E. (1993). Single-sex schooling: What is the issue? In D. K. Hollinger & R. Adamson (Eds.), *Single-sex schooling: Proponents speak* (pp. 39–46). Washington, DC: U.S. Department of Education.

Lee, V. E., & Bryk, A. S. (1986). Effects of single-sex secondary schools on student achievement and attitudes. *Journal of Educational Psychology,* 78, 381–395.

Lee, V. E., & Bryk, A. S. (1989). Effects of single-sex schools: Response to Marsh. *Journal of Educational Psychology,* 81, 647–650.

Lee, V. E., Marks, H. M., & Byrd, T. (1994). Sexism in single-sex and coeducational secondary school classrooms. *Sociology of Education,* 67, 92–120.

Lockheed, M., Thorpe, M., Brooks-Gun, J., Casserly, P., & McAloon, A. (1985). *Sex differences in middle school mathematics, science and computer science: What do we know?* Princeton, NJ: Educational Testing Service.

Ma, X., & Kishor, N. (1997). Attitude toward self, social factors, and achievement in mathematics: A meta-analytic review. *Educational Psychology Review,* 9, 89–120.

Maccoby, E. E. (1966). *The development of sex differences.* Stanford, CA: Stanford University Press.

Mael, F. A. (1998). Single-sex and coeducational schooling: Relationships to socioemotional and academic development. *Review of Educational Research,* 68(2), 101–129.

Maple, S. A., & Stage, F. K. (1991). Influences on the choice of math/science major by gender and ethnicity. *American Educational Research Journal,* 28(1), 37–60.

Marsh, H. W. (1989). Effects of attending single-sex and coeducational high schools on achievement, attitudes, behaviors and sex differences. *Journal of Educational Psychology,* 81, 70–85.

Marsh, H. W., & Yeung, S. A. (1998). Longitudinal structural equation models of academic self-concept and achievement: Gender differences in the development of math and English constructs. *American Educational Research Journal,* 35(4), 705–738.

Massey, D. S., & Denton, N. (1993). *American apartheid: Segregation and the making of the underclass.* Cambridge, MA: Harvard University Press.

Mayer, S. E., & Jencks, C. (1989). Growing up in poor neighborhoods: How much does it matter? *Science* 243, 1441–1445.

McLaughlin, M. W., Irby, M. A., & Langman, J. (1994). *Urban sanctuaries: Neighborhood organizations in the lives and futures of inner-city youth.* San Fransisco: Jossey-Bass.

Meece, J. L., Parsons, J. E., Kazcala, C. M., Goff, S. B., & Futterman, R. (1982). Sex differences in math achievement: Toward a model of academic choice. *Psychological Bulletin 91*, 324–348.

Mulkey, L. M., Catsambis, S., & Steelman, L. C. (2002). *Getting 'psyched-up': Gender, middle school tracking, and social psychological characteristics as predictors of the high school mathematics trajectory.* Paper presented at the International Sociological Association conference, Brisbane, Australia.

Muller, C. (1998). Gender differences in parental involvement and adolescents' mathematics achievement. *Sociology of Education, 71*, 336–256.

National Center for education statistics (NCES). (2002). *Digest of education statistics 2001.* Washington, DC: U.S. Department of Education, Office of Educational Research and Improvement.

National Science Foundation. (1988). *Women and minorities in science and engineering.* (NSF-86-301). Washington, DC: Author.

Oakes, J. (1990). Opportunities, achievement and choice: Women and minority students in science and mathematics. *Review of Research in Education, 16*, 153–222.

Ogbu, J., & Simons, H. D. (1998). Voluntary and involuntary minorities: A cultural-ecological theory of school performance with some implications for education. *Anthropology and Education Quarterly, 29*(2), 155–188.

Ornstein, P. (1994). *Schoolgirls: Young women, self-esteem, and the confidence gap.* New York: Doubleday.

Papanastasiou, C. (2000). Internal and external factors affecting achievement in mathematics: Some findings from TIMSS. *Studies in Educational Evaluation, 26*, 1–7.

Parcel, T. L., & Menaghan, E. G. (1994a). Early parental work, family social capital, and early childhood outcomes. *American Journal of Sociology, 99*(4), 972–1009.

Parcel, T. L., & Menaghan, E. G. (1994b). *Parents' jobs and children's lives.* New York: Aldine.

Riordan C. (1990). *Girls and boys in school: Together or separate?* New York: Teachers College Press.

Sadker, D., & Sadker, M. (1995). *Failing at fairness: How America's schools shortchange girls,* New York: Scribner's.

Sadker, M., Sadker, D., & Klein, S. (1991). The issue of gender in elementary and secondary education. *Review of Research in Education 17*, 269–334.

Sampson, R. J. (2000). The neighborhood context of investing in children: Facilitating mechanisms and undermining risks. In *Securing the future: Investing in children from birth to college.* New York: Russell Sage.

Science Service. (1998). *Westinghouse science talent search science service data base.* Westinghouse Foundation.

Sewell, W. H., Haller, A. O., & Portes, A. (1969). The educational and early occupational attainment process. *American Sociological Review, 34*, 82–92.

Seymour, E., & Hewitt, N. (1997). *Talking about leaving: Why undergraduates leave the sciences.* Boulder, CO: Westview Press.

Slaughter, D. T., & Epps, E. G. (1987). The home environment and academic achievement of black American children and youth: An overview. *Journal of Negro Education, 56*(1), 3–20.

Spencer, S. J. (1999). *Cultural images and stereotype threat: The effect of media images on women's math performance and career selection.* Oxford, England: European Association of Experimental Social Psychology.

Steinberg, L. (1998). *Adolescence.* New York: McGraw Hill Publishing Co.

Steincamp, M. W., & Maehr, M. L. (1984). Gender differences in motivational orientations towards achievement in school science: A Quantitative synthesis. *American Educational Research Journal, 21*(1), 39–59.

Thorne, B. (1986). Girls and boys together . . . but mostly apart: Gender arrangements in elementary schools. In W. Hartrip & Z. Rubin (Eds.), *Relationships and Development* (p. 468). Hillsdale, NJ: Lawrence Erlbaum Associates.

Tidball, M. E. (1980). Women's colleges and women achievers revisited. *Signs: Journal of Women in Culture and Society, 5*, 504–517.

Useem, E. L. (1992). Middle school and math groups: Parents' involvement in children's placement. *Sociology of Education, 65*(4), 263–279.

Walker, E. N. (2001). *On time and off track? Advanced mathematics course-taking among high school students.* Unpublished doctoral dissertation, Graduate School of Education, Harvard University, Boston.

Wang, J., & Wildman, L. (1995). An empirical examination of the effects of family commitment in education on student achievement in seventh grade science. *Journal of Research in Science Teaching, 32*(8), 833–37.

Weis, L. (1990). *Working class without work: High school students in a de-industrializing economy.* Albany: State University of New York Press.

Willingham, W., Cole, N. S., Lewis, C., & Leung, S. W. (1997). Test performance. In W. W. Willingham & N. S. Cole (Eds.), *Gender and fair assessment* (pp. 55–126). Mahwah, NJ: Lawrence Erlbaum Associates.

Willis, P. (1977). *Learning to labour: How working class kids get working class jobs.* England: Saxon House.

Zeldin, A. L., & Pajares, F. (2000). Against the odds: Self-efficacy beliefs of women in mathematical, scientific, and technological careers. *American Educational Research Journal, 37*(1), 215–246.

12

"I can, but I don't want to"

The Impact of Parents, Interests, and Activities on Gender Differences in Math

Janis E. Jacobs, Pamela Davis-Kean, Martha Bleeker, Jacquelynne S. Eccles, and Oksana Malanchuk

Although the mathematics performance gap between males and females has narrowed over the past decade (e.g., Hall, Davis, Bolen, & Chia; 1999; Hyde, 1997; National Center for Education Statistics [NCES], 2001), there continues to be a gulf between the number of women and men who pursue college degrees in engineering, physical sciences, computer sciences, and mathematics (Bae & Smith, 1996; Higher Education Research Institute, 1996; Stumpf & Stanley, 1996). Furthermore, women who hold bachelor's degrees in science and engineering are less likely than men with similar degrees to actually be employed in those fields; women constitute only 23% of the science and engineering labor force (National Science Foundation [NSF], 2000). The underrepresentation of women is especially evident in the physical sciences, where women comprise only 9% of employed engineers and 10% of employed physicists (NSF, 2000).

In light of diminishing performance differences, the continuing gender gap in math/science educational and career choices suggests that such choices are based on much more than achievement (Linver, Davis-Kean, & Eccles, 2002). Numerous theories dealing with competence, expectancy, and control beliefs provide explanations for performance on different kinds of achievement tasks; however, many of these theories do not systematically address another important motivational question: What makes the individual *want* to do math or science? Even if individuals feel competent, they may not want to pursue it. Over the past 20 years, we have used the Eccles' parent socialization model to consider the role played by parents in children's achievement choices in a variety of domains. In this chapter, we use this perspective to consider gender differences in children's math and science achievement choices and the environment provided by parents to support children's interests in math and science. We begin by reviewing the theoretical perspective and previous work to support it, and then we present new evidence related to the "gendered" nature of the math/science opportunities and expectations that parents provide for their children.

Theoretical Perspective

According to some of the modern expectancy-value theories (e.g., Eccles et al., 1983; Feather, 1982; Wigfield & Eccles, 1992), an individual's values for particular goals and tasks can help explain *why* a child chooses one field of study over another. Eccles (Parsons) and her colleagues elaborated and tested an expectancy-value model of activity choice (e.g., Eccles, 1987; Eccles, Adler, & Meece, 1984; Eccles & Wigfield, 1995; Eccles [Parsons] et al., 1983; Meece, Parsons, Kaczala, Goff, & Futterman, 1982; Meece, Wigfield, & Eccles, 1990) that focuses on the social-psychological influences on choice and persistence. According to this model, the key determinants of choice will be the relative value and perceived probability of success of each available option. Expectancies and values are assumed to directly influence performance and task choice, and to be influenced by task-specific beliefs, such as self-perceptions of competence, perceptions of the task demands, and the child's goals (both short- and long-term) and self-schemas. These social cognitive variables, in turn, are influenced by the child's perceptions of other peoples' attitudes and expectations for them, gender roles and activity stereotypes, and their own interpretations of their previous experiences with achievement outcomes. Finally, the child's perceptions are influenced by the greater cultural milieu, socializers' beliefs, their own aptitudes or talents, and their previous achievement-related performances.

Various aspects of this model have been confirmed in the domain of mathematics (e.g., Eccles, 1987; Eccles et al.,1984; Eccles, Wigfield, Harold, & Blumenfeld, 1993; Meece et al., 1982; Wigfield, Eccles, Mac Iver, Reuman, & Midgley, 1991), and our findings make it clear that task values play an important role in future plans to pursue math and science. In addition, we have found that key determinants of value are parents' attitudes and behaviors, children's self-perceptions, and gender role expectations (e.g., Eccles [Parsons] et al., 1983; Jacobs, 1991; Jacobs & Eccles, 1992). In this chapter, we briefly review previous research focusing on the importance of gender and parents' roles in children's achievement choices, and we then turn to some recent findings to illustrate these aspects of achievement choices.

Parent Socialization Model

Although many experiences and a variety of socializers help shape children's values, we focus primarily on the role of parents. Over the years, numerous studies have linked parenting practices to children's achievement motivation (see Eccles, Wigfield, & Schiefele, 1998, for review); however, few researchers have focused on how parents motivate their children to do different things or to value different activities.

The Eccles (Parsons) et al. (1983) model of parent socialization is presented in Fig. 12.1. As indicated in the model, we believe that characteristics of the parents, family, and neighborhood, and characteristics of the child, will influence parents' behaviors and their general beliefs about the world, as well as their specific beliefs about the child. We expect these beliefs to then influence their parenting behaviors, which, in turn, will affect child outcomes. Examples of each of these constructs are given in Fig. 12.1. Although the model is drawn in a linear fashion and the original model (Eccles [Parsons] et al., 1983) proposed a causal sequence, it is important to acknowledge that parents' and children's outcomes are likely to influence each other reciprocally and that different beliefs depicted as a single construct in the model are likely to influence each other (e.g., gender role stereotypes and personal values).

We focus on the three boxes in the middle of Fig. 12.1, depicting parents' general beliefs and behaviors, parents' child-specific beliefs, and parenting behaviors. Although several examples of each construct are listed in Fig. 12.1 we focus only on the following four ways in which parents influence their children: (1) by the general social-emotional climate they offer and by their general childrearing beliefs; (2) by providing specific experiences for the child (e.g., enrollment in lessons, involvement in church activities); (3) by modeling involvement in valued activities; and (4) by communicating their perceptions of the child's abilities and expectations for performance.

According to this model, the environment, role modeling, and messages that parents provide regarding the value they attach to science and math activities are expected to influence children's motivation to pursue those fields. Over time, children develop their own level of interest in math and science and integrate these interests or values into their self-systems. Ultimately, the values that are incorporated into one's self-beliefs will affect future task choices (it is important to remember, however, that the influence between self-beliefs and values is bidirectional). Parents' roles may shift in this process from providing exposure, opportunities, and role modeling of math and science activities at early ages to providing encouragement and guidance for activities that continue to be supportive of the child's developing interest in math/science (if there is a lack of interest, we would expect less encouragement in the field of math). We have tested and found support for each of the four components of parent influence (e.g., Eccles, 1994; Eccles [Parsons] et al., 1983; Jacobs, 1991; Jacobs & Eccles, 1985, 1992; Jacobs, Finken, Griffin, & Wright, 1998). Our findings on each are briefly reviewed in the following sections.

Social-Emotional Climate and General Beliefs

Positive parent–child relationships have often been connected with successful parental socialization. Although we have not emphasized this construct, Eccles, Early, Frasier, Belansky, & McCarthy (1996) found that

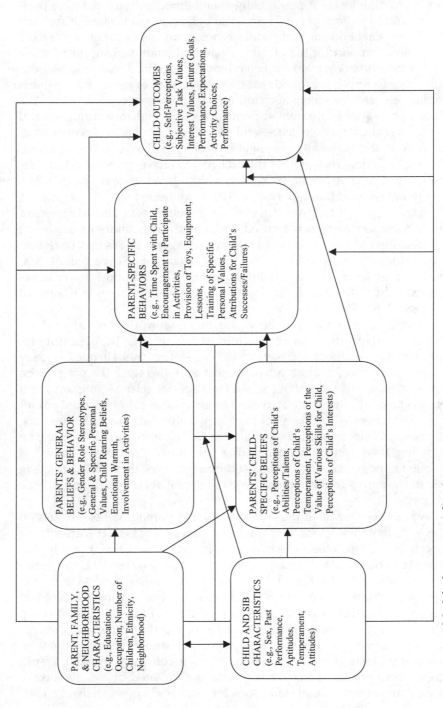

FIGURE 12.1. Model of parent socialization.

perceived high levels of connectedness and emotional support were positively related to both psychological and behavioral indicators of successful development during early adolescence, particularly for girls. We have also found support for the impact of parental emotional support during childhood on later adolescent behaviors and parent–adolescent relationships. For example, we found that parents' reports of perceived closeness to their elementary school-age children are positively related to the children's perceptions of parent support, affection, and monitoring several years later during adolescence, and negatively related to perceptions of parental strictness and involvement in problem behaviors (Jacobs, Hyatt, Tanner, & Eccles, 1998). Other researchers also have emphasized the importance of positive parent–child relationships (Connell & Wellborn, 1991), emotional support (Deci & Ryan, 1985), or connectedness (Barber, Olsen, & Shagle, 1994) for children's mental health, self-esteem, and achievement motivation. Our work has focused on the nature of children's emotional relationships with their parents, and how these connections may be related to developing values and activity choices. As might be expected, perceptions of high levels of connectedness and emotional support from parents are related positively to both psychological and behavioral indicators of successful development.

Parents also provide messages about their own worldviews and values, either directly by discussing them or indirectly through the opportunities they provide and the interpretations they give. The values in question may range from specific values for particular activities (e.g., the parent who loves science and talks about it, watches special science programs, and enrolls the child in science activities) to general world beliefs and values (e.g., the parent who doesn't believe girls should do math because it is for boys). Children are likely to discern the parents' values by noticing how free time is spent, by comparing how much time, money, or effort goes into one activity vs. another, and from conversations with parents in which the parent conveys enthusiasm or interest about one topic, but little about another.

We have documented the indirect effects of parents' general beliefs on the goals that they set for their children in the area of gender-stereotyping (Jacobs, 1991; Jacobs & Eccles, 1992). We investigated the relationships between parents' gender-based stereotypes, their beliefs about their own children's abilities, and their children's self-perceptions and performance in two studies (Jacobs, 1991; Jacobs & Eccles, 1992). The first study focused on stereotypes, beliefs, and performance related to mathematical ability only. The second study involved three domains of ability (mathematics, sports, and social). Parents' gender stereotypes in both studies and in all domains directly influenced their perceptions of their children's abilities, resulting in more positive perceptions for children favored by the stereotypes (e.g., daughters for social skills, sons for math and sports skills). Parents' perceptions, in turn, influenced their children's performance and their self-perceptions of their abilities in each domain, even after controlling for the child's previous performance. These findings suggest that parents hold general beliefs (stereotypes) that influence the way in which they interpret their children's performance, depending on individual characteristics of the children, such as gender. More importantly, their interpretations of that performance are conveyed to their children and tend to influence the children's self-perceptions and grades, ultimately carrying more weight than previous performance. In a follow-up to that study, we found that parents' gender stereotypes about math had long-lasting effects on their children's career choices (Bleeker & Jacobs, 2004). In this study, daughters of mothers who held stereotypes about male math abilities when their children were in the sixth grade were less likely to choose physical science careers than other more traditional science careers (e.g., nursing) or nonscience careers.

Provision of Specific Experiences for the Child

Parents structure children's experiences in a variety of ways that should impact self and task values, skill acquisition, preferences, and choice. We have found that exogenous child and family characteristics (e.g., parents' income, education, child gender, age) influence the experiences parents provide for their children primarily through their impact on parents' perceptions of their children's abilities and interests, and on parents' valuing of the activity domain. For example, parents were more likely to provide extra sports experiences for their children if they believed that the children were interested in the activity and had sports ability (Fredericks, 1999). This is a good example of the reciprocal nature of parent–child attitudes: parents are using the feedback they receive from the child, as well as their own assessment of the child, to inform their decisions about which opportunities to provide.

This has sometimes been described as the "opportunity structure" provided by parents. Although most children have the opportunity to be exposed to mathematics and science in school, parents may provide earlier math-related activities, play math games with the child, and encourage involvement in extra math or science activities (e.g., specialized clubs or competitions as the child gets older). The type of opportunities provided will depend on many factors – what is available in the community or school, economic resources, and time constraints (single parents, two-earner families, and families with many children may have less time to devote to their child's participation in extracurricular activities). Participation in extracurricular activities has been associated with socioeconomic class (e.g., Coleman, 1961; Hollingshead, 1949). Participation in activities also may raise an individual's status within the school, extend the child's social network, and even serve as a protective factor against dropping out (e.g., Czikszentimihalyi, Rathunde, & Whalen, 1993; Eder & Parker, 1987; Kinney, 1993; Mahoney & Cairns, 1997). Therefore, parents' decisions to provide or to curtail particular opportunities may have an impact that reaches beyond the child's activity values and perceptions of competence.

Not surprisingly, parents often provide experiences for their children that fit existing expectations for gender-appropriate activities. For example, in a study by Altenburg-Caldwell, Jacobs, & Eccles (1999), we found that parents provide equal numbers of organized activities during early middle childhood for girls and boys, but that the activities provided differ by gender. Similar effects are likely to be found in the math and science domains.

Modeling Involvement in Valued Activities

The importance of role models in socializing behavior has been well documented in the developmental literature (e.g., Bandura & Walters, 1963). According to this work, parents exhibit behaviors that children may later imitate and adopt as part of their own repertoire. The influence of role models may include the messages they provide about their beliefs regarding their own abilities and about their values in general, and previous work suggests that children perceive these messages accurately. The ways in which parents spend their time, the choices they make between available activities, and the sense of self-competence that they project send strong messages to their children about activities that are valued and about acceptable ways to spend time. To test this facet of parental influence, we include numerous indicators of parents' practices and involvement in different types of activities in our research. Findings from one of our earlier studies lend support to this concept. We found that children's perceptions of their parents' enjoyment of math were significantly correlated with the parents' self-reports of past and present math ability, math difficulty, and the effort needed to do well in math. In addition, children who saw their parents do household math (e.g., balancing a checkbook) believed that their parents liked math more than those whose parents did not engage in math activities at home (Eccles-Parsons, Adler, & Kaczala, 1982). Another marker of parental valuing of an activity is their involvement in related activities with the child. For example: Are parents involved in math and science activities with the child? Do they help with homework in these areas? Does their involvement vary by gender? Others have found that parental involvement influences children's leisure activities and achievement behaviors because it communicates parents' perceptions about the value of the activity, as well as their beliefs about the child's ability in that arena (Ginsburg & Bronstein, 1993; Larson, Dworkin, & Gillman, 2001).

Communicating Ability Perceptions, Values, and Future Expectations

Another way in which parents influence their children's task values is by acting as "interpreters of reality" through the messages they provide regarding their perceptions of their children's world and experiences (Eccles, Lord, Roeser, Barber, & Jozefovicz, 1997; Goodnow & Collins, 1990; Phillips, 1987). When children are young, they are not particularly good at assessing their own competence (Nicholls, 1978), so they must rely on their parents' interpretations of their performance as a major source of information about their competence. We have found that parents' perceptions of their children's abilities and their expectations for the child's future success have a large impact on children's developing perceptions of self-competence (e.g., Eccles-Parsons et al., 1982; Jacobs & Eccles, 1992). In these studies, parents' perceptions of their children's abilities, their expectations for their children's success, and their gender stereotypes predict children's self-perceptions of competence and their actual achievement, even after previous indicators of achievement are controlled. In addition, parents' inappropriately low estimations of their children's competence are related to children's lower self-perceptions of their competence in the same areas. Due to the links between self-competence and values, the accuracy of parents' interpretations are critical to children's continued interest, participation, and ultimate valuing of an activity. However, we know that many things will influence parents' interpretations, including the values and expectations within their culture. Although parents are clearly forming their opinions about the child's ability based on objective indicators such as grades and sports competitions, it appears that the direction of influence for perceptions of competence is from parents to children and that parents' views of their children's abilities are quite stable over time (Yoon, Wigfield, & Eccles, 1993).

The Role of Gender

As we have already indicated, much of our research has focused on the role gender (both their own gender and that of their child) plays in influencing children's choices, self-perceptions, and values, and also in the way it influences parents' views of their children and parental behavior in the way they structure the environment for either boys or girls. We have found gender-role stereotypic differences for sports, social activities, English, and music (Eccles et al., 1989, 1993; Jacobs, Lanza, Osgood, Eccles, & Wigfield, 2002; Wigfield et al., 1991) across age groups. As a child, one of the ways to express one's gender identity is by participating in and valuing gender-appropriate activities. Data from our longitudinal Childhood and Beyond (CAB) study (Altenburg-Caldwell, Jacobs & Eccles, 1999) suggests that participation in activities during elementary school is highly gender typed. Girls participate significantly more than boys in art activities, hobbies, clubs, and individual competitive sports; however, boys participate in team sports significantly more than girls. Not surprisingly, this behavioral instantiation of their social identities is related to children's intrinsic values. For example, children who participate the most in team sports, not only value sports the most, but value the arts the least; and those who participate in the arts, have the lowest values for sports.

In addition, we know that perceptions of math competence and values for math are often different for girls and boys, especially at the youngest ages. Previous theories and research have suggested that the gap widens as children get older; however, in a recent study we found that, although males' have higher self-perceptions of math ability than females in the early grades, those differences decrease with age so that by the 12th grade the differences are gone (Jacobs et al., 2002). These results, indicating that gender differences decline with age, complement and extend earlier shorter-term longitudinal studies (e.g., Eccles et al., 1989; Wigfield et al., 1991; Wigfield, Eccles, Yoon, & Harold, 1997). The findings are also consistent with those reported by Marsh, showing no age-related changes in gender differences in general self-concept (Marsh, 1993) and no gender differences in developmental models (Marsh & Yeung, 1997, 1998). However, as suggested at the beginning of this chapter, these findings are at odds with what is known about gender differences in career and educational choices. We believe that the answer may be found in gender-differentiated family support for math/science that results in gender differences in interest in these topics.

Current Questions

We described our general conceptualization of the ways in which parents might influence children's decisions to pursue one achievement domain over another and the role that gender is likely to play; however, there has been little information in the literature on specific parenting practices related to achievement in math/science and little focus on parents' values and attitudes. To fill in some of the gaps in our knowledge about parenting practices and attitudes related to math and science achievement, we present data that address the following questions: (1) does parent support for extracurricular math/science activities vary by sex and grade?, (2) are parents' math-promotive behaviors and attitudes about math related to children's later interest in math and later performance in math?, and (3) are parents' gender stereotypes related to children's interests in math/science?

EVIDENCE

Description of Dataset

The CAB longitudinal data set was collected in Michigan with the goal of investigating the development of children's self-perceptions, task values, and activity choices (Eccles et al., 1983). Beginning in 1987, children ($n = 864$), parents ($n = 550$), and teachers ($n = 70$) were recruited through

10 elementary schools. All children in kindergarten, grade 1, and grade 3 were asked to participate, and 75% of the children both agreed to participate and obtained parental permission. A cross-sequential design was employed in which three cohorts of children were followed longitudinally across the elementary, middle, and high school years. The original sample consisted of 53% girls and 47% boys, and these proportions remained the same throughout the waves of data collection (kindergarten thru 3 years post-high school). Participants were interviewed almost every year between 1987 and 2000 (due to lack of funding there was no data collection in years 1991–3). A similar set of protocols and questions were used at every wave of data collection with additions and deletions made based on the changing ages of children. Information about income provided by the school districts indicates that the children were from middle-class backgrounds with average family income around $50,000 at the initial time of data collection. Over 95% of the children were European American. Attrition in the sample was due mostly to children moving away from the school districts sampled, although every effort was made to relocate children each year, and the longitudinal sample included children who continued to live in the same general area, even if they no longer attended participating schools.

Does Parent Support for Extracurricular Math/Science Activities Vary by Sex and Grade?

Our model suggests that parents may convey the importance of math and science to their children in a variety of ways. They may model their own interest in math and science by spending time on such activities at home. They may also show support of these topics by working on math/science activities with their children, or by providing toys, books, and games on these topics. In the CAB project, we asked parents to report on each of these methods of socializing children about the importance and value of math/science. Mothers' reports can be seen in Fig. 12.2, indicating that they were significantly ($p \leq 0.001$) more likely at every grade to purchase math/science items for sons than for daughters, regardless of child's grade in school.

We also asked parents how much time they spent working on math and science activities with their children. Mothers were significantly more likely than fathers to report involvement in children's math/science activities in kindergarten ($F(1, 78) = 15.28, p < 0.001$), first grade ($F(1, 210) = 5.13, p < 0.05$), second grade ($F(1, 200) = 5.09, p < 0.05$), and third grade ($F(1, 239) = 5.19, p < 0.05$), but mothers and fathers spent similar amounts of time on math with their children after grade three. As children got older, both mothers and fathers indicated significantly less involvement in children's

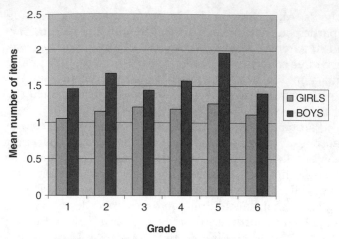

FIGURE 12.2.   Math/science items purchased for child during last year.

math/science activities (F $(1, 247) = 15.75$, $p < 0.001$). Although some gender differences were found, these were not consistent by parent or grade.

Finally, to examine parental modeling of involvement in math/science, we asked parents how much time they spent around the house on math/science activities themselves. In this sample, parents did not report spending much time on these activities (just over one hour per week on average), and time spent by mothers and fathers did not differ significantly.

Are Parents' Math-Promotive Behaviors and Attitudes About Math Related to Children's Later Self-Perceptions of Ability and Actual Achievement?

Our previous research has shown that parents' specific beliefs about their children and their general beliefs about the world (i.e., gender stereotypes) influence children's own beliefs about their abilities and their achievement behaviors (Jacobs, 1991; Jacobs & Eccles, 1992). We wanted to know if parent socialization practices regarding math and science might contribute to the prediction of these previously tested relationships between parent and child beliefs. To test this, we developed a composite variable that included math/science items purchased by the mother (mothers' reports were used due to the larger sample size and nonindependence of father reports), mothers' involvement in math/science activities themselves, and mothers' involvement in such activities with their children. We used linear regression to test the effects of mothers' math/science purchases, activities with their child, and modeling on children's later math/science GPA. We also included mothers' values for achievement in math/science. To control for mothers' perceptions of their children's abilities and interests, we included those two variables in the model. Not surprisingly, the positive beta weights for these variables indicate that children, who reported the highest self-perceptions of math ability, have the highest math/science GPA a year later (see Table 12.1). More important for the topic at hand is the fact that mothers' math-promotive behaviors were significantly related to later achievement, even after controlling for children's self-perceptions of ability and interest. It is interesting to note that mothers' values for math/science do not make a significant independent contribution to the model after children's beliefs and parenting practices have been included.

Are Parents' Gender Stereotypes about Math Related to Children's Later Interest in Math?

Our earlier work and the Eccles model of parent socialization describe a prominent role for parents' general worldviews, as well as their perceptions of their own children. We investigated this topic in an earlier study with another data set, and found that both mothers' and fathers' gender stereotypes about math had a large influence on their beliefs about their own children's abilities, as well as the children's later self-perceptions of their abilities in math. Because the gap between males' and females' achievement in math has narrowed (e.g., Catsambis, 1999, Hyde, 1997; Marsh & Yeung, 1998; Serbin, Zekowitz, Doyle, & Gold, 1990) and females are participating in some areas of science in greater numbers (e.g., Burkam, Lee, &

TABLE 12.1. *Role of Mother's Math/Science Promotive Activities and Child Attitudes on Math/Science GPA, One Year Later*

Variable	B	SE B	β
Block 1[1]			
Child gender	−0.14	0.44	−0.02
Grade	1.3	0.18	0.33***
Block 2[2]			
Child's math interest (Y2)	−0.13	0.12	−0.06
Child's self-perception of math ability (Y2)	0.59	0.23	0.13**
Block 3[3]			
Mother's math/science items, activities, and modeling (Y2)	0.37	0.15	0.11**
Mother's value for math/science	0.22	0.16	0.07

[1] R^2 for Block 1 = 0.11
[2] R^2 for Blocks 1 & 2 = 0.13
[3] R^2 for Blocks 1, 2, & 3 = 0.15
** $p < 0.01$
*** $p < 0.001$

TABLE 12.2. *Role of Parent Gender Stereotypes on Child Math Interest,*
One Year Later

Variable	MOM			DAD		
	B	SE B	β	B	SE B	β
Block 1[1]						
Child gender	0.17	0.16	0.05	0.19	0.19	0.06
Gender stereotype (Y3)	−0.23	0.08	−0.14***	0.00	0.10	0.02
Interaction of child gender and gender stereotype	0.17	0.15	0.05	0.37	0.20	0.11*
Grade	−0.30	0.06	−0.23***	−0.26	0.07	−0.20***
Block 2[1]						
Parent's perception of child's math ability (Y3)	0.33	0.07	0.23***	0.35	0.09	0.22***

[1] R^2 for Mothers' Block 1 = 0.08, R^2 for Fathers' Block 1 = 0.06;
[2] R^2 for Mothers' Blocks 1 & 2 = 0.13, R^2 for Fathers' Blocks 1 & 2 = 0.11
* $p < 0.05$
** $p < 0.01$
*** $p < 0.001$

Smerdon, 1997; NCES, 2001), we expected to find fewer gender stereotypes favoring males than we have found previously.

Using the CAB data, we constructed a regression model in which we used mother's gender stereotype, child's grade, and child's past perception of math ability to predict interest in math. Table 12.2 describes the results. The negative beta weights for both mother's gender stereotype and child's grade indicate that children who are younger and children who have mothers with less traditional views about gender are more likely to indicate interest in the domain of math. The positive beta weight for past perception of math ability supports past findings that indicate that children who are more positive about their abilities in math are also more likely to be interested in math. Child's gender and math/science activities were not related to interest. For the model using data from fathers, the interaction of father's gender stereotype and child's gender, child's grade, and child's earlier perceptions of math ability were significant predictors of child's interest in math. Once again, the negative beta weight for child's grade indicates that younger children are more interested in math. The positive beta weight for the interaction of father's gender stereotype and child's grade indicates that girls' interest in math decreases as fathers' gender stereotypes increase, whereas boys' math interest increases as fathers' gender stereotypes increase (see Fig. 12.3). Once again, the positive beta weight for past perceptions of math ability indicates that children who

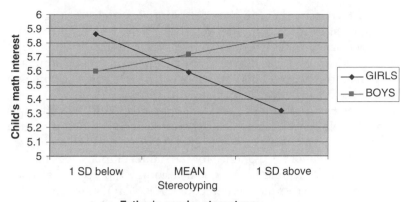

FIGURE 12.3. Influence of father's gender stereotype on child's interest in math.

are more positive about their abilities in math are also more likely to be interested in math.

CONCLUSION

In this chapter, we used the Eccles' parent socialization model to consider the role played by parents in children's math/science achievement choices. We focused on gender differences in children's math and science attitudes and achievement, and on the environment provided by parents to support girls' and boys' interests in math and science. We began by reviewing the theoretical perspective and our previous work, indicating that key determinants of children's self-perceptions and values for math are parents' attitudes and behaviors, children's self-perceptions, and gender-role expectations (e.g., Eccles, 1987; Eccles et al., 1993; Eccles [Parsons] et al., 1983; Jacobs, 1991; Jacobs & Eccles, 1992; Wigfield et al., 1991).

We then presented new evidence related to the "gendered" nature of the math/science opportunities and expectations that parents provide for their children. Parents appear to provide more math-supportive environments for their sons than for their daughters by purchasing more math/science toys for sons, spending more time on math/science with sons, and holding higher perceptions of their sons' than daughters' math abilities as well as gender-typed worldviews about natural talent in math. We also provided evidence of the relations between children's earlier math interests, self-perceptions, and activities and their later math/science GPAs, and between parents' gender stereotypes and child-specific beliefs and the child's later interest in math. These longitudinal findings emphasize the importance of the middle childhood years for later math/science achievement choices. If girls are not interested in math and science at early ages or if they believe that their parents do not value their competence in those topics, they may be less likely to pursue them as they get older. Research has suggested that girls' interest in math continues to decline across high school even when their performance (as measured by grades) is higher than the boys' (Linver, Davis-Kean, & Eccles, 2002). Thus, even if girls are performing at high levels in math, the likelihood that they will be interested in pursuing math-related majors in college is low.

Although the Eccles' theoretical model of parent socialization attempts to describe the relationships between the multifaceted contexts provided by parents, the interactions of parents and children, and what children bring to the mix, most of the evidence for the model emphasizes only one part of the picture at a time because it is a complex process that takes place over years and across many interactions. It is clear that much of what parents do is in response to their perceptions of their children and may be elicited by the child; thus, the process of providing a math-supportive environment may begin with the child in many cases. Although the process might be somewhat different if the child initiates it, we cannot assume that children who begin by valuing math necessarily maintain that interest and involvement without some parental support and/or encouragement.

The general conclusion that we draw from our work is that, although girls' performance and self-perceptions of ability suggest that they feel competent in math, they are less likely than boys to find it intrinsically interesting and their parents are less likely to create math-supportive or math-promotive environments for them. It appears, instead, that the achievement environment in many homes is a gendered environment and that messages from parents about achievement continue to be sent through gender-typed filters.

References

Altenburg-Caldwell, K., Jacobs, J. E., & Eccles, J. S. (1999, June). *Gender differences in activity involvement: Relations between activities, self-beliefs, and gender-typing*. Paper presented at the annual meeting of the American Psychological Society, Denver, CO.

Bae, Y., & Smith, T. M. (1996). *Issues in focus: Women in mathematics and science*. Washington, DC: National Center for Educational Statistics.

Bandura, A., & Walters, R. H. (1963). *Social learning and personality development*. New York: Holt, Rinehart, & Winston.

Barber, B. K., Olsen, J. E., & Shagle, S. C. (1994). Associations between parental psychological and behavioral control and youth internalized and externalized behaviors. *Child Development, 65*, 1120–1136.

Bleeker, M. M., & Jacobs, J. E. (2004, March). Achievement in math and science: Do mother's beliefs matter twelve years later? *Journal of Educational Psychology, 96*(1).

Burkham, D. T., Lee, V. E., & Smerdon, B. A. (1997). Gender and science learning early in high school: Subject matter and laboratory experiences. *American Educational Research Journal, 34*(2), 297–331.

Catsambis, S. (1999). The path to math: Gender and racial-ethnic differences in mathematics participation from middle school to high school. In L. A. Peplau & S. C. DeBro (Eds.), *Gender, culture, ethnicity: Current research about women and men* (pp. 102–120). Mountain View, CA: Mayfield Publishing.

Coleman, J. S. (1961). *The adolescent society.* New York: Free Press.

Connell, J. P., & Wellborn, J. G. (1991). Competence, autonomy, and relatedness: A motivational analysis of self-system processes. In R. Gunner & L. A. Sroufe (Eds.), *Minnesota symposia on child psychology* (Vol. 23, pp. 43–77). Hillsdale, NJ: Lawrence Erlbaum Associates.

Czikszentimihaliyi, M., Rathunde, K., & Whalen, S. (1993). *Talented teenagers: The roots of success and failure.* New York: Cambridge University Press.

Deci, E. L., & Ryan, R. M. (1985). *Intrinsic motivation and self-determination in human behavior.* New York: Plenum Press.

Eccles, J. S. (1987). Gender roles and women's achievement-related decisions. *Psychology of Women Quarterly, 11,* 135–172.

Eccles, J. S. (1994). Understanding women's educational and occupational choices: Applying the Eccles et al. model of achievement-related choices. *Psychology of Women Quarterly, 18,* 585–609.

Eccles, J. S., Adler, T. F., & Meece, J. L. (1984). Sex differences in achievement: A test of alternative theories. *Journal of Personality and Social Psychology, 46,* 26–43.

Eccles, J. S., Early, D., Frasier, K., Belansky, E., & McCarthy, K. (1996). The relation of connection, regulation, and support for autonomy to adolescents' functioning. *Journal of Adolescent Research, 12,* 263–286.

Eccles, J. S., Lord, S. E., Roeser, R. W., Barber, B. L., & Jozefowicz, D. M. (1997). The association of school transitions in early adolescence with developmental trajectories through high school. In J. Schulenberg, J. L. Maggs, & K. Hurrelmann (Eds.), *Health risks and developmental transitions during adolescence.* New York: Cambridge University Press.

Eccles, J. S., & Wigfield, A. (1995). In the mind of the achiever: The structure of adolescents' academic achievement related-beliefs and self-perceptions. *Personality and Social Psychology Bulletin, 21,* 215–225.

Eccles, J. S., Wigfield, A., Flanagan, C., Miller, C., Reuman, D., & Yee, D. (1989). Self-concepts, domain values, and self-esteem: Relations and changes at early adolescence. *Journal of Personality, 57,* 283–310.

Eccles, J. S., Wigfield, A., Harold, R., & Blumenfeld, P. (1993). Age and gender differences in children's achievement self-perceptions during the elementary school years. *Child Development, 64,* 830–847.

Eccles, J. S., Wigfield, A., & Schiefele, U. (1998). Motivation to succeed. In W. Damon (Ed.), Handbook of child psychology, N. Eisenberg (Vol. Ed.), *Social, emotional, and personality development.* New York: Wiley.

Eccles (Parsons), J., Adler, T. F., Futterman, R., Goff, S. B., Kaczala, C. M., Meece, J. L., & Midgley, C. (1983). Expectancies, values, and academic behaviors. In J. T. Spence (Ed.), *Achievement and achievement motivation* (pp. 75–146). San Francisco: W. H. Freeman.

Eccles-Parsons, J., Adler, T. F., & Kaczala, C. M. (1982). Socialization of achievement attitudes and beliefs: Parental influences. *Child Development, 53,* 322–339.

Eder, D., & Parker, S. (1987). The cultural production and reproduction of gender: The effect of extracurricular activities on peer-group culture. *Sociology of Education, 60,* 200–214.

Feather, N. T. (1982). Expectancy-value approaches: Present status and future directions. In N. T. Feather (Ed.), *Expectations and actions: Expectancy-value models in psychology* (pp. 395–420). Hillsdale, NJ: Erlbaum.

Fredericks, J. (1999). *"Girl-Friendly" Family contexts: Socialization into math and sports.* Unpublished doctoral dissertation. Ann Arbor: University of Michigan.

Ginsburg, G. S., & Bronstein, P. (1993). Family factors related to children's intrinsic/extrinsic motivational orientation and academic performance. *Child Development, 64*(5), 1461–1474.

Goodnow, J. J., & Collins, W. A. (1990). *Development according to parents: The nature, sources, and consequences of parents' ideas.* London: Erlbaum.

Hall, C. W., Davis, N. B., Bolen, L. M., & Chia, R. (1999). Gender and racial differences in mathematical performance. *Journal of Social Psychology, 139*(6), 677–689.

Higher Education Research Institute. (1996). *The American freshman: National norms for Fall, 1996.* Los Angeles: University of California, Graduate School of Education and Information Studies.

Hollingshead, A. B. (1949). *Elmstown's youth: The impact of social classes on adolescents.* New York: Wiley.

Hyde, J. S. (1997). Gender differences in math performance: Not big, not biological. In M. R. Walsh (Ed.), *Women, men, & gender: Ongoing debates* (pp. 271–287). New Haven, CT: Yale University Press.

Jacobs, J. E. (1991). The influence of gender stereotypes on parent and child math attitudes: Differences across grade-levels. *Journal of Educational Psychology, 83*, 518–527.

Jacobs, J. E., & Eccles, J. S. (1985). Gender differences in math ability: The impact of media reports on parents. *Educational Researcher, 14*, 20–25.

Jacobs, J. E., & Eccles, J. E. (1992). The influence of parent stereotypes on parent and child ability beliefs in three domains. *Journal of Personality and Social Psychology, 63*, 932–944.

Jacobs, J. E., Finken, L. L., Griffin, N. L., & Wright, J. D. (1998). The career plans of science-talented rural adolescent girls. *American Educational Research Journal, 35*, 681–704.

Jacobs, J. E., Hyatt, S., Tanner, J., & Eccles, J. (1998). *Lessons learned at home: Relations between parents' child-rearing practices and children's achievement perceptions.* Paper presented at the annual meeting of the American Educational Research Association, San Diego, CA.

Jacobs, J. E., Lanza, S., Osgood, D. W., Eccles, J. S., & Wigfield, A. (2002). Changes in children's self-competence and values: Gender and domain differences across grades one through twelve. *Child Development, 73*, 509–527.

Kinney, D. A. (1993). From nerds to normals: The recovery of identity among adolescents from middle school to high school. *Sociology of Education, 66*, 21–44.

Larson, R., Dworkin, J., & Gillman, S. (2001). Facilitating adolescents' constructive use of time in one-parent families. *Applied Developmental Science, 5*(3), 143–157.

Linver, M., Davis-Kean, P. E., & Eccles, J. S. (2002, March). *Influences of gender on academic achievement.* Paper presented at the Society for Research on Adolescence, New Orleans, LA.

Mahoney, J. L., & Cairns, R. B. (1997). Do extracurricular activities protect against early school dropout? *Developmental Psychologist, 33*, 241–253.

Marsh, H. W. (1993). Relations between global and specific domains of self: The importance of individual importance, certainty, and ideals. *Journal of Personality and Social Psychology, 65*(5), 975–992.

Marsh, H. W., & Yeung, A. S. (1997). Organization of children's academic self-perceptions: Reanalysis and counter-interpretations of confirmatory factor analysis results. *Journal of Educational Psychology, 89*(4), 752–759.

Marsh, H. W., & Yeung, A. S. (1998). Longitudinal structural equation models of academic self-concept and achievement: Gender differences in the development of math and English constructs. *American Educational Research Journal, 35*(4), 705–738.

Meece, J. L., Eccles-Parsons, J., Kaczala, C. M., Goff, S. E., & Futterman, R. (1982). Sex differences in math achievement: Toward a model of academic choice. *Psychological Bulletin, 91*, 324–348.

Meece, J. L., Wigfield, A., & Eccles, J. S. (1990). Predictors of math anxiety and its consequences for young adolescents' course enrollment intentions and performances in mathematics. *Journal of Educational Psychology, 82*, 60–70.

National Center for Education Statistics (NCES). (2001). *Digest of Educational Statistics: Postsecondary Education.* Web site can be accessed at http://nces.ed.gov/.

National Science Foundation (NSF). (2000). *Women, minorities, and persons with disabilities in science and engineering.* (NSF 00–327). Arlington, VA.

Nicholls, J. G. (1978). The development of the concepts of effort and ability, perceptions of academic attainment, and the understanding that difficult tasks require more ability. *Child Development, 49*, 800–814.

Phillips, D. A. (1987). Socialization of perceived academic competence among highly competent children. *Child Development, 58*, 1308–1320.

Serbin, L. A., Zelkowitz, P., Doyle, A., & Gold, D. (1990). The socialization of sex-differentiated skills and academic performance: A mediational model. *Sex Roles, 23*, 613–628.

Stumpf, H., & Stanley, J. (1996). Gender related differences on the College Board's advanced placement and achievement tests, 1982–1992. *Journal of Educational Psychology, 88*, 353–364.

Wigfield, A., & Eccles, J. (1992). The development of achievement task values: A theoretical analysis. *Developmental Review, 12*, 265–310.

Wigfield, A., Eccles, J., Mac Iver, D., Reuman D., & Midgley, C. (1991). Transitions at early adolescence: Changes in children's domain-specific self-perceptions and general self-esteem across the transition to junior high school. *Developmental Psychology, 27*, 552–565.

Wigfield, A., Eccles, J. S., Yoon, K. S., & Harold, R. D. (1997). Change in children's competence beliefs and subjective task values across the elementary school years: A 3-year study. *Journal of Educational Psychology, 89*(3), 451–469.

Yoon, K. S., Wigfield, A., & Eccles, J. S. (1993, April). *Causal relations between mothers' and children's beliefs about math ability: A structural equation model.* Paper presented at the annual meeting of the American Educational Research Association.

13

Gender Effects on Mathematics Achievement

Mediating Role of State and Trait Self-Regulation

Eunsook Hong, Harold F. O'Neil, and David Feldon

Gender differences in achievement have been the focus of many studies across different domains (e.g., Halpern, 2000; Willingham & Cole, 1997). Mathematics especially has received much attention due to its fundamental importance in modern society, its observed performance gap in favor of males on many academic tasks, and its minority of female experts in related fields (Halpern, 2000). Other chapters in this book provide a discussion of possible reasons for these gender differences in mathematics (e.g., critical thinking, biopsychosocial reasons, spatial ability, talent, personality). The focus of this chapter is on the role of self-regulation.

In a general sense, self-regulation is any effort to alter or sustain one's own pattern of behavior (Baumeister, Heatherton, & Tice, 1994). Within the academic context, however, self-regulated learning has been characterized by motivational, cognitive, and metacognitive strategies that specifically facilitate academic achievement (Bandura, 1993; McCombs, 1984). We explore mediating roles of students' trait and state self-regulation in academic tasks and of students' test anxiety to further our understanding of the gender gap in students' mathematics achievement.

Traits are considered relatively enduring predispositions or characteristics of people (e.g., intelligence, aptitude, or self-regulation), whereas states are attributes of individuals that are relatively changeable, thus representing dimensions of intraindividual variability over time or occasions (Spielberger, 1975). The distinction is important because individuals' traits are highly predictive of their state characteristics, although manifestations of state characteristics are highly dependent on the environment and circumstances of the specific instance. Weiner and his colleagues (Weiner, 1985; Weiner, Freize, Kukla, Reed, & Rosenbaum, 1971) examined effort, a component of self-regulation, and determined that state effort varied significantly with different times and situations, but that overall effort (trait) can be evaluated as laziness or industriousness with great stability over time. Hong (1995, 1998b) examined the viability of a state-trait distinction in self-regulation and found that, although the factor structures were invariant across the models, there was a significant difference in the stability of subjects' state and trait self-regulation behaviors. Thus, we have generalized the key constructs from an affective domain (e.g., state and trait anxiety) to a cognitive domain (e.g., state and trait self-regulation).

Two major issues need to be understood in the gender and self-regulation area. First, if males outperform females on standardized math tests, then one would predict that males' trait self-regulation would be higher than females' because more self-regulation in general should result in better standardized math test performance. This logic assumes that standardized math tests represent an average of learning experiences over an extended period of time. In addition, it would be expected that trait test anxiety would be lower for males because high test anxiety would depress standardized test performance.

An alternative explanation for males outperforming females on standardized math tests would be that such tests are administered at a single point in time (i.e., a test dropped out of the sky). Thus, males would be more influenced by state self-regulation and state anxiety, not trait self-regulation and trait anxiety. The literature on stereotypes (Blascovich, Spencer, Quinn, & Steele, 2001; Steele, 1997; Steele & Aronson, 1995), which indicates that stimulation of racial or ethnic stereotypes can depress standardized test performance, would support this explanation of a state phenomenon.

Second, if females outperform males on school achievement measures (grades, homework, teacher-made tests), one would predict that females' trait self-regulation would be higher than males' and that trait test anxiety would be lower. Like the alternative explanation for gender effects on standardized math tests, one could argue that it would be a trait issue as most classroom measures (grades, exams) represent performance across time. Thus, our predictions of gender effects on standardized test performance vs. school achievement measures depend on individual difference variables of trait or state self-regulation and test anxiety. More empirical work is needed to sort out these various possible theoretical explanations.

In this chapter, we present briefly the background of gender differences in mathematics achievement, test anxiety, and academic self-regulation, and relationships among them. We then provide validated and easy-to-use scales for measuring students' trait and state self-regulation to increase the number of studies investigating these phenomena. Last, we report findings from a study that examined mediating roles of state and trait self-regulation, as well as state and trait test anxiety, on gender differences in mathematics achievement.

GENDER DIFFERENCES IN MATHEMATICS ACHIEVEMENT

Gender differences in academic mathematics performance, especially in grades nine to twelve, have been well documented since the early 1960s (e.g., Fennema, 1974; Flanagan et al., 1964; Halpern, 2002; Kupermintz, Ennis, Hamilton, Talbert, & Snow, 1995; Schildkamp-Kuendiger, 1982). Research findings on gender difference in mathematics at the elementary and secondary levels vary widely, from a significant gender difference favoring males (Cahan & Ganor, 1995; Fennema, 1984; Martin & Hoover, 1987; Seegers & Boekaerts, 1996) to no difference (Caporrimo, 1990; Senk & Usiskin, 1983). At the college level, some studies have shown a lack of significant relationship between gender and mathematical ability (Cooper & Robinson, 1989; Hong & Karstensson, 2002). In an international student assessment reported in 2000, 15-year-old males performed better on the mathematics portion in half of the countries where the test was administered. However, the remaining half, which included the United States, did not show significant gender differences in mathematics performance (Organisation for Economic Co-Operation and Development, 2000).

Of the studies that found gender differences in mathematics, the type of measures used in the studies has been one of the elements that differentiated the gender–mathematics relationship (Willingham & Cole, 1997). In an extensive review of the literature, Kimball (1989) reported that although males are usually found to perform significantly better on standardized tests, females from middle school through university tend to perform significantly higher at all levels of mathematics courses (Deboer, 1984; Hanna & Sonnenschein, 1985; Rech, 1996; Stockard & Wood, 1984). Further, upon categorizing mathematics courses by content as more advanced (analytical geometry, calculus, probability and statistics, and elementary functions) and less advanced (algebra, plane geometry, and trigonometry), Kimball found that women's grade advantage increased in more advanced courses. Conversely, analyses of major testing programs, including the ACT-Math, the SAT-Math, National Education Longitudinal Study (NELS), and High School and Beyond (HSB), indicated that standard mean differences or effect sizes were between 0.27 and 0.45 favoring men (Willingham & Cole, 1997).

Gender differences also vary depending on skill subsets. Although the algebra items significantly favored females, males performed significantly better on number and computation, data analysis, and geometry and measurement items (Garner & Engelhard, 1999). Females in grades 10 and 12 outperformed males in logic and geometric reasoning, but males scored better on items testing scale and three-dimensional solid geometry (Pattison & Grieve, 1984). However, there is conflicting evidence by Snow and Ennis (1996). Females were stronger in computation than males, but males performed better on inferential reasoning tasks. Further, males improved their inferential reasoning skills at a significantly greater rate and to a significantly greater level than females throughout high school (Kupermintz et al., 1995). These conflicting research findings warrant continued investigations in this area with rigorous design of research approaches.

GENDER DIFFERENCES IN TEST ANXIETY

Gender differences in test anxiety have been shown in numerous studies, with females in general reporting higher anxiety than males (Bander & Betz, 1981; Benson, Bandalos, & Hutchinson, 1994; Hembree, 1988; Lussier, 1996; Pintrich & De Groot, 1990). Liebert and Morris's (1967) two-factor conceptualization of test anxiety – worry and emotionality – has been supported by various research studies (e.g., Benson & Tippets, 1990; Morris, Davis, & Hutchings, 1981; O'Neil & Abedi, 1992; O'Neil & Fukumura, 1992; Zeidner, 1990). Worry (i.e., the cognitive concern about test taking and performance, such as negative expectations and preoccupation with performance and potential consequences) has shown a stronger inverse relationship with test performance than emotionality (i.e., perceived physiological reactions to testing situations such as nervousness; Liebert & Morris, 1967; Powers, 1987; Zeidner, 1990; Zeidner & Nevo, 1992). Although there was a significant relationship between worry and emotionality within and between testing occasions, these elements were independent (Hong, 1999). Gender differences were also indicated in the two elements of test anxiety: In a test of high school science students, males reported similar levels of worry and emotionality, whereas females demonstrated disproportionately higher levels of worry (Williams, 1996).

Worry and emotionality have differential impacts on achievement. Worry is the test anxiety component that has shown a consistent and strong inverse relationship with performance, whereas emotionality has either a weak or no relationship with performance (e.g., Morris et al., 1981; O'Neil & Abedi, 1992; Powers, 1987; Zeidner & Nevo, 1992). However, other factors such as item difficulty and feedback were found to have moderating effects on the strength of relationship between worry/emotionality and test performance (e.g., Kim & Rocklin, 1994; Morris & Fulmer, 1976).

SELF-REGULATION, GENDER, AND MATHEMATICS ACHIEVEMENT

Students' self-regulatory skills have been shown to correlate with academic achievement (Kitsantas, 2002; Schunk & Swartz, 1993; Zimmerman & Kitsantas, 1999). Kitsantas (2002), for example, examined the relationship between test performance of college students in a psychology course and self-regulatory behaviors and strategies before, during, and after test taking. It was found that high scorers on the tests used a higher number of self-regulatory strategies overall than did low scorers. Specifically, planning, goal-setting, and help-seeking behaviors prior to tests were associated with high test performance. High scores also covaried with the utilization of planning strategies more frequently during the tests.

Self-regulated learners systematically use metacognitive, motivational, and behavioral strategies to accomplish academic tasks (Zimmerman, 1986, 1989, 1990). Specifically, self-regulated learners plan, self-monitor, and self-evaluate at various stages of the learning process (metacognitive component), and are also competent and self-efficacious, expend effort, and have less anxiety (motivational components). Bandura (1993) asserted that self-directed learning requires motivation as well as cognitive and metacognitive strategies. Self-efficacy, enhanced by the use of cognitive and metacognitive strategies, provides the motivational basis for further self-regulated learning (Zimmerman, 1990). Self-regulated learners not only report high self-efficacy, but also display high levels of effort and persistence during learning (Bandura, 1993; Zimmerman, 1990).

Pintrich and De Groot (1990) contended that there are three key components to self-regulated classroom performance: metacognitive strategies, management and control of effort, and conceptualization of learning strategies. In their study of seventh-grade science and English students, they evaluated performance on classroom assignments against student self-reports of self-regulation and motivational components, including test anxiety. Their findings indicated that, although there was a relationship between self-regulation and motivational beliefs, self-regulation more directly influenced performance on assignments. Zimmerman and Martinez-Pons (1988, 1990) also found significant relationships between the use of self-regulatory learning strategies and achievement and between students' use of self-regulation and their motivation.

Consistent with Zimmerman's (1986, 1989, 1990) theory of self-regulated learning, we have isolated two significant higher-order factors in the assessment of self-regulated learning: metacognition and motivation (Hong & O'Neil, 2001). Metacognition, as conceptualized in Flavell's (1976, 1979) research, entails monitoring and awareness of one's own learning processes through activities such as planning and self-checking (e.g., Borkowski & Burke, 1996; Brown, Bransford, Ferrara, & Campione, 1983; Zimmerman & Martinez-Pons, 1988). Metacognitive planning is representative of goal setting for specific learning outcomes. As Zimmerman (2000) explained, "The goal systems of highly self-regulated individuals are organized hierarchically, such that process goals operate as proximal regulators of more distal outcomes" (p. 17). Such goal-setting behaviors have been observed to facilitate the successful completion of basic computation skills (Das, Naglieri, & Kirby, 1994; Naglieri & Gottling, 1995, 1997) and long-division problem sets during time-restricted study sessions (Locke & Latham, 1990). Beyond simply guiding learning behaviors in a prescriptive sense, interim goal steps have been found to improve self-efficacy for people who set and execute them because such individuals frequently approach and attain interim goals (Bandura & Schunk, 1981; Manderlink & Harackiewicz, 1984). Specifically, in the realm of mathematics, this effect was observed in conjunction with an increase in students' intrinsic interest.

Complementing the planning process in metacognition is self-monitoring or self-checking. According to Carver and Scheier (1981), there is a constant feedback loop that operates to check action outcomes against planned interim actions. If such self-observation is insufficient or attends to irrelevant details, students' progress in acquiring or performing new skills will be hindered, as the need for modifications to their actions will not be recognized. The monitoring process extends beyond the execution itself and includes the conditions that surround it and the effects that it produces (Zimmerman & Paulsen, 1995).

Turning to the motivation factor, we also focus on effort and self-efficacy in this chapter. Bandura (1993) argues that effort is necessary in order to bring tasks to completion in the event of distractions, stress, or other performance-inhibiting factors. In academic self-regulation research, effort is measured by items on self-report instruments. Subjects respond via Likert scale to items such as "When work is hard, I either give up or study only the easy parts" (Pintrich & De Groot, 1990) and "I work hard to do well even if I don't like a task" (O'Neil, Baker, Ni, Jacoby, & Swigger, 1994).

Effort has been demonstrated to increase the accuracy of assessments and academic performance (Neuberg, 1989; Volet, 1997). Neuberg (1989) instructed one group of subjects to exert extra effort in attending to and gathering information from interaction partners, and compared their performance recalling and drawing conclusions about the information elicited. Participants in the control group were given similar instruction, but were not told explicitly to exert effort. As a result, the performance of the control group was significantly lower than that of the experimental group. In another example (Keinan, 1987), research participants were instructed to complete multiple-choice tests under varying levels of stress. As the stress required some of the subjects' mental effort to process, it was expected that performance would degrade as the level of stress increased. Consistent with this hypothesis, subjects failed to adequately evaluate all possible choices before responding, and the frequency of incorrect responses varied with the magnitude of the stress variable.

Associated with, but distinct from, effort is self-efficacy. Bandura (1997) defined self-efficacy as "beliefs in one's capabilities to organize and execute the courses of action required to manage prospective situations" (p. 2). Put simply, self-efficacy is an individual's belief regarding his or her own ability to succeed at a particular task. Extensive research examining the construct's role in predicting performance, course selection, and perseverance has been supported across a wide variety of domains (Pajares, 1996). In college mathematics, it has been found that students' self-efficacy in the subject is a better predictor of interest and selection of course enrollment and majors than either previous performance or expectations of outcome (Hackett, 1985; Hackett & Betz, 1989; Lent, Lopez, & Bieschke, 1991, 1993; Pajares & Miller, 1994, 1995).

The relationship between self-efficacy and academic endeavors attempted also manifests itself in other motivational constructs and performance indicators. In a number of experimental studies, it has been found that people with high levels of self-efficacy exert more effort significantly more often than those with low self-efficacy (e.g., Bandura, 1993; Pintrich & Schrauben, 1992; Schunk, 1984). Analyzing the role of academic self-efficacy through path analysis, Zimmerman, Bandura, and Martinez-Pons (1992) found that it influenced achievement directly (0.21) and further impacted it by raising students' achievement goals (0.36). Likewise, self-efficacy in mathematics accounted for performance (0.46) directly and indirectly through persistence (0.30) (Schunk, 1984). It has also been demonstrated that self-efficacy significantly mediates the relationships between performance and general ability, previous mathematics performance, and gender (Pajares & Kranzler, 1995).

Studies examining gender differences in self-regulation are relatively few. As noted above, Zimmerman and Martinez-Pons (1990) observed gender effects on self-efficacy and self-regulation strategy selection, where females demonstrated greater use of monitoring, environmental structuring, goal setting, and planning, but reported lower self-efficacy than males. Ablard and Lipschultz (1998) investigated gender differences in self-regulated learning by the type of strategy. Their qualitative findings indicated that females demonstrated significantly higher levels of self-regulated learning with advanced problem-solving strategies. Females also demonstrated a significantly stronger mastery orientation, although no difference was found for performance orientation. Further, females' overall measures of self-regulated learning were higher than those of males, and females used strategies that optimized the immediate environment and personal regulation.

We believe that more progress in this area of gender and self-regulation research can be had if valid questionnaire measures of trait and state self-regulation are available. Currently, the best available questionnaire for this purpose is the Motivational Strategies Learning Questionnaire (Pintrich & De Groot, 1990). However, this questionnaire does not reflect a trait-state distinction among constructs, which we believe is essential. Thus, we began a development effort to create a state version of a self-regulation questionnaire (see O'Neil & Abedi, 1996) and a trait version (see O'Neil & Herl, 1998, and Appendix A, this chapter). The questionnaire in Appendix

A is recommended for research purposes and represents our "final" version of the self-regulation questionnaire.

RELIABILITY AND VALIDITY OF A MEASURE OF SELF-REGULATION

This section reports reliability and validity data on a self-report measure of trait self-regulation (see Appendix A). The validation procedures for both state and trait self-regulation measures were similar. Due to space limitations, we present the validation information for the trait measure only. As part of our ongoing research and development effort to develop new measures for alternative assessments, we have been designing, developing, and validating a set of self-regulation measures for use with such assessments. The data reported in this section are from a series of studies using both U.S. and international samples of convenience.

Theoretical Framework

The research adapted the models and measures of several educational psychologists (e.g., Bandura, 1993; Borkowski & Muthukrishna, 1992; Everson, Smodlaka, & Tobias, 1994; Paris, Cross, & Lipson, 1984; Pintrich & De Groot, 1990; Pressley & Afflerbach, 1995; Schunk, 1995; Tobias & Everson, 1995; Zimmerman, 1994) to serve as a relevant framework on self-regulation. Similar to Zimmerman (1995), we define self-regulation to consist of metacognition and motivation. Metacognition is defined as consisting of planning and self-assessment or self-monitoring, and motivation is defined as consisting of effort and self-efficacy.

We have created a measure of trait self-regulation that can be administered in 10 to 15 minutes. The stability of this construct and the brief administration time make it practical for teachers to use in the classroom to help them better assess the needs of individual students. Conversely, a state self-regulation measure might prove useful for identifying and assessing context-dependent factors of variability in individual students' performance. Using constructs from state-trait anxiety theory (Spielberger, 1975) as an analogy, we have formulated a set of self-report, domain-independent trait and state measures (O'Neil & Abedi, 1996) of self-regulation.

A trait conception for motivational skills (or "self-efficacy for learning") has been documented by Kanfer, Ackerman, and Heggestad (1996). An excellent self-rating scale on motivational beliefs and self-regulated learning, the Motivational Strategies for Learning Questionnaire (MSLQ; Pintrich & De Groot, 1990; Pintrich, Smith, Garcia, & McKeachie, 1993) was developed to examine factors that influence academic performance in college students. The MSLQ uses three general constructs in the motivational scales (expectancy, value, and affect) and three general scales in the learning strategies component (cognitive, metacognitive, and resource management). The

metacognitive component was evaluated by a single subscale that measures planning, monitoring, and regulating. However, as indicated earlier,
the MSLQ does not explicitly address either the state-trait distinction or
individual components of metacognitive constructs (e.g., planning), which
we believe are critical in the measurement of self-regulation.

Questionnaire Development

The trait self-regulation questionnaire consists of four subscales: planning, self-checking, self-efficacy, and effort. The metacognition (planning
and self-checking) and effort items were written by our research group. The
self-efficacy items were adapted from Pintrich and De Groot's (1990) intrinsic motivation scale (with Dr. Pintrich's permission). Definitions of the
constructs follow. *Planning* is the behavior of setting a goal (either assigned
or self-directed) and arranging actions to achieve the goal. *Self-monitoring*,
or *self-checking*, is a mechanism to evaluate and confirm goal achievement.
Self-efficacy is a person's confidence in being able to accomplish a particular
task. *Effort* is the extent to which a person works hard on a task.

As with our adaptation of state and trait constructs from the state-trait
anxiety theory (Spielberger, 1975, 1983) to define trait self-regulation, our
approach to determining reliability and validity for our trait self-regulation
measure is also based on an analogy from state-trait anxiety theory. Spielberger (1972) discussed two important requirements of trait anxiety measures: reliability (consistency, stability), and a positive relationship to state
measures of anxiety. With respect to trait self-regulation, we view similar
requirements to be brevity, reliability, and relationships to state measures of
self-regulation. The trait scale must be brief as we try to minimize student
time in assessment. Our approach to validation relies heavily on construct
validity techniques, as well as content validity.

The trait self-regulation inventory was administered to multiple groups
of students in 12 successive studies to examine its psychometric characteristics. A common statistical methodology was employed. In each study,
descriptive statistics such as means and standard deviations were obtained
for each item and each subscale. Classical measures of reliability, such as
Cronbach's alpha and item-remainder coefficients, were computed. To further evaluate the internal consistency of items, a principal components factor analysis with varimax rotation was also performed on the items within
each subscale to see whether any of the subscales was multidimensional.
It was expected that there would be only one factor per scale. Items were
eliminated so there was no significant reduction in the reliability or validity indices of the subscales. In most of the studies, a confirmatory factor
analysis was also conducted. The resulting revised scale was used in the
next study. A set of achievement tests (mainly in mathematics) were used

as criterion measures to determine the construct validity relationship between achievement and the various aspects of self-regulation.

With one exception, the results of analyses for the trait self-regulation subscales indicated acceptable alpha coefficients (0.81 to 0.86 for planning from four studies – e.g., O'Neil & Herl et al., 1998; Kosmicki, 1993; 0.75 to 0.82 for self-checking from four studies – e.g., O'Neil & Herl et al., 1998; Kosmicki, 1993; −0.84 to 0.91 for self-efficacy from six studies, e.g., Huang, 1996; Wang, 1997; and 0.77 to 0.91 for effort from ten studies – e.g., Huang, 1996; Kosmicki, 1993; Wang, 1997). All final subscales consisted of no more than eight items, for brevity. The majority of the construct validity predictions were supported and have been reported in various publications. For example, in all cases, self-efficacy and effort were positively related, and for studies conducted in Taiwan, both effort and self-efficacy were related to performance, as predicted.

In summary, the analyses showed that all subscales had sufficient reliability and validity to be useful for research purposes. Such a trait scale could be used to conduct research in gender or international comparisons, in program evaluation, or as an outcome measure for the teaching of higher-order thinking skills. As mentioned earlier, we have provided this trait measure in Appendix A.

GENDER EFFECTS ON MATHEMATICS ACHIEVEMENT: MEDIATING ROLES OF STATE AND TRAIT SELF-REGULATION AND TEST ANXIETY

In this section, we present a research study that examined mediating roles of self-regulation and test anxiety. The purpose of the study was to understand gender differences in mathematics achievement by providing some empirical findings to begin to resolve various alternative explanations of the roles of gender and self-regulation in mathematics. Although the criterion measure, the math test (a teacher-made test that represented a relatively long period of learning), was given at a single point in time, we expected that males would have higher levels of self-regulation and lower state anxiety than females, thus resulting in superior performance for males on this math test.

Consistent with our definition, self-regulation in this study represents a higher-order construct that consists of two component constructs. That is, self-regulation, a third-order factor, consisted of two second-order constructs (metacognition and motivation), with planning and self-checking as the first-order factors for metacognition, and effort and self-efficacy for motivation. The third-order self-regulation framework was adopted from previous research (Hong, 1995; Hong & O'Neil, 2001). Whereas the invariance of factor structures of state and trait self-regulation was evident from a multigroup analysis, the two models (i.e., a state model and a

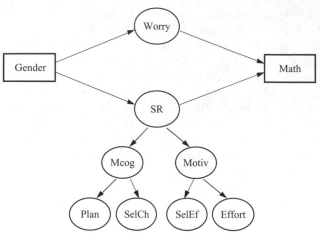

FIGURE 13.1. Model 1 for both state and trait measures . (SR = self-regulation; Mcog = metacognition; Motiv = motivation; SelCh = self-check; SelEf = self-efficacy.)

trait model) showed differential stability (Hong, 1998b). As expected, trait self-regulation remained more stable over time than state self-regulation. Similar findings were also obtained for state and trait test anxiety (Hong, 1998b).

In the study, gender effects on math achievement were examined with self-regulation and the worry component of test anxiety as two mediating variables. In examining relationships among gender, worry, self-regulation, and math achievement, both state and trait models were investigated. That is, the relationships were examined with state worry and state self-regulation in one model, and with trait worry and trait self-regulation in another model. In addition, two different path models were investigated (see Fig. 13.1 for Model 1 and Fig. 13.2 for Model 2). The only difference between Model 1 and Model 2 is that a hypothesized direct effect of gender on math performance was added in Model 2. The two alternative path models were tested because of conflicting findings regarding the gender–math relationship. Altogether, four hypothesized models – state and trait models for path Model 1 and those for path Model 2 – were examined in the study. It was predicted that gender would have a direct effect on both worry and self-regulation, and that worry and self-regulation, in turn, would have direct effects on math performance. In addition, Model 2 predicts a direct effect of gender on math performance. As *state* vs. *trait* differences in relationships among the four constructs have not been examined previously, we explored whether these hypothesized relationships among the four constructs would be different across the state and trait models.

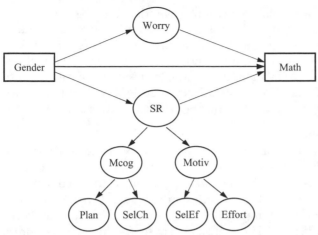

FIGURE 13.2. Model 2 for both state and trait measures. (SR = self-regulation; Mcog = metacognition; motiv = Motivation; SelCh = self-check; SelEf = self-efficacy.)

Participants and Procedure

The sample consisted of 209 eleventh-grade males ($n = 149$) and females ($n = 60$) from two Korean high schools. The two schools selected were typical high schools in the capital of South Korea. A school entrance examination process does not exist at the high school level in South Korea, and students are assigned to a particular high school located within the area of their residence. The students from the two participating schools represented a broad range of socioeconomic background. Students were assigned to classes based on their average achievement in selected subject matter areas (e.g., mathematics, Korean language and literature) at the end of the previous school year, thus generating similar class average scores.

The state and trait self-regulation questionnaires were group administered during two regular class periods in each school. The state questionnaire was administered to participating students immediately after a mathematics examination, with instructions to indicate how they thought during the mathematics test. The trait questionnaire was administered about a week before the state questionnaire was administered, with instructions to students to indicate how they generally think in situations where they solve general academic tasks. No remuneration or extra credit was provided for participating in the study.

Measures

To measure *state* and *trait* self-regulation in academic performance, a modified version of O'Neil and Abedi's (1996) self-regulatory inventory was used. The original self-regulatory inventory was developed by O'Neil and his colleagues (1992, 1996), and measured state and trait metacognitive skills and effort use (see "Reliability and Validity of a Measure of Self-Regulation" in this chapter). Although most of the items used in this study were adopted from O'Neil and his associates, trait self-efficacy items were adapted from the Generalized Self-Efficacy, a scale developed and validated by Schwarzer (1993) and Wegner, Schwarzer, and Jerusalem (1993).

State Self-Regulation

The state self-regulation measure, adapted from O'Neil and Abedi (1996), consisted of 23 items that assessed participants' perceived state self-regulation skills as measured immediately after they completed a mathematics examination. Each of the four first-order state self-regulation constructs (planning, self-checking, self-efficacy, and effort) and state worry consisted of three indicators. The complete item set for the state measure is presented in Appendix B. Participants responded to the state items by rating themselves on the following four-point scale: (1) *not at all*, (2) *somewhat*, (3) *moderately so*, and (4) *very much so*. Thus, the state scale defines a continuum of increasing levels of intensity in worry and self-regulatory behavior, with low scores indicating a low level of worry or self-regulatory activities during the exam and high scores indicating intense worry or a high level of self-regulatory activities during the exam. Internal consistency estimates (coefficient alpha) of the subscales of the state self-regulation questionnaire were state planning (0.76), state self-checking (0.68), state self-efficacy (0.76), state effort (0.80), and state worry (0.72). These estimates are considered acceptable for the current research.

Trait Self-Regulation

The trait self-regulation measure consisted of 34 items that assessed participants' perceived trait self-regulation skills. Again, each of the first-order trait self-regulation and trait worry constructs consisted of three indicators. The trait items used in this research were similar to those provided in Appendix B, except for the self-efficacy and worry items. Participants responded to each *trait* item by rating themselves on the following scale: (1) *almost never*, (2) *sometimes*, (3) *often*, and (4) *almost always*. Thus, the traits were measured on a frequency dimension, with low/high scores indicating a low/high level of worry or self-regulation activity in general task-oriented situations that are relatively stable over time. Internal consistency estimates (coefficient alpha) of the subscales of the trait self-regulation questionnaire ranged were trait planning (0.77), trait self-checking (0.61), trait self-efficacy (0.85), trait effort (0.83), and trait worry (0.79).

Mathematics Achievement

Mathematics scores were gathered from the classroom teachers. Students within each school took the same mathematics test. However, because the two schools in the study used different math tests, mathematics scores given by the teachers were standardized within each school.

Data Analysis

We first examined state and trait measurement models separately using confirmatory factor analysis (CFA). Then, a structural equation model (SEM) was employed to investigate the direct and indirect effects among variables. The hypothesized third-order CFA models and SEM models were tested with the EQS program (Bentler, 2002). The measurement models were examined in ascending order, beginning with the first-order model, to determine factor correlations that might explain the hierarchical structure of the model. The evaluation of model adequacy was based on the chi-square statistic, CFI, IFI, RMSEA, inspection of the values of standardized residuals, and the results of LM tests and Wald tests.[1] In addition, the first author's knowledge of the data, as well as theoretical aspects of research in self-regulation and test anxiety, were considered in evaluating the model adequacy (see Jöreskog, 1971, for this rationale).

Measurement Models

The first-, second-, and third-order CFA models were examined to test our theoretical views regarding self-regulation.

First-Order Factor Model
Both the state and the trait model represented a good fit to the data, with fit indices of 0.98 for each. All free parameters were reasonable and statistically significant. A few factor loading parameters were suggested for addition according to the LM statistics; however, based on the overall good fit and theoretical meaningfulness of the model, no changes were made to the original first-order model. Factor correlations among the five first-order factors are presented in Table 13.1 for the state and trait measurement

---

[1] Model adequacy was evaluated by a number of fit indexes reported by the EQS program (Bentler, 2002). Among the fit indexes, Bentler's comparative fit index (CFI) was recommended by Bentler (1990) and Gerbing and Anderson (1993). The CFI ranges from 0 to 1, and a value greater than 0.90 indicates an acceptable fit to the data. The CFI and incremental fit index (IFI) avoid the normed fit index's underestimation of fit with small samples and the large sampling variability of the nonnormed fit index (Bentler, 1992). Values of Root Mean Square Error of Approximation (RMSEA) between 0.05 and 0.08 indicate a fair fit (Browne & Cudeck, 1993; MacCallum, Browne, & Sugawara, 1996). The Lagrange Multiplier (LM) test evaluates the statistical necessity of the restrictions (fixed parameters) – that is, whether some of the fixed parameters in the model could be freed – whereas the Wald test is used to evaluate whether some of the free parameters in the model could be restricted (Bentler, 1992).

TABLE 13.1. *Factor Correlations Among the Five First-Order Constructs*

Factors	Planning	Self-Checking	Self-Efficacy	Effort	Worry
State measure					
Planning	—	0.76^b	0.57^b	0.74^b	0.32^b
Self-checking		—	0.25^a	0.63^b	0.47^b
Self-efficacy			—	0.56^b	0.02
Effort				—	0.12
Worry					—
Trait measure					
Planning	—	0.96^b	0.64^b	0.66^b	0.17
Self-checking		—	0.66^b	0.76^b	0.27^a
Self-efficacy			—	0.66^b	−0.14
Effort				—	−0.04
Worry					—

^{a} $p < 0.01$.
^{b} $p < 0.001$.

models. In both models, factor correlations among the self-regulation-related constructs were all statistically significant. However, worry did not have a significant relationship with the self-efficacy and effort constructs in either the state or the trait model, or with trait planning. The pattern of factor correlations, excluding the worry factor, indicated higher-order factors might exist within the self-regulatory factors.

Second-Order Factor Model

The first-order factor model was respecified to include the two second-order factors, metacognition and motivation, in place of first-order factor covariances among the four self-regulatory factors. Both the state and trait second-order CFA models fit the data well again, with fit indices of 0.97 (state) and 0.98 (trait). The factor correlations of the two second-order factors (metacognition and motivation) were 0.87 and 0.86, $ps < 0.001$, for the state and trait model, respectively. However, the correlations of worry with the two self-regulatory factors were lower in magnitude, as compared with that of the within self-regulatory factors: 0.41, $p < 0.001$ and 0.22, $p < 0.02$, between metacognition and worry for state and trait measures, respectively, and 0.12 and −0.11, both nonsignificant, between motivation and worry for state and trait measures, respectively. The pattern indicates there existed a higher-order factor that generated significant covariance between metacognition and motivation.

Third-Order Factor Model

The state and trait models again provided a good fit to the data, with fit indices of 0.96 for both models. The factor correlation between self-regulation and worry was statistically significant, 0.32, $p < 0.01$, for the state model, but nonsignificant, 0.14, for the trait model. Estimates of the factor loadings were relatively large and statistically significant, with the smallest loading of 0.61 and 0.56 for the state and trait model, respectively.

With these results from the confirmatory factor analyses of the state and trait models, we next examined the hypothesized structural model, in which the third-order self-regulation factor and the first-order worry factor were separated, to test the relationships among gender, self-regulation, worry, and mathematics achievement.

Structural Models

To examine the goodness of fit of the two hypothesized models, the third-order factor model was respecified by imposing the structure of each model (see Figs. 13.1 and 13.2). Gender and mathematics achievement variables were included, and the structural regression paths that represent the direct and indirect relationships were imposed.

Structural Model with State Measures

Each of the two hypothesized state structural models represented a reasonable fit to the current data (fit indices were equal to or large than 0.93). However, the direct effect of gender on mathematics achievement in Model 2 was not statistically significant. Thus, Model 2 was selected for further examination. The LM statistics identified a parameter to be added to Model 2: a path from the first-order self-checking construct to worry. Although this relationship is theoretically not well established so far, it is reasonable to surmise that students who self-check frequently might worry more because in the process of checking their answers, they might worry more about their performance. Thus, this path was added to Model 2 and subjected to the goodness-of-fit test.

The final state structural model provided a better fit to the data compared to the original Model 2 (fit indices were 0.98). All structural regression coefficients presented in this model were statistically significant. Significant direct effects of gender on worry and self-regulation were observed ($ps < 0.05$), with female students having higher state worry and a lower level of self-regulation than did male students. Worry and self-regulation, in turn, had significant effects on mathematics achievement ($ps < 0.001$).

This model, along with the estimates of standardized regression coefficients, factor loadings, and residual variances, is presented in Fig. 13.3 (figures not in parentheses are state measures; for clarity, loadings on the first-order factors were not included Fig. 13.3). The parameter estimates were all reasonable and statistically significant. Variance (R^2) in worry anxiety accounted for by gender was 0.26. However, only 3% of the variance in self-regulation was accounted for by gender, indicating no substantially

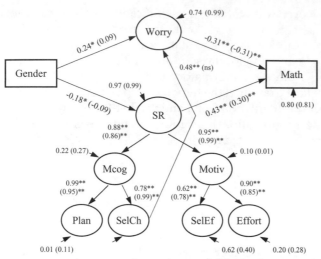

FIGURE 13.3. A structural equation model for both state and trait measures. Values not in parentheses are those from the state model and those in parentheses are from the trait model. (SR = self-regulation; Mcog = metacognition; Motiv = motivation; SelCh = self-check; SelEf = self-efficacy.) $^*p < 0.05$. $^{**}p < 0.001$.

important differences of self-regulation between males and females. Variance in mathematics scores attributed by worry and self-regulation was 0.23. Estimates of factor loadings in the measurement model part of the full structural model were relatively large and statistically significant, ranging from 0.62 to 0.99.

Structural Model with Trait Measures

Each of the two hypothesized trait structural models represented a marginal fit to the current data. In both Model 1 and Model 2, gender effects on worry and self-regulation were not statistically significant. In addition, as found in the state model, gender had no direct effect on mathematics achievement in Model 1. Although Model 2 is a slightly better fit than Model 1, the trait model does not have the hypothesized path structure originating from gender, indicating no statistical or substantial differences between males and females in their trait worry and trait self-regulation. Worry and self-regulation, however, had significant effects on mathematics achievement in the trait model ($ps < 0.001$). Variance (R^2) in mathematics scores attributed by worry and self-regulation was 0.19. For the purpose of comparing state and trait paths, this trait model, along with the estimates of standardized regression coefficients, factor loadings, and residual variances, is presented in Fig. 13.3 (figures in parentheses are trait measures). Estimates of factor loadings in the measurement model part of the full structural model were relatively large and statistically significant, ranging from 0.56 to 0.99.

GENDER GAP IN MATHEMATICS ACHIEVEMENT: LOOKING INTO THE SOURCES OF THE GAP

The study examined direct and indirect effects of gender on mathematics achievement with worry and self-regulation as mediating variables. We represented self-regulation as a third-order construct that includes both metacognition and motivation. The intent was to examine whether an over-all level of self-regulation as a combined measure of distinguishable but highly related traits of metacognition and motivation would have a me-diating role between gender and mathematics achievement. That is, the intent was to determine whether students who are highly metacognitive and highly motivated would achieve highly in mathematics. For both the state and trait factor models, the third-order self-regulation model was con-firmed. The relationship between trait worry and trait self-regulation was not significant. However, state worry showed a weak, positive relationship, indicating that during the mathematics test, students who self-regulated also worried about their performance or vice versa.

The noteworthy results in this study were the differences in gender effects found between state and trait worry and between state and trait self-regulation. Gender differences were found as expected in both state worry and state self-regulation favoring males. Unexpectedly, neither trait worry nor trait self-regulation differed across gender.

Female students reported having higher state worry while they were taking the mathematics exam than their male counterparts. The gender difference in test anxiety has been evidenced in previous research, with females reporting higher anxiety than males (Benson et al., 1994; Hembree, 1988; Lussier, 1996; Malpass, O'Neil, & Hocevar, 1999). However, a gender difference in worry was not evident in general task-oriented situations (i.e., trait anxiety). This finding was unexpected as the vast majority of research (e.g., Hembree, 1988) indicated a gender effect size of 0.33 with mainly trait measures. For example, in a previous study by Hong and Karstens-son (2002) with college students, females reported higher trait worry than males, although the effect size was small. In the current study, the partic-ipants were Korean high school students. Whether the difference in pop-ulation examined in the studies (Korean vs. U.S. students, high school vs. college) has made differences in the findings would be a worthy area for future investigation.

The effects of gender on self-regulation showed the same pattern in regard to the state and trait measures. Male students reported higher self-regulation activities during the mathematics examination (i.e., state self-regulation) than did female students. On this point, even for studies using similar measures, the research literature is inconsistent. For example, in Malpass et al. (1999), gender differences were not present in state metacognition but were present in self-efficacy, with males reporting higher self-efficacy. In the current study, state self-regulation included state self-efficacy. It should be noted that the current effect sizes were very small, thus requiring more studies in this area to increase our understanding. Male and female students did not differ in their overall trait self-regulation. In their review of gender effects on self-regulation, Ablard and Lipschultz (1998) found that females' overall measure of self-regulated learning was higher than that of males. However, Ablard and Lipschultz did not identify the state or trait situation of the studies reviewed, the domains of the studies were not all mathematics, and operational definitions of self-regulation might not have been the same as those used in the current study. In Malpass et al.'s and the current studies, the domain examined was mathematics. It is not clear whether students' self-regulatory behaviors were influenced by the domain (i.e., mathematics).

In the state model, students who engaged in self-checking tended to worry more than those who did not self-check during the test. It can be speculated that self-checking of the test items and thinking about the uncertainty concerning the accuracy of answers might have caused students to worry. Both state and trait worry and self-regulation had significant impacts on mathematics achievement. Students who worried during the exam, as well as those who had a tendency to worry when taking tests in general, did poorly on the mathematics exam in the study. The negative effect that test anxiety, especially the worry component, has on test performance has been evidenced in numerous studies (e.g., Hong, 1999; Kim & Rocklin, 1994; Malpass et al., 1999; Morris et al., 1981; O'Neil & Abedi, 1992; Zeidner & Nevo, 1992). The current study adds more evidence to the theory of the worry–performance relationship.

Students who reported self-regulating while solving mathematics problems (i.e., state self-regulation) and those having a tendency to self-regulate in general task-oriented situations (i.e., trait self-regulation) performed better on the mathematics achievement test. The effects of self-regulation in both state and trait situations were strong, possibly in part because the self-regulation construct in this study represented both students' metacognitive activities, as measured by their planning and self-checking behaviors, and their motivation, as measured by their self-efficacy and effort.

Different patterns of relationships between state and trait worry and self-regulation measures with gender and with mathematics achievement in this study indicate that understanding both state and trait attributes of student characteristics is important in determining individual differences in learning and performance. In the mathematics area, female high school Korean students seemed to experience higher state worry than male students during testing, whereas trait worry was not different across gender.

SUMMARY AND CONCLUSION

The study of gender and self-regulation effects on mathematics performance is highly complex and requires simultaneous evaluation of many relevant variables to develop a comprehensive understanding of the diverse findings in the literature. The current study attempted to include several constructs (state and trait anxiety and self-regulation) in an effort to search for mediating effects on gender gap in mathematics performance. Whereas there were no significant direct or indirect effects of gender on mathematics performance, worry and self-regulation (both state and trait) had significant effects. That is, regardless of gender, students who plan, monitor, expend effort, and have self-efficacy tend to have high achievement scores in mathematics. However, students who worry in general or while taking tests tend to have low mathematics performance scores. That is, regardless of the gender status, students' test anxiety affects mathematics achievement. Thus, both male and female students would benefit from reducing worry and increasing self-regulation skills for improving mathematics achievement.

That both trait and state worry and self-regulation had direct effects on mathematics achievement indicates that trait measures, as well as state measures, are useful in predicting performance. Hong and O'Neil (2001), in their construct validation study of the trait self-regulation questionnaire, stressed the importance of understanding what self-regulatory traits students bring into their classrooms. Trait and state self-regulation are highly related, with trait attributes affecting the level of state characteristics (Hong, 1998a, 1998b). With a good understanding of students' traits, teachers might be better equipped to further provide self-regulation strategies instructions for their students.

Gender differences in state constructs may indicate that developing gender equity in mathematics may be approached by addressing the gender gap in state worry and self-regulation. Although the indirect effect of gender on mathematics performance was not statistically significant in the current study, the significant direct effect of worry and self-regulation on mathematics performance warrants in-depth investigations of the gender gap in worry and self-regulation.

Readers should be reminded that the participants in the study were 11th graders from Korea. Thus, our findings and interpretations might only apply to this specific population. Whether both trait and state measures of self-regulation and test anxiety would be significant in other cultures and ages would be worthy of future research. Likewise, whether the no gender difference in trait measures found in the study would hold in other cultures and ages also warrants further investigation.

APPENDIX A

Trait Thinking Questionnaire

Scales	Items
Planning	1, 5, 9, 13, 17, 21, 25, 29
Self-checking	2, 6, 10, 14, 18, 22, 26, 30
Effort	3, 7, 11, 15, 19, 23, 27, 31
Self-efficacy	4, 8, 12, 16, 20, 24, 28, 32

Trait Thinking Questionnaire

Name (please print): _____

Teacher: _____ Date: _____

Directions: A number of statements that people have used to describe themselves are given below. Read each statement and indicate how you generally think or feel on learning tasks by marking your answer sheet. There are no right or wrong answers. Do not spend too much time on any one statement. Remember, give the answer that seems to describe how you *generally* think or feel.

	Almost Never	Sometimes	Often	Almost Always
1. I determine how to solve a task before I begin.	1	2	3	4
2. I check how well I am doing when I solve a task.	1	2	3	4
3. I work hard to do well even if I don't like a task.	1	2	3	4
4. I believe I will receive an excellent grade in this course.	1	2	3	4
5. I carefully plan my course of action.	1	2	3	4
6. I ask myself questions to stay on track as I do a task.	1	2	3	4
7. I put forth my best effort on tasks.	1	2	3	4
8. I'm certain I can understand the most difficult material presented in the readings for this course.	1	2	3	4
9. I try to understand tasks before I attempt to solve them.	1	2	3	4

(continued)

	Almost Never	Sometimes	Often	Almost Always
10. I check my work while I am doing it.	1	2	3	4
11. I work as hard as possible on tasks.	1	2	3	4
12. I'm confident I can understand the basic concepts taught in this course.	1	2	3	4
13. I try to understand the goal of a task before I attempt to answer.	1	2	3	4
14. I almost always know how much of a task I have to complete.	1	2	3	4
15. I am willing to do extra work on tasks to improve my knowledge.	1	2	3	4
16. I'm confident I can understand the most complex material presented by the teacher in this course.	1	2	3	4
17. I figure out my goals and what I need to do to accomplish them.	1	2	3	4
18. I judge the correctness of my work.	1	2	3	4
19. I concentrate as hard as I can when doing a task.	1	2	3	4
20. I'm confident I can do an excellent job on the assignments and tests in this course.	1	2	3	4
21. I imagine the parts of a task I have to complete.	1	2	3	4
22. I correct my errors.	1	2	3	4
23. I work hard on a task even if it does not count.	1	2	3	4
24. I expect to do well in this course.	1	2	3	4
25. I make sure I understand just what has to be done and how to do it.	1	2	3	4
26. I check my accuracy as I progress through a task.	1	2	3	4
27. A task is useful to check my knowledge.	1	2	3	4
28. I'm certain I can master the skills being taught in this course.	1	2	3	4
29. I try to determine what the task requires.	1	2	3	4
30. I ask myself how well am I doing as I proceed through tasks.	1	2	3	4
31. Practice makes perfect.	1	2	3	4
32. Considering the difficulty of this course, the teacher, and my skills, I think I will do well in this course.	1	2	3	4

APPENDIX B

State Self-Regulation and State Worry

Planning	1. I tried to understand the goals of the exam questions before I attempted to answer.
	2. I made sure I understood just what had to be done and how to do it.
	3. I determined how to solve the exam questions.
	4. I tried to determine what the exam required.
	5. I developed a plan for the solution of most of the exam questions.
	6. I thought through the steps in my mind.
Self-checking	1. I checked my work while I was doing it.
	2. I corrected my errors.
	3. I almost always knew how much of the test I had left to complete.
	4. I kept track of my progress.
	5. I checked the accuracy as I progressed through the exam.
Self-efficacy	1. I expect to do very well on this exam.
	2. I had no doubts about my capability to do well on this exam.
	3. I think I will receive a good score on this exam.
	4. I am sure I did an excellent job on the questions on this exam.
	5. I understand the content on which we were tested today quite well.
	6. Even when the questions were difficult, I knew I could succeed.
Effort	1. I concentrated as hard as I could when taking the exam.
	2. I worked hard on the exam.
	3. I kept working, even on difficult questions.
	4. I put forth my best effort.
	5. I tried to do my best on the exam.
	6. I did not give up, even though the exam was hard .
Worry	1. I thought my score would be so bad that everyone, including myself, would be disappointed.
	2. I was afraid I should have studied more for this exam.
	3. I was not happy with my performance.
	4. I felt regretful about my performance on the exam.
	5. I was concerned about what would happen if I did poorly.
	6. I did not feel very confident about my performance on the exam.

AUTHORS' NOTE

The work reported herein was funded in part under the Educational Research and Development Centers Program, PR/Award Number R305B960002, as administered by the Office of Educational Research and

Improvement, U.S. Department of Education. The findings and opinions expressed in this report do not reflect the positions or policies of the National Institute on Student Achievement, Curriculum, and Assessment, the Office of Educational Research and Improvement, or the U.S. Department of Education.

Address correspondence and requests for reprints to Dr. Eunsook Hong, Department of Educational Psychology, University of Nevada, Las Vegas, 4505 Maryland Parkway, Las Vegas, NV 89154-3003. Phone: 702-895-3246; fax: (702) 895-1658. E-mail: ehong@nevada.edu.

References

Ablard, K. E., & Lipschultz, R. E. (1998). Self-regulated learning in high-achieving students: Relations to advanced reasoning, achievement goals, and gender. *Journal of Educational Psychology, 90*, 94–101.

Bander, R. S., & Betz, N. E. (1981). The relationship of sex and sex role to trait and situationally specific anxiety types. *Journal of Research in Personality, 15*, 312–322.

Bandura, A. (1993). Perceived self-efficacy in cognitive development and functioning. *Educational Psychologist, 28*, 117–148.

Bandura, A. (1997). *Self-efficacy: The exercise of control.* New York: Freeman.

Bandura, A., & Schunk, D. H. (1981). Cultivating competence, self-efficacy, and intrinsic interest through proximal self-motivation. *Journal of Personality and Social Psychology, 41*, 586–598.

Baumeister, R. F., Heatherton, T. F., & Tice, D. M. (1994). *Losing control: How and why people fail at self-regulation.* San Diego, CA: Academic Press.

Benson, J., Bandalos, D., & Hutchinson, S. (1994). Modeling test and anxiety among men and women. *Anxiety, Stress & Coping: An International Journal, 7*, 131–148.

Benson, J., & Tippets, E. (1990). Confirmatory factor analysis of the test anxiety inventory. In C. Spielberger & R. Dias-Guererro (Eds.), *Cross cultural anxiety* (Vol. 4, pp. 149–156). New York: Hemisphere/Taylor-Francis.

Bentler, P. M. (1990). Comparative fit indices in structural models. *Psychological Bulletin, 107*, 238–246.

Bentler, P. M. (1992). On the fit of models to covariances and methodology. *Psychological Bulletin, 112*, 400–404.

Bentler, P. M. (2002). *EQS 6.0 for Windows.* Encino, CA: Multivariate Software, Inc.

Blascovich, J., Spencer, S. J., Quinn, D., & Steele, C. (2001). African Americans and high blood pressure: The role of stereotype threat. *Psychological Science, 12*, 225–229.

Borkowski, J. G., & Burke, J. (1996). Trends in the development of theories, models, and measurement of executive functioning: Views from an information processing perspectives. In G. R. Lyon & N. A. Krasnegor (Eds.), *Attention, memory, and executive functioning* (pp. 235–262). Baltimore, MD: P. H. Brookes.

Borkowski, J. G., & Muthukrishna, N. (1992). Moving metacognition into the classroom: "Working models" and effective strategy teaching. In M. Pressley, K. R. Harris, & J. T. Guthrie (Eds.), *Promoting academic competence and literacy in school* (pp. 477–501). San Diego, CA: Academic Press.

Brown, A. L., Bransford, J. D., Ferrara, R. A., & Campione, J. C. (1983). Learning, remembering, and understanding. In P. H. Mussen (Series Ed.) & J. H. Flavell & E. M. Markman (Vol. Eds.), *Handbook of child psychology: Vol. 3. Cognitive development* (4th ed., pp. 77–166). New York: Wiley.

Brown, M. W., & Cudeck, R. (1993). Alternative ways of assessing model fit. In K. A. Bollen & J. S. Long (Eds.), *Testing structural equation models* (pp. 111–135). Beverly Hills, CA: Sage.

Cahan, S., & Ganor, Y. (1995). Cognitive gender differences among Israeli children. *Sex Roles, 32,* 469–484.

Caporrimo, R. (1990, August). *Gender, confidence, math: Why aren't the girls "where the boys are?"* Paper presented at the annual meeting of the American Psychological Association, Boston.

Carver, C. S., & Scheier, M. F. (1981). *Attention and self-regulation: A control theory approach to human behavior.* New York: Springer-Verlag.

Cooper, S. E., & Robinson, D. A. (1989). The influence of gender and anxiety on mathematics performance. *Journal of College Student Development, 30,* 459–461.

Das, J. P., Naglieri, J. A., & Kirby, J. R. (1994). *Assessment of cognitive processes.* Needham Heights, MA: Allyn & Bacon.

Deboer, G. E. (1984). A study of gender effects in the science and mathematics course-taking behavior of a group of students who graduated from college in the late 1970s. *Journal of Research in Science Teaching, 21,* 95–103.

Everson, H. T., Smodlaka, I., & Tobias, S. (1994). Exploring the relationship of test anxiety and metacognition on reading test performance: A cognitive analysis. *Anxiety, Stress, and Coping, 7,* 85–96.

Fennema, E. (1974). Mathematics learning and the sexes: A review. *Journal of Research in Mathematics Education, 5,* 126–139.

Fennema, E. (1984). Girls, women, and mathematics. In E. Fennema & M. J. Ayre (Eds.), *Women and education: Equity or equality* (pp. 137–164). Berkeley, CA; McCutchan.

Flanagan, J. C., Davis, F. B., Dailey, J. T., Shaycroft, M. F., Orr, D. B., Goldberg, I., & Neyman, C. A., Jr. (1964). *Project TALENT: One-year follow-up studies* (Final report for Cooperative Research Project No. 635, U.S. Office of Education). Pittsburgh, PA: University of Pittsburgh.

Flavell, J. H. (1976). Metacognitive aspects of problem solving. In L. Resnick (Ed.), *The nature of intelligence.* Hillsdale, NJ: Erlbaum.

Flavell, J. H. (1979). Metacognition and cognitive monitoring: A new area of cognitive-developmental inquiry. *American Psychologist, 34,* 906–911.

Garner, M., & Engelhard, G., Jr. (1999). Gender differences in performance on multiple-choice and constructed response mathematics items. *Applied Measurement in Education, 12,* 29–51.

Gerbing, D. W., & Anderson, J. (1993). Monte Carlo evaluations of goodness-of-fit indices for structural equation models. In K. A. Bollen & J. S. Long (Eds.), *Testing structural equation models* (pp. 40–65). Newbury Park: Sage.

Hackett, G. (1985). The role of mathematics self-efficacy in the choice of math-related majors of college women and men: A path analysis. *Journal of Counseling Psychology, 32,* 47–56.

Hackett, G., & Betz, N. E. (1989). An exploration of the mathematics self-efficacy/mathematics performance correspondence. *Journal for Research in Mathematics Education, 20,* 261–273.

Halpern, D. F. (2000). *Sex differences in cognitive abilities* (3rd ed.). Mahwah, NJ: Erlbaum.

Halpern, D. F. (2002). *The development of adult cognition: Understanding constancy and change in adult learning* (Report prepared for the U.S. Army Research Institute).

Hanna, G. S., & Sonnenschein, J. L. (1985). Relative validity of the Orleans-Hanna Algebra Prognosis Test in the prediction of girls' and boys' grades in first-year algebra. *Educational and Psychological Measurement, 45,* 361–367.

Hembree, R. (1988). Correlates, causes, effects and treatment of test anxiety. *Review of Educational Research, 58,* 47–77.

Hong, E. (1995). A structural comparison between state and trait self-regulation models. *Applied Cognitive Psychology, 9,* 333–349.

Hong, E. (1998a). Differential stability of individual differences in state and trait test anxiety. *Learning and Individual Differences, 10,* 51–69.

Hong, E. (1998b). Differential stability of state and trait self-regulation in academic performance. *Journal of Educational Research, 91,* 148–158.

Hong, E. (1999). Test anxiety, perceived test difficulty, and test performance: Temporal patterns of their effects. *Learning and Individual Differences, 11,* 431–447.

Hong, E., & Karstensson, L. (2002). Antecedents of state test anxiety. *Contemporary Educational Psychology, 27,* 348–367.

Hong, E., & O'Neil, H. F., Jr. (2001). Construct validation of a trait self-regulation model. *International Journal of Psychology, 36,* 186–194.

Huang, D. (1996). *The role of parental expectation, effort, and self-efficacy in the achievement of high and low track high school students in Taiwan.* Unpublished doctoral dissertation, University of Southern California, Los Angeles.

Jöreskog, K. G. (1971). Simultaneous factor analysis in several populations. *Psychometrika, 36,* 409–426.

Kanfer, R., Ackerman, P. L., & Heggestad, E. D. (1996). Motivational skills and self-regulation for learning: A trait perspective. *Learning and Individual Differences, 8,* 185–209.

Keinan, G. (1987). Decision making under stress: Scanning of alternatives under controllable and uncontrollable threats. *Journal of Personality and Social Psychology, 52,* 639–644.

Kim, S. H., & Rocklin, T. (1994). The temporal patterns of worry and emotionality and their differential effects on test performance. *Anxiety, Stress & Coping: An International Journal, 7,* 117–130.

Kimball, M. M. (1989). A new perspective on women's math achievement. *Psychological Bulletin, 105,* 198–214.

Kitsantas, A. (2002). Test preparation and performance: A self-regulatory analysis. *The Journal of Experimental Education, 70,* 101–113.

Kosmicki, J. J. (1993). *The Effect of Differential Test Instructions on Math Achievement, Effort, and Worry of Community College Students (Test Anxiety).* Unpublished doctoral dissertation, University of Southern California, Los Angeles.

Kupermintz, H., Ennis, M. M., Hamilton, L. S., Talbert, J. E., & Snow, R. E. (1995). Enhancing the validity and usefulness of large-scale educational assessments: I. NELS:88 mathematics achievement. *American Educational Research Journal, 32,* 525–554.

Lent, R. W., Lopez, F. G., & Bieschke, K. J. (1991). Mathematics self-efficacy: Sources and relation to science-based career choice. *Journal of Counseling Psychology, 38,* 424–430.

Lent, R. W., Lopez, F. G., & Bieschke, K. J. (1993). Predicting mathematics-related choice and success behaviors: Test of an expanded social cognitive model. *Journal of Vocational Behavior, 42,* 223–236.

Liebert, R. M., & Morris, L. W. (1967). Cognitive and emotional components of test anxiety: A distinction and some initial data. *Psychological Reports, 20,* 975–978.

Locke, E. A., & Latham, G. P. (1990). *A theory of goal setting and task performance.* Englewood Cliffs, NJ: Prentice-Hall.

Lussier, G. (1996). Sex and mathematical background as predictors of anxiety and self-efficacy in mathematics. *Psychological Reports, 79,* 827–833.

MacCallum, R. C., Browne, M. W., & Sugawara, H. M. (1996). Power analysis and determination of sample size for covariance structure modeling. *Psychological Methods, 1,* 130–149.

Malpass, J. R., O'Neil, H. F., Jr., & Hocevar, D. (1999). Self-regulation, goal orientation, self-efficacy, worry, and high-stakes math achievement for mathematically gifted high school students. *Roeper Review, 21,* 281–288.

Manderlink, G., & Harackiewicz, J. M. (1984). Proximal versus distal goal setting and intrinsic motivation. *Journal of Personality and Social Psychology, 47,* 918–928.

Martin, D. J., & Hoover, H. D. (1987). Sex differences in educational achievement: A longitudinal study. *Journal of Early Adolescence, 7,* 65–83.

McCombs, B. L. (1984). Processes and skill underlying continuing intrinsic motivation to learn: Toward a definition of motivational skills training interventions. *Educational Psychologist, 19,* 199–218.

Morris, L. W., Davis, M. A., & Hutchings, C. H. (1981). Cognitive and emotional components of anxiety: Literature review and a revised worry-emotionality scale. *Journal of Educational Psychology, 73,* 541–555.

Morris, L. W., & Fulmer, R. S. (1976). Test anxiety (worry and emotionality) changes during academic testing as a function of feedback and test importance. *Journal of Educational Psychology, 68,* 817–824. (ERIC Document Reproduction Service No. EJ156041).

Naglieri, J. A., & Gottling, S. H. (1995). A cognitive education approach to math instruction for the learning disabled: An individual study. *Psychological Reports, 76,* 1343–1354.

Naglieri, J. A., & Gottling, S. H. (1997). Mathematics instruction and PASS cognitive processes: An intervention study. *Journal of Learning Disabilities, 30,* 513–520.

Neuberg, S. L. (1989). The goal of forming accurate impressions during social interactions: Attenuating the impact of negative expectancies. *Journal of Personality and Social Psychology, 56,* 374–386.

O'Neil, H. F., & Abedi, J. (1992). Japanese children's trait and state worry and emotionality in a high-stakes testing environment. *Anxiety, Stress & Coping, 5,* 253–267.

O'Neil, H. F., & Abedi, J. (1996). Reliability and validity of a state metacognitive inventory: Potential for alternative assessment. *Journal of Educational Research, 89,* 234–245.

O'Neil, H. F., Baker, E. L., Ni, Y., Jacoby, A., & Swigger, K. M. (1994). Human benchmarking for the evaluation of expert systems. In H. F. O'Neil, Jr. & E. L. Baker (Eds.), *Technology assessments in software applications* (pp. 13–45). Hillsdale, NJ: Erlbaum.

O'Neil, H. F., Jr., & Fukumura, T. (1992). Relationship of worry and emotionality to test performance in a Juku environment. *Anxiety, Stress, and Coping: An International Journal, 5*, 241–251.

O'Neil, H. F., Jr., & Herl, H. E. (1998, April). *Reliability and validity of a trait measure of self-regulation.* Presented at the annual meeting of the American Educational Research Association, San Diego, CA.

O'Neil, H. F., Sugrue, B., Abedi, J., Baker, E. L., & Golan, S. (1992). *Final report of experimental studies on motivation and NAEP test performance* (Report to NCES, Grant No. RS90159001). Los Angeles: University of California, Center for Research on Evaluation, Standards, and Student Testing.

Organisation for Economic Co-Operation and Development. (2000). *Knowledge and skills for life: First results from PISA 2000.* Paris: Author.

Pajares, F. (1996). Self-efficacy beliefs in academic settings. *Review of Educational Research, 66*, 543–578.

Pajares, F., & Kranzler, J. (1995). Self-efficacy beliefs and general mental ability in mathematical problem solving. *Contemporary Educational Psychology, 20*, 427–444.

Pajares, F., & Miller, M. D. (1994). The role of self-efficacy and self-concept beliefs in mathematical problem solving: A path analysis. *Journal of Educational Psychology, 86*, 193–203.

Pajares, F., & Miller, M. D. (1995). Mathematics self-efficacy and mathematics outcomes: The need for specificity of assessment. *Journal of Counseling Psychology, 42*, 190–198.

Paris, S. G., Cross, D. R., & Lipson, M. Y. (1984). Informed strategies for learning: A program to improve children's reading awareness and comprehension. *Journal of Educational Psychology, 76*, 1239–1252.

Pattison, P., & Grieve, N. (1984). Do spatial skills contribute to sex differences in different types of mathematical problems? *Journal of Educational Psychology, 76*, 678–689.

Pintrich, P. R., & De Groot, E. V. (1990). Motivational and self-regulated learning components of classroom academic performance. *Journal of Educational Psychology, 82*, 33–40.

Pintrich, P. R., & Schrauben, B. (1992). Students' motivational beliefs and their cognitive engagement in classroom academic tasks. In D. H. Schunk & J. L. Meece (Eds.), *Student perceptions in the classroom* (pp. 149–183). Hillsdale, NJ: Erlbaum.

Pintrich, P. R., Smith, D. A., Garcia, T., & McKeachie, W. J. (1993). Reliability and predictability of the motivated strategies for learning questionnaire (MSLQ). *Educational & Psychological Measurement, 53*, 801–813.

Powers, D. E. (1987). *Test anxiety and the GRE general test* (Report No. 86-45). Princeton, NJ: Educational Testing Service.

Pressley, M., & Afflerbach, P. (1995). What readers can do when they read: A summary of the results from the on-line self-report studies of reading. In M. Pressley & P. Afflerbach (Eds.), *Verbal protocols of reading: The nature of constructively responsive reading* (pp. 31–82). Hillsdale, NJ: Erlbaum.

Rech, J. F. (1996). Gender differences in mathematics achievement and other variables among university students. *Journal of Research & Development in Education, 29*, 73–76.

Schildkamp-Kuendiger, E. (Ed.). (1982). *An international review of gender and mathematics*. Columbus: Ohio State University. (ERIC Document Reproduction Service No. ED222326).

Schunk, D. H. (1984). Self-efficacy perspective in achievement behavior. *Educational Psychologist, 19*, 48–58.

Schunk, D. H. (1995, August). *Development of strategic competence through self-regulation of attributions*. Paper presented at the annual meeting of the American Psychological Association, New York.

Schunk, D. H., & Swartz, C. W. (1993). Goals and progress feedback: Effects on self-efficacy and writing achievement. *Contemporary Educational Psychology, 18*, 337–354.

Schwarzer, R. (1993). *Measurement of perceived self-efficacy: Psychometric scales for cross-cultural research*. Berlin: Forschung an der Freie Universität Berlin.

Seegers, G., & Boekaerts, M. (1996). Gender-related differences in self-referenced cognitions in relation to mathematics. *Journal for Research in Mathematics Education, 27*, 215–240.

Senk, S., & Usiskin, Z. (1983). Geometry proof writing: A new view of sex differences in mathematics ability. *American Journal of Education, 91*, 187–201.

Snow, R., & Ennis, M. (1996). Correlates of high mathematical ability in a national sample of eighth graders. In C. Benbow & D. Lubinski (Eds.), *Intellectual talent: Psychometric and social issues* (pp. 301–327). Baltimore: Johns Hopkins University Press.

Spielberger, C. D. (1972). *Anxiety: Current trends in theory and research*. Oxford, UK: Academic Press.

Spielberger, C. D. (1975). Anxiety: State-trait process. In C. D. Spielberger & I. G. Sarason (Eds.), *Stress and anxiety* (Vol. 1, pp. 115–143). Washington, DC: Hemisphere.

Spielberger, C. D. (1983). *Manual for the State-Trait Anxiety Inventory (Form Y)*. Palo Alto, CA: Consulting Psychologist Press.

Steele, C. (1997). A threat in the air: How stereotypes shape intellectual identity and performance. *American Psychologist, 52*, 613–629.

Steele, C., & Aronson, J. (1995). Stereotype threat and the intellectual test performance of African Americans. *Journal of Personality and Social Psychology, 69*, 797–811.

Stockard, J., & Wood, J. W. (1984). The myth of female underachievement: A reexamination of sex differences in academic achievement. *American Educational Research Journal, 21*, 825–838.

Tobias, S., & Everson, H. (1995, April). Development and validation of an objective measure of metacognition. In W. E. Montague (Chair), *Issues in metacognitive research and assessment*. Symposium conducted at the annual meeting of the American Educational Research Association, San Francisco.

Volet, S. E. (1997). Cognitive and affective variables in academic learning: The significance of direction and effort in students' goals. *Learning and Instruction, 7*, 235–254.

Wang, S.-L. (1997). *The role of perceived beliefs in effort, self-efficacy, and task value on high school students' effort and math achievement in Taiwan*. Unpublished doctoral dissertation, University of Southern California, Los Angeles.

Wegner, M., Schwarzer, R., & Jerusalem, M. (1993). Generalized self-efficacy (scale translated in English). In R. Schwarzer (Ed.), *Measurement of perceived self-efficacy: Psychometric scales for cross-cultural research*. Berlin: Freie Universität Berlin.

Weiner, B. (1985). An attribution theory of achievement motivation and emotion. *Psychological Review, 92*, 548–573.

Weiner, B., Friez, I. H., Kukla, A., Reed, L., & Rosenbaum, R. M. (1971). *Perceiving the causes and success of failure*. Morristown, NJ: General Learning Press.

Williams, J. E. (1996). Gender-related worry and emotionality test anxiety for high-achieving students. *Psychology in the Schools, 33*, 159–162.

Willingham, W. W., & Cole, N. S. (1997). *Gender and fair assessment*. Mahwah, NJ: Erlbaum.

Zeidner, M. (1990). Does test anxiety bias scholastic aptitude test performance by gender and sociocultural group? *Journal of Personality Assessment, 55*, 145–160.

Zeidner, M., & Nevo, B. (1992). Test anxiety in examinees in a college admission testing situation: Incidence, dimensionality, and cognitive correlates. In K. A. Hagtvet, A. Knut, & T. B. Johnsen (Eds.), *Advances in test anxiety research* (Vol. 7, pp. 288–303). Hillsdale, NJ: Erlbaum.

Zimmerman, B. J. (1986). Becoming a self-regulated learner: Which are the key subprocesses? *Contemporary Educational Psychology, 11*, 307–313.

Zimmerman, B. J. (1989). A social cognitive view of self-regulated academic learning. *Journal of Educational Psychology, 81*, 329–339.

Zimmerman, B. J. (1990). Self-regulated learning and academic achievement: An overview. *Educational Psychologist, 25*, 3–17.

Zimmerman, B. J. (1994). Conceptual framework for self-regulation. In D. H. Schunk & B. J. Zimmerman (Eds.), *Self-regulation of learning and performance: Issues and educational applications* (pp. 3–21). Hillsdale, NJ: Erlbaum.

Zimmerman, B. J. (1995). Self-regulation involves more than metacognition: A social cognitive perspective. *Educational Psychologist, 30*, 217–221.

Zimmerman, B. J. (2000). Attaining self-regulation: A social cognitive perspective. In M. Boekaerts, P. R. Pintrich, & M. Zeidner (Eds.), *Handbook of self-regulation* (pp. 13–39). San Diego: Academic Press.

Zimmerman, B. J., Bandura, A., & Martinez-Pons, M. (1992). Self-motivation for academic attainment: The role of self-efficacy beliefs and personal goal setting. *American Educational Research Journal, 29*, 663–676.

Zimmerman, B. J., & Kitsantas, A. (1999). Acquiring writing revision skill: Shifting from process to outcome self-regulatory goals. *Journal of Educational Psychology, 91*, 241–250.

Zimmerman, B. J., & Martinez-Pons, M. (1988). Construct validation of a strategy model of student self-regulated learning. *Journal of Educational Psychology, 80*, 284–290.

Zimmerman, B. J., & Martinez-Pons, M. (1990). Student differences in self-regulated learning: Relating grade, sex, and giftedness to self-efficacy and strategy use. *Journal of Educational Psychology, 82*, 51–59.

Zimmerman, B. J., & Paulsen, A. S. (1995). Self-monitoring during collegiate studying: An invaluable tool for academic self-regulation. In P. Pintrich (Ed.), *New directions in college teaching and learning: Understanding self-regulated learning* (Vol. 63, pp. 13–27). San Francisco: Jossey-Bass.

14

Gender Differences in Mathematics Self-Efficacy Beliefs

Frank Pajares

In the early 1940s, at the height of behaviorism's influence on American psychology and education, learning theorists began to propose theories of social learning and imitation that rejected behaviorist notions of associationism in favor of drive reduction principles (e.g., Miller & Dollard, 1941). Although these theories were instrumental in emphasizing the role that social processes play on human learning and functioning, they failed to take into account the creation of novel responses or the processes of delayed and nonreinforced behaviors. In 1963, Bandura and Walters proposed a theory of social learning that broadened the frontiers of existing theories with the now familiar principles of observational learning and vicarious reinforcement. Bandura (1977, 1986) later proposed a view of human functioning that accorded a central role to cognitive, vicarious, self-regulatory, and self-reflective processes in human adaptation and change. In this sociocognitive perspective, individuals are viewed as proactive and self-regulating rather than as reactive and controlled by biological or environmental forces.

Social cognitive theory is rooted in a view of human agency in which individuals are proactively engaged in their own development and can make things happen by their actions. Key to this sense of agency is the fact that, among other personal factors, individuals possess self-beliefs that enable them to exercise a measure of control over their thoughts, feelings, and actions, that "what people think, believe, and feel affects how they behave" (Bandura, 1986, p. 5). Bandura provided a view of human behavior in which the beliefs that people have about themselves are critical elements in the exercise of control and personal agency. Thus, individuals are viewed both as products and as producers of their own environments and of their social systems.

SELF-EFFICACY BELIEFS

Bandura (1986, 1997) contended that, of all self-beliefs, it is the beliefs that individuals hold about their competence, or *self-efficacy* beliefs, that powerfully influence the choices people make, the effort they expend, how long they persevere in the face of challenge, and the degree of apprehension they bring to the task at hand. He defined self-efficacy beliefs as "people's judgments of their capabilities to organize and execute courses of action required to attain designated types of performances" (Bandura, 1986, p. 391). What people know, the skills they possess, or the attainments they have previously accomplished are often poor predictors of subsequent attainments because the beliefs that they hold about their abilities powerfully influence the ways in which they will behave.

The process of creating and using self-efficacy beliefs is intuitive: individuals engage in behaviors, interpret the outcomes of their actions, use the interpretations to develop beliefs about their capability to engage in subsequent behaviors in similar domains, and act in concert with the beliefs created. In school, for example, the beliefs that students develop about their academic capabilities help determine what they do with the knowledge and skills they possess. Consequently, their academic performances are in large part the result of what students actually come to believe that they have accomplished, are accomplishing, and can accomplish in the future. Moreover, self-efficacy beliefs are critical determinants of how well knowledge and skills are acquired in the first place.

In addition to influencing human functioning directly, self-efficacy beliefs mediate the effect of other determinants of behavior on subsequent behavior such that, when these determinants are controlled, self-efficacy judgments are typically better predictors of human performance. Other self-beliefs and motivation constructs (e.g., self-concept, interest, perceived value, anxiety) are viewed as common mechanisms of personal agency in the sense that they, like self-efficacy beliefs, also influence an outcome. However, from a social cognitive perspective, the influence of these mechanisms on behavior are mediated by self-efficacy judgments – that is to say, their influence is partly due to the confidence with which individuals approach a task. Self-efficacy judgments also mediate the effect of variables such as gender and prior experience or achievement on the common mechanisms. That is, when gender and prior experience are controlled, self-efficacy is a stronger predictor not only of a related outcome, but also of common mechanisms such as anxiety, self-concept, perceived value, and other motivation constructs.

How Self-Efficacy Beliefs Are Created

Individuals form their self-efficacy beliefs by interpreting information primarily from four sources. The most influential source is the interpreted result of one's previous performance, or mastery experience. Individuals engage in tasks and activities, interpret the results of their actions, use the interpretations to develop beliefs about their capability to engage in subsequent tasks or activities, and act in concert with the beliefs created. Typically, outcomes interpreted as successful raise self-efficacy; those interpreted as failures lower it. Of course, people who possess a low sense of efficacy often discount their successes rather than change their self-belief. Even after individuals achieve success through dogged effort, some continue to doubt their efficacy to mount a similar effort.

People also form their self-efficacy beliefs through the vicarious experience of observing others perform tasks. This source of information is weaker than mastery experience in helping create self-efficacy beliefs, but, when people are uncertain about their own abilities, they become more sensitive to it. The effects of modeling are particularly relevant in this context, especially when the individual has little prior experience with the task. Even experienced and self-efficacious individuals, however, will raise their perceived self-efficacy even higher if models teach them better ways of doing things. Vicarious experience is particularly powerful when observers see similarities in some attribute and then assume that the model's performance is diagnostic of their own capability. For example, a girl is more likely to increase her mathematics self-efficacy on seeing a woman model exhibit mathematical prowess than on seeing a male model do so. In this case, gender is the attribute for assumed similarity. Observing the successes of such models contributes to the observers' beliefs about their own capabilities ("If they can do it, so can I."). Conversely, watching models with perceived similar attributes fail can undermine the observers' beliefs about their own capability to succeed. When people perceive the model's attributes as highly divergent from their own, the influence of vicarious experience is greatly minimized. It bears noting that people seek out models who possess qualities they admire and capabilities to which they aspire. A significant model in one's life can help instill self-beliefs that will influence the course and direction that life will take.

Individuals also create and develop self-efficacy beliefs as a result of the social persuasions they receive from others. These persuasions can involve exposure to the verbal judgments that others provide. Persuaders play an important part in the development of an individual's self-beliefs. But social persuasions should not be confused with knee-jerk praise or empty inspirational homilies. Effective persuaders must cultivate people's beliefs in their capabilities while at the same time ensuring that the envisioned success is attainable. And, just as positive persuasions may work to encourage and empower, negative persuasions can work to defeat and weaken self-efficacy beliefs. In fact, it is usually easier to weaken self-efficacy beliefs through negative appraisals than to strengthen such beliefs through positive encouragement.

Somatic and emotional states such as anxiety, stress, arousal, and mood states also provide information about efficacy beliefs. People can gauge their degree of confidence by the emotional state they experience as they contemplate an action. Strong emotional reactions to a task provide cues about the anticipated success or failure of the outcome. When they experience negative thoughts and fears about their capabilities, those affective reactions can themselves lower self-efficacy perceptions and trigger additional stress and agitation that help ensure the inadequate performance they fear. Of course, judgments of self-efficacy from somatic and emotional states are not necessarily linked to task cues. Individuals in a depressed mood lower their efficacy independent of task cues. One way to raise self-efficacy beliefs is to improve physical and emotional well-being, and reduce negative emotional states. Because individuals have the capability to alter their own thinking and feeling, enhanced self-efficacy beliefs can, in turn, powerfully influence the physiological states themselves. As Bandura (1997) has observed, people live in psychic environments that are primarily of their own making.

The sources of self-efficacy information are not directly translated into judgments of competence. Individuals interpret the results of events, and these interpretations provide the information on which judgments are based. The types of information people attend to and use to make efficacy judgments, and the rules they employ for weighting and integrating them, form the basis for such interpretations. Thus, the selection, integration, interpretation, and recollection of information influence judgments of self-efficacy.

How Self-Efficacy Beliefs Influence Human Functioning

A strong sense of efficacy enhances human accomplishment and personal well-being in countless ways. First, self-efficacy beliefs influence the choices people make and the courses of action they pursue. Individuals tend to select tasks and activities in which they feel competent and confident, and to avoid those in which they do not. Unless people believe that their actions will have the desired consequences, they have little incentive to engage in those actions. How far will an interest in architecture take a student who feels hopeless in geometry? Whatever factors operate to influence behavior, they are rooted in the core belief that one has the capability to accomplish that behavior.

Self-efficacy beliefs also help determine how much effort people will expend on an activity, how long they will persevere when confronting obstacles, and how resilient they will be in the face of adverse situations. The higher the sense of efficacy, the greater the effort, persistence, and resilience. People with a strong sense of personal competence approach difficult tasks as challenges to be mastered rather than as threats to be avoided.

They have greater intrinsic interest and deep engrossment in activities, set themselves challenging goals and maintain strong commitment to them, and heighten and sustain their efforts in the face of failure. Moreover, they more quickly recover their sense of efficacy after failures or setbacks, and attribute failure to insufficient effort or deficient knowledge and skills that are acquirable.

Self-efficacy beliefs also influence an individual's thought patterns and emotional reactions. High self-efficacy helps create feelings of serenity in approaching difficult tasks and activities. Conversely, people with low self-efficacy may believe that things are tougher than they really are, a belief that fosters anxiety, stress, depression, and a narrow vision of how best to solve a problem. This function of self-beliefs can also create the type of self-fulfilling prophecy in which one accomplishes what one believes one can accomplish. That is, the perseverance associated with high self-efficacy is likely to lead to increased performance, which, in turn, raises one's sense of efficacy and spirit, whereas the giving-in associated with low self-efficacy helps ensure the very failure that further lowers confidence and morale. As a consequence, self-efficacy beliefs are strong determinants and predictors of the level of accomplishment that individuals finally attain. For these reasons, Bandura (1997) argued that self-efficacy beliefs constitute the key factor of human agency.

Self-Efficacy and Related Constructs

Self-beliefs specific to one's perceived capability are prominent in motivation research. These include task-specific self-concept, self-concept of ability, academic self-concept, expectancies, expectancy beliefs, expectancy for success, performance expectancies, perceptions of competence, perceptions of task difficulty, self-perceptions of ability, ability perceptions, perceived ability, self-appraisals of ability, perceived control, subjective competence, and confidence. Self-efficacy and these constructs are similar in that they are each beliefs about one's perceived capability; they differ in that self-efficacy is typically defined in terms of individuals' perceived capabilities to attain designated types of performances and achieve specific results. Depending on what is being managed, the events over which personal influence is exercised may entail regulation of one's own motivation, thought processes, affective states and actions, or changing environmental conditions. Self-efficacy beliefs are sensitive to these contextual factors. As such, they differ from other competence beliefs in that self-efficacy judgments are both more task- and situation-specific and in that individuals make use of these judgments in reference to some type of goal. Consequently, self-efficacy is generally assessed at a more microanalytic level than are other competence beliefs that, although they can be domain specific, typically represent more global and general self-perceptions (see Pajares, 1997).

Self-efficacy judgments vary in level, strength, and generality, and these dimensions prove important in determining appropriate measurement. In the academic area of mathematics, a self-efficacy instrument may ask students to rate their confidence to solve specific mathematics problems, perform particular mathematics-related tasks (such as determining the amount of sales tax on a purchase, calculating interest due on a savings account), or succeed in various mathematics-related courses. Self-efficacy items are worded in terms of *can*, a judgment of capability, rather than of *will*, a statement of intention.

Self-efficacy beliefs differ in predictive power depending on the outcome they are asked to predict. In general, efficacy beliefs best predict the outcomes that most closely correspond with such beliefs. Thus, understanding that beliefs differ in generality is crucial to understanding efficacy assessment. Reasonably precise judgments of capability matched to a specific outcome afford the greatest prediction and offer the best explanations of behavioral outcomes because these are typically the sorts of judgments that individuals use when confronted with behavioral tasks. To this end, if the purpose of a study is to achieve explanatory and predictive power, self-efficacy judgments should be consistent with and tailored to the domain of functioning and/or task under investigation (see Bandura, 2001; Pajares & Miller, 1995). This is especially critical in studies that attempt to establish causal relations between beliefs and outcomes. All this is to say that capabilities assessed and capabilities tested should be similar capabilities. Because of the specificity and correspondence required between self-efficacy beliefs and related outcomes, all-purpose or global instruments of the type prevalent in self-belief research are neither developed nor encouraged by self-efficacy theorists. It is this attention to contextual specificity and correspondence that also serves to differentiate the self-efficacy construct from other motivation constructs that aim to assess perceptions of capability.

During the 25 years since Bandura (1977) first introduced the construct, the predictive and mediational role of self-efficacy has received extensive support from a growing body of findings from diverse fields (Bandura, 1997; Schunk & Pajares, 2002; and see Stajkovic & Luthans, 1998, for meta-analysis of research on the relationship between self-efficacy and achievement). The depth of this support prompted Graham and Weiner (1996) to conclude that self-efficacy has proven to be a more consistent predictor of behavioral outcomes than have other self-beliefs. Self-efficacy has also received increasing attention in educational research, primarily in studies of academic motivation (Pintrich & Schunk, 2002). The area of mathematics has received special attention in self-efficacy research for a number of reasons. Mathematics holds a valued place in the academic curriculum; it is prominent on high-stakes measures of achievement generally used for level placement, for entrance into special programs, and for college admissions; and it has been called a "critical filter" for students in pursuit of scientific and technical careers at the college level (Sells, 1980). Moreover, mathematics self-efficacy has been acknowledged as a strong predictor of students' selection of math-related activities and pursuit of math-related majors and careers (Hackett, 1995).

MATHEMATICS SELF-EFFICACY

In early studies, confidence in learning mathematics, a globally assessed conceptual forerunner to mathematics self-efficacy, was consistently found to predict mathematics-related behavior and performance (see Hackett, 1985; Reyes, 1984). In general, these findings were important in establishing the first confidence–performance relationships. Correlations in these studies ranged from .20 to .72 (e.g., Aiken, 1970a, 1970b, 1972, 1974; Armstrong, 1980; Crosswhite, 1972; Fennema & Sherman, 1976, 1977, 1978; Hendel, 1980; Sherman, 1980; Sherman & Fennema, 1977; Smead & Chase, 1981). In keeping with Bandura's cautions regarding assessment, mathematics self-efficacy has more recently been assessed in terms of individuals' judgments of their capabilities to solve specific mathematics problems, perform mathematics-related tasks, and succeed in mathematics-related courses (Betz & Hackett, 1983). The growing career literature is especially concerned with the latter judgments.

Researchers have demonstrated that self-efficacy beliefs predict numerous mathematics outcomes, whether these outcomes are criterion-referenced test scores or aptitude/achievement indexes (e.g., score on a standardized achievement test), and that these beliefs play the mediational role posited by Bandura (e.g., Bandura & Schunk, 1981; Bong, 2002; Hackett, 1985; Hackett & Betz, 1989; Lent, Lopez, & Bieschke, 1991; Norwich, 1986; Pajares, 1996a; Pajares & Graham, 1999; Pajares & Kranzler, 1995; Pajares & Miller, 1994, 1995; Randhawa, 1994; Randhawa, Beamer, & Lundberg, 1993; Siegel, Galassi, & Ware, 1985; Zimmerman, Bandura, & Martinez-Pons, 1992; and see Pajares, 1996b; Schunk, 1991, for reviews). Moreover, mathematics self-efficacy typically predicts mathematics performances to a greater degree than do variables such as mathematics self-concept, mathematics anxiety, previous mathematics experience, perceived value of mathematics, or self-efficacy for self-regulatory practices. Pajares and Kranzler (1995) found that the influence of self-efficacy on mathematics performance was as strong as that of general mental ability.

Another oft-reported finding is that most students tend to overestimate their mathematics capabilities. Hackett and Betz (1989) found that 54% of the men and 44% of the women overestimated their capability, whereas only 16% of the men and 18% of the women underestimated. Pajares and Miller (1994) similarly found that 57% of the men and 58% of the women overestimated their mathematics capability (and see Pajares, 1996a; Williams, 1994).

GENDER DIFFERENCES IN MATHEMATICS SELF-EFFICACY

Literature on the relationship between gender and mathematics performance is abundant in psychology and education. Although early findings consistently showed that boys outperformed girls in most areas of mathematics (see Maccoby & Jacklin, 1974), national attention was not focused on the issue until findings were substantiated by Benbow and Stanley (1980, 1982, 1983) in a series of studies in which boys outperformed girls on standardized tests of mathematics ability. The media attention these findings received encouraged the view that men were superior in this area (see Jacklin, 1989). Subsequently, Eccles and her associates conducted a series of studies that showed that differences in performance were attributable to factors such as mathematics anxiety, gender-stereotyped parental beliefs, and students' perceived value of mathematics (see Eccles, Adler, & Kaczala, 1982; Eccles, Adler, & Meece, 1984; Eccles & Jacobs, 1986; Eccles, Kaczala, & Meece, 1982). Other researchers have posited that these differences are attributable to factors such as previous experience with mathematics, parental expectations, opportunity to learn, mathematics attitudes and self-beliefs, or speed of math-facts retrieval (see Beal, 1994, 1999; Fennema, 1980; Fennema & Sherman, 1977, 1978; Lapan, Boggs, & Morrill, 1989; Pedro, Wolleat, Fennema, & Becker, 1981).

Although, on average, males slightly outperform girls in formal testing situations and girls outperform boys in obtaining high grades in mathematics classes (Beal, 1999), recent findings suggest that gender differences in mathematics achievement up to the high school level have diminished (Eisenberg, Martin, & Fabes, 1996). Nonetheless, gender differences in the mathematics competence self-perceptions of American and of European students may still be prevalent (see Stipek, 2002; Wigfield, Eccles, & Pintrich, 1996). Early studies suggested that boys were more confident in their mathematics skills than were girls. For example, in a study of over 1,200 high school students, Fennema and Sherman (1977) reported that boys had more positive attitudes toward mathematics, including greater confidence in their ability to learn mathematics. In a subsequent study of 1,320 middle school students, they again found boys more confident. When they compared their middle and high school results, they found that these differences in confidence increased as students progressed from grades 6 to 11. Early studies also showed that, by middle school, boys began to rate mathematics as more useful than did girls (Fennema & Sherman, 1977; Hilton & Berglünd, 1974) and that girls' perceptions of usefulness decline throughout high school (Sherman, 1980).

It seems that boys and girls report equal confidence in their mathematics ability during elementary school, but, by high school, boys tend to report higher confidence (Eccles, 1983). Even by middle school, boys often rate themselves more efficacious than do girls (Pintrich & De Groot, 1990; Reis & Park, 2001; Seegers & Boekaerts, 1996; Wigfield, Eccles, MacIver, Reuman,

& Midgley, 1991). Gifted girls are especially likely to understimate their competence in mathematics (Eccles et al., 2000; Pajares, 1996a; Reis & Park, 2001; Siegle & Reis, 1998). This gender difference in mathematics confidence has sometimes been called the "confidence gap" (see Sadker & Sadker, 1994), and the middle school years have been identified as the time during which this gap between girls' and boys' self-perceptions of ability emerges (Fennema & Hart, 1994; Wigfield et al., 1991). These findings are consistent with those from the United Kingdom, where men consistently expect better grades on university examinations than do women (Erkut, 1983; Vollmer, 1984, 1986a, 1986b; and see Matsui, Matsui, & Ohnishi, 1990).

Researchers focusing on mathematics self-efficacy or task-specific perceptions of competence have typically reported that male students express higher mathematics self-efficacy than do female students (e.g., Gwilliam & Betz, 2001; Hackett, 1985; Lapan et al., 1989; Lent, Brown, Gover, & Nijjer, 1996; Lent, Lopez, & Bieschke, 1993; Lussier, 1996; Post-Kammer & Smith, 1985; Randhawa, 1994; Randhawa, Beamer, & Lundberg, 1993; Williams, 1994), a finding that led Betz and Hackett (1983) to conclude that "math-related cognitions are suggested both theoretically and empirically to be important moderators of sex differences in major and career choice behavior" (p. 343). Boys express stronger judgments of their mathematics capability than do girls even after controlling for achievement in mathematics (Seegers & Boekaerts, 1996). In addition, female students have lower self-efficacy than do male students both about their computer skills (Jorde-Blom, 1988; Miura, 1987; Vasil, Hesketh, & Podd, 1987) and about their prospects to succeed in mathematics-, science-, and technology-related careers (Hackett, 1985; Hackett & Betz, 1989; Lent, Brown, & Larkin, 1984, 1986; Miura, 1987; and see Hackett, 1995, for a review).

In a series of studies focusing on students' self-efficacy to solve mathematics word problems, Pajares and his colleagues have obtained inconsistent results regarding gender differences. Pajares and Miller (1994) found that male undergraduates reported stronger self-efficacy in their capabilities than did female undergraduates, but the men also obtained higher scores on the mathematics performance measure, suggesting that their higher self-efficacy was warranted. Pajares and Kranzler (1995) investigated the mathematics self-efficacy of 329 high school students and found that boys and girls did not differ either in their capability to solve mathematics word problems or in the strength of their self-efficacy beliefs. Moreover, boys and girls displayed similar overconfidence. The inconsistency may in part be accounted for by the fact that college students are better able to assess what they know and do not know than are high school students.

Pajares (1996b) examined the interplay between self-efficacy judgments and the mathematical problem-solving of middle school students mainstreamed in algebra classes. Mathematics self-efficacy made an independent contribution to the problem-solving performance of regular education students ($\beta = 0.387$) and of gifted students ($\beta = 0.455$) in a path model that controlled for the effects of math anxiety, cognitive ability, mathematics grades, self-efficacy for self-regulatory learning, and gender. Pajares also found that regular education girls reported lower self-efficacy despite receiving higher grades in mathematics and obtaining similar scores as did the boys on the problem-solving measure. There were no gender differences in the mathematics self-efficacy of gifted girls and boys, despite the fact that gifted girls obtained significantly higher scores on the performance measure. In other words, girls expressed lower confidence when performance scores did not warrant it and similar confidence when performance scores warranted greater confidence. Although most students were biased toward overconfidence, girls were less biased in that direction, and gifted girls were biased toward underconfidence. The implications for gifted girls are especially troubling, as other researchers have reported similar low self-efficacy for gifted girls compared with boys, accompanied by negative changes in girls' interest and motivation over time (Malpass, O'Neil, & Hocevar, 1999; Reis & Park, 2001; Siegle & Reis, 1998; Terwilliger & Titus, 1995). For example, Junge and Dretzke (1995) studied the mathematics self-efficacy of gifted high school students and reported that gifted boys were overconfident on a greater number of items than were gifted girls, and that gifted girls were only overconfident on items involving stereotypical female activity.

Consistent with previous findings, Pajares (1996a) also found that most students were generally overconfident about their ability to solve the problems, and regular education students and gifted boys were biased toward overconfidence. Girls, however, were overconfident on fewer items than were boys, less biased toward overconfidence, and more accurate in their self-perceptions. These results suggest that girls' self-beliefs more accurately reflected their capability. Such accuracy may be a two-edged sword, however. Bandura (1986) argued that some overestimation of capability is useful because it increases effort and persistence. Mean bias scores of gifted girls revealed that they had a general tendency toward underconfidence, and a third of the gifted girls were to some degree underconfident in their capability to solve mathematics problems that they could indeed solve. Accurate self-perceptions may enable students to more accurately assess their problem-solving strategies, but the danger of "realistic" self-appraisals is that they may be purchased at the cost of lower optimism and lower levels of self-efficacy's primary functions – effort, persistence, and perseverance.

Pajares and Graham (1999) assessed the mathematics problem-solving self-efficacy of entering middle school students and found that, after controlling for math anxiety, mathematics self-concept, self-regulation, perceived value of mathematics, mathematics engagement, and standardized achievement in mathematics, girls showed lower self-efficacy than boys at the start of the academic year, but not at the end of the year. As with Pajares (1996a), the difference in self-efficacy at the start of the year existed, despite no differences in mathematics performance.

Gender differences in mathematics self-efficacy have been found in African American college undergraduates, with men reporting stronger mathematics self-efficacy perceptions than women (Gainor & Lent, 1998). Post, Stewart, and Smith (1991) found that, although all students reported lower self-efficacy, confidence, interest, and consideration of math/science occupations than for nonmath/science occupations, both self-efficacy and interests predicted consideration of a math/science major for African American men, but only interests predicted consideration of a math/science major for women. Males also reported greater confidence, self-efficacy, interests, and consideration for math/science careers than did females. Females reported greater interest, however, for nonmath/science careers than males. According to the authors, these findings support the assertion that gender, rather than race, might be the reason that African American females are underrepresented in careers of a mathematic and scientific nature.

Some researchers have failed to find gender differences in mathematics self-efficacy indexes. For example, Middleton and Midgley (1997) detected no gender differences in the mathematics self-efficacy of sixth-grade students. Similarly, Fouad and Smith (1996) found that the mathematics self-efficacy beliefs of middle school boys and girls did not differ in a path model that included age, interest, outcome expectations, and intentions to enroll in a mathematics-related career. Lopez and Lent (1992) found no differences in the reported sources of the mathematics self-efficacy beliefs of high school students. And Busch (1995) detected no gender differences in the mathematics self-efficacy of students of business administration.

In summary, findings on gender differences in mathematics self-efficacy coincide on four points:

1. Most researchers found that male students report stronger mathematics self-efficacy beliefs than do female students, although it bears emphasizing that a number of researchers have failed to find differences. In most cases, results strongly depend on the variables included in regression models or path analyses.
2. When differences are detected, it seems that they start during middle school and accentuate as students grow older.
3. Gender differences in mathematics self-efficacy do not favor female students at any level of schooling.
4. The differences favoring boys often are found when girls and boys have similar mathematics achievement indexes, or even when girls have higher achievement than do boys.

CONCLUSION

As I have outlined in this chapter, the relationship between gender and mathematics self-efficacy has been a focus of self-efficacy research. In general, researchers report that male students tend to be more confident than are female students in academic areas related to mathematics, science, and technology, despite the fact that achievement differences in these areas are either diminishing, have disappeared, or even favor girls in early academic levels. Before engaging in a discussion of the educational implications that emanate from these findings, however, it bears noting that gender differences in self-efficacy are confounded by a number of factors. First, many gender differences in academic self-beliefs are nullified when variables such as previous achievement or opportunity to learn are controlled (see Cooper & Robinson, 1991; Lent et al., 1986; Pajares, 1996b; Zimmerman & Martinez-Pons, 1990). For example, Lent et al. (1991) reported that men were more self-efficacious about their capability to succeed in mathematics-related college courses. However, when the researchers regressed self-efficacy on the source variables with gender as the last step, gender no longer entered the equation as a significant predictor. Lent et al. suggested that this may be because men tend to enroll in more mathematics courses prior to college and so have a greater opportunity to develop their mathematics skills and efficacy percepts. Benson (1989) also found that men reported higher mathematics self-efficacy and also suggested it was a function of women having taken fewer mathematics courses. Hackett (1985) found a direct effect of gender on years of high school mathematics and from this prior experience to self-efficacy in a path analysis.

A second confounding factor is the tendency of boys and girls to adopt a differing stance when responding to self-efficacy instruments. Researchers have observed that boys tend to be more self-congratulatory in their responses, whereas girls tend to be more modest (Wigfield et al., 1996). Noddings (1996) suggested that boys and girls may use a different "metric" when providing confidence judgments, adding that these sorts of ratings may represent more of a promise to girls than they do to boys. If this is the case, actual differences in confidence are masked or accentuated by such response biases (Wigfield et al., 1996; and see Flynn, 1988, for a feminist perspective on gender issues in academic contexts).

A third confounding factor lies in the manner in which gender differences in self-efficacy are typically assessed and reported. Traditionally, students are asked to provide judgments of their confidence that they possess certain academic skills or can accomplish academic tasks. Differences in average level of confidence reported are interpreted as gender differences in self-efficacy. Pajares and his colleagues asked students to provide self-efficacy judgments about their writing ability in the traditional manner but also to make comparative judgments regarding their actual ability versus that of other boys and girls in their class and in their school (Pajares, Miller, & Johnson, 1999; Pajares & Valiante, 1999). Consistent with established findings, although girls outperformed the boys, girls and boys reported equal self-efficacy. When students were asked whether they were better writers than their peers, however, girls expressed that they were better writers than were the boys in their class and in their school. That is, regardless of the ratings that boys and girls provided on the self-efficacy measure, it was clear that girls considered themselves better writers than the boys. This phenomenon was found both at the elementary and middle school levels. If researchers are to continue to explore gender differences in self-beliefs, they will need to address that issue with questions that will provide these sorts of insights (see Schwarz, 1999).

Yet another confounding factor deals with the nature of the self-belief that may be undergirding gender differences. Numerous researchers have argued that some gender differences in social, personality, and academic variables may actually be a function of gender orientation – the stereotypic beliefs about gender that students hold – rather than of gender (Eisenberg et al., 1996; Hackett, 1985; Harter, Waters, & Whitesell, 1997; Matsui, 1994). For example, gender differences in variables such as moral voice or empathy tend to disappear when gender stereotypical beliefs are accounted for (Harter et al., 1997; Karniol, Gabay, Ochion, & Harari, 1998). Eccles's (1987) model of educational and occupational choice posits that cultural milieu factors such as students' gender role stereotypes are partly responsible for differences in course and career selection and in confidence beliefs and perceived value of tasks and activities. In a line of inquiry by Matsui and associates, female college students reported lower self-efficacy than did male students for male-dominated careers such as mathematics and higher levels of self-efficacy for female-dominated occupations (Matsui, 1994; Matsui, Ikeda, & Ohnishi, 1989). Nosek, Banaji, and Greenwald (2002) demonstrated that the more that girls identified themselves as stereotypically female and identified mathematics as a male domain the more likely they were to report negative attitudes toward mathematics.

To determine the degree to which gender differences in motivation and achievement are a function of gender stereotypic beliefs rather than of gender, Pajares and Valiante (2001) asked students to report how strongly they identified with characteristics stereotypically associated with males or females in American society. Results revealed that holding a feminine orientation was associated with writing self-efficacy and rendered nonsignificant gender differences in writing self-concept, self-efficacy for self-regulation, perceived value of writing, and writing task goals. This suggests that gender differences in academic motivation may in part be accounted for by differences in the beliefs that students hold about their gender rather than by their gender per se (also see Pajares & Valiante, 2002).

Social cognitive theory does not endow gender self-beliefs with agentic and motivating properties (Bussey & Bandura, 1999), but neither does it endow gender itself with such properties. Researchers have long observed that areas such as mathematics, science, and technology are typically viewed by students as being within a male domain (Fennema & Sherman, 1978; Nosek et al., 2002; and see Eisenberg et al., 1996). In these areas, a masculine orientation is associated with confidence and achievement because masculine self-perceptions are themselves imbued with the notion that success in these areas is a masculine imperative (Eccles, 1987; Hackett, 1985). One challenge before educators is to alter students' views of academic subjects so they are perceived as relevant and valuable both to girls and boys. A challenge for all educators, and for the broader culture, is to continue to expound and model gender self-beliefs that encompass both the feminine expressiveness and the masculine instrumentality that are critical to a balanced self-view.

Gender differences are also related to developmental level. There is little evidence for differences in self-efficacy among elementary school students. For older students, gender differences should not be expected when students are able to derive clear performance information about their capabilities or progress in learning (Schunk & Pajares, 2002). Schunk and Lilly (1984) asked middle school students to report their self-efficacy to learn a novel mathematics task, after which the students received instruction and opportunities to practice the task. Although girls initially reported lower self-efficacy than did boys, following the instruction, girls and boys did not differ in achievement or self-efficacy for solving problems. The feedback conveyed to students that they were learning and raised girls' self-efficacy to that of boys.

Gender differences in self-efficacy can arise not from the specific skills themselves but rather from their linkage to contexts (Bandura, 1997). Although female students typically judge their self-efficacy for mathematics or science occupations lower than do male students, these differences can disappear when female students report their self-efficacy for performing the same mathematics- and science-related skills in everyday activities (Matsui & Tsukamoto, 1991). Female students also typically report lower self-efficacy for occupations requiring quantitative skills, but differences disappear when self-efficacy for the quantitative activities are made on stereotypically feminine tasks (Betz & Hackett, 1983; Junge & Dretzke, 1995).

Gender differences can arise as a function of home, cultural, educational, and mass media influences. Parents often underestimate their daughters' academic competence and hold lower expectations for them (Phillips & Zimmerman, 1990). Parents can also act differentially with respect to mathematics and science, portraying them as male domains (Bandura, 1997; Meece & Courtney, 1992; Nosek et al., 2002). As girls enter middle and high school, the perception of mathematics as a masculine domain may lower their interest in it and begin to undermine the belief that these are subjects in which they can excel and in which they can succeed in later life.

Students who lack confidence in skills they possess are less likely to engage in tasks in which those skills are required, and they will more quickly give up in the face of difficulty. If it is indeed the case that many girls have unwarranted lower self-efficacy in their mathematics capabilities and potential than do boys, it seems that young women may be especially vulnerable in this area. Recall that researchers have demonstrated that self-efficacy beliefs influence the choice of majors and career decisions of college students (Hackett, 1995). In some cases, underestimation of capability, not lack of competence or skill, is responsible for avoidance of math-related courses and careers, and this is more likely to be the case with women than with men. When this is the case, efforts to identify and alter these inaccurate judgments, in addition to continued skill improvement, should prove beneficial.

Zeldin and Pajares (2000) explored the personal stories of women who excelled at careers in areas of mathematics, science, and technology to better understand the ways in which their self-efficacy beliefs influenced their academic and career choices. They found that verbal persuasions and vicarious experiences nourished the self-efficacy beliefs of girls and women as they set out to meet the challenges required to succeed in male-dominated academic domains. Findings suggested that girls develop higher mathematics self-efficacy in homes and classrooms in which parents and teachers stress the importance and value of mathematical skills, encourage girls to persist and persevere in the face of academic and social obstacles, and break down stereotypical conceptions regarding academic domains. Parents and teachers should also convey the message that academic success is a matter of desire, effort, and commitment rather than of gender or established social structure. They should also provide models that validate that message. All who would seek to be caring agents in the lives of young women should be especially reflective and proactive in this regard, especially since individuals often convey stereotypical and maladaptive messages to girls in unintentional but subtle ways.

References

Aiken, L. R. (1970a). Attitudes toward mathematics. *Review of Educational Research, 40*, 551–596.

Aiken, L. R. (1970b). Nonintellective variables and mathematics achievement: Directions for research. *Journal of School Psychology, 8*, 28–36.

Aiken, L. R. (1972). Research on attitudes toward mathematics. *Arithmetic Teacher, 19*, 229–234.

Aiken, L. R. (1974). Two scales of attitude toward mathematics. *Journal for Research in Mathematics Education, 5*, 67–71.

Armstrong, J. M. (1980). *Achievement and participation of women in mathematics: An overview.* Denver: Education Commission of the States.

Bandura, A. (1977). Self-efficacy: Toward a unifying theory of behavioral change. *Psychological Review, 84,* 191–215.

Bandura, A. (1986). *Social foundations of thought and action: A social cognitive theory.* Englewood Cliffs, NJ: Prentice Hall.

Bandura, A. (1997). *Self-efficacy: The exercise of control.* New York: Freeman.

Bandura, A. (2001). *Guide for constructing self-efficacy scales.* Available from Frank Pajares, Emory University.

Bandura, A., & Schunk, D. H. (1981). Cultivating competence, self-efficacy, and intrinsic interest through proximal self-motivation. *Journal of Personality and Social Psychology, 41,* 586–598.

Bandura, A., & Walters, R. H. (1963). *Social learning and personality development.* New York: Rinehart and Winston.

Beal, C. R. (1994). *Boys and girls: The development of gender roles.* New York: McGraw Hill.

Beal, C. R. (1999). Introduction: Special issue on the math-fact retrieval hypothesis. *Contemporary Educational Psychology, 24,* 171–180.

Benbow, C. P., & Stanley, J. C. (1980). Sex differences in mathematics ability: Fact or artifact? *Science, 210,* 1262–1264.

Benbow, C. P., & Stanley, J. C. (1982). Consequences in high school and college of sex differences in mathematical reasoning ability: A longitudinal perspective. *American Educational Research Journal, 19,* 598–622.

Benbow, C. P., & Stanley, J. C. (1983). Sex differences in mathematical reasoning ability: More facts. *Science, 222,* 1029–1031.

Benson, J. (1989). Structural components of statistical test anxiety in adults: An exploratory study. *Journal of Experimental Education, 57,* 247–261.

Betz, N. E., & Hackett, G. (1983). The relationship of mathematics self-efficacy expectations to the selection of science-based college majors. *Journal of Vocational Behavior, 23,* 329–345.

Bong, M. (2002). Predictive utility of subject-, task-, and problem-specific self-efficacy judgments for immediate and delayed academic performances. *Journal of Experimental Education, 70,* 133–162.

Busch, T. (1995). Gender differences in self-efficacy and academic performance among students of business administration. *Scandinavian Journal of Educational Research, 39,* 311–318.

Bussey, K., & Bandura, A. (1999). Social cognitive theory of gender development and differentiation. *Psychology Review, 106,* 676–713.

Cooper, S. E., & Robinson, D. A. G. (1991). The relationship of mathematics self-efficacy beliefs to mathematics anxiety and performance. *Measurement and Evaluation in Counseling and Development, 24,* 4–11.

Crosswhite, F. J. (1972). *Correlates of attitudes toward mathematics.* National Longitudinal Study of Mathematical Abilities, Report No. 20. Palo Alto, CA: Stanford University Press.

Eccles, J. (1983). Expectancies, values, and academic behavior. In J. T. Spencer (Ed.), *Achievement and achievement motivation* (pp. 75–146). San Francisco: W. H. Freeman.

Eccles, J. (1987). Gender roles and women's achievement-related decisions. *Psychology of Women Quarterly, 11,* 135–172.

Eccles, J., Adler, T., & Kaczala, C. M. (1982). Socialization of achievement attitudes and beliefs: Parental influences. *Child Development, 53,* 310–321.

Eccles, J., Adler, T., & Meece, J. L. (1984). Sex differences in achievement: A test of alternate theories. *Journal of Personality and Social Psychology, 46,* 26–43.

Eccles, J., Barber, B., Jozefowicz, D., Malenchuk, O., & Vida, M. (2000). Self-evaluations of competence, task values, and self-esteem. In N. Johnson, M. Roberts, & J. Worrell (Eds.), *Girls and adolescence* (pp. 53–84). Washington, DC: American Psychological Association.

Eccles, J., & Jacobs, J. E. (1986). Social forces shape math attitudes and performance. *Signs, 11,* 367–389.

Eccles, J., Kaczala, C. M., & Meece, J. L. (1982). Socialization of achievement attitudes and beliefs: Classroom influences. *Child Development, 53,* 322–339.

Erkut, S. (1983). Exploring sex differences in expectancy, attributions, and academic achievement. *Sex Roles, 9,* 217–231.

Eisenberg, N., Martin, C. L., & Fabes, R. A. (1996). Gender development and gender effects. In D. C. Berliner & R. C. Calfee (Eds.), *Handbook of educational psychology* (pp. 358–396). New York: Simon & Schuster Macmillan.

Fennema, E. (1980). Sex-related differences in mathematics achievement: Where and why. In L. H. Fox, L. Brody, & D. Tobin (Eds.), *Women and the mathematical mystique* (pp. 76–93). Baltimore: Johns Hopkins University Press.

Fennema, E., & Hart, L. E. (1994). Gender and the JRME. *Journal for Research in Mathematics Education, 25,* 648–659.

Fennema, E., & Sherman, J. A. (1976). Fennema-Sherman Mathematics Attitude Scales: Instruments designed to measure attitudes toward the learning of mathematics by females and males. *JSAS Catalog of Selected Documents in Psychology* (Ms. No. 1225), *6,* 31.

Fennema, E., & Sherman, J. A. (1977). Sex-related differences in mathematics achievement, spatial visualization, and affective factors. *American Educational Research Journal, 14,* 51–71.

Fennema, E., & Sherman, J. A. (1978). Sex-related differences in mathematics achievement and related factors: A further study. *Journal for Research in Mathematics Education, 9,* 189–203.

Flynn, E. A. (1988). Composing as a woman. *College Composition and Communication, 39,* 423–435.

Fouad, N. A., & Smith, P. L. (1996). A test of a social cognitive model for middle school students: Math and science. *Journal of Counseling Psychology, 43,* 338–346.

Gainor, K. A., & Lent, R. W. (1998). Social cognitive expectations and racial identity attitudes in predicting the math choice intentions of Black college students. *Journal of Counseling Psychology, 45,* 403–413.

Graham, S., & Weiner, B. (1996). Theories and principles of motivation. In D. C. Berliner & R. C. Calfee (Eds.), *Handbook of educational psychology* (pp. 63–84). New York: Simon & Schuster Macmillan.

Gwilliam, L. R., & Betz, N. E. (2001). Validity of measures of math- and science-related self-efficacy for African Americans and European Americans. *Journal of Career Assessment, 9,* 261–281.

Hackett, G. (1985). The role of mathematics self-efficacy in the choice of math-related majors of college women and men: A path analysis. *Journal of Counseling Psychology, 32,* 47–56.

Hackett, G. (1995). Self-efficacy in career choice and development. In A. Bandura (Ed.), *Self-efficacy in changing societies* (pp. 232–258). New York: Cambridge University Press.

Hackett, G., & Betz, N. E. (1989). An exploration of the mathematics self-efficacy/mathematics performance correspondence. *Journal for Research in Mathematics Education, 20,* 261–273.

Harter, S., Waters, P., & Whitesell, N. (1997). Lack of voice as a manifestation of false self-behavior among adolescents: The school setting as a stage upon which the drama of authenticity is enacted. *Educational Psychologist, 32,* 153–173.

Hendel, D. D. (1980). Experimental and affective correlates of math anxiety in adult women. *Psychology of Women Quarterly, 5,* 219–230.

Hilton, T. L., & Berglünd, G. W. (1974). Sex differences in mathematics achievement: A longitudinal study. *Journal of Educational Research, 67,* 231–237.

Jacklin, C. N. (1989). Female and male: Issues of gender. *American Psychologist, 44,* 127–133.

Jorde-Blom, P. (1988). Self-efficacy expectations as a predictor of computer use: A look at early childhood administrators. *Computers in the School, 5,* 45–63.

Junge, M. E., & Dretzke, B. J. (1995). Mathematical self-efficacy gender differences in gifted/talented adolescents. *Gifted Child Quarterly, 39,* 22–26.

Karniol, R., Gabay, R., Ochion, Y., & Harari, Y. (1998). Is gender or gender-role orientation a better predictor of empathy in adolescence. *Sex Roles, 39,* 45–59.

Lapan, R. T., Boggs, K. R., & Morrill, W. H. (1989). Self-efficacy as a mediator of investigative and realistic general occupational themes on the Strong-Campbell Interest Inventory. *Journal of Counseling Psychology, 36,* 176–182.

Lent, R. W., Brown, S. D., Gover, M. R., & Nijjer, S. K. (1996). Cognitive assessment of the sources of mathematics self-efficacy: A thought-listing analysis. *Journal of Career Assessment, 4,* 33–46.

Lent, R. W., Brown, S. D., & Larkin, K. C. (1984). Relation of self-efficacy expectations to academic achievement and persistence. *Journal of Counseling Psychology, 31,* 356–362.

Lent, R. W., Brown, S. D., & Larkin, K. C. (1986). Self-efficacy in the prediction of academic performance and perceived career options. *Journal of Counseling Psychology, 33,* 265–269.

Lent, R. W., Lopez, F. G., & Bieschke, K. J. (1991). Mathematics self-efficacy: Sources and relation to science-based career choice. *Journal of Counseling Psychology, 38,* 424–430.

Lent, R. W., Lopez, F. G., & Bieschke, K. J. (1993). Predicting mathematics-related choice and success behaviors: Test of an expanded social cognitive model. *Journal of Vocational Behavior, 42,* 223–236.

Lopez, F. G., & Lent, R. W. (1992). Sources of mathematics self-efficacy of high school students. *The Career Development Quarterly, 41,* 3–12.

Lussier, G. (1996). Sex and mathematical background as predictors of anxiety and self-efficacy in mathematics. *Psychological Reports, 79,* 827–833.

Maccoby, E., & Jacklin, C. (1974). *Psychology of sex differences.* Stanford, CA: Stanford University Press.

Malpass, J., O'Neil, H., & Hocevar, D. (1999). Self-regulation, goal orientation, self-efficacy, worry, and high-stakes math achievement for mathematically gifted high school students. *Roeper Review, 21,* 281.

Matsui, T. (1994). Mechanisms underlying sex differences in career self-efficacy expectations of university students. *Journal of Vocational Behavior, 45*, 177–184.

Matsui, T., Ikeda, H., & Ohnishi, R. (1989). Relations of sex-typed socializations to career self-efficacy expectations of college students. *Journal of Vocational Behavior, 35*, 1–16.

Matsui, T., Matsui, K., & Ohnishi, R. (1990). Mechanisms underlying math self-efficacy learning of college students. *Journal of Vocational Behavior, 37*, 225–238.

Matsui, T., & Tsukamoto, S. (1991). Relation between career self-efficacy measures based on occupational titles and Holland codes and model environments: A methodological contribution. *Journal of Vocational Behavior, 38*, 78–91.

Meece, J. L., & Courtney, D. P. (1992). Gender differences in students' perceptions: Consequences for achievement-related choices. In D. H. Schunk & J. L. Meece (Eds.), *Student perceptions in the classroom* (pp. 209–228). Hillsdale, NJ: Lawrence Erlbaum Associates.

Middleton, M. J., & Midgley, C. (1997). Avoiding the demonstration of lack of ability: An underexplored aspect of goal theory. *Journal of Educational Psychology, 89*, 710–718.

Miller, N. E., & Dollard, J. (1941). *Social learning and imitation.* New Haven, CT: Yale University Press.

Miura, I. T. (1987). The relationship of self-effcicacy expectations to computer interest and course enrollment in college. *Sex-Roles, 16*, 303–311.

Noddings, N. (1996, April). *Current directions in self research: Self-concept, self-efficacy, and possible selves.* Symposium presented at the meeting of the American Educational Research Association, New York.

Norwich, B. (1986). Assessing perceived self efficacy in relation to mathematics tasks: A study of the reliability and validity of assessment. *British Journal of Educational Psychology, 56*, 180–189.

Nosek, B. A., Banaji, M. R., & Greenwald, A. G. (2002). Man = male, Me = female, therefore math ≠ me. *Journal of Personality and Social Psychology, 83*, 44–59.

Pajares, F. (1996a). Role of self-efficacy beliefs in the mathematical problem-solving of gifted students. *Contemporary Educational Psychology, 21*, 325–344.

Pajares, F. (1996b). Self-efficacy beliefs in academic settings. *Review of Educational Research, 66*, 543–578.

Pajares, F. (1997). Current directions in self-efficacy research. In M. Maehr & P. R. Pintrich (Eds.), *Advances in motivation and achievement* (Vol. 10, pp. 1–49). Greenwich, CT: JAI Press.

Pajares, F., & Graham, L. (1999). Self-efficacy, motivation constructs, and mathematics performance of entering middle school students. *Contemporary Educational Psychology, 24*, 124–139.

Pajares, F., & Kranzler, J. (1995). Self-efficacy beliefs and general mental ability in mathematical problem-solving. *Contemporary Educational Psychology, 26*, 426–443.

Pajares, F., & Miller, M. D. (1994). The role of self-efficacy and self-concept beliefs in mathematical problem-solving: A path analysis. *Journal of Educational Psychology, 86*, 193–203.

Pajares, F., & Miller, M. D. (1995). Mathematics self-efficacy and mathematics performances: The need for specificity of assessment. *Journal of Counseling Psychology, 42*, 190–198.

Pajares, F., Miller, M. D., & Johnson, M. J. (1999). Gender differences in writing self-beliefs of elementary school students. *Journal of Educational Psychology, 91,* 50–61.

Pajares, F., & Valiante, G. (1999). Grade level and gender differences in the writing self-beliefs of middle school students. *Contemporary Educational Psychology, 24,* 390–405.

Pajares, F., & Valiante, G. (2001). Gender differences in writing motivation and achievement of middle school students: A function of gender orientation? *Contemporary Educational Psychology, 26,* 366–381.

Pajares, F., & Valiante, G. (2002). Students' self-efficacy in their self-regulated learning strategies: A developmental perspective. *Psychologia, 45, 211–221.*

Pedro, J. D., Wolleat, P., Fennema, E., & Becker, A. D. (1981). Election of high school mathematics by females and males: Attributions and attitudes. *American Educational Research Journal, 2, 207–218.*

Phillips, D. A., & Zimmerman, M. (1990). The developmental course of perceived competence and incompetence among competent children. In R. J. Sternberg & J. Kolligian, Jr. (Eds.), *Competence considered* (pp. 41–66). New Haven, CT: Yale University Press.

Pintrich, P. R., & De Groot, E. V. (1990). Motivational and self-regulated learning components of classroom academic performance. *Journal of Educational Psychology, 82,* 33–40.

Pintrich, P. R., & Schunk, D. H. (2002). *Motivation in education: Theory, research, and applications* (2nd ed). Englewood Cliffs, NJ: Prentice Hall.

Post, P., Stewart, M. A., & Smith, P. L. (1991). Self-efficacy, interest, and consideration of mathscience and non-mathscience occupations among Black freshmen. *Journal of Vocational Behavior, 38,* 179–186.

Post-Kammer, P., & Smith, P. L. (1985). Sex differences in career self-efficacy, consideration, and interest of eighth and ninth graders. *Journal of Counseling Psychology, 32,* 63–81.

Randhawa, B. S. (1994). Self-efficacy in mathematics, attitudes, and achievements of boys and girls from restricted samples in 2 countries. *Perceptual and Motor Skills, 79,* 1011–1018.

Randhawa, B. S., Beamer, J. E., & Lundberg, I. (1993). Role of mathematics self-efficacy in the structural model of mathematics achievement. *Journal of Educational Psychology, 85,* 41–48.

Reis, S. M., & Park, S. (2001). Gender differences in high-achieving students in math and science. *Journal for the Education of the Gifted, 25,* 52–73.

Reyes, L. H. (1984). Affective variables and mathematics education. *The Elementary School Journal, 84,* 558–581.

Sadker, M., & Sadker, D. (1994). *Failing at fairness: How America's schools cheat girls.* New York: Charles Scribner's Sons.

Schunk, D. H. (1991). Self-efficacy and academic motivation. *Educational Psychologist, 26,* 207–231.

Schunk, D. H., & Lilly, M. W. (1984). Sex differences in self-efficacy and attributions: Influence of performance feedback. *Journal of Early Adolescence, 4,* 203–213.

Schunk, D. H., & Pajares, F. (2002). The development of academic self-efficacy. In A. Wigfield & J. Eccles (Eds.), *Development of achievement motivation* (pp. 15–31). San Diego, CA: Academic Press.

Schwarz, N. (1999). Self-reports: How the questions shape the answers. *American Psychologist, 54,* 93–105.

Seegers, G., & Boekaerts, M. (1996). Gender-related differences in self-referenced cognitions in relation to mathematics. *Journal for Research in Mathematics Education, 27,* 215–240.

Sells, L. W. (1980). The mathematical filter and the education of women and minorities. In L. H. Fox, L. Brodey, & D. Tobin (Eds.), *Women and the mathematical mystique* (pp. 66–75). Baltimore: Johns Hopkins University.

Sherman, J. (1980). Mathematics, spatial visualization, and related factors: Changes in girls and boys, grades 8–11. *Journal of Educational Psychology, 72,* 476–482.

Sherman, J., & Fennema, E. (1977). The study of mathematics by high school girls and boys: Related variables. *American Educational Research Journal, 14,* 159–168.

Siegel, R. G., Galassi, J. P., & Ware, W. B. (1985). A comparison of two models for predicting mathematics performance: Social learning versus math aptitude-anxiety. *Journal of Counseling Psychology, 32,* 531–538.

Siegle, D., & Reis, S. M. (1998). Gender differences in teacher and student perceptions of gifted students' ability and effort. *Gifted Child Quarterly, 41,* 39–47.

Smead, V. S., & Chase, C. I. (1981). Student expectations as they relate to achievement in eighth grade mathematics. *Journal of Educational Research, 75,* 115–120.

Stajkovic, A. D., & Luthans, F. (1998). Self-efficacy and work-related performances: A meta-analysis. *Psychological Bulletin, 124,* 240–261.

Stipek, D. J. (2002). *Motivation to learn* (4th ed). Boston: Allyn & Bacon.

Terwilliger, J. S., & Titus, J. C. (1995). Gender differences in attitudes and attitude changes among mathematically talented youth. *Gifted Child Quarterly, 39,* 29–35.

Vasil, L., Hesketh, B., & Podd, J. (1987). Sex differences in computing behaviour among secondary school pupils. *New Zealand Journal of Educational Studies, 22,* 201–214.

Vollmer, F. (1984). Sex differences in personality and expectancy. *Sex Roles, 11,* 1121–1139.

Vollmer, F. (1986a). The relationship between expectancy and academic achievement: How can it be explained? *British Journal of Educational Psychology, 56,* 64–74.

Vollmer, F. (1986b). Why do men have higher expectancy than women? *Sex Roles, 14,* 351–362.

Wigfield, A., Eccles, J., MacIver, D., Reuman, D., & Midgley, C. (1991). Transitions at early adolescence: Changes in children's domain specific self-perceptions and general self-esteem across the transitions to junior high school. *Developmental Psychology, 27,* 552–565.

Wigfield, A., Eccles, J. S., & Pintrich, P. R. (1996). Development between the ages of 11 and 25. In D. C. Berliner & R. C. Calfee (Eds.), *Handbook of educational psychology* (pp. 148–185). New York: Simon & Schuster Macmillan.

Williams, J. E. (1994). Gender differences in high-school students efficacy-expectation performance discrepancies across 4 subject-matter domains. *Psychology in the Schools, 31,* 232–237.

Zeldin, A. L., & Pajares, F. (2000). Against the odds: Self-efficacy beliefs of women in mathematical, scientific, and technological careers. *American Educational Research Journal, 37,* 215–246.

Zimmerman, B. J., Bandura, A., & Martinez-Pons, M. (1992). Self-motivation for academic attainment: The role of self-efficacy beliefs and personal goal setting. *American Educational Research Journal, 29,* 663–676.

Zimmerman, B. J., & Martinez-Pons, M. (1990). Student differences in self-regulated learning: Relating grade, sex, and giftedness to self-efficacy and strategy use. *Journal of Educational Psychology, 82,* 51–59.

15

Gender Differences in Mathematics

What We Know and What We Need to Know

Ann M. Gallagher and James C. Kaufman

The true nature of the relationship between gender and mathematics is much more complex than most people have been led to believe. Differences are found in relatively few aspects of mathematics performance (as noted by several authors in this volume), and when they are found, their causes are varied and often elusive. Indeed, individual differences in ability and achievement *within* gender are probably much larger than the differences *between* genders.

Yet, there persists a monolithic stereotype that girls don't like math and aren't as good at it as boys. This common perception is a poor reflection of reality and is likely to discourage girls from engaging in mathematics study and thus to limit opportunities for women in mathematics and related fields. Why do data from some standardized tests of mathematics show a gender gap, while nontest data show women matching or exceeding men in the classroom? Chapters in this book explore the issue from a variety of disciplines and perspectives. Some use a cognitive processing perspective, others use the lens of social psychology, and others bring in aspects of education and environment. Taken together, these perspectives complement each other in painting a picture of how the gender gap in test performance arises despite the many areas of gender parity in performance and ability.

BACKGROUND ISSUES

Chipman's personal history of her involvement in research on gender and mathematics chronicles the factors influencing early research efforts in this area, and presents some important contemporary issues that illustrate the complexity and contradictory nature of the evidence for and against gender differences in performance and participation. We chose her chapter for our introduction because we wanted readers to be aware, upfront, of the inconsistency of findings, the large overlap between men's and women's skills and abilities, and the many areas in which male and female performance is similar.

In her conclusion, Chipman raises the fundamental question of whether research focused on gender *differences*, as opposed to *similarities*, is likely to reinforce current stereotypes rather than help to dispel them. Others in this volume (Caplan and Caplan in Chapter 2; Halpern, Wai, and Saw in Chapter 3) and elsewhere have also raised this concern. Both Chipman and Caplan and Caplan advocate that researchers stop focusing on gender differences because current stereotypes about women and mathematics have been so resistant to change, regardless of research findings that refute them. As these authors note, the popular press is much more eager to publicize findings that confirm stereotypes, and thus to perpetuate them, than they are to dispel them with evidence that they are false.

In Chapter 3, Halpern, Wai, and Saw, however, point out that "stereotypes and prejudice will not be eradicated if we refuse to examine data" (p. 50). Although the popular press may distort the practical significance of findings in gender differences research, they argue, the only way to invalidate stereotypes is to provide compelling evidence of where differences occur and where they do not occur, and to understand the causes of the differences. This evidence will provide important input for the development of better and more equitable methods of teaching, assessment, and learning.

Both Halpern et al. and the Caplans raise the issue of theoretical perspective and the nature/nurture argument. Although the Caplans suggest that biological determinism is the underlying motivation behind much of the research that seeks to examine gender differences in performance or cognitive processing, we disagree with this point of view. Instead, we propose that the true motivation lies in our refusal to believe that one sex is "better" or "smarter" than the other, and that the myriad skills required to do mathematics may be somewhat differently distributed across the sexes, irrespective of the origins of those differences. Researchers examining differences in performance that are evident in both high-stakes assessments and in a few other tasks related to mathematics (e.g., three-dimensional mental rotation) seek to identify the sources of these differences so more informed decisions can be made about the design of the assessments and the interpretation of their results. That is, they seek to provide information that will contribute to fairer assessments.

For example, the construct "mathematical reasoning" is only vaguely defined in most testing organizations that produce measures of this construct. Specifications for the contents of such tests are often based more on historical precedent than on theoretical work defining which cognitive processes are critical components of mathematical or quantitative reasoning and which are not. A case in point is spatial ability. As Nuttall, Casey, and Pezaris point out in Chapter 6, performance on the SAT-M is dependent to some extent on spatial skills. There is, however, no evidence that spatial skills are actually necessary or important in solving complex mathematical problems of the type students encounter in college-level or graduate-level mathematics (the performance that the SAT-M and GRE general Quantitative test were designed to predict).

An example of one generally irrelevant element in most high-stakes mathematics assessments is the "speediness" element. Most of these tests require students to respond to unfamiliar (and sometimes contrived) mathematical questions in less than two minutes each. The relationship between effectiveness in math problem solving and speediness is unclear. On spatial tasks, which use many of the same cognitive processes as solving mathematical problems, Kaufman (1979) showed that quicker problem solvers tend to be better problem solvers (as measured by the Block Design, Picture Arrangement, and Object Assembly subtests on the WISC-R). However, many would argue that using shortcuts might actually lead to poorer performance in solving higher-level mathematics problems that can require days or weeks to solve. According to Kessel and Linn (1996), mathematicians value the persistence required for this kind of extended problem solving over speedy, less considered solutions.

By identifying how specific skills contribute to performance on a test, researchers can foster dialog about the importance of those skills in predicting actual performance. These discussions may lead to changes in test content or interpretation, which will ultimately make them fairer and more accurate assessments of mathematics.

SOCIALIZATION ISSUES

As Halpern et al. argue in their chapter, dichotomizing theories about the sources of gender differences in mathematics into those predicated on nature or biology vs. those based on nurture or society presents a false sense that these effects can, in fact, be separated. Indeed, much of the debate about nature vs. nurture has been perpetuated in the mass media – much as they continue to fuel the gender and math stereotypes. Regardless of where theories fall on the continuum from nature to nurture, most psychologists agree that a complex activity, such as mathematical problem solving or reasoning, cannot in any sense be attributable solely to either alone. Even theories attributing differences purely to socialization should recognize the biological elements that prompt differential experiences.

One of the first pieces of information that a family receives about a newborn is the sex of the baby (regardless of how definitive that determination is). This one piece of information sets in motion a lifetime of culturally based expectations and sanctions. In a review of the literature from social, educational, and cognitive psychology that examines antecedents of gender differences in performance on mathematics tests, Gallagher (1998) notes that children are socialized from birth into male or female "cultures" based on their sex classification. Different sets of behaviors are either rewarded or discouraged by parents, teachers, and peers, depending on the gender group to which a child has been assigned. Because "assignment" to these groups is never random, it is impossible to completely separate the effects due to socialization from any effects that may be due to biology. We may thus never be certain that differences in behavior result purely from socialization or purely from biological causes.

One important aspect of theories that present socialization as a contributor to performance differences is that differences in socialization are usually viewed as somewhat more amenable to change than are biological factors (although changing cultural beliefs takes time). Indeed, as Chipman and Halpern et al. point out in Chapters 1 and 3, respectively, substantial progress toward change has been made over the past 20 years, as evidenced by rates of participation of women in mathematically intensive occupations such as accounting or economics, to the point where these fields now contain equal or greater numbers of women than men.

Other work in this volume by Jacobs et al. (Chapter 12) and by Pajares (Chapter 14) discusses in detail research illuminating how various societal factors act to undermine girls' interest and feelings of self-efficacy in mathematics. Both of these chapters cover work that helps to explain why greater numbers of girls and women opt out of mathematical activities even when their actual performance is equal to that of the boys and men who persist. Both chapters conclude that parents and other key adults in girls' lives are likely to influence their degree of persistence in mathematics.

Parjares's chapter draws the link between lower math self-efficacy in women and their gender self-concept. He challenges educators to "desex" academic subjects so these effects will not come into play, and he challenges society at large to model gender roles that include both instrumental and expressive elements to allow both sexes to hold a more balanced self-view. In Chapter 12, Jacobs et al. illustrate how parents' attitudes and behaviors shape their children's self-perceptions and valuing of mathematics. Parents' gender stereotypes and beliefs about their child's ability in math appear to be related to the child's later interest in math.

Catsambis examines these same phenomena from a sociological perspective, discussing family influences on girls' decisions to persist in math, as well as influences of their schools and communities. Research examining organizational features, social interactions, assessment, and curriculum in schools points to facets of these variables that exacerbate or diminish gender differences in math participation and performance. Although, as Catsambis points out, there are few studies examining community influences on math participation, there is some evidence to suggest that community

environments can influence students' educational decisions. This is especially true during adolescence, when children begin spending more time
away from home.

In Chapter 13, Hong, O'Neil, and Feldon discuss work that has been
done examining the role of self-regulation and test anxiety in math test performance. They discuss the importance of the distinction between "state"
(temporary) and "trait" (longer-term) math anxiety to understanding its
relationship to performance. These authors present data to validate a measure of state and trait self-regulation, and then report on a study using
that instrument to look at the relationship of planning, self-checking, self-
efficacy, effort, and worry variables to mathematics performance. Their
findings indicate that, for the Korean high school students in their sample,
the relationship between these constructs is the same for both males and
females. That is, students who plan, monitor, expend effort, and have
high self-efficacy generally score higher on mathematic achievement tests.
Those students who show high levels of test anxiety (or who are anxious
people) will perform worse. However, Hong et al. found that state worry
(but not trait worry) was higher for females during testing. These findings suggest that the state/trait distinction may be an important one for
understanding how test anxiety may differ by gender.

Another variable that interacts with gender and math performance is
ethnicity. In Chapter 10, Walters and Brown discuss the finding that gender differences on high-stakes tests tend to be largest among Hispanic and
European American students, and smallest among African American students (the gap among Asian American students falls in between). Hispanic
students tend to show the largest gender gap in attitudes toward math, with
females showing less positive attitudes. Walters and Brown hypothesize
that one possible reason for this larger gap might be the patriarchal nature
of many Hispanic households. Both Walters and Brown and Catsambis
(Chapter 11) point out that in mathematics classroom achievement, the
gap is reversed among African American students, with women achieving
at higher levels than men.

The relationship among ethnicity, gender, and mathematics performance is complex. Research on stereotype threat discussed in four chapters
of this volume (Walters and Brown in Chapter 10; Catsambis in Chapter 11;
Davies and Spencer in Chapter 8; and Ben-Zeev et al. in Chapter 9) suggests that under controlled conditions, performance of almost any group,
even that of white males, can be affected. Stereotype threat research is
a natural outgrowth of research on the effects of socialization on performance and participation in mathematics. This work examines how societal
stereotypes can affect an individual's performance in a high-stakes testing
environment. Davies and Spencer (Chapter 8) review research confirming the existence of a stereotype threat construct, and discuss how and
when it affects performance of test takers in specific ethnic and gender

groups. It is particularly interesting to note that under specific conditions, even test-takers generally considered to be in the "majority" group (e.g., white males) can be affected by this phenomenon. In Chapter 9, Ben Zeev et al. discuss work examining the physiological changes that result from stereotype threat and how these changes affect cognitive performance. According to Ben Zeev et al., when a stereotyped individual feels stress from a testing situation, the resulting physiological "threat" response may lead to higher cortisol levels released by the pituitary gland. This increase in cortisol levels leads to intellectual underperformance.

Findings have, as yet, only been replicated in laboratory settings (as opposed to "real" testing situations). The few studies that have been done in authentic high-stakes testing environments (e.g., Stricker & Bejar, in press) have not been successful in manipulating performance gaps. Nonetheless, this work brings to light the existence of the stereotype threat effect and begins to explore the mechanisms by which it affects test performance.

COGNITIVE PROCESSING

Just as there may be several social and cultural factors contributing to a gender gap in mathematics, differences in cognitive processing may also account for some portion of gender differences in mathematics test performance. Royer and Garofoli (Chapter 5) focus on speed of mathematics fact retrieval and mental rotation[1] skill as predictors of performance on the SAT-M, whereas Nuttall et al. (Chapter 6) focus on the relationship of spatial ability (including mental rotation skill) to performance, and examine a hypothetical genetic component underlying these skills.

According to work conducted and reviewed by Royer and Garofoli, math fact retrieval – or the ability to respond quickly and accurately to simple addition, subtraction, multiplication, and division problems – is positively associated with mathematics test performance on tests like the SAT-M. Royer and Garofoli hypothesize that this type of retrieval, in conjunction with mental rotation skill, explains an important proportion of variance in performance of groups based on gender. This hypothesis is based on the notion that speed of processing in these two areas allows more cognitive "space" to be devoted to representing and constructing a solution to mathematics problems.

An underlying assumption of this hypothesis is that fact retrieval speed is a causal factor in test performance. It is also possible, however, that speed of fact retrieval may actually be a byproduct of greater interest, experience, and motivation in mathematics – which could also result in superior test

---

[1] Measures of this skill are generally based on speed of response as opposed to accuracy (which generally shows no difference). The subject is asked to identify a target (an abstract three-dimensional object) that has been rotated in space from a set of similar objects.

performance. Although Royer and Garofoli's work documents a relationship among speed of fact retrieval, spatial skill, and performance on the SAT-M, it does not fully address the question of the direction of causality in that relationship. It is possible that males may be quicker at fact retrieval or spatial tasks because they have more practice (e.g., sports statistics, block-building games), and/or because they are more interested in mathematics and more confident in their own mathematics ability. Other affective factors (which are discussed later in this chapter) might also produce similar results.

Studies that focus on mathematics and spatial training would help to shed light on the nature of this relationship. Work cited by Newcomb, Mathason, and Terlecki (2002) indicates that spatial skill can be improved with training. In a discussion of a meta-analysis conducted by Baenninger and Newcomb (1989), these authors point out that although long-term training (e.g., training that lasted at least one semester) appears to benefit males and females equally (increasing speed of mental rotation in both groups), the asymptote for such training may or may not be at the same level for both groups. If females are trained in fact retrieval and spatial skills, and their skills increase to a level equal to that of males, will their performance on high-stakes tests like the SAT-M or the GRE general Quantitative test improve? The answer to this question would provide important information about how these skills are related.

In Chapter 6, Nuttall et al. review several studies documenting the relationship of mental rotation ability to performance on high-stakes standardized tests such as the SAT-M. These authors propose a genetic mediator to the acquisition of spatial skills in females that does not affect skill acquisition in males. According to their hypothesis, because of sex-linked inherited traits that affect cerebral lateralization (as indicated by handedness), females who possess these traits will benefit more than from training in spatial skills than those who don't possess the trait. Nuttall et al. have begun to test this hypothesis in their research examining spatial abilities of college-age men and women in mathematics and science majors (who are assumed to have more experience with spatial tasks), as compared with the abilities of students in other fields.

Using family information on handedness as an indicator of the genetic component related to spatial ability, Nuttall et al. found that female math/science majors with the specific combination of sex-linked genetic indicators performed at a level equal to males on the mental rotation test. These females also performed significantly better than other female math/science majors who did not posses the genetic indicators. Although findings of this study do suggest that there may be a relationship among cerebral lateralization, spatial ability, and mathematics ability, it is not entirely clear whether explicit training in spatial skills would improve the performance of all females. To answer this question, we await results of studies examining this issue using the mathematics program developed by these authors to incorporate spatial thinking into a mathematics curriculum.

We applaud Nuttall et al. for working to incorporate findings from their research into materials that can be used in teaching. The gap between research findings and practical applications for teachers is often quite large. Research does not usually result in changes to curricula. Curricula that focus on developing cognitive skills hold promise for changing gender differences in mathematics test performance. We eagerly await the next lines of research in this direction.

OUR WORK

Work by Gallagher (Gallagher & De Lisi, 1994; Gallagher et al., 2000; Gallagher, Levin, & Cahalan, 2002) has also found spatial skills to be an important element in performance on tests like the SAT-M and the GRE general Quantitative test. This work indicates that, in addition to spatial abilities, differences in test performance also involve other cognitive processes. We propose that some of these cognitive differences could stem from affective factors that may overlap and interact with each other, such as stereotype threat, self-confidence, and personality. In studies examining gender differences in performance on specific types of items on the GRE, Gallagher et al. (2002) classified test questions according to the cognitive demands of their solutions, and then compared the size of performance differences (impact[2]) for male and female examinees on the different item categories. Although significant differences that were found were small (effect sizes ranged from 0.1 to 0.17), one must bear in mind that questions used in this test (and other high-stakes tests) are closely monitored for group differences in performance before they are used in a scored test section. Questions with large differences thus are generally not included in the test score. The fact that we found any performance differences consistent with our predictions – but *not* related to overall question difficulty –

---

[2] For each item, effect size was calculated using the following equation:

$$d = \frac{\overline{X}_f - \overline{X}_m}{\sqrt{\dfrac{SD_m^2 + SD_f^2}{2}}}$$

where $\overline{X}_f$ is the mean percent correct for female examinees, $\overline{X}_m$ is the mean percent correct for male examinees, and SD_f and SD_m are the respective standard deviations for female and male examinees. Thus, positive values indicate that the item is more likely to favor female test takers and negative values indicate that the item is more likely to favor male test takers. This formula is less dependent on subgroup sample sizes than a formula using weighted standard deviations (Willingham & Cole, 1997, p. 21).

indicates that differences in the cognitive skills brought to bear in solving test questions can, at least partially, account for differences in test scores.

With regard to our findings related to spatial ability, results indicated that the most consistent general effects on performance appear when spatial strategies are optional; that is, on questions for which other types of strategies can lead to a correct answer, but for which a spatial strategy provides some advantage in speed or accuracy. Our research also found that, in addition to involving spatial skills, items with the most consistent gender differences in performance were those that *look* like standard textbook questions but that actually require unusual solution strategies.

Questions with the *least* impact were generally equally as difficult as high-impact questions, but required a different set of cognitive skills. Lower impact questions were those that:

- Required labeling the problem as a specific type of problem, and/or retrieving a formula or routine that should be known from memory but was not immediately apparent. (We used this only for nonobvious cases; obvious, standard retrieval problems were coded using the next category.)
- Were typical textbook problems – the context was familiar, frequently seen in mathematics coursework; the solution path was one that was generally associated with the context.
- Were multistep problems that required accuracy and a systematic approach. For example, the problem required two successive calculations, and the second calculation used information from the first calculation.
- Required reading and comprehension of mathematics such as using (applying) a newly defined function or understanding the properties of an algebraic expression.

Although differences in performance on the various question types were significant, the size of the effect was fairly small (as noted above), indicating substantial variation *within* and overlap *between* gender groups.

One thing that is interesting to note is the reduced performance difference in mathematical problems requiring reading or on problems placed in a real-life context. Theories about information processing and thinking styles offer some interesting hypotheses for differences in performance across ethnicities, culture, and gender. Cohen and Ibarra (Chapter 7) discuss multicontext theory and its possible role in the differential performance of underrepresented groups (including females) on standardized tests. This theory (originally developed by Hall, 1959) suggests that one component of the performance gap may result from what they call cultural conflict.

According to this theory, cultural conflict arises when an individual's culture is not well matched with the culture of an organization (such as a school or workplace). The culture in which an individual is raised influences the kinds of cues that a person uses to interpret the world, learn new material, and communicate with others. Individuals belonging to certain ethnic minority groups such as African Americans and Hispanics, as well as females, tend to use high levels of context in interpreting the world. In contrast, European Americans and males tend to take a low-context approach. High-context individuals tend to use multiple sources of information, such as nonverbal cues, social interactions, and other streams of information surrounding an event, to interpret its meaning. Communication among high-context individuals is often indirect, and messages are implicit. In contrast, low-context individuals tend to be more reductionist in their methods, relying on objective facts and words, and their style of communication is more direct. Work by Ibarra (2001) suggests that standardized tests are a medium that is more aligned with low-context cultures than with high-context cultures, and that this may help to explain differentially lower performance for groups of individuals (e.g., females and minority students) from high-context cultures.

In addition to the multicontext theory, work on thinking styles also suggests that males and females as a group may use and attend to different aspects of a given situation or set of information. Thinking styles are ways people characteristically respond to or interpret information or problems. They are not abilities, but rather reflect a preference for how people choose to use their abilities (Sternberg, 1997).

Bruner's (1986) work in this area makes a distinction between paradigmatic and narrative modes of thought. Paradigmatic thought is logical and scientific; narrative thought seeks connections and sees the world as a story. If paradigmatic thought is concerned with capturing "what is," then narrative thought is focused more on "what may be." Bruner's dichotomy is structurally similar to several other models. Some of these similar models include Spence's (1989) distinction between narrative truth and historical validity, Epstein's cognitive-experiential self theory (e.g., Pacini & Epstein, 1999), and multicontext theory discussed by Cohen and Ibarra in this volume.

Work by Kaufman (2002) using Bruner's theory to study creative writers and journalism students may shed some light on gender differences in how events or materials are interpreted. Results of this work indicated that creative writers used more narrative thought than journalists (as expected), but paradigmatic thought interacted with gender. Male journalists used significantly more paradigmatic thought than male creative writers, but no significant differences were observed for females – even when personality and motivation factors were controlled.

Why would the paradigmatic variable be a successful predictor of writing interest for men, but not for women? Kaufman's findings suggest that, although male journalists and male creative writers approach a sentence writing task in different ways, female journalists and female creative writers may not necessarily treat the tasks differently. Even if a female journalist approached the sentence writing task from a paradigmatic thinking style, this paradigmatic thought would then be filtered through an inherently narrative perspective. The resulting finding of an effect for men, but no effect for women, is consistent with this idea (as is the absence of any interaction in narrative thought). In keeping with work by Gallagher (Gallagher & De Lisi, 1994; Gallagher et al., 2002), Kaufman's research found gender differences in preferences for qualitatively different solution strategies.

In short, females as a group may tend to prefer narrative thought or highly contextualized verbally based strategies – even when dealing with stimuli that are better solved with paradigmatic thought. If so, this may explain the differences found on many math items requiring reductionist thinking, spatial abilities, or concrete solution patterns. Such a preference may give women an advantage in verbal performance, but may be harmful in solving mathematical problems. The most harm may occur in timed tests – including most standardized tests – in which the extra minutes spent "converting" a paradigmatic problem into a narrative framework may require more time.

NEW AVENUES FOR RESEARCH

We think it possible that once academic preparation is controlled, the cognitive differences that appear to have been found in strategy use could be found to be largely the result of differences in affective factors. Many of these factors such as confidence, self-efficacy, and the effects of stereotype threat, are discussed in the earlier chapters in this book. Certain aspects of personality or temperament may also come into play in strategy selection and susceptibility to stereotype threat (or other potentially deleterious affective factors) in high-stakes test performance, although there has been little research examining the relationship between these two factors and mathematics achievement and test performance.

Factors such as lower self-confidence (as discussed by Pajares in Chapter 14 and Catsambis in Chapter 11) and stereotype threat (discussed by Davies and Spencer in Chapter 8, and by Ben Zeev et al. in Chapter 9) are likely to produce more conservative problem-solving styles in a high-stakes testing environment. It is conceivable that personality or temperament would mediate a person's level of susceptibility to the detrimental effects of these factors. Although little work has been done to look at the relationship between temperament or personality variables and mathematics achievement or test performance, a few studies indicate this may be a promising avenue to pursue. It is especially appealing because it has the potential to take the onus off of one's gender per se, and instead place it on variables that may be correlated with gender but are not necessarily sex-linked characteristics.

Davis and Carr (2002), in one of the few studies examining the relationship between performance in mathematics and temperament, found that impulsivity and inhibition were differentially related by gender to strategies used by seven-year-olds in solving arithmetic problems. Boys who were rated as having an "easy" temperament (e.g., low impulsive) were more likely than boys rated as "difficult" (high impulsive) to use retrieval strategies as opposed to manipulative strategies in solving simple arithmetic problems. Among girls, however, there was no relationship between strategy use and temperament, and girls tended to use manipulative strategies more than retrieval. Previous work by these same authors (Carr, Jessup, & Fuller, 1999) indicates that parents and teachers explicitly teach manipulative strategies to students at this age level. It is conceivable, then, that girls are using the strategies they have been taught and have seen taught to others around them, while boys are autonomously using "quicker" strategies (such as retrieval). This tendency on the part of females to "follow the rules" may stem from temperament or personality factors.

Indeed, a meta-analysis of research examining gender differences among adults in "Big Five" personality variables[3] (Costa & McCrae, 2001) across various cultures found that, among many other things, women tended to be more compliant (a facet of agreeableness) than men. It seems likely that students who are more compliant would be more likely to use strategies they were taught in class than to use self-invented shortcuts. This parallels findings by Gallagher and De Lisi (1994) that females are more apt to prefer solution strategies they were taught in school over unconventional strategies devised on the spot. It also accords with suggestions noted above by Davis and Carr (2002) regarding problem-solving strategies used by young children.

Another aspect of personality and temperament that could be relevant to performance on high-stakes tests is risk taking behavior or sensation/ excitement seeking. It is conceivable that test takers who are less willing to take risks may be slower and more systematic in their solution strategies. They may also be less comfortable taking educated guesses on multiple-choice tests. Among their many findings, Costa and McCrae (2001) report that males are significantly higher in excitement seeking.

There is other evidence to suggest that risk taking in academic situations may vary by sex. Sorrentino, Hewitt, and Raso-Knott (1992) investigated risk taking in a game situation (a ring-toss game). Findings of their study indicate that when given a choice in risk level (with success at the higher risk levels indicating higher proficiency), males were more likely to choose high-risk levels, whereas females were more likely to choose low-risk levels. A meta-analysis by Byrnes, Millar, and Schafer (1999) examining risk-taking behavior in a number of different types of activities found similar results. These authors report that the largest difference between males and

---

[3] The "Big Five" variables are extraversion, neuroticism, openness to experience, agreeableness, and conscientiousness.

females in risk taking was on intellectual tasks involving mathematical or spatial skill. On these tasks, males preferred higher risk conditions (difficulty) than did females. As in Sorentino et al., the only pay-off for success on these tasks was "proof" of higher ability.

In a study examining strategy use on multiple-choice (MC) vs. free-response (FR) test questions, Gallagher (1992) found that females used computational or algorithmic strategies on both question formats, whereas males varied strategies from one format to the other, using algorithmic strategies on FR questions and less computational strategies on MC questions (including working the question backward from the given options). Males were also more likely to guess at answers than were females, and females were more likely than males to use the question's options to detect calculation errors in answers they had generated independently with algorithmic strategies. Taken together with other findings, these findings suggest that on high-stakes tests, females may be more cautious in their approach to problem solving, and that this caution may cost them valuable time. These findings also coincide with the risk-taking findings discussed above.

The chapters by Byrnes (Chapter 4) and Halpern et al. (Chapter 3) offer comprehensive theories for the sources of gender differences in performance and participation in mathematics. Both theories include multiple types of factors that help explain gender differences in performance and participation. Byrnes proposes a "Three Conditions Model of Achievement," in which he argues that children perform better in academic areas when they have exposure (where they are regularly given the opportunity to learn), motivation, and ability. Byrnes then follows gender differences in mathematics across these three facets. Halpern et al. propose a psychobiosocial model in response to the notion that "nature" and "nurture" stand at opposite ends of a single continuum. Their model shows biological and psychosocial variables influencing each other. The psychobiosocial model includes such biological factors as brain development, genetic influences, and hormonal secretion, as well as such psychosocial factors as experiences and the environment.

CONCLUSION

Why is it important to study gender and mathematics? We believe it is important in order to foster equity and validity in assessment development and use. Standardized tests of mathematics are widely used for high-stakes admissions decisions and academic awards. It is critical that those who construct and use the tests be aware of threats to validity and of the test's limitations.

According to the *Standards for Educational and Psychological Testing* (American Educational Research Association, 1999), "Validity refers to the degree to which evidence and theory support the interpretations of test scores entailed by proposed uses of the test" (p. 9). Messick's (1995) definition of validity explicitly incorporates social values as an important component of a unified conception of validity. What Messick calls the consequential basis for validity and test use focuses on the values associated with scoring an score use, and with the outcomes of testing. This represents an expansion of the previous definitions of validity and acts as the link between the values and expectations of stakeholder and the operational use of test scores – what it means to do well or poorly on a particular test. Key concerns of this element of validity are intended and unintended social and psychological impact that the use of the test may have on test takers, score users, and others.

As noted earlier in this chapter, specifications for the contents of many large-scale standardized ability tests (e.g., the SAT and GRE) are based more on historical precedent than on in-depth analyses of the cognitive processes and skills required for successful performance in the domains they are intended to assess.[4] Therefore, information about group differences (in this case, gender differences) in how information is processed, or about differences in levels of experience with specific types of materials, can foster discussion and empirical research focused on the importance of these elements to predicting performance. Such research findings can inform decisions about what is to be covered by the test, what cognitive processes are to be assessed and how the test scores should be used. Without this level of scrutiny and public debate, changes to enhance the fairness of large-scale standardized tests would be made at random with unpredictable results.

One definition of whether a measure is fair is the extent to which the score includes variables that are relevant to the construct being measured – in other words, a measure is fair to the extent that it minimizes error variance (Kaufman & Boodoo, 2003). In the case of the SAT-M or the GRE general Quantitative test, research discussed in this book suggests that some portion of scores may be attributable to factors other than mathematical ability. We hope that this book serves to stimulate discussions about both the validity of the content of standardized mathematics tests and the consequences associated with using such tests in high-stakes decisions.

High-stakes standardized tests were originally created with the intent of opening up opportunities to those who were not part of the privileged class. To a large degree, they have been successful in that mission. Most people now agree that admission to higher education should be based on merit and not on privilege or connections, as was the case 75 years ago. If used in conjunction with other indicators of ability or accomplishment,

---

[4] This is less so for achievement tests, of which the newer ones often have a structural or cognitive rationale for what is included.

standardized tests can, indeed, provide valuable information about an individual. One problem, however, is that they are too often NOT used in conjunction with other indicators. The use of standardized tests is ever more pervasive in our educational system. For this reason, it is important that we continue to evaluate the validity of such tests for predicting future academic success.

Some of the factors discussed in this book that influence the gender-based score gap in mathematics could potentially be manipulated to change the size of that gap, but they must first be subject to policy evaluations regarding their importance to predicting performance. For instance, the elimination of the need for spatial skills could potentially shrink the gender gap on some mathematics tests, but before this is done, consensus must be reached in the mathematics community regarding the relevance of specific spatial skills to predicting mathematics performance in college or graduate school. Other factors such as stereotype threat are likely to be much more difficult to manipulate, and may take many years for any type of change to be implemented. We believe, however, that beginning a dialogue about how the tests may be modified is essential, and we hope that our book has been a continuing step in this direction.

References

American Educational Research Association, American Psychological Association, and the National Council on Measurement in Education. (1999). *Standards for educational and psychological testing*. Washington, DC: American Educational Research Association.

Baenninger, M., & Newcomb, N. (1989). The role of experience in spatial test performance: A meta-analysis. *Sex Roles, 20*, 327–344.

Bruner, J. (1986). *Actual minds, possible worlds*. Cambridge, MA: Harvard University Press.

Byrnes, J. P., Millar, D. C., & Schafer, W. D. (1999). Gender differences in risk taking: A meta-analysis. *Psychological Bulletin, 125*, 367–383.

Carr, M., Jessup, D. L., & Fuller, D. (1999). Gender differences in first-grade mathematics strategy use: Parent and teacher contributions. *Journal for Research in Mathematics Education, 30*, 20–46.

Costa, P. T., & McCrae, R. R. (2001). Gender differences in personality traits across cultures: Robust and surprising findings. *Journal of Personality and Social Psychology, 81*, 322–331.

Davis, H., & Carr, M. (2002). Gender differences in mathematics strategy use: The influence of temperament. *Learning and Individual Differences, 13*, 83–95.

Gallagher, A. M. (1992). Sex differences in problem-solving strategies used by high-scoring examinees on the SAT-M. (ETS RR 92-2). Princeton, NJ: Educational Testing Service.

Gallagher, A. M. (1998). Gender and antecedents of performance in mathematics testing. *Teachers College Record, 100*, 297–314.

Gallagher, A. M., & De Lisi, R. (1994). Gender differences in Scholastic Aptitude Test: Mathematics problem solving among high-ability students. *Journal of Educational Psychology, 86,* 204–211.

Gallagher, A. M., De Lisi, R., Holst, P. C., McGillicuddy-De Lisi, A. V., Morley, M., & Cahalan, C. (2000). Gender differences in advanced mathematical problem solving. *Journal of Experimental Child Psychology, 75,* 165–190.

Gallagher, A. M., Levin, J., & Cahalan, C. (2002). *Cognitive patterns of gender differences on mathematics admissions tests* (ETS RR 96-17). Princeton, NJ: Educational Testing Service.

Hall, E. T. (1959). *The silent language.* Greenwich, CT: Fawcett.

Ibarra, R. A. (2001). *Beyond affirmative action: Reframing the context of higher education.* Madison: University of Wisconsin Press.

Kaufman, A. S. (1979). Role of speed on WISC-R performance across the age range. *Journal of Consulting and Clinical Psychology, 47,* 595–597.

Kaufman, J. C. (2002). Narrative and paradigmatic thinking styles in creative writing and journalism students. *Journal of Creative Behavior, 36*(3), 201–220.

Kaufman, J. C., & Boodoo, G. M. (2003). *Enhancing fairness: A new look at creativity in assessment.* Manuscript in preparation.

Kessel, C., & Linn, M. C. (1996). Grades or scores: Predicting future college mathematics performance. *Educational Measurement: Issues and Practice, 15*(4), 10–14.

Messick, S. (1995). Validity of psychological assessment: Validation of inferences from persons' responses and performances as scientific inquiry into score meaning. *American Psychologist, 50,* 741–749.

Newcomb, N. S., Mathason, L., & Terlecki, M. (2002). Maximization of spatial competence: More important than finding the cause of sex differences. In A. McGillicuddy-De Lisi & R. De Lisi (Eds.), *Biology, society, and behavior: The development of sex differences in cognition* (pp. 183–206). Westport: Ablex.

Pacini, R., & Epstein, S. (1999). The relation of rational and experiential information processing styles to personality, basic beliefs, and the ratio-bias phenomenon. *Journal of Personality & Social Psychology, 76,* 972–987.

Sorrentino, R. M., Hewitt, E. C., & Raso-Knott, P. A. (1992). Risk-taking in games of chance and skill: Informational and affective influences on choice behavior. *Journal of Personality and Social Psychology, 62,* 522–533.

Spence, D. P. (1989). Narrative appeal vs. historical validity. *Contemporary Psychoanalysis, 25,* 517–524.

Sternberg, R. J. (1997). *Thinking styles.* New York: Cambridge University Press.

Stricker, L. J., & Bejar, I. I. (in press). Test difficulty and stereotype threat on the GRE general test. *Journal of Applied Social Psychology.*

Willingham, W. W., & Cole, N. S. (1997). *Gender and fair assessment.* Mahwah, NJ: Erlbaum.

Author Index

Subject Index